T3-AKC-549

CATHER STUDIES

WITHDRAWN

Series Editor

1988–2004

Susan J. Rosowski, University of Nebraska–Lincoln

2005–

Guy Reynolds, University of Nebraska–Lincoln

Board Members

Elizabeth Ammons, Tufts University

Marilyn Arnold, Brigham Young University, Emerita

Blanche H. Gelfant, Dartmouth College

David Stouck, Simon Fraser University

James Woodress, University of California–Davis,

   Emeritus

VOLUME 6

Cather Studies

History, Memory, and War

EDITED BY STEVEN TROUT

To Larry,
who helped make it
possible.

3-16-07

Steven Trout

UNIVERSITY OF NEBRASKA PRESS

LINCOLN & LONDON

© 2006 by the Board of Regents of the University of Nebraska

All rights reserved

Manufactured in the United States of America

∞

The series Cather Studies is sponsored by the University of Nebraska–Lincoln
in cooperation with the Willa Cather Pioneer Memorial and Educational
Foundation.

ISSN: 1045-9871

ISBN-13: 978-0-8032-9464-6

ISBN-10: 0-8032-9464-6

Frontispiece:
Willa Cather wearing a Civil War cap in the 1880s.
Nebraska State Historical Society Photograph Collections.

In memory of Susan J. Rosowski

CONTENTS

EDITORIAL POLICY

Cather Studies, a forum for Cather scholarship and criticism, is published biennially by the University of Nebraska Press. Submissions are invited on all aspects of Cather studies: biography, various critical approaches to the art of Cather, her literary relationships and reputation, the artistic, historical, intellectual, religious, economic, political, and social backgrounds to her work. Criteria for selection will be excellence and originality. Manuscripts may vary in length from 4,000 to 12,000 words and should conform to the MLA *Style Manual,* 1998 edition. Please submit manuscripts in duplicate, accompanied by return postage; overseas contributors should enclose international reply coupons. Because *Cather Studies* adheres to a policy of anonymous submission, please include a title page providing author's name and address and delete identifying information from the manuscript. Manuscripts and editorial correspondence should be addressed to Guy Reynolds, Editor, *Cather Studies,* Department of English, University of Nebraska–Lincoln, Lincoln NE 68588-0333.

Introduction

S T E V E N   T R O U T

As Mary Chinery points out in the final essay of this volume, some of the American troops who landed at Normandy on June 6, 1944, carried with them the compact, but unabridged, Armed Services edition of a particularly rich and powerful American novel—Willa Cather's *Death Comes for the Archbishop*. We do not know how much welcome distraction, to say nothing of solace, Cather's text provided these soldiers, how much her words meant, or failed to mean, when read in the midst of Operation Overlord. One would like to think, however, that at least a few of the GIs who carried *Death Comes for the Archbishop* with them during the opening phase of the liberation of Europe took comfort in the spiritual austerity of Cather's narrative or, at the very least, found a momentary refuge from war's horrors in a faraway landscape of mesas, piñons, and adobe. Hopefully, some of these servicemen responded to the text in the same manner as the wounded veteran of the Battle for the Philippines described at the opening of Chinery's essay: this soldier decided to keep reading even after discovering (contrary to the book's title) that *Death Comes for the Archbishop* was not a murder mystery. To his surprise, he "liked it anyway."

That Cather was there, albeit vicariously, at the D-Day landings and in the midst of the Pacific island campaigns should not surprise us. Indeed, as far as her connections to twentieth-century history are concerned, we might as well, as the saying goes, expect the unexpected. Now fading is the once widely held view of Cather as a writer who separated herself from the historical present (to the degree to which this was possible) and who remained aloof from the ideological pressures and preoccupations of her day. Over the past two decades, scholars equipped with the methodologies of

New Historicism and cultural studies have turned this conception on its head, replacing the solitary, politically indifferent artist with a cultural *participant* whose works embrace, reject, or redefine, by turns, the dominant values and beliefs located in her contemporary milieu. If this ideologically alert body of scholarship has at times placed too much emphasis on measuring Cather's alignment with current political orthodoxies (as Joan Acocella charges), it has also vastly expanded the ways in which her fiction can be enjoyed, understood, and taught. No longer sealed away from politics, ideology, and material culture, Cather's texts now *say* much more than they once did. As read by New Historicists and culture critics, they speak of themes central to the so-called American century and to our own historical moment—themes such as empire, migration, multiculturalism, changing gender roles, sexual orientation, ecological awareness, and war.

The latter subject, whose importance in Cather's life and writings has only recently attracted scholarly notice, serves as the focus for this collection. Cather was not, of course, what we think of as a war writer (i.e., an eyewitness to military violence or to its immediate aftermath for whom armed conflict is subsequently a central artistic concern). She did not hear a shot fired in anger even once during her seventy-four years, and direct depictions of combat appear in only two of her narratives—in the Civil War story "The Namesake" (1907) and, more notoriously, in *One of Ours* (1922), long regarded as one of her weakest novels. On the surface, Cather's acquaintanceship with Mars was slight and, if anything, detrimental to her art. However, as the fourteen essays assembled here demonstrate, an author does not have to be a "war writer" in order to produce work that registers the cultural and personal impact of mass violence, particularly during the first half of an especially war-torn century. Though Cather turned her artistic gaze directly to the battlefield just twice during her career as a fiction writer, war forms an important component in virtually everything she wrote.

The sheer number of armed conflicts evoked in her fiction is perhaps unprecedented in American literature. In *My Ántonia* (1918), a work whose sudden moments of violence and grotesquery arguably reflect the world war that raged during its composition, Jim

Burden inhabits a landscape that has been crisscrossed by conquistadors both old and new—by Coronado, whose memory is
tellingly connected to a rusty weapon, and, more recently, by the
U.S. Army, which has killed or displaced the Native Americans
whose ghostly horse ring Jim sees outlined in the snow. Wars of
imperialist aggression also form part of the backdrop for other
Cather novels, including *Death Comes for the Archbishop* (1927),
where the Mexican-American conflict of 1848 is essential to the
plot (as the event that brings Latour's future archdiocese under
American political control) and where the U.S. military's genoci-
dal campaign against the Navajos receives a disturbingly impartial
portrayal; *A Lost Lady* (1923), where, in a scene loaded with historical resonance, Cather depicts a railroad tycoon nonchalantly
entering Indian territory and planting a stake to mark the location
of his future home (more than anything, it was the railroad that
led to the near eradication of the Plains Indians in the 1860s and
1870s); and *Shadows on the Rock* (1931), where Cather recreates a
seventeenth-century New World city that is also an imperial for-
tress. The American Civil War, the central historical event for the
generation that included Cather's parents, figures prominently not
only in "The Namesake," which offers a gory picture of battle,
but also in *Sapphira and the Slave Girl* (1940), which records the
conflict's repercussions within the deeply divided community of
Back Creek Valley, Virginia, the writer's home until age nine. In
addition, veterans of the Blue and the Gray, invariably portrayed
as dignified and kindly old men, are scattered throughout Cather's
Nebraska fiction, along with references to their monuments and
meeting halls.

Even more significant are the many moments when World War I,
the conflict that had the greatest personal impact on Cather, enters
into her fictional world. The events of 1914 to 1918 are, of course,
central to *One of Ours*, which focuses on a Nebraska farmer turned
doughboy, and to *The Professor's House* (1925), which in describing a professional historian's response to four years of unprecedented slaughter memorably sums up the War to End All Wars as
"the great catastrophe." Yet World War I appears in other works
as well, often in passages that seem incidental initially but grow in
significance upon rereading. For example, in *Lucy Gayheart* (1935),

Harry Gordon momentarily escapes thoughts of his lost opportunity for happiness with Lucy by plunging into the "war work" offered by the Red Cross and by Herbert Hoover's Food Conservation Program (177). Ultimately Gordon serves overseas with a volunteer ambulance unit (à la Ernest Hemingway and John Dos Passos). And then there are the multiple references to the war in short stories such as "The Old Beauty" (1948), a late (and underappreciated) work whose full meaning only becomes clear when, as Janis P. Stout demonstrates in her contribution to this collection, we read it as an account of a world broken in two by unthinkable violence—a world that went on breaking for Cather until the very end of her life.

The ubiquity of armed conflict whether as a main theme or as a background feature in Cather's writings reflects her historical context, reading, and artistic preoccupations. Indeed, it would be surprising, given the historical events that transpired shortly before and during her lifetime, if Cather's fiction did not touch upon military matters frequently. Born three years before the Battle of Little Bighorn, the last large-scale clash between the U.S. Army and Plains Indians, and just eight years after Lee's surrender at Appomattox, Cather lived to see warfare move onto a terrifying global scale. Judging from her letters—which contain, as Stout has demonstrated in her calendar of Cather's correspondence, with references to conflicts past, present, and future—she seems to have thought of war on a regular basis (particularly after 1914), and few American conflicts from 1861 to 1945 failed to intersect with her life in some significant fashion. As a child and then as an adolescent, Cather witnessed the rituals and pageantry through which Civil War veterans, both Southern and Northern, commemorated the war of their youth, and she soaked up family stories of her lost uncle, William Seibert Boak, a Confederate mortally wounded at Manassas. While in her early teens in the 1880s, Cather created a visual testimony to her fascination with the Civil War by donning a soldier's kepi, perhaps her uncle's, for a Red Cloud photographer (see the frontispiece). Further evidence of her deep-seated interest in the War between the States surfaced during her career as a journalist: in 1900 she offered a highly fictionalized account of her meeting with Stephen Crane in 1895 and recollected a detailed discussion of *The Red Badge of Courage*. (Her familiarity with Crane's war writing shows up elsewhere as well: in 1898 she wrote a scathing review of his poetry volume *War is Kind,* and in 1926 she provided an introduction for his Spanish-American War dispatches collected under the title *Wounds in the Rain and Other Impressions of War.*)

More than three decades after Cather donned the headdress of a Civil War soldier, a very different conflict captured her attention and prompted the most intensive research she ever conducted as a fiction writer. While composing the story of Claude Wheeler, a character partially inspired by the writer's first cousin Grosvenor P. Cather (killed on the Western Front in 1918), she interviewed dozens of soldiers, absorbed most of the major works of World War I literature available by the early 1920s, and even traveled to the battlefields of France, where she saw firsthand the vast cemeteries and swaths of shell-pounded countryside left in the war's wake. However, exorcizing the personal trauma of World War I proved difficult for Cather, and one novel alone could not contain her thoughts on such a shattering historical event. She continued to reflect on "the great catastrophe" throughout the 1920s and 1930s, both in her fiction and in her correspondence, and she contemplated the approach of World War II with weariness and dread (even as she hoped the United States would shake off its isolationism). As James Woodress has observed, Cather's grim thematic concerns in her final novel—paralysis, lust, and betrayal—perhaps have much to do with the violent historical background against which she wrote (483). Three wars arguably inform *Sapphira and the Slave Girl*—the American Civil War, which Cather weaves directly into her narrative; World War I, a central source for her darkening vision during the final third of her life; and World War II, whose opening stages, dominated by fascist victories, were contemporaneous with the novel's composition.

Arranged chronologically, beginning with the American Civil War and ending with World War II, the fourteen essays in this collection examine the presence of armed conflict in Cather's life and art from several theoretical perspectives—ranging from New Historical to formalist—and vary widely in terms of scope and methodology. The essays arc, however, grouped together by common themes and interpretive concerns. Central to the first four is the issue of memory, both personal and cultural, an issue made all the more fascinating by Cather's complex liminality. As a southerner and northerner, Nebraskan and New Yorker, regionalist and Europhile, realist and modernist, Cather provides a particularly rich case study in how a literary artist negotiates often conflicting cultural traditions and ideologies. Among the many questions that *Cather Studies 6* explores are the following: How did Cather *remember* the various conflicts that intersected with her life? And how did her individual memory interact with cultural memory?

Ann Romines starts us down the beckoning path that leads out from such questions with her essay "Willa Cather's Civil War: A Very Long Engagement." Noting that Cather was "the particular target" of Southern Lost Cause mythology, Romines traces Cather's ambivalent attitudes toward her Civil War inheritance all the way from her Virginia childhood to *Sapphira and the Slave Girl,* written almost a lifetime later. As Romines convincingly demonstrates, Cather's final novel turns upside down many of the conventions of Southern Civil War commemoration and nostalgic Southern fiction such as Margaret Mitchell's *Gone With the Wind* (published in 1936, the year that Cather began work on her own depiction of the Old South). A book "without battle scenes or youthful male heroism," *Sapphira* "contains none of the saleable staples of Civil War art." And, even more important, the narrative violates a central Lost Cause taboo by openly confronting the ideological issue at the heart of the war—slavery. At the same time, however, Romines notes instances when the novel resurrects pro-Southern Reconstruction-era stereotypes, as when, for example, the former slave Tap falls prey to an evil carpetbagger and an ignorant Yankee jury. With its many contradictions, *Sapphira* ultimately demonstrates "how difficult and freighted a process the telling of Civil War stories (still) is."

The issue of memory also stands at the heart of Michael Gorman's "Jim Burden and the White Man's Burden: *My Ántonia* and Empire." Just where and how, this essay provocatively asks, are Native Americans *remembered* in Cather's novel of triumphant European settlement on the Great Plains? Do the wars of imperialist aggression that cleared the way for communities such as Black

Hawk receive any recognition in the text? Gorman persuasively argues that the relative absence of references to Native Americans in Jim Burden's narration is, in itself, revealing; indeed, it invites an ironic reading of Cather's often blind and deluded protagonist. Seldom conscious of Nebraska's original inhabitants (his contemplation of the fading horse circle is a rare exception), Jim prefers to define the Plains as virgin territory, as land without human history, as a nothingness waiting to be made into something. The historical realities of violence and displacement that Jim conveniently ignores enter the novel only symbolically—through his slaying of the rattlesnake, an indigenous creature that stands for both the Sioux Indians (whose tribal name was understood in 1918 to mean "venomous snake") and the nation of Spain, an imperial competitor defeated by the United States in 1898.

Margaret Anne O'Connor's essay, "The Not-So-Great War: Cather Family Letters and the Spanish-American War," focuses on memory in a different way. Utilizing materials only recently made available, as part of the George Cather Ray Collection at the University of Nebraska–Lincoln, O'Connor examines the letters that G. P. Cather (later the model for Claude Wheeler) received from several Webster County soldiers who served in the Spanish-American conflict. Ironically, the martial enthusiasm that G. P. later displayed, as he rushed into the ranks of the first American division to reach the Western Front (he would meet his fate in the first American battle of the war), perhaps reflects his failed memory: his turn-of-the-century correspondents described a military experience made up primarily of boredom, discomfort, sickness, and fear. By 1917 G. P. had forgotten the lessons contained in their testimony. Willa Cather, on the other hand, did not forget the ugly side of war as she came to know it during the writing of *One of Ours*, and her novel of the First World War ends, appropriately enough, with a soldier's letters in the hands of a grieving mother who sees through her son's illusions.

Titled "Between Two Wars in a Breaking World: Willa Cather and the Persistence of War Consciousness," Janis P. Stout's essay deals with the burden of memory. Drawing upon Cather's correspondence and published writings (particularly neglected short stories and essays) from the interwar decades, Stout argues that

Cather never fully recovered from the "shock" of World War I, with its ten million casualties and host of industrialized horrors, and that her sense of living in a world forever broken by war colored virtually everything she wrote after 1918. In particular, Stout locates evidence of Cather's war consciousness in the stories "Uncle Valentine" (1925), "Double Birthday" (1929), and "The Old Beauty" (1948), as well as the essay "148 Charles Street" (1936). From this bold, exploratory analysis, a new version of Cather emerges. In his landmark study *The Great War and Modern Memory* (1975), Paul Fussell focuses on the way in which British literary artists responded to the historical and cultural ruptures produced my mass slaughters like the 1916 Battle of the Somme. According to Fussell, the grotesque realities of the Western Front fostered a volatile mode of interpretation that he terms "modern memory," a mode characterized in part by stark, ironic dichotomies (e.g., cavalry versus machine guns, bloodthirsty generals versus Christlike troops, optimistic strategy versus stalemate and disaster). Stout posits a similar dynamic at work within Cather's creative imagination, which abounds in its own extreme dichotomies and incessant breakages. No one who reads this exciting analysis will see Cather's post–World War I fiction the same way again.

The next five essays in this volume all focus on *One of Ours*, a controversial book that has finally come into its own as a sophisticated, if ambivalent, statement on war and its construction within early-twentieth-century American culture. One signal of the novel's belated recognition as a major work came in 2002, when the University of Nebraska–Lincoln hosted a daylong conference titled "Great Passions, Great Aspirations: Willa Cather and World War I." Most of the papers and panels featured at that memorable event focused on *One of Ours*, and they revealed a text that is remarkably multi-layered—even by Cather standards. Originally presented at the Great Passions, Great Aspirations conference, Pearl James's essay, "The 'Enid Problem': Dangerous Modernity in *One of Ours*," plunges us straight into the novel's formidable complexity by focusing on a character who has become something of a critical lightning rod—Claude Wheeler's wife, Enid Royce. Arguing that "*One of Ours* conflates a nostalgia for 'natural' pre-industrial frontier life with a nostalgia for traditional femininity," James presents Enid as a "dangerous New Woman," whose defiance of traditional gender roles brings her inevitably into conflict with her husband. Other critics have made similar observations. However, what sets James's analysis apart is the depth and specificity with which she links Enid's threatening modernity, in all its many facets, to the turbulent background of wartime America. Enid's "scientific domestic economy," for example, "reflects the discourse used to mobilize women on the home front, in their kitchens, parlors, and gardens." Likewise, Enid's accomplished handling of an automobile (Claude, one notes, relinquishes that masculine holy of holies, the driver's seat) evokes the entry of American women into the Motor Corps, one of many wartime expediencies that destabilized conventional notions of gender. By establishing such connections, James offers the most thorough analysis to date of a character whose disappearance halfway though the narrative belies her many connections to the war that ultimately destroys Claude.

Bayliss Wheeler, one of Cather's most unpleasant creations, receives a similarly thorough and detail-rich analysis from Celia M. Kingsbury. Titled "'Squeezed into an Unnatural Shape': Bayliss Wheeler and the Element of Control in *One of Ours*," Kingsbury's essay establishes Claude's neo-materialistic, pleasure-killing older brother as a small-town version of Henry Ford and John Harvey Kellogg, American moguls driven by a socially sanctioned "desire to acquire and control." Likening Frankfort to a Foucaultian panopticon, with Bayliss as its "enforcer and executioner," Kingsbury notes the many nuances that go into this repellent character's portraiture—his connection, for example, with German *Kultur* as it was constructed by American propagandists and his ironic kinship with Enid, his near Doppelganger.

The other three essays on *One of Ours* all focus on the novel's most problematic section—Books IV and V, where Cather depicts her protagonist's service in the American Expeditionary Forces. Dismissing this portion of the text, combined with some expression of regret that Cather did keep her story in Nebraska, became standard in the negative reviews that the novel received in 1922, and scholars today remain divided when it comes to determining the success or failure of Cather's rendering of military life. However, anyone who doubts the intricacy of Cather's artistry in the second half of her most controversial novel would do well to study Mary R. Ryder's essay, "'As Green as Their Money': The Doughboy Naïfs in *One of Ours*," an exceptionally close reading that locates unexpected significance in what seems, at first sight, to be entirely clichéd language. Zeroing in on Cather's back-and-forth references to American soldiers as "men" and as "boys," Ryder demonstrates that Claude and his companions "must . . . play a double role in the national imagination." Citing numerous World War I propaganda posters, Ryder concludes that *men*, as defined within wartime discourse, were robustly masculine—trained killers who endured and inflicted violence. *Boys*, on the other hand, were innocent, clumsy, and soft—the perfect signifiers for propaganda that played up the moral purity and disinterestedness of American intervention. Tested in the manly arena of combat but still a child in his understanding of French culture (as well as the geopolitical realities of World War I), Claude moves uneasily between these two discursive roles and becomes in the process "the prototype" of the American soldier.

Mark A. Robison and Debra Rae Cohen shed additional light on the war chapters in *One of Ours* by considering the related themes of recreation and tourism. Robison's essay, "Recreation in World War I and the Practice of Play in *One of Ours*," situates Cather's novel within a unique cultural context— "the curious intersection between war efforts and the ideas emerging in the new field of recreation." After offering a detailed account of the early-twentieth-century recreation movement, which worked to provide American adults with opportunities for healthy outdoor play, and the U.S. War Department's emphasis on morale building amusements and diversions, Robinson demonstrates that Claude's sense of joy in Books V and VI has little to do with combat (thus, he is not, contrary to Stanley Cooperman's influential interpretation, a true war lover). Instead, Robinson ties Claude's contentment to the recreational opportunities offered by the American Expeditionary Forces—to the musical performances, culturally enriching travel, games, and quiet walks that Claude enjoys as a soldier. Meticulously researched, Robison's contribution to this volume represents New Historicism at its best and breaks entirely new scholarly ground. In "Culture and the 'Cathedral': Tourism as Potlatch in *One of Ours*," Debra Rae Cohen offers a theoretically sophisticated discussion of the tourist/traveler trope, both as it operates in Cather's novel and in the World War I writings of other American women authors. As Cohen demonstrates, Claude Wheeler's shifting qualifications as a tourist one moment and a traveler the next ultimately destabilize the distinction that Cather employs. Moreover, Claude's journey through wartime France, as part of an overfed, oversupplied army, illustrates "the mechanism of potlatch, the deceptive mechanism of competitive 'wastage' of capital central to the theories of George Bataille." A dense reading anchored in both deconstruction and cultural theory, Cohen's essay provides a new interpretive framework for Claude's overseas experiences.

Three years after drawing the fire of indignant male critics, who were incensed to see a noncombatant, a woman no less, venture into the territory of war literature, Cather returned to the subject of World War I in a major novel but this time in a manner that leaves the conflict's thematic importance more implied than explicit. Cather's decision to make the "great catastrophe" practically invisible in *The Professor's House* has prompted questions ever since. Just how central to the narrative is World War I? Does the war function chiefly as a plot device, a means to separate Tom Outland from his mentor and, ultimately, to kill him off? Or is the war connected in subtle but essential ways to the novel's treatment of the St. Peter family and its concern with technology and science? Four contributors to this volume—Susan Meyer, Jennifer Haytock, Wendy K. Perriman, and Steven Trout—provide answers to these questions, and taken together, their essays forcefully suggest that without the presence of World War I, however shadowy or "unnamed," *The Professor's House* would be a very different novel indeed.

In "On the Front and at Home: Wharton, Cather, the Jews, and the First World War," Susan Meyer focuses on the Professor's Jewish son-in-law, Louie Marsellus, and, in response to critics who have accused Cather of anti-Semitism, sets this character alongside representations of Jews in American wartime and postwar discourse. In particular, she contrasts Marsellus with the repellently

STEVEN TROUT

drawn Jews featured in Edith Wharton's World War I novel *A Son at the Front* (1923) and concludes that Cather's character ultimately reflects an "ambivalence about what constitutes the most appropriate human response to [the] 'great catastrophe.'"

Jennifer Haytock's "Looking at Agony: World War I in *The Professor's House*" focuses on Tom Outland's decision to join the French Foreign Legion, the impact of his death on Godfrey St. Peter, and the disturbing conception of "civilization" that Cather's novel offers. Arguing that Outland is less callow at the time of his enlistment than most critics have acknowledged, Haytock attributes his departure not to propaganda-inspired idealism but to his realization (achieved as he studies the mesa dwellers' extinction) that cultures unwilling to wage war face certain annihilation. Haytock then shifts the discussion to Outland's mentor and convincingly establishes that St. Peter "fails to find a way to mourn Tom specifically. . . . Instead of grieving, the Professor simply cuts himself off from his past." St. Peter's inability to confront the loss of Outland reflects the emotional numbness that slowly envelops him during Book I of the novel and that leaves him, in the end, tied to his family, not by love but by a sense of duty. Thus, *The Professor's House* offers "difficult, even heretical, truths: that war, though pointless, is unavoidable and that family love may wear out and die. Both of these points seem to be contrary to 'civilization,' but Cather suggests instead that 'civilization' is created by an impersonal feeling of responsibility rather than by individual and unreliable loyalties."

Cather's treatment of war-related science, technology, and commerce receives attention in Wendy K. Perriman's "Cather's Literary Choreography: The 'Glittering Idea' of Scientific Warfare in *The Professor's House*" and Steven Trout's "Rebuilding the Outland Engine: A New Source for *The Professor's House*." Both essays stress the spongelike nature of Cather's artistic imagination, which absorbed and recycled details drawn from every imaginable cultural venue—from ballet performances to daily newspapers. Perriman focuses on Cather's love of ballet and the likely influence of dance-based "plots, themes, twists, reversals, and techniques" on her fiction. In the case of *The Professor's House*, Perriman casts the sinister link between Outland's scientific study and World War

I aviation as an ironic reversal of the positivistic message contained in the ballet *Excelsior* (1881), a widely performed work that Cather almost certainly encountered between 1908 and 1914. An allegory depicting the triumph of scientific enlightenment over the dark forces of ignorance and violence, *Excelsior* personified pre–World War I optimism. *The Professor's House,* on the other hand, shows that science and destruction are linked. The ballets *Jeux* (1913) and *Faust* (1848), Perriman goes on to demonstrate, probably influenced Cather as well. These two works supplied motifs that ultimately find their way into Cather's depiction of the St. Peter family, as well as the homoeroticism that runs throughout her narrative. Likewise focused on scientific development and on the issue of Cather's artistic sources, Trout's essay posits a connection between the Outland engine, credited in *The Professor's House* with "revolutionizing aviation," and the Liberty engine, one of the United States' most publicized technological contributions to the Allied war effort. Although the two machines are dissimilar in many respects, Trout contends that the production history of the Liberty engine, as extensively covered in the *New York Times,* may have offered Cather a positive image of the "pep and can-do spirit" of American manufactures and, at the same time, "turned her thoughts to the fuzzy morality of wartime contract procurement." Thus, "even the most seemingly fanciful of Cather's fictions—an implausibly revolutionary aircraft engine—has a complex basis in her material culture."

Mary Chinery's "Wartime Fictions: Willa Cather, the Armed Services Editions, and the Unspeakable Second World War" forms an appropriate coda to this collection by showing how Cather helped provide much-needed diversion for American soldiers during World War II. After agreeing in 1943 to contribute a section of *Death Comes for the Archbishop* to a servicemen's anthology edited by New York theater critic Alexander Woollcott, Cather went on to authorize the reprinting of several of her best-known novels in cheaply made, ultra-compact Armed Services editions. As Chinery observes, Cather's willingness in this instance to see her work distributed in paperback form was unprecedented. Utterly dictatorial when it came to the physical presentation of her writing (right down to the type style, width of margins, and weight of paper),

Cather hated the notion of cheap soft-cover printings, denied requests from analogy editors as a matter of course, and blocked radio readings of her fiction that might well have expanded her audience. Thus, her participation in the Armed Services editions program reflected her deeply felt desire to serve the Allied war effort in the best way that she could. And, as it turns out, her generosity brought unforeseen rewards. Though she may not have known so at the time, the distribution of her novels among thousands of book-ravenous soldiers greatly expanded her visibility as an author and arguably helped elevate her name within the American literary canon.

More work on the braided themes of history, memory, and war in Cather's writing remains to be done, and it is hoped that the essays provided here, many of them by authors who have only recently fallen under Cather's spell, will suggest further avenues of inquiry and thereby attract still more newcomers to Cather scholarship. With this desire, the late Susan J. Rosowski would be in accord. The series editor of Cather Studies from its inception until her death in 2004, Susan worked tirelessly to bring fresh faces and ideas into an always vibrant and ever-expanding community of scholars and friends. Without her encouragement, this volume would not have been possible. Without her leadership, Cather's reputation would not be what it is today.

WORKS CITED

Acocella, Joan. *Willa Cather and the Politics of Criticism.* Lincoln: U of Nebraska P, 2000.

Cather, Willa. *Death Comes for the Archbishop.* New York: Knopf, 1927.

———. "Double Birthday." *Forum* 81 (February 1929): 78–92

———. *A Lost Lady.* New York: Knopf, 1923.

———. *Lucy Gayheart.* New York: Knopf, 1935.

———. *My Ántonia.* Boston: Houghton, 1918.

———. "The Namesake." 1907. *Willa Cather's Collected Short Fiction, 1892–1912.* Ed. Virginia Faulkner. Lincoln: U of Nebraska P, 1965. 137–46.

———. "The Old Beauty." *The Old Beauty and Others.* New York: Knopf, 1948. 3–72.

———. "148 Charles Street." *Not Under Forty*. New York: Knopf, 1936. 52-75.

———. *One of Ours*. New York: Knopf, 1922.

———. *The Professor's House*. New York: Knopf, 1925.

———. *Sapphira and the Slave Girl*. New York: Knopf, 1940.

———. *Shadows on the Rock*. New York: Knopf, 1931.

———. "Uncle Valentine." *Woman's Home Companion* (February 1925): 60-85.

———. "When I Knew Stephen Crane." 1900. *The World and the Parish, Willa Cather's Articles and Reviews, 1893-1902*. Ed. William M. Curtin. Lincoln: U of Nebraska P, 1970. 776.

Cooperman, Stanley. *World War I and the American Novel*. Baltimore: The Johns Hopkins UP, 1967.

Fussell, Paul. *The Great War and Modern Memory*. London: Oxford UP, 1975.

Stout, Janis P. *A Calendar of the Letters of Willa Cather*. Lincoln: U of Nebraska P, 2002.

Woodress, James. *Willa Cather: A Literary Life*. Lincoln: U of Nebraska P, 1987.

Willa Cather's Civil War
A Very Long Engagement

ANN ROMINES

Willa Cather's story "The Namesake" was published in
1907, soon after her move to New York City as an editor of the
influential *McClure's Magazine*. With a volume of poems and one
of stories published and a career at the center of American literary
and publishing culture opening up in front of her, Cather appears
in this story to be thinking about what makes an artist "American," about what an American artist's resources are. In the story
a group of young, male American artists gather in Paris around a
successful sculptor, Lyon Hartwell, who seems to epitomize what
it means to be an American artist: "to mean all of it, from ocean
to ocean" (137). To these young men, who have come from various
U.S. locales (but not from the South, where Cather was born), a
Paris studio is the place where they imagine that they can become
players in the exhilarating game of American art in which Hartwell is so brilliantly succeeding. "Never had the game seemed so
enchanting, the chance to play it such a piece of unmerited, unbelievable good fortune" (138). Hartwell's success has been built
on a series of iconic images of male heroism drawn from the con-
tinuum of U.S. history; he has "thrown up in bronze all the restless,
teeming force of that adventurous wave still climbing westward in
our own land across the waters . . . his *Scout*, his *Pioneer*, his *Gold
Seekers*, and those monuments in which he had invested one and
another of the heroes of the Civil War with such convincing dignity and power." The height of Hartwell's achievement is his latest
work, *The Color Sergeant*, which will be "cast in bronze, intended
as a monument for some American battlefield. . . . It was the figure

of a young [Union] soldier running, clutching the folds of a flag, the staff of which had been shot away." The figure is full of "splendid action and feeling" (139). The description of Hartwell's work emphasizes that he has achieved both artistic and marketplace success, tapping into postbellum America's appetite to memorialize its own legendary (and recent) history, particularly through the monumental sculpture that commemorated the Civil War.[1]

For the aspiring acolytes who cluster around Hartwell in his Paris studio, expatriation seems one of the rules of the game, and a summons "home" to America, such as one of their number has received, is a disaster that threatens their status as artists. Hartwell responds to his young friend's departure with a story about his discovery of his own U.S. "citizenship" as a source of his deepest feelings and his art, as expressed in *The Color Sergeant*. He was born in Italy, son of an expatriate father and a mother who died early and had no acknowledged influence on her son. His father was an unsuccessful sculptor ("I dare say you've not heard of him") who remained in Rome until his death, "chipping away at his Indian maidens and marble goddesses, still gloomily seeking the thing for which he had made himself the most unhappy of exiles." When the Civil War broke out, he did not return home to Pennsylvania to enlist in the Union army, and was thus considered a "renegade" by his family (140). For Hartwell, his father seems to embody the dark side of expatriation, and his conventional female subjects cut him off from the sanctioned narrative of U.S. male heroism. He is the problematic noncombatant ancestor—and yet Hartwell is clearly the beneficiary of his father's ambitions and profession and of the Roman education that his father decreed for him.[2]

As a young man whose career as a sculptor was just beginning to flourish, Hartwell was also summoned back to the United States by family duty: his father's sister, nearly helpless from a "cerebral disease," needed his care. At the lonely family house the only connection he feels is to a portrait of a dead uncle for whom he was named but never met. This namesake enlisted in the Union army at fifteen and died as a color sergeant bearing the flag a year later. Since the aunt can summon up few memories of her soldier brother, who is buried in the orchard, Hartwell pieces together the story of his brief career and heroic death from "an old soldier in the village" and a comrade's newspaper account of the boy's death. Hartwell also begins to read Civil War history in books collected by his grandfather. To Hartwell, this uncle—whose name he shares and whose identity thus seems to be entwined with his own—"seemed to have possessed all the charm and brilliance allotted to his family and to have lived up its vitality in one splendid hour" (143–44). Then, in response to the stimulus of a powerful national impulse—Decoration Day on May 30, an observance that began in 1865 and grew to an important national ritual of Civil War remembrance by the late nineteenth century—the aunt rouses herself to commemoration: she instructs Hartwell to run up the "big flag" on the uncle's grave and goes with him to decorate the grave with "garden flowers" (see fig. 1). That day, Hartwell at last discovers the trunk—marked with the name they share—in which the dead boy's mother packed away her son's belongings: clothing, toys, war letters, and a textbook embellished with his childish drawings of military paraphernalia, a "Federal flag" and lines from the national anthem. Clutching this book, which suddenly gives him the sense that he "knows" his uncle, Hartwell spends the night sitting at the soldier's grave, as the flag tosses above him in the dark. It is a rending, overwhelming experience:

> It was the same feeling that artists know when we, rarely, achieve truth in our work; the feeling of union with some great force, of purpose and security, of being glad that we have lived. For the first time I felt the pull of race and blood and kindred, and felt beating within me things that had not begun with me. It was as if the earth under my feet had grasped and rooted me, and were pouring its essence into me. I sat there until the dawn of morning, and all night long my life seemed to be pouring out of me and running into the ground. (146)

Hartwell has found his "citizenship," the other half of his inheritance, the meaning of his name, and his nationality. For the first time in his life he feels rooted, tied by kinship and by passion to a national and familial tradition that is not purely personal: "things that had not begun with me." The earth, which contains his uncle, asserts its claim on him, "pouring its essence" into Hartwell, and

Fig. 1. This turn-of-the-century postcard commemorates Decoration Day with some of the iconography that had become associated with that holiday, established to honor Civil War dead. The central wreath is a conventional tribute to heroism, and the U.S. and Confederate flags are of equal size and importance, suggesting that both armies are honored. The flags become the clothing of the central young woman, implying that memorializing is a female task. Ruth Rogers Romines Collection, courtesy of the author.

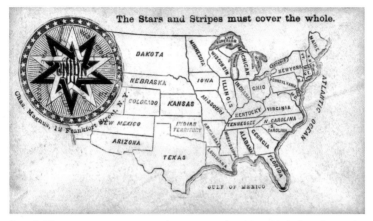

Fig. 2. This commemorative envelope, printed in New York City during the Civil War years, underlines the importance of the U.S. flag ("The Stars and Stripes must cover the whole" map of U.S. territories and states—even the seceded states) and of UNION, the word emblazoned across the red, white, and blue star at upper left. Collection of the author.

he responds in kind, in imagery that suggests both semen and blood, both life and death, as his life "seemed to be pouring out of me and running into the ground." For Hartwell, this is not only an experience of discovering and acknowledging family and national connections; it is also his making, as a specifically American artist.

Federal language emphasized that the Civil War was fought to "preserve the Union." A typical bit of ephemera from the Civil War years, a decorated envelope printed in New York, is emblazoned with a red, white, and blue star with "UNION" at its center, superimposed on a map of the entire United States, including the seceded states. Above is this legend: "The Stars and Stripes must cover the whole" (see fig. 2). The language that describes Hartwell suggests these same Union priorities: as an artist, he means "all of it," the *whole* nation "from ocean to ocean" and the "adventurous wave" of its settlement and defense. When his work succeeds in achieving "truth," Hartwell says, he has a "feeling of union." As an artist, then, he can memorialize both his uncle and the cause for which the young color sergeant died, "with the flag settling about him" (176). On many levels, Hartwell has found a way, through his art, to preserve the Union. And yet he does so as an expatriate

American artist, living out the legacies of both the soldier uncle and the noncombatant father.

In her sympathetic portrait of Lyon Hartwell, Cather invented an American artist born in 1854 who was able to draw sustenance from both a native and an expatriate heritage and whose art responds powerfully to the national priorities of his time, of which a central event was the Civil War. As David W. Blight writes, "The most immediate legacy of the war was its slaughter and how to remember it" (64). This legacy of loss and memory created Hartwell's market—all those battlefield monuments—and his private/public epiphany is occasioned by a national observance, Decoration Day. According to Blight, "Decoration Day, and the ways in which it was observed, shaped Civil War memory as much as any other cultural ritual" (65). In addition, as he sought his namesake's story, Hartwell participated in other memorial rituals that Americans observed in the years after the war: he heard and read stories by veterans; he studied Civil War histories; he examined the relics of the dead soldier preserved (as was customary) by his female relatives. Participating in such rituals, and producing art that will become a part of them, Hartwell—even though he is in France—can achieve a powerful (and lucrative) union with his culture.

As we read the narrative of Cather's career, "The Namesake" might first seem to reveal a thirty-some-year-old writer examining a model for her own career as American artist, and in particular claiming the Civil War and its remembrance as a subject. In fact, few American writers of her generation so fully owned that subject, by inheritance, as Cather. Her father, Charles Cather, and her paternal uncle, George Cather, had been noncombatants in the war. The Cather family, living in Frederick County in the Shenandoah Valley of Virginia, a region that saw heavy and constant combat, supported the Union cause. The two sons briefly moved into West Virginia near the war's end, to avoid the Confederate draft, but neither joined the Union army. (Cather's father was only seventeen when the war ended.) However, Cather's three maternal uncles all joined the Confederate army, and one of them died in 1862, at nineteen, of wounds received at Second Manassas.[3] Cather's mother, Mary Virginia Boak Cather, and her maternal grandmother, Rachel Seibert Boak, told stories of this family war hero, and his sword, uniform, and a Confederate flag were preserved as family relics. Civil War stories from both sides of the family—the Union Cathers and the Confederate Boaks—were a staple component of Cather's childhood and adolescence, both in her Virginia birthplace and later in Nebraska, and a famous photograph of adolescent Cather in a Confederate cap suggests that she may have used the family relics to enact such stories herself. In some ways, Cather's own inheritance replicates Hartwell's, with combatant and noncombatant ancestors, relics of a dead hero preserved by loving women, and a repertoire of war stories in fact far more extensive than the expatriate Hartwell's.[4]

A few years before the story "The Namesake," Cather had published a poem of the same title, which was closer than Hartwell's story to her own family legacy. In it, a somewhat androgynous young speaker stands at the grave of a young uncle, a Confederate war casualty, whose name he bears.[5] The speaker resembles the dead soldier ("with hair like mine") and, in ringing couplets, he expresses his eagerness to share the hero's military life ("help you hold your gun") and death, leaving his "girl" behind to share the soldier's "bed of glory," a grave. However, this young speaker is no self-abnegating mourner, caught up in a death wish—instead he looks toward his own future, aiming to "be winner at the game / Enough for two who bore the name." He intends to be a player, and he is drawn to "the game" as powerfully as are the young artists who cluster around Hartwell in Paris.

Cather's poem, when originally published in 1902, had this dedication: "To W.L.B., of the Thirty-Fifth Virginia." As Bernice Slote observes, "W.L.B. could refer only to Cather's maternal grandfather, William Lee Boak [who had died well before the war, in 1854], and, like the 'Thirty-Fifth' was clearly an error that was corrected in 1903," with publication in *April Twilights*, to "To W.S.B. of the Thirty-Third Virginia" (55). Cather's biographers have assumed that this corrected dedication refers to her dead Confederate uncle, William Seibert Boak, who was indeed a member of "the Thirty-Third Virginia." However, that uncle's name was actually James William Boak, as his military records and tombstone confirm. (Another Confederate uncle was Jacob Seibert Boak, but he survived the war.) Apparently young Cather was confused about some of the details of her family's Civil War history and her own Confederate genealogy when she made this slight but telling alteration in her uncle's name. Also, by this time she had adopted "Sibert" (an alternate spelling used by some family members) as her own middle name. She would continue to be Willa Sibert Cather professionally until mid-career and personally until the end of her life. So she needed a namesake with the Seibert name. In addition, Cather had been called "Willie" by family and close friends since babyhood. One source for the nickname was her female namesake, paternal aunt Wilella Cather, who died of diphtheria in 1869 at the age of four; Wilella too had been called "Willie" by the Cather family. (Cather herself had changed her given name from "Wilella" to "Willa" when, as a child, she altered the inscription in the family Bible.) But "Willie" may have honored her mother's dead brother, James William, who was also called by that nickname, as well as her father's dead sister. The fact that Cather, early in her career, produced two works titled "The Namesake" suggests that an identification with a namesake was a special issue for her, and one that linked her to the Civil War.

Of the two works, the 1907 story is the more rich and complex; it foreshadows Cather's great fiction to come. But it also implies—if one reads autobiographical elements in both poem and story, as most critics have—that Cather is revising away some of the complications of her actual genealogy as it was reflected in her name. "Wilella/Willa/Willie" suggests a name both inherited and chosen, with androgynous possibilities. "Cather" ties her to her paternal tradition of noncombatant support of the Union cause. And by adding "Sibert" to her name, she evoked her slave-owning Virginia Seibert ancestors and her ties to her beloved Confederate Grandmother Boak (who was born a Seibert), as well as the Confederate soldier. To make the Civil War ancestor a Union soldier eliminates most of these conflicting loyalties and makes possible Hartwell's personal and artistic act of union with the dead soldier, a union that advances his career—as the publication of the story in a major national magazine, *McClure's*, may well have advanced Cather's career.[6] As Lisa Marcus has suggested, "Perhaps Cather, more cosmopolitan and worldly in 1907, recognized that her dedication to her dead Confederate relative was problematic"

(108). In her story, Cather proposed a model for Civil War art that seemed to promise success in the early-twentieth-century market where she was positioning herself and to offer options for writing some of the Civil War stories that were part of her own rich legacy.

However, as we know, those stories did not follow. Instead, the Civil War is remarkably absent from Cather's oeuvre until her last novel, published in 1940. *Sapphira and the Slave Girl* spans the years between 1856 and 1881, and it is set in Cather's ancestral Virginia (one of the most heavily contested areas of the war), where she spent her first years, 1873–83. Here, at last, was Cather's Civil War novel, following closely upon such notable Civil War fictions as *Absalom, Absalom!* and *Gone with the Wind*, both published in 1936, the year that Cather began to write *Sapphira*. But this Civil War novel is one without battle scenes or youthful male heroism of the sort celebrated in *The Color Sergeant*. Nor does it feature exhausted women such as Hartwell's aunt, wasted in body and in memory, for whom Decoration Day—devoted to Civil War memories—is the most important day of the year, or elderly male veterans full of war stories, such as the one who tells Hartwell about his uncle. In Cather's novel, all these saleable staples of Civil War art are notably absent. In fact, the war itself is absent; *Sapphira* comprises 269 pages set on a slaveholding Virginia plantation/farm in 1856, followed by a 20-page epilogue set twenty-five years later. The war years are a powerful absence at the center of the book.

Cather had been a child of Reconstruction, born eight years after the war's end. According to Bertram Wyatt-Brown, "When the Civil War came to its bloody end, the white people of the Confederacy felt the shame of defeat, a sense of profound hopelessness, and a fear of the future" (230). Reconstruction measures established Union martial law in the South; these measures required the rewriting of state constitutions to accommodate the changed legal status of African Americans, attempted to broaden the bases of public education, and encouraged economic recovery. But, as Joseph M. Flora has written, in the South this "Reconstruction history was readily subsumed under the myth of Reconstruction that portrayed Reconstruction efforts as totally wrong and resulting in state governments . . . composed of Negroes ill-prepared for office, 'carpetbaggers,' . . . and 'scalawags'" (727). Southern historians William J. Cooper and Thomas E. Terrill add that white "Southerners came to view Reconstruction as a Tragic Era" and "salved wounds of defeat and feelings of massive wrong with this and other legends: the Lost Cause . . . the Old South" (383, 389). As a child in a postwar white Southern family, Cather was the particular target of this mythology; if it was to survive (as it did), children of her generation would need to absorb and perpetuate it. Many Southerners—particularly women—organized to combat the "intrusions" of Reconstruction with educational projects aimed specifically at white children (Clinton 182-84). And, as a female relative of men who had fought for the Confederacy, Cather inherited the obligation to memorialize them (as she did in her poem "The Namesake") and the cause for which they fought—another postwar women's project that was especially prominent in Virginia, where there are 223 Confederate memorials, more than in any other state.

Frederick County had suffered severely in the war. It was considered "mandatory for the Confederacy to hold this region that . . . was bountifully productive of . . . wheat, beef, leather, horses, cloth—but also was strategically placed and shielded by the Blue Ridge so that a Confederate Army in Winchester and the northern [Shenandoah] Valley would always threaten not only Washington but also Maryland and Pennsylvania" (Colt 8). Thus the county's major town, Winchester (only eleven miles west of the Cathers' home in Back Creek Valley), "from the summer of 1861 through the fall of 1864 . . . knew the occupation or threatening proximity of one army or the other." No other town of this size saw so much action during those four years (Colt 8-9). Although many Frederick Countians had been Union sympathizers at the war's beginning, by its end, "the majority of citizens were firmly aligned with the South, primarily because of the harsh treatment they had received from Union troops" (Kalbian 73). After Appomattox, Frederick County's Confederate soldiers "came home to a wasteland— no trees, no fences, no barns, no mills. . . . A great many people had invested their all—what was not in the ravaged land—in Confederate money and bonds. There was no remaining capital to fuel new enterprises" (Colt 19).

In this climate the noncombatant, Unionist Cathers fared better than many of their neighbors. Their home, Willow Shade, was not significantly damaged, and they had not lost sons or property or suffered severe financial reverses during the war, as many of their neighbors had. After the war, Cather's grandfather, William Cather, was appointed sheriff by the occupying Union troops; he hired his own sons and nephew as deputies, and the family remained financially stable. There are persistent rumors that this good luck was resented in Back Creek Valley. In 1872 members of the William Cather family began to emigrate to Nebraska, seeking better crops, financial opportunity, and a healthier climate for daughters who suffered from tuberculosis. Cather's young parents, Charles and Mary Virginia, along with Grandma Boak, remained in Frederick County and ran the profitable family sheep farm at Willow Shade—until 1883, when their sheep barn burned (there were rumors of arson). Within a few weeks, the family moved to Nebraska; Cather was nine years old. As recently as 1952 a Frederick County woman claimed that the Charles Cather family "left this country and moved to Red Cloud because of some mean low down gossip" (Hannum)—possibly suggesting that Reconstruction tensions spurred their removal.

During Cather's childhood in Frederick County, so recently embattled, among persons who had experienced the conditions of war at close hand, stories of the war and the circumstances that preceded it were a cultural staple. And in the Cather household, most of the storytellers appear to have been women. Mary Virginia Boak told stories of her Confederate brothers, particularly the dead one. Marjorie Anderson, the family servant in both Virginia and Nebraska, had several brothers in the Confederate army; she is evoked as Mahailey, a teller of Virginia war tales, in *One of Ours* (Lewis 11–12). A favorite great-aunt, Sidney Cather Gore, prototype for the abolitionist Mrs. Bywaters in *Sapphira*, hid soldiers from both armies in her "rambling garrets" (*Sapphira* 274); Cather surely heard such stories from her, as well as from both her grandmothers. In a 1969 interview, Cather's Red Cloud friend Carrie Miner Sherwood—then almost one hundred years old—recalled the stories told by Rachel Boak, who died in 1893:

We were just as fond of Grandmother Boak, Willie's maternal grandmother, as the Cathers were. She was a little Southern lady who had lived through the war. She held us spellbound with first-hand accounts of the Civil War. As I remember it [incorrectly], she had sons in both armies.

We loved to have her tell and retell about the time the soldiers took possession of their home near Shenandoah [sic], Virginia. And how, at night, she would go with supplies for the boys to the Confederate camp, and the following night take supplies to the Union camp. (Hoover 150)

In a letter to a friend at the time of *Sapphira*'s publication, Cather also said that the stories told by her Grandmother Boak and by "Aunt Till," a former slave who had belonged to Rachel Boak's parents, provided her understanding of antebellum Back Creek Valley (Cather to Dorothy Canfield Fisher).

So it seems apparent that much of the material for Cather's Civil War novel was a product of the Reconstruction years and those that immediately followed and the patterns of storytelling—both private and published—that those years produced. One of the earliest and most successful of Southern writers from those years was a Shenandoah Valley veteran and novelist, John Esten Cooke, whom Cather's parents presumably admired: his books were in their library, and they named one of their sons John Esten Cather. Cooke wrote from a romantic Confederate perspective, celebrating such Shenandoah Valley heroes as Stonewall Jackson and Turner Ashby, and he developed a national audience. According to Blight, "Combining literary ambition with a genteel Lost Cause outlook, Cooke demonstrated that some soldiers were ready early to refashion war memories into cultural and political dividends" (157)—dividends such as Cather celebrated in Hartwell's Civil War sculpture. By the 1880s, Blight argues, "reconciliation" was the desired theme of Civil War literature for both Southern and Northern readers. "The war was drained of evil, and to a great extent, of cause or political meaning." For the most part, "the ideological character of the war, especially the reality of emancipation, had faded from American literature." Such a literature denied "that the war and its aftermath were all about race" (215,

217, 221). Even such a masterly psychological study of the war as Stephen Crane's *The Red Badge of Courage* (1895) shared this ideological emptiness—as did Hartwell's *The Color Sergeant.*

Coming of age in the late nineteenth century as an artist, and as an artist who might write about the Civil War, Cather must have been bombarded with conflicting precedents. From Rachel Boak and "Aunt Till," she heard of the "slave girl" Nancy's cruel harassment and difficult escape—as well as Till's hagiographic tales (very much in the romantic "faithful slave" mode) of the "Master" and "Mistress" who owned Nancy and Till herself. Were the postwar years—when Nancy memorably returned to Back Creek Valley for a reconciliatory visit—a period of calm and reunion, or of angry tensions that may have helped to precipitate the Cathers' departure for Nebraska? "Lost Cause" ideology would have pushed Cather to memorialize Southern heroics, as epitomized in the soldier-uncle of her poem, while the national market for benign "reconciliation" would have enjoined her to drain ideology—and particularly issues of race—from Civil War art. No wonder that, after the publication of her two versions of "The Namesake," Cather eschewed the Civil War for thirty years!

When Cather began to write *Sapphira,* she was sixty-three and an established major "player" in the game of American letters. At that point she was more than ready to set her own priorities. Perhaps the most striking feature of her 1940 Civil War novel is that it contradicts most of the precedents that might have constrained her in the late nineteenth and early twentieth centuries. The major portion of the novel, set in 1856, foreshadows the coming war in Sapphira and Henry Colbert's slaveholding household. As Henry agonizes over whether slavery is morally (and religiously) justifiable and whether his marriage vows obligate him to keep his wife's human property enslaved, the invalid Sapphira becomes jealous of her husband's obvious attachment to the innocent "slave girl" Nancy and invites a sexually predatory nephew, Martin, for a long visit, with the apparent hope that he will rape Nancy. Meanwhile, Sapphira and Henry's adult daughter, Rachel, who has opposed slaveholding since her childhood, decides (with the help of local Quaker connections to the Underground Railroad) to help the terrified Nancy escape to Canada. Nancy leaves without saying a word about her intentions to her own mother, Till (Sapphira's most trusted slave), or to anyone else in the slave community, and proud Till is reduced to surreptitiously asking Rachel about her own daughter's welfare. Surmising Rachel's aid to Nancy, Sapphira cuts off relations with her daughter. They are partially, formally reconciled only when Rachel loses one of her young daughters to diphtheria and Sapphira is so ill that she needs her daughter's constant attendance. The minute Sapphira dies, Henry frees all her slaves (he had offered to free his capable assistant, Sampson, earlier, and Sampson refused the offer, preferring the security of his life as a slave).

In this trenchant plot, Cather shows how the institution of slavery blights white and black family and marital relations, invoking the sexual anger of white women who observed or suspected white men's sexual relations with slave women and resultant mulatto children, like Nancy, as well as the family splits that were exacerbated by the war, especially in border regions like the northern Virginia county where Cather's family lived, and economic conflict between slaves and poor white laborers. As Tomas Pollard has shown, the political events of the 1850s that culminated in war in 1861 are very much a presence in this novel (38–45). The text invokes the "severe Fugitive Slave Law" of 1850; "Its very injustice had created new sympathizers for fugitives, and opened new avenues of escape," facilitating Nancy's departure (222). In addition, Horace Greeley's abolitionist *New York Tribune*, which Mrs. Bywaters subscribes to and shares with her friend Rachel, is an important presence in the book. However, slavery is never openly debated in *Sapphira*; instead, it is a silencing, isolating force, muffling the rapport between Rachel and her father and preventing a loving understanding between Nancy and Till, to mention only two examples. When the novel was published, Cather wrote to her old (and Southern) friend Viola Roseboro' that she had wanted to explore something "Terrible" in her book, an estranging force beneath the surfaces (often pleasant) of domestic life. *Sapphira* makes it very clear that a rending conflict is coming and that the issue of slavery, grounded in race, will be at its center. The war is not "drained of evil"; instead, the "Terrible" presence of evils grounded in slavery blights, at least partially, almost every relationship in the book.

Cather's actual picture of the Civil War years is folded into the novel's epilogue. This picture does not emphasize local and family military heroes, such as the "Namesake" uncles. Nancy's nemesis, Martin Colbert, was a Confederate casualty. Rachel Blake reports of her cousin, "He'd got to be a captain in the cavalry, and the Colberts made a great to-do about him after he was dead, and put up a monument. But I reckon the neighbourhood was relieved" (290). Heroic trappings—rank and monument—do not obliterate Martin's local reputation as a lazy, predatory rake, and Martin is not mourned by his Southern neighbors.

The story of another Confederate casualty, a Back Creek Valley boy, emphasizes his pitiful suffering, not heroism:

> When Willie Gordon, a Rebel boy from Hayfield, was wounded in the Battle of Bull Run, it was [antislavery] Mr. Cartmell, Mrs. Bywaters's father, who went after him in his hay-wagon, got through the Federal lines, and brought him home. While the boy lay dying from gangrene in a shattered leg, . . . the Hayfield people, regardless of political differences, came in relays, night and day, and did the only thing that relieved his pain a little: they carried cold water from the springhouse and with a tin cup poured it steadily over his leg for hours at a time. (274)

The character of Mr. Cartmell, who brings the wounded soldier home, is based on Cather's great-grandfather James Cather, and the story of his neighborly act of kindness was probably a family tale. In addition, some of Frederick County's local Civil War historians believe that Willie Gordon was probably based on the Boak family war casualty, James William ("Willie") Boak. The name "Willie," with its strong personal and family ties, would have been a significant choice for Cather, and possibly a private signal of kinship to this character, who died a few days after Second Manassas, as her uncle had. In *One of Ours,* Mahailey (whose prototype was Marjorie Anderson) tells a similar story of one her Confederate brothers, whom she says her mother brought home from Bull

Run in a wagon to die "by inches" of gangrene in just the same way (1107–08). Cather seldom repeated incidents so closely in her fiction; the two publications of this sad little tale of a Civil War casualty suggest that it had made a powerful impression on her, perhaps because she heard it frequently as a child.

Sapphira's one gesture toward full-scale glorification of (Confederate) war heroism also occurs in the epilogue. It is the account of "young Turner Ashby of [neighboring] Fauquier County, who held the Confederate line from Berkeley Springs to Harpers Ferry, —so near home that word of his brilliant cavalry exploits came out to Back Creek with the stage-driver" (275). Brigadier General Ashby was admired, Cather writes, by both Union and Confederate supporters, and he became Frederick County's most-venerated war hero; the local chapter of the United Daughters of the Confederacy is named for him. Addressing her 1940 readers, Cather adds that Ashby died leading a "victorious charge," on June 6, 1862, and that "Even today, if you should be motoring through Winchester on the sixth of June, and should stop to see the Confederate cemetery, you would probably find fresh flowers on Ashby's grave [an elaborate monument erected by 'The ladies of Winchester' in 1881]. He was all that the old-time Virginians admired: *Like Paris handsome and like Hector brave.* And he died young. 'Shortlived and glorious,' the old Virginians used to say" (275). In this passage, Cather subtly acknowledges her close knowledge of Frederick County's Civil War mythology. In Winchester, Confederate Memorial Day is celebrated on the anniversary of Turner Ashby's death—to this day, Ashby's grave is indeed decorated with flowers on this date, and all the cemetery's surrounding graves, including the nearby grave of J. W. Boak, are marked with Confederate flags (see fig. 3). Addressing her present-day (1940) readers who may be indulging in the new pastime of Civil War automobile tourism, Cather repeats the florid language that glorified Ashby's war exploits, but she discreetly distances herself from that language, attributing it to "the old-time Virginians." She acknowledges Americans' continued interest in the mythology of Civil War heroism (as had recently been amply demonstrated by public enthusiasm for the book and film version of *Gone with the Wind*), and, in the mode of much post–Reconstruction Civil War fiction, she makes

Fig. 3. This photograph was taken in Stonewall Confederate Cemetery, Winchester, Virginia, on June 7, 2001, the day after the observance of Confederate Memorial Day, which is celebrated in Winchester on June 6, the anniversary of General Turner Ashby's death in battle in 1862. As Cather mentions in the epilogue to *Sapphira and the Slave Girl*, Ashby's large tomb (inscribed THE BROTHERS ASHBY) is decorated with flowers, and all the graves in the cemetery are decorated with small Confederate flags. One of the small adjacent tombstones marks the grave of Willa Cather's uncle, James William Boak. Photograph by the author.

no mention of the issues for which the war was fought, emphasizing personal heroic style instead.

Female heroism, however, is more explicitly celebrated—or at least noted—in the novel. What we know of the Virginia stories of the war years that were told in the Cather/Boak family suggests that they provided some precedents and models for daring female behavior. Carrie Miner Sherwood's memories of Grandmother Boak's tales to her grandchildren emphasize Rachel Boak's audacious nighttime forays into the camps of both armies to nurture hungry soldiers. And Sidney Cather Gore kept voluminous journals during the war years that chronicle her tireless efforts to provide food, spiritual guidance, and medical care for both Union and Confederate troops, at her home and at the hospitals in Winchester and nearby, as well as her anguished efforts to reconcile her Union political principles with her warm sympathy for the suffering of Confederate neighbors. In 1923 Sidney Gore's youngest son, James Howard Gore, edited and published his mother's journals, and since Cather regularly visited and corresponded with this cousin, it seems likely that she would have read his edition of Sidney Gore's journals, as well as hearing stories from her aunt (with whom she stayed on her first return visit to Virginia in 1896). In *Sapphira*, both Rachel Boak and Sidney Gore, as Rachel Blake and Mrs. Bywaters, act on their antislavery principles in ways that are audacious and dangerous, as Rachel engineers her mother's slave's escape from slavery and Mrs. Bywaters openly subscribes to an abolitionist newspaper and then hides fugitive Confederate soldiers in her house. They are models of active heroism that is *not* "drained of ideology." And, as I'll argue later in this essay, there are heroic elements in Nancy's story as well: her return was a "thrilling" story of personal achievement that Cather remembered throughout her life. These women characters in *Sapphira* offer alternative conceptions of what a "war hero" might be. Beyond the generic monument and "great to-do" that memorialized Martin Colbert, they suggest a heroism of principled activism that addresses the core issues of the Civil War instead of ignoring them.

The writing of *Sapphira* had a double purpose for Cather. First, it allowed her to plumb the Terrible as it was grounded in her own family's Virginia history and in the domestic and local life that she experienced at Willow Shade in her own early years. Thus, as I've said, the book does confront, in many ways, the central issues for which the war was fought, particularly slavery. In fact, as several critics have observed, *Sapphira* is the most politically confrontational of Cather's novels. But Cather also wrote this novel for solace and escape. The late 1930s were the worst period of her life, she told friends. Her favorite brother, Douglass, died in June 1938—her first loss of a sibling. A few months later, the great romance of her life, Isabelle McClung Hambourg, also died. In addition, Cather was distraught over the news of the developing war in Europe, where she had many friends. Work on *Sapphira* was a solace, she said, and she wrote much more material than she could use, simply for the relief of writing about her nineteenth-century

Virginia home. Thus *Sapphira* is, in many ways, a novel of war and loss written to escape war and loss.

This is evident in the sometimes contradictory picture of war and Reconstruction that emerges from the epilogue. Cather acknowledges little antagonism among Frederick Countians: "The war made few enmities in the country neighbourhoods," she writes (274), an assertion that seems at least partially to contradict her own family history. The pervasive postwar "shame of defeat" and "profound hopelessness" described by a later historian, Wyatt-Brown, are absent from Cather's account of the returning Frederick County "Rebel" soldiers; they "were tired, discouraged, but not humiliated or embittered by failure. The country people accepted the defeat of the Confederacy with dignity, as they accepted death when it came to their families. Defeat was not new to these men"—they were farmers, and accustomed to crop failures (276). The "lost cause" is subsumed in the ongoing (and perhaps comforting) rhythms of nature and agriculture. In the novel, unlike Southern mythology of Reconstruction horrors, there are almost no appearances by carpetbaggers, scalawags, or other demonized figures—"Mrs. Bywaters was still the postmistress. She had not been removed in the 'carpetbag' period, when so many questionable Government appointments were made" (274). The postwar changes seem mostly positive, and Old South traditions don't appear to hamper young adults of Cather's parents' generation: "This new generation was gayer and more carefree than their forebears, perhaps because they had fewer traditions to live up to" (277). One of those abandoned traditions would have been slavery, of course; anxiety about slaveholding was a major reason why Rachel Blake and Henry Colbert ("forebears" of Cather's mother) were seldom gay and carefree before the war.

The centerpiece of the epilogue, of course, is "Nancy's Return," seen through the eyes of Cather as a child of five. Nancy left Frederick County in secret defiance of Virginia and U.S. law, as an abused and terrified slave girl. Cather's text suggests an almost causal relation between Nancy's escape and the Civil War, "which came on so soon after Nancy ran away" (273). Nancy returns, around 1881, as a self-possessed, prosperous Canadian woman, a legendary hero in young Cather's household. "Well,

ANN ROMINES

Nancy child, you've made us right proud of you," Cather's grandmother Rachel says (283). Openly visiting her mother, Till, and
the descendants of her former owner, Nancy is evidence of all
that the Civil War has made possible. In fact, she is a triumph
of personal reconstruction. Having remade herself as a Northern woman with fashionable clothes, British-accented speech, a
secure job, and a mixed-race marriage and family, she can now return to claim the best resources of her Southern childhood. For
young Cather, Nancy is an important first acquaintance with a successful urban woman who can move from region to region and
still retain her selfhood. Indeed, Nancy may be seen in this autobiographical narrative as one of young Cather's first models for
her own peripatetic, multi-regional life in the post-Reconstruction
United States. Yet, at the same time, little Willa betrays the marks
of her postbellum conditioning as an heir of the Confederacy: she
is suspicious of Nancy's precise Northern speech and prefers the
"shade of deference" in Nancy's voice "when she addressed my
mother"—the granddaughter of Nancy's owner (284). The child
entirely approves of her family's hospitality to Nancy and Till:
after the white Cathers have eaten, the black visitors are served
at a segregated second table. Intentionally or not, Cather's picture
of "Nancy's Return" shows us both the changed possibilities that
had opened up for African Americans after the war and the constraints that still existed, especially in the South—and that were
taking legal shape in Jim Crow laws.

The epilogue's picture of other African Americans after the war
contrasts even more vividly with the rather calm and placid view
of the Reconstruction years that Cather constructs. Some work
for the families that formerly owned them; Cather's father employs some of Sapphira's former slaves. One mill worker, Sampson ("Master's steadiest man" [288]), has made a successful life
for himself and his family in Pennsylvania, but he is homesick for
the grist mill where he was a slave and for Virginia cooking. He
tells Till, "I ain't had no real bread since I went away." Where he
works, "the machines runs so fast an' gits so hot, an' burns all the
taste out-a the flour" (289). Sampson's story suggests that even
the ablest of former slaves may be displaced and unhappy outside

the Old South, where they must contend with the facts of industrialization.

Even worse is the tale of another freed slave, "Tap, the jolly mill boy . . . whom everybody liked."

> People said he hadn't been able to stand his freedom. He went to town . . . and picked up various jobs. . . . Early in the Reconstruction time a low German from Pennsylvania opened a saloon and pool hall in Winchester, a dive where negroes were allowed to play, and gambling went on. One night after Tap had been drinking too much, he struck another darky on the head with a billiard cue and killed him. (290)

Tap was hanged for this crime, despite local white farmers' testimony to his "good character." "Mrs. Blake and Till always said it was a Yankee jury that hanged him; a Southern jury would have known there was no real bad in Tap" (290).

The implications of this story, corroborated by the two old women, white and black, who were young Cather's major early teachers, are the most appalling of Southern Reconstruction–era dogma: a "low" outsider—a carpetbagger Northerner and immigrant—has created a dangerous public space where the races mix, and when Tap impulsively kills "another darky" there, "no real bad" has been done, according to the native white men of the neighborhood. Tap's story expresses the postwar Southern ideology summarized by Eric J. Sundquist: "Emancipation, it was argued, had ushered in an age of childlike loss of direction, mental and physical decline, and a propensity for violence on the part of blacks" (336).

The most complex portrayal of an African American in Cather's epilogue is Till. Matilda Jefferson, the prototype for Till, had been a slave in the household of Jacob and Ruhamah Seibert and remained there, after emancipation, until Ruhamah's death in 1873. Thereafter, from the evidence of Cather's letters and the epilogue, she lived on in the cabin that had been her slave dwelling and often visited or worked in Cather's parents' household. In the 1856 portion of *Sapphira*, Till is Sapphira's housekeeper and personal slave. She is an austere and taciturn figure who appears estranged from the slave community. Her strongest attachments are to white women: the English housekeeper who trained her and her mistress, Sapphira. She never tells stories, not even to her daughter, Nancy. But the Till of the epilogue is in many ways transformed into a typical figure from postbellum literature. As an erect, "spare, neat little old darky" (280), Till is a physical refusal of the buxom, maternal "mammy" stereotype so popular in postwar fictions of the Old South. But in other ways, she replicates that type: as a lovingly remembered member of Cather's Virginia household, she is a benign presence, tenderly solicitous of the white child's every desire—such as little Willa's wish to witness the reunion of Nancy and Till—even when it inconveniences herself and her own child, Nancy.

Such solicitude is tellingly reminiscent of one of the best-known post-Reconstruction Southern storytellers, Joel Chandler Harris's Uncle Remus. Blight says that Harris's first Uncle Remus book, *Uncle Remus: His Songs and Sayings* (the best-selling American book of 1880), "may have set the literary tone for the reconciliationist eighties" (228). Cather's family apparently shared in the national enthusiasm for Uncle Remus; in "Old Mrs. Harris," Mr. Templeton, a character based on Cather's father, tells an Uncle Remus tale to his receptive children. Uncle Remus's rapt and indulged listener is, like the young Willa of the epilogue, a white child, the descendant of Remus's former owners. Remus also puts himself at the child's disposal, and, just as Till invokes her mistress "Miss Sapphy," Remus's ultimate authority is the antebellum "ole Miss." The little boy's family encourages his visits to Uncle Remus's cabin; Willa's parents leave her at Till's former slave cabin to "hear the old stories." According to Robert Hemenway, "The Uncle Remus stories create a racial utopia. . . . Uncle Remus's cabin constitutes one of the most secure and serene environments in American literature, . . . and Uncle Remus reassured Southern whites . . . [that]free black people would love, not demand retribution" (19–20). Till's cabin is a similarly protected space, and Till's stories about her master and mistress are full of lovingly remembered detail and respect for her owners; she never speaks a word to young Willa that might be interpreted as criticism of the institution of slavery as she experienced it.

Cather makes Till's evaluation of Sapphira the ending of her epilogue. Till recounts Sapphira's brave, solitary death from heart disease, in her parlor, as a triumph of whiteness and of class: the "fine folks" of Sapphira's privileged girlhood on a Loudoun County plantation came for her, "and she went away with them" (294). Till concludes that Sapphira should have never left her original antebellum home for the more volatile border territory of Frederick County, where there was no settled social and economic hierarchy and "nobody was anybody much" (295). In other words, Till defends (at least for her mistress) the seemingly fixed world of a prosperous antebellum plantation, a world that is (unlike the 1856 Back Creek of the novel's major action) untouched by the tensions that will erupt in the Civil War.

According to Blight, in the Uncle Remus stories, "Harris's achievement was to create a world where on the one hand the Civil War never really needed to have happened, but on the other, all the deception, cunning, and bare-bones competition the underdogs of life could muster was necessary for their very survival" (228–29). In Uncle Remus's tales, of course, the wily trickster Brer Rabbit epitomizes the survival strategies employed by economic "underdogs," particularly slaves. In *Sapphira*, Till's stories to little Willa also evoke an antebellum world where there was no necessity for a Civil War, and Till conspires with Willa's grandmother to ensure that the child remains ignorant of "deception, cunning" and desperate survival strategies. For example, when the name of Martin Colbert comes up in the child's hearing, Rachel Blake gives Nancy and Till a glance "that meant it was a forbidden subject" (290), and the little girl hears nothing of Sapphira's animosity to her slave girl, Martin's relentless pursuit, and Nancy's desperate strategies to evade him. The doubleness of the Uncle Remus stories, Blight says, epitomizes the reconciliationist agenda of the 1880s. Perhaps it is not surprising that *Sapphira* shows a similar duplicity, since it is grounded in the stories Cather first heard in Reconstruction Virginia.

Of those stories, Cather says in her epilogue, "I soon learned that it was best never to interrupt with questions,—it seemed to break the spell. Nancy [during her visit] wanted to know what had happened during the war, and what had become of everybody,—

and so did I" (288). Sapphira does not fully tell us the story of "what happened during the war" in Cather's ancestral Virginia. But it does give us a powerful sense of why the war happened and of "what had become of everybody"—how lives of white and black Virginians were forever changed. To piece together that story from the censored memories of white and black elders, like Till and Rachel Blake, demanded intense and strategic listening on the part of young Cather (as well as the research and reflection of the mature novelist). Till's stories also required close attention to nuances of tone and to "hints that she dropped unconsciously" (292). Looking and listening to all that was said and not said, the child must have received her first lessons in the telling of stories about the Civil War and the years before and after and all of the rigors and restrictions that accompanied such stories.

Cather was sixty-seven—the approximate age of her Grandmother Boak and "Aunt Till" in the epilogue—when *Sapphira* was published. Clearly, the popular priorities of youthful male heroism and nationalist art that she had explored in the two versions of "The Namesake," her first efforts to write out of her own Civil War history, no longer engaged her. But the priorities of "race and blood and kindred" still did. In her last novel she takes her place among the family women, telling the stories of the "what had happened during the war, and what had become of everybody."[7] And, although Till appears to have the (evasive) last word, in the novel's famous final note, printed on the last page after "THE END", and signed by the present-day novelist, WILLA CATHER, (in capitals slightly larger than "THE END"), Cather foregrounds her own memories, through her use of "Frederick County surnames," which she heard from her parents in early childhood. "The names of those unknown persons sometimes had a lively fascination for me," she says (295)—and some of them have been incorporated into the novel. I read this idiosyncratic note as Cather's reminder to us that this is her material, and she is the surviving storyteller now. *Sapphira and the Slave Girl* is, among many other things, Cather's Civil War story. In it, she acknowledges her personal history and that of her community and nation and reminds us of how difficult and freighted a process the telling of Civil War stories (still) is.

NOTES

1. In a recent essay Steven Trout also discusses "The Namesake" in terms of Cather's interest in the Civil War and ultimately World War I. See "From 'The Namesake' to *One of Ours:* Willa Cather on War," ALR 27 (Winter 2005): 117–40.

2. Cather's account of Lyon Hartwell's career bears a resemblance to the career of Augustus Saint-Gaudens (1848–1907), arguably the best American sculptor of his time, who, in the Shaw Memorial installed on Boston Common in 1897, created the best-known and most admired work of Civil War memorial sculpture. An American citizen, Saint-Gaudens was the son of immigrant parents and studied in both Rome and Paris; like Lyon Hartwell, he lived in Paris for a portion of his career, which was launched by a much-praised memorial to Union admiral David Farragut in Madison Square Garden. The Shaw Memorial commemorated a Union officer and the African American regiment he led; it had special significance for Saint-Gaudens, who worked on it for more than twenty years. When the memorial was at last unveiled, in an elaborate and widely publicized ceremony that included important speeches by William James and Booker T. Washington, the *Boston Transcript* hailed it (as Blight has noted) as bringing "new artistic fervor to Civil War memorialization" (Blight 338–443; *The Shaw Memorial* 20–23, passim).

As a professional journalist and a voracious reader, Cather would undoubtedly have been aware of the Shaw Memorial's unveiling. In her first year as an editor of *McClure's* (1906–07), Cather lived in Boston, not far from the Boston Common, where the Shaw Memorial was installed, and almost certainly saw it there. This was the year during which "The Namesake" was published and, presumably, written. It is also interesting to note that a selection of Saint-Gaudens' letters was published in *McClure's* in 1908, the year after his death. So there are many reasons to presume that Willa Cather knew of this notable sculptor's career as a creator of Civil War memorials and might have it in mind as one of her sources for the figure of Lyon Hartwell.

3. Family stories say that Mary Virginia Boak, Cather's mother, had four brothers in the Confederate army (see Bennett 5). Census records confirm that there were four Boak brothers old enough to serve in the Civil War; however, the oldest Boak brother, George Washington Boak, died of illness in 1858. Confederate records confirm that the other three Boak brothers did serve.

4. For biographical details, I have largely relied on Bennett, Woodress, and Romines.

5. See Marcus (105) on the gender ambivalence of this poem.

6. "The Namesake," published in the March 1907 issue, was the sec-

ond Cather story to appear in *McClure's*. The first was "The Sculptor's Funeral," published in January 1905.

7. Marcus makes a similar point (117).

WORKS CITED

Bennett, Mildred. "Willa Cather's Virginia 1873–1883." *Willa Cather Pioneer Memorial Newsletter* 25 (1981): 5–10.

Blight, David W. *Race and Reunion: The Civil War in American Memory.* Cambridge: Harvard UP, 2001.

Cather, Willa. Letter to Dorothy Canfield Fisher. October 14, 1940. Bailey-Howe Library, University of Vermont, Burlington.

———. Letter to Viola Roseboro'. December 18, 1940. Alderman Library, University of Virginia, Charlottesville.

———. "The Namesake." *April Twilights (1903)*. Ed. Bernice Slote. Lincoln: U of Nebraska P, 1968. 25–26.

———. "The Namesake." 1907. *Willa Cather's Collected Short Fiction, 1892–1912*. Ed. Virginia Faulkner. Lincoln: U of Nebraska P, 1965. 137–46.

———. *One of Ours.* 1922. *Early Novels and Stories.* New York: Library of America, 1987. 939–1297.

———. *Sapphira and the Slave Girl.* New York: Knopf, 1940.

Clinton, Catherine. *Tara Revisited: Women, War, and the Plantation Legend.* New York: McGraw-Hill, 1996.

Colt, Margaretta Barton. *Defend the Valley: A Shenandoah Family in the Civil War.* New York: Orion, 1994.

Cooper, William J., and Thomas E. Terrill. *The American South: A History.* 2nd ed. New York: McGraw-Hill, 1996.

Flora, Joseph M. "Reconstruction." *The Companion to Southern Literature.* Ed. Joseph M. Flora and Lucinda H. MacKethan. Baton Rouge: Louisiana State UP, 2002.

Gore, James Howard. *My Mother's Story: Despise Not the Day of Small Things.* Philadelphia: Judson P, 1923.

Hannum [sp?], H. C. Letter to Mrs. W. A. Sherwood. January 17, 1952. Willa Cather Pioneer Memorial and Educational Foundation Archives, Red Cloud, Nebraska.

Harris, Joel Chandler. *Uncle Remus: His Songs and Sayings.* 1880. New York: Penguin, 1982.

Hemenway, Robert. Introduction. *Uncle Remus: His Songs and Sayings,* by Joel Chandler Harris. New York: Penguin, 1982.

Hoover, Sharon, ed. *Willa Cather Remembered.* Lincoln: U of Nebraska P, 2002.

Kalbian, Maral S. *Frederick County, Virginia: History through Architecture*. Winchester VA: Winchester-Frederick County Historical Society, 1999.

Lewis, Edith. *Willa Cather Living: A Personal Record*. 1953. Lincoln: U of Nebraska P, 2000.

Marcus, Lisa. " 'The Pull of Race and Blood and Kindred': Willa Cather's Southern Inheritance." *Willa Cather's Southern Connections: New Essays on Cather and the South*. Ed. Ann Romines. Charlottesville: UP of Virginia, 2000. 98–119.

Pollard, Tomas. "Political Silence and His'try in *Sapphira and the Slave Girl*." *Willa Cather's Southern Connections: New Essays on Cather and the South*. Ed. Ann Romines. Charlottesville: UP of Virginia, 2000. 38–53.

Romines, Ann. "Historical Essay: *Sapphira and the Slave Girl*." *Sapphira and the Slave Girl*, by Willa Cather. Nebraska Scholarly Edition. Lincoln: U of Nebraska P, forthcoming.

The Shaw Memorial: A Celebration of an American Masterpiece. Cornish NH: Eastern National, 2002.

Sundquist, Eric J. *To Wake the Nations: Race in the Making of American Literature*. Cambridge: Harvard UP, 1993.

Woodress, James. *Willa Cather: A Literary Life*. Lincoln: U of Nebraska P, 1987.

Wyatt-Brown, Bertram. *The Shaping of Southern Culture: Honor, Grace, and War, 1760s-1890s*. Chapel Hill: U of North Carolina P, 2001.

Jim Burden and the
White Man's Burden
My Ántonia and Empire

MICHAEL GORMAN

Recent harvests in American history and letters have
yielded an almost universal acknowledgement: the pioneer myth
of the American West has been cultivated in a soil broken and
furrowed by the colonizing impulse of empire. Each narrative of
western settlement is rooted in a "legacy of conquest" (Limerick) informing the text, and exposing this legacy demands re-
covering lost texts and rereading familiar works within their ideological contexts. Nowhere is this challenge more complex—or
more rewarding—than in reading Willa Cather, a writer simultaneously celebrated for her depiction of pioneers and respected
for her historical authenticity. The bounty from this garden has
been sampled often in the last decade and a half. Mike Fischer has
unearthed the "burden of imperialism" in Cather's pioneer texts;
Joseph Urgo has considered Cather's acceptance of America's imperial stance; and Deborah Karush has discussed the "nostalgic
vision" with which Cather viewed the frontier. These studies demonstrate the veracity and continuing vitality of Guy Reynolds's
assertion that "Cather's novels fictionalize the transfer of European empires to America and the subsequent growth of American
empire" (46). My trespass into this field attempts to reveal how
Cather's most enduring pioneer text—My Ántonia—reconciles the
insular conception of the nineteenth-century United States with
the post–Spanish-American War reality, reflecting America's transition from continental to global power. I argue in particular that
with the Great War as its immediate subtext, this novel reaches

back to the closing years of the American frontier and the influx of European immigrants to the Plains states, projecting an image of the nation and legitimizing its status as "European" power.

The original introduction (1918) to *My Ántonia* is an intricate frame for what some critics regard as a simple country novel. Like the openings to Daniel Defoe's *Robinson Crusoe* and Nathaniel Hawthorne's *The Scarlet Letter*, it operates as a narrative of transmission establishing a fictionalized origin for the text. The most obvious effect of the introduction is the distance it establishes between Cather and her story. In the opening pages, an unnamed female narrator credits Jim Burden, a childhood acquaintance, for writing the tale. By making Jim "legal counsel for one of the great Western railways" (x), Cather complicates his perspective through its association to the controversial role the railroad played in Indian-white relations, western settlement patterns, and resource exploitation.

The introduction situates the production of Jim's manuscript in the immediate present (1916–18), synchronous to the novel's actual composition. As the dates of its composition suggest, *My Ántonia* is a highly charged exercise of political memory. Written as the First World War ravaged Europe and cast as the reminiscence of middle-aged Jim Burden, it is a "prehistory" reconstructing the 1880s and early 1890s from the verge of America's entrance into the Great War. Cather further complicates the account by making its teller a rural Nebraskan turned successful New York attorney and infusing the memory of his prairie childhood with a wholehearted acceptance of progress (the Yankee credo) and a fair share of romantic yearning:

> As for Jim, no disappointments have been severe enough to chill his naturally romantic and ardent disposition. This disposition, though it often made him seem very funny when he was a boy, has been one of the strongest elements in his success. He loves with a personal passion the great country through which his railway runs and branches. His faith in it and his knowledge of it have played an important part in its development. He is always able to raise capital for new enterprises in Wyoming or Montana, and has helped young men

out there to do remarkable things in mines and timber and oil. If a young man with an idea can once get Jim Burden's attention, can manage to accompany him when he goes off into the wilds hunting for lost parks or exploring new canyons, then the money which means action is usually forthcoming. Jim is still able to lose himself in those big Western dreams. (xi)

The speaker in the introduction claims that Jim "loves with a personal passion the great country through which his railway runs and branches," yet his infatuation for this territory is clearly an obsession to exploit its resources for material gain like the despicable Wick Cutter of *My Ántonia* and other characters appearing in Cather's oeuvre (e.g., Bayliss Wheeler in *One of Ours* and Ivy Peters in *A Lost Lady*). While described as one who loves exploring "lost parks" or "new canyons," Jim appreciates these marvels with a mercenary eye like the Spanish conquistador Francisco Vásquez de Coronado (1510–54), who figures so prominently in his adolescent figuration of Nebraska. Notwithstanding the "naturally romantic" character attributed to James Quayle Burden, the "big Western dreams" in which he loses himself equal not innocent adventure but economic conquest: raising capital for ventures that "do remarkable things in mines and timber and oil." Like Coronado's famed 1540–41 expedition from New Spain to present-day Kansas in search of the legendary Seven Cities of Gold, Jim's frequent travels to the West are speculative in nature and rooted in colonialism.

Cather plants U.S. expansionism squarely in Jim's retrospective, which allegorizes America's displacement of the Plains Indians and the Spanish Empire. Although they do not figure explicitly in the novel, the history and culture of the Plains Indians form a palimpsest occasionally—and tellingly—exposed in the text, especially when considering the impact federal policies like the 1862 Homestead and Pacific Railroad acts and the 1887 Dawes Act had upon the original inhabitants of Nebraska. Equally significant are suggestive allusions in the novel to Spain's presence in North America. Such rhetoric and imagery hints to America's wresting the mantle of empire from Spain in the 1898 Spanish-American War and suggest that, in addition to absorbing Spain's colonial holdings in the Caribbean and Pacific, the United States has inherited Spanish obligations in Europe. In other words, within the pastoral and nostalgic account ascribed to Jim, Cather traces the United States' cultural heritage and its rise to global power—a genealogy suggesting that America has a duty, as de facto European state, to participate in the Great War.

TAKING POSSESSION

Despite the sentimentality with which this novel has been received traditionally, Cather scholars—reflecting America's long history of distrusting jurists—have treated Jim's narrative as a suspect document. While narratologists have pointed to the intricate layering involved in the tale's construction and transmission, feminist readings have focused on the relationship between Jim and his subject, Ántonia. Among the vanguard in questioning Jim's reliability as a narrator is Susan J. Rosowski, who asserts in *The Voyage Perilous: Willa Cather's Romanticism* (1986) that Jim's allegiance as an adult is not to Ántonia but to his own ideas; when the circumstances in Ántonia's life conflict with his beliefs or intentions, he "denies the reality" (89).

What Rosowski perceives in Jim's treatment of Ántonia can also be witnessed in his construal of western American history; just as Cather builds tension into Jim's thoughts about Ántonia in order to deconstruct the myths about women to which he subscribes (Rosowski 89), she undermines his interpretation of history. Although *My Ántonia* accurately projects an image of the United States as empire, statements attributed to Jim consistently disregard the political maneuvers—most obviously the incidents involving the removal and genocide of the American Indians—contributing to his nation's hemispheric ascendancy and growing global prominence.

Jim's initial observation about the rolling grasslands reveals the superficial understanding of Plains history Cather imposes on him. On the ride from the train station in Black Hawk to his grandparents' homestead, the orphaned traveler peers from the wagon bed into the dark night and concludes, "There seemed to be nothing to see; no fences, no creeks or trees, no hills or fields. If there was a road, I could not make it out in the faint starlight. There was nothing but land: not a country at all, but the material out of which countries are made. No, there was *nothing* but land" (7, italics added). In subtle strokes, Jim Burden erases the inhabitants preexisting the arrival of European settlers from his memoir. The black night, which he suggestively labels "utter darkness" (5) and later "empty darkness" (7), functions like a geopolitical tabula rasa, an ideological blackboard with the previous record wiped clean and awaiting the next lesson to be inscribed.

Jim's language echoes a common sentiment in American literature and political ideology: that of the frontier as a virgin land waiting to be settled. On one level his reflections about the prairie's barrenness suggest the youthful ignorance of a ten year old on his inaugural visit to the Plains. Yet beneath this childish observation lurks the willful blindness that Cather writes into the adult narrating this episode. Deborah Karush notes that Cather's novels promote a "fantasy of unrestrained expansion" by using child narrators to impart nostalgic accounts of "the frontier as a vast, empty space . . . conveniently devoid of Native Americans" (30). Jim's reflections certainly fit this pattern. He specifically equates the emptiness of the prairie landscape to its lack of infrastructure and agrarian development. Progress requires improvement to the land: it demands fences, fields, and roads. At the time he is credited with writing the story of Ántonia, Jim is implicitly involved in the exigencies of progress. As a railroad attorney, his career would entail what Patricia Nelson Limerick cleverly calls "the drawing of lines and the marking of borders" (55): through legal sleight of hand, he would have turned *land* into *property*. Successful performance of his duties would necessitate an intimate familiarity with the territorial statutes, congressional legislation, and military involvement making the land grants to the railroads possible.

Competing experiences of dispossession and possession figure prominently in the early chapters of *My Ántonia*. In one sense, Cather's entire tale charts Jim's individual journey from banishment and divestiture to acquisition, and, accordingly, in its earliest appearance, Nebraska is Jim's Paradise Lost. Upon disembarking from the train at Black Hawk, Jim and the immigrant family he sees huddling together on the station platform are enveloped by cold and "utter darkness" despite the red glow emanating from the locomotive firebox. The night's imposing blackness and the steam engine's smoldering fire evoke Miltonic images of Hell encountered by Satan and his minions after being exiled from Heaven to a "Dungeon horrible, on all sides round / As one great Furnace flam'd, yet from those flames / No light, but rather darkness visible / [. . . .] / As far remov'd from God and light of Heav'n / As from the Center thrice to th' utmost Pole" (*Paradise Lost*, Book I, ll.61–74). Disoriented by his new surroundings, Jim gazes toward Heaven and contemplates his fate. As he looks up at the unfamiliar expansive sky, "the complete dome of heaven all there was of it," Jim concludes "that the world was left behind, that we had got over the edge of it, and outside man's jurisdiction" (7). His remarks a few lines later extend upon this phrasing: "Between that earth and that sky I felt erased, blotted out. I did not say my prayers that night: here, I felt, what would be would be" (8). The orphaned boy feels that he has traveled not merely beyond the authority of men but beyond the influence of Heaven—no need for prayers since they can no longer be heard, let alone answered.

Cather's wording—being "erased and blotted out"—indicates a profound sense of alienation. Though his initial thoughts reflect the idea of being exiled, Jim's views about his new surroundings soon move from the nihilistic toward the existential. His life in the West will be what he *makes* of it—what he takes and claims title to, including Ántonia. His determination to make his own world is reflected in the final lines of the introduction, when the speaker points out how he corrected the working title of the manuscript by adding "My" to the original inscription, "Ántonia" (xiii). Before his narrative even begins, Cather establishes not only Jim's impulse to acquire but also his awareness of the role semantics play in acquisition. Of course, this is a lesson a successful railroad attorney in an age of phenomenal railway expansion would know well: to procure anything legitimately it must be first recognized and named. Ántonia Shimerda, "this girl [who] seemed to mean . . . the country" (xi–xii), embodies the West. By having Jim prefix the title of his manuscript with the first-person singular possessive pronoun, Cather deepens the parallel between Jim's judicious claim to Ántonia and the territory absorbed by his burgeoning nation throughout the nineteenth century.

The convergence of verbal expression and possession makes its most conspicuous appearance in the novel when Jim and his grandmother visit the primitive dugout homestead of their new neighbors. Shortly after they arrive, Ántonia Shimerda takes Jim's hand and they race away from the adults to the edge of a ravine, followed by Yulka, Ántonia's younger sister. The ensuing encounter is incredibly Edenic. "'Name? What name?' she asked, touching me on the shoulder. I told her my name, and she repeated it after me and made Yulka say it. She pointed into the gold cottonwood tree behind whose top we stood and again, 'What name?'" (25). Hidden from everyone and everything but the red grass, blue sky, and yellow cottonwood, Jim names the things around him on that breezy autumn afternoon with the assurance of Adam in the Garden. While an exercise in discovery for Ántonia, this lesson displays Jim's powers of recognition and identification, deliberately recalling Genesis 1:28–2:19, where God bestows dominion over the earth to humankind and has Adam christen "every living creature." As he confidently identifies all Ántonia points to, Jim verbally demonstrates his familiarity with the prairie environment, a territory to which he initially felt alien, and proves himself less a stranger to the surrounding landscape than the oldest daughter of the Bohemian family.

Teaching English to the Shimerda girls plays a pivotal role in Jim's recovery of what he lost, namely, his identity associated with a sense of place, after being orphaned and moving from the lush wooded hills of Virginia to the open, wine-colored grassland of Nebraska. At the entreaty of Ántonia's father, Jim continues the English tutorials until she turns fifteen, when events (including her father's suicide) force her to abandon language learning and attend to chores at the farm (116–17). Jim's thoughts about teaching Ántonia read like a parody of George Bernard Shaw's *Pygmalion*. During the lessons Jim attempts to exercise authority over Ántonia in a fashion similar to the way phonetics Professor Henry Higgins lords over Eliza Doolittle in Shaw's 1913 comedy.[1] "Much as I like Ántonia," Jim writes, "I hated a superior tone that she sometimes took with me. She was four years older . . . and had seen more of the world; but . . . I resented her protecting manner. Before the autumn was over she began to treat me more like an equal and to defer to me in other things than reading lessons" (41). Like Professor Higgins, Jim wants to influence his student in more than language matters, and he soon gets his wish.

The desired change in Ántonia's opinion of him was brought about by an event of mock-epic proportions. With Ántonia to act as his damsel in distress, Jim instinctively reenacts the legend of St. George and slays "a circus monstrosity" of a rattlesnake with a borrowed spade (44). Though he and Otto Fuchs, the Burdens' Austrian farmhand, later realize the cold autumn day and the age of the snake took away its "fight," Jim is pleased with the immediate result: it "was enough for Ántonia. She liked me better," he notes happily, "she never took a supercilious air with me again. I had killed a big snake—I was now a big fellow" (47–48). Once recognized by Ántonia as both linguistic and prairie authority, Jim is empowered to mold her to the extent possible, not *in* his own *image* but *through* his own *imagination*. At this point, she has become both his inspiration and his invention and, like other resources in the West, will become subject to his exploitation.

THE DEAD SNAKE:
COMMEMORATION AND APPROPRIATION

In addition to enhancing Jim's esteem in Ántonia's eyes, the dead snake links Nebraska's agricultural present to its frontier past. During the post-mortem examination of the unfortunate rattler, Jim uses all "five and a half feet" of its carcass to instruct Ántonia in rudimentary herpetology and Plains history: "He had twelve rattles, but they were broken off before they began to taper, so I insisted that he must once have had twenty-four. I explained to Ántonia how this meant that he was twenty-four years old, that he must have been there when white men first came, left on from *buffalo and Indian times*. As I turned him over I began to feel proud of him, to have a kind of respect for his age and size. He seemed like the ancient, eldest Evil" (45–46, italics added).

This seemingly insignificant episode where Jim kills a rattlesnake with a spade borrowed from the Russian immigrants Pavel and Peter functions on a figurative level. Jim's victory allegorizes America's decimation of the American Indians and Spanish colonial enterprise.

Not only does this passage reflect the legacy of what Werner Sollors in *Beyond Ethnicity* (1986) has deemed the "cult of the vanishing Indian," it also echoes the rhetoric of the "black legend," the defamatory discourse criticizing Spain's colonial enterprise during the Spanish-American War. Metaphorically, the rattlesnake Jim encounters symbolizes the obstacles facing American continental expansion and hemispheric hegemony. Competing claims to the land and the armed resistance formed by parties opposed to the United States realizing its manifest destiny constituted the chief impediment to the new nation's growth in size and influence. The snake denotes the challenges Plains Indians (primarily the Lakota Sioux) and Spain (including its former colony Mexico) posed to American territorial advances, while Jim's violent method of dispatching the reptile reflects federal strategies employed to achieve hemispheric supremacy.

As Jim marvels at the size and the age of the rattler, concluding that it was "left on from buffalo and Indian times," Cather somewhat uncannily (if incidentally) evokes Henry H. Cross's 1898 oil painting *Victim of Fate,* in which a seriously wounded buffalo has climbed to the crest of a hill to stand near the contorted body of a recently deceased Plains Indian warrior (see fig. 1 on p. 52). Depictions of dying indigenes, like the fallen hunter in Cross's canvas, were widespread in the nineteenth century. In the final decades of the 1800s, "epitaphs" for the Lakota and other Great Plains tribes were especially popular in painting, sculpture, popular literature, and Wild West shows. Despite its sentimentality and conventional theme, Cross's painting reflects a reality exploited by American expansionists: the fortunes of the bison and the Plains cultures were inextricably linked. The decimation of the great herds, expedited by hunters hired by the railroads to provide meat for the construction crews, precipitated the decline in the power of the Arapaho, Cheyenne, Kiowa, Lakota, Pawnee, and other Plains nations.

Relegating buffalo and Indians to extinction is a logical extension of Jim's earlier conclusion regarding the "emptiness" of the landscape. Informing his utterance is the erroneous—but popularly accepted and widely promoted—assumption that the American bison and the Plains Indians are extinct, that their times have passed in the scant twenty-four years since the arrival of the "white men." The phrasing Cather attributes to Jim reflects racist underpinnings allowing Americans to dismiss Plains cultures and seriously endangered herding animals in the same breath and betrays his acceptance of the popular representation of native peoples collectively as a "vanishing" race.[2]

Jim's slaying of the serpent gains further significance by considering the term "Sioux," a name Cather never allows him to utter. According to its etymology, "Sioux" is an abbreviated form of "Naddouessioux," the French transliteration of the Ojibwa epithet for their principal enemies to the west.[3] Since its earliest appearance in seventeenth-century French documents, "Sioux" has been regarded by whites as a synonym for a venomous snake.[4] Popular and scholarly sources at the time of *My Ántonia*'s release in 1918 also accepted this interpretation. In Native American studies the decade prior to the publication of *My Ántonia*, few scholars and studies were as influential as ethnologist Frederick Webb Hodge and the *Handbook of American Indians North of Mexico*, which he edited from 1907 to 1910. The *Handbook* defines "Sioux" as "a French-Canadian abbreviation of the Chippewa *Nadowe-is-iw*, a diminutive of *nadowe*, 'an adder,' hence 'an enemy.' *Nadoweisiw-eg* is the diminutive plural. The diminutive singular and plural were applied to the Dakota, and to the Huron to distinguish them from the Iroquois proper, the true 'adders' or 'enemies'" (1:376, 2:577). Notwithstanding the significant regional and cultural distinctions differentiating the speakers of three mutually intelligible dialects, they became known collectively and derogatively as Sioux, a frozen curse derived from an Ojibwa expression denoting a venomous snake.[5]

At the time of European contact, the Dakota, Nakota, and Lakota peoples inhabited territory ranging from the upper reaches of the Mississippi River to the eastern slopes of the Big Horn Mountains. The Pawnee may have been the most numerous people in central Nebraska when Spanish and French first arrived, but in the

MICHAEL GORMAN

second half of the nineteenth century, the Lakota (Teton Sioux) of western Nebraska, South Dakota, and eastern Wyoming came to represent the greatest threat to American expansion. Not only did they comprise the largest contingent in the force that defeated Custer at the 1876 Battle of Little Bighorn, the three most famous Indian figures in America at that time—Sitting Bull, Crazy Horse, and Red Cloud—were Lakota. By declining to name specific tribes in Jim's account, Cather further delineates Jim's character. Jim's usage of the misnomer "Indian" in *My Ántonia* suggests his disinterest in issues affecting the native peoples of western Nebraska and North America in general, betraying instead an acceptance of the wider U.S. Indian policy directed toward the containment and cultural assimilation of the Plains Indians as well as the allotment of "surplus" tribal lands.

Jim's slaughter of the rattlesnake resembles the dirty political reality in which his future employer, the railroad, was complicit. In other words, Jim's vicious beating and near beheading of the aged sidewinder corresponds to the manner in which the U.S. military and railway industry colluded to eliminate Native American claims to territory in the Central Great Plains. While the rattlesnake serves as the namesake for all members of the Great Sioux Nation (and, by extension, other Plains Indians), the spade represents the superior technology and complex strategy—involving homesteading, railroad grants, and Indian policy—used to eliminate the native presence and supplant it with European settlement, agricultural development, and exploitation of natural and mineral resources.

As Richard Slotkin recognizes in *The Fatal Environment* (1985), particularly close ties were established between the railroad and the U.S. military; in fact, General Philip Sheridan vociferously promoted extending the railroads west, for he theorized that the railroad would contribute to the elimination of the buffalo and eventual decimation of the Sioux and other native inhabitants of the Plains who depended on buffalo as a source of food, shelter, and clothing (408, 427). Sheridan's theory was deadly accurate; nothing contributed more to the erosion of the Plains Indian cultures than the railroad, which not only brought meat and hide hunters west but also led to settlement and agricultural development that disrupted migration patterns of the buffalo and divided the great bison herds into lesser northern and southern herds.

The future railroad attorney's mortal wielding of the spade also mirrors the devastating effect of federal legislation designed to appropriate native lands. The deleterious legacy of the 1887 Dawes Allotment Act on America's native population is well documented. Even more devastating for the Plains cultures was congressional passage of the Homestead and Pacific Railroad acts in 1862. These remain for Native Americans two of the most insidious bills ever drafted and passed since they worked in tandem to expropriate Indian lands and to populate the West with European immigrants and Americans willing to migrate. In *Native American History* (1996), Judith Nies declares these acts of legislation to be the "two most influential laws in overturning Indian treaties and opening western Indian lands to settlement," making special note of the 174 million acres of "public lands" and subsequent land charters granted to transcontinental railroad companies (268). The railroads, in turn, promoted the settlement and development of the Great Plains, eventually pushing to extend into lands—notably Paha Sapa, the sacred Black Hills, which Red Cloud's Lakota Sioux along with their Cheyenne and Arapaho allies were assured by the 1868 Treaty of Fort Laramie.

Throughout the narrative, the language Cather assigns to Jim hints to the violent history of the Central Plains that preceded large-scale settlement, reminding readers of the recent campaign to contain the western tribes and appropriate the land they formerly controlled. Once, after concluding an English lesson and escorting her home as far as Squaw Creek, Jim and Ántonia stood in silence mesmerized by the beauty of the setting sun upon the stubble fields and stacks of hay—evidence of European occupation and agrarian development of the Plains: "As far as we could see, the miles of copper-red grass were drenched in sunlight that was stronger and fiercer than at any other time of the day. The blond cornfields were red gold, the haystacks turned rosy and threw long shadows. The whole prairie was like the bush that burned with fire and was not consumed. That hour always had the exultation of victory, of triumphant ending, like a hero's death—heroes who died young and gloriously. It was a sudden transfiguration, a lifting-up of day" (38-39). Jim has come to view the settlement of the Plains in quasi-religious terms. For him, the developed landscape offers a covenant as sacred as the one revealed to Moses. Nebraska itself is evidence of the "manifest destiny" awaiting a new generation of chosen people.[6] Close scrutiny of this passage indicates that realizing this destiny will only come after much sacrifice and migration—for immigrants and native inhabitants alike. The name of the creek running between the Burden and Shimerda farms is an oblique reminder of western Nebraska's former inhabitants relegated to Pine Ridge and Rosebud reservations just across the border in South Dakota. In this context, the glorious deaths Jim envisions are likely to be those of Custer and his Seventh Cavalry troops, who died at the 1876 Battle of Little Bighorn in a recent effort to eliminate the native threat to "progress." Along with 211 soldiers, the man known as the "Boy General" lost his life in the campaign waged to open the Black Hills to mining and settlement interests.[7] Posthumously, Custer achieved his goal: the Black Hills were opened, and the European culture and industry transfigured the former "savage" land, just as John Gast depicted in *American Progress*, his 1872 canvas personifying Progress on her westward course.

"As I turned him [the dead snake] over," Jim recalls, "I began to feel proud of him, to have a kind of respect for his age and size" (45). The respect that Jim accords the rattler after killing it mirrors the nobility American writers and artists, since Washington Irving's essay "Philip of Pokanoket" (1814), had projected upon dead or dying Indians.[8] Although nominally appearing to lament the passing of the American Indians, the art and literature devoted to Native American themes, in Jill Lepore's words, "mourned these losses as inevitable and right" (210). Case in point: the antebellum art and literature lamenting the elimination or removal of eastern tribes had virtually no effect on the treatment of Native Americans encountered by U.S. citizens and federal agencies in the trans-Mississippi West after the Civil War. Moreover, at the close of the century, when the First Nations of the Great Plains and the Southwest had been removed or contained and American expansionists began coveting Hawaii and Spain's colonial possessions, Indian subjects in art were still represented heroically as a doomed race, perhaps culminating in *The End of the Trail* (1894), James Earle Fraser's award-winning sculpture depicting a slouching Plains Indian rider upon his equally exhausted mount. Although the Indians were portrayed as vanishing, the popular motif was not, nor, as its presence in *My Ántonia* indicates, did it appear likely to vanish in the twentieth century.[9]

In the nineteenth century, commemorating the "vanishing American" and celebrating European territorial supremacy merged in the practice of naming American communities. Innumerable European settlements across the United States in the nineteenth century were named for Indian tribes (like Omaha, Nebraska, and Cheyenne, Wyoming) or for famed American Indian leaders (like Red Cloud, Nebraska, and Pontiac, Michigan). Cather, reflecting this cultural phenomenon, names the nearest community to the Burden farm Black Hawk, after the Sauk (Sac) leader, Ma-ka-tai-me-she-kia-kiak, who unsuccessfully resisted the influx of European settlers and miners into his people's territory. As scholars have long recognized, the community Cather names Black Hawk is a fictional version of her Nebraskan hometown, actually named Red Cloud for the talented Teton Sioux strategist who forced the United States to sign the 1868 Treaty of Fort Laramie after effectively closing the Bozeman Trail to American advancement.[10] Renaming her south-central Nebraskan community Black Hawk displaces the most recent struggles between the United States and American Indians (the Plains Wars) in time and locale, making it seem like the Indian wars were concluded several decades earlier (1832) east of the Mississippi (Illinois Territory). *My Ántonia*, therefore, literally removes the nations known generically by the whites as the Plains Indians from the territory they occupied less than a decade before Jim Burden's (and Cather's own) arrival.

Cather allows Jim only a vague acknowledgement of the people formerly living on the prairie surrounding Black Hawk: "Beyond the pond on the slope that climbed to the cornfield, there was, faintly marked in the grass, a great circle where the *Indians* used to ride" (60, italics added). By limiting Jim's description of the people formerly living in Nebraska to the abstract term "Indian," Cather eliminates specific controversies affecting the Lakota and other Plains natives from his narrative. Specifically, she diminishes the controversy surrounding the 1887 Dawes Act, which, in favor of promoting further agricultural and industrial development of the Central Plains, reduced title to lands granted Plains Indians by treaty. The West, then, can be seen as settled, the indigenous inhabitants as "vanished" or subsumed as Domestic Dependent Nations under the aegis of the Republic. *My Ántonia* is rhetorically freed to pursue its economic interests and cultural obligations in Europe in the midst of the Great War.

THE SNAKE AS REFLECTION OF SPAIN

Despite the romanticism with which Jim initially celebrates his annihilation of the snake, experience has provided him a more accurate lens to view the episode. In hindsight, he interprets his vanquishing of the reptile more pragmatically, as a keen legal professional who wisely understands that myriad capricious elements contribute to every victory:

> Subsequent experiences with rattlesnakes taught me that my first encounter was fortunate in circumstance. My big rattler was old, and had led too easy a life; there was not much fight in him. He had probably lived there for years, with a fat prairie dog for breakfast whenever he felt like it, a sheltered home, even an owl-feather bed, perhaps, and he had forgot that the world doesn't owe rattlers a living. A snake of his size, in fighting trim, would be more than any boy could handle. So in reality it was a mock adventure; the game was fixed for me by chance, as it probably was for many a dragon-slayer. I had been adequately armed by Russian Peter; the snake was old and lazy; and I had Ántonia beside me, to appreciate and admire. (47–48)

As an adult, Jim recognizes that several factors irrelevant to his martial skill contributed to the lopsided defeat of the serpent. The corpulent snake had become complacent and corrupt, undeserving of the bounty from which it benefited for so long. Jim's characterization of the snake as lazy hunter echoes the reasoning of

American leaders like Senator Dawes who believed the traditional hunting economies of Plains nations unsuitable to the goal of assimilation and designed legislation to force the native inhabitants to adopt an agricultural lifestyle. At the same time, Jim's unsympathetic description of the rattlesnake resembles rhetoric the American press and politicians voiced of Spain during the Spanish-American War.

Wartime understanding of the Spanish Empire was shaped by a defamatory discourse that can be traced to sixteenth-century anti-Spanish sentiment based in religious differences (Protestants versus Papists) and competition to control the seas and acquire territory in the New World. In "American Ideology: Visions of National Greatness and Racism" (1992), Michael H. Hunt describes the influence the "black legend" and "its condemnatory view of the Spanish character" exercised on the American consciousness, noting its prominence in textbooks, comics, "political rhetoric," and national policy (20). Simply put, according to the tradition, Spain was backward, negligent, and cruel: an imperial power that never grew out of feudalism. "More broadly understood," Hunt writes, "the legend stood for all those undesirable characteristics that were Spain's unfortunate legacy to much of the New World" (21).

The impact of this rhetoric relied upon the contrast drawn between the republican virtues of Anglo-Saxon powers like Great Britain and the United States and the tyranny of the Spanish Empire. Empires who fail to profit their colonial subjects have no legitimacy. Consequently, U.S. involvement in the Spanish-American War was predicated on America's duty to confer abstract benefits—namely, democracy and progress—on Spain's former colonies. Before and after the Spanish-American War, the War Hawks—including future president Teddy Roosevelt, Republican senators Henry Cabot Lodge and Albert J. Beveridge, and naval mastermind Alfred Thayer Mahan—invoked the "black legend" to rationalize America's "crusade" against Spain. The following excerpt from an 1898 justification for the war serves as a vivid example of the centuries-old Spanish rhetoric: "Spain has been tried and convicted in the forum of history. Her religion has been bigotry, whose sacraments have been solemnized by the faggot and the rack. Her statesmanship has been infamy: her diplomacy, hypocrisy: her wars have been massacres: her supremacy has been a blight and a curse, condemning continents to sterility, and their inhabitants to death" (qtd. in Hunt 21). Most commonly levied against Spain were accusations of brutality, vampirism, and neglect of her colonial possessions—charges justifying America's participation in the war. Likewise, inherent iniquity and indolence contribute to the perdition of the rattlesnake in *My Ántonia*. It is characterized as evil (42) and lazy (43), having preyed too long among its hapless victims, the prairie dogs and burrowing owls, through a parasitical living arrangement that mirrors the *reconcentrado* strategy instituted and maintained in rural Cuba by the Spanish military.

In *The Reckless Decade* (1995), popular historian H. W. Brands describes *los reconcentrados* as "Spanish established fortified camps and towns into which Cuban peasants were herded from the countryside; access to these camps was strictly controlled, with the idea that any guerrillas who came into the camps would be unable to get out and cause mischief and any person who stayed outside must be a guerrilla and therefore would be subject to capture or killing" (305). With an eye on Cuba's sugar industry, expansionists in the United States criticized Spain's handling of the rebellion, expressly attacking the policy of the concentration camps and casting the commander of Spanish forces in Cuba, General Valeriano Weyler, as the epitome of the "black legend." Weyler was depicted by William Randolph Hearst's *New York Journal* as a "brute" who could not contain "his carnal, animal brain from running riot with itself in inventing tortures and infamies of bloody debauchery," while Joseph Pulitzer's *New York World* pleaded for a "nation wise . . . brave . . . and strong enough to restore peace in this bloodsmitten land" (qtd. in Brands 307). Such one-sided accounts of the Cuban Insurrection pressured the United States to deliver Cuba from Spanish villainy, specifically the cold-blooded conduct of General Weyler. When it finally entered the fray, the United States accomplished the task in four months (April to August 1898). In the papers at least, the United States liberated Cuba and the Philippines from Spanish despotism. The war with Spain proved to be, like Jim's encounter with the sidewinder, a "mock adventure" against a once formidable adversary no longer in "fighting trim."

The imagery and language employed in the snake episode draw powerfully on the legacy of nineteenth-century American imperialism. An attentive reading of the passage reveals compelling figurative parallels to American removal/containment of the Plains tribes and U.S. participation and successful resolution of the Spanish-American War. By crushing the idle serpent with a simple sod-breaking tool used by industrious homesteaders, Jim reenacts the United States' displacement of Native Americans and Spaniards, peoples Americans have traditionally regarded as obstacles to expansion and dismissed as shiftless.

SPAIN'S BEQUEST: UNEARTHING THE LEGACY OF CONQUEST

While child narrators (like Jim Burden) in Cather's fiction help authenticate the myth of manifest destiny, Cather's frequent reference to archeology and history legitimate America's position as a global power and heir to the Spanish Empire. Through allusion to archeology and invocation of epic, *My Ántonia* actually reinforces former Spanish claims to the American West, now inhabited by American and European settlers, only to support the transfer of imperial responsibility.[11]

In "Selling Relics, Preserving Antiquities" (1995), Howard Horwitz recognizes that "ethnology, anthropology and archaeology —overlapping emergent disciplines—were nationalist enterprises dedicated to discovering the fundamental racial and cultural characteristics of America and Americans" (362). Jim's manuscript, likewise, serves nationalist enterprises by reflecting America's European inheritance while dismissing native influences. Although Cather introduces "the great circle where the Indians used to ride" (60) into Jim's reminiscence, he remains unable or unwilling to assign it to a specific Plains Indian people. His lack of specificity suggests an indifference to indigenous civilizations as well as an ignorance of current practices in anthropology promoted by Columbia University professor Franz Boas. By 1915 the Boasian approach, stressing intensive study of localized cultures, had begun to supplant comparative methods in anthropology that reified scientific racism so popular after Darwin. The result, as Robert F. Berkhofer Jr. notes in "White Conception of Indians," was that indigenous Americans were studied "as tribes and as cultures not as the Indian" (543). The absence of native artifacts, combined with Jim's inability to interpret traces left by Plains Indian tribes, weakens indigenous claims to the land now inhabited by definable groups of European settlers—Austrians, Bohemians, Danes, Norwegians, Russians, and Swedes—that Jim befriends in Nebraska.

In a break from study the summer before enrolling at the University of Nebraska, Jim Burden attends a picnic with "the hired girls"—Ántonia Shimerda, Lena Lingard, Tiny Soderball, and Anna Hansen—and entertains the four young immigrant women with a myth Ántonia characterizes as "how the Spanish *first* came here [to Nebraska], like you and Charley Harling used to talk about" (235, italics added):[12]

They sat under a little oak, Tony . . . and the other girls . . . listened to the little I was able to tell them about Coronado and his search for the Seven Golden Cities. At school we were taught that he had not got so far north as Nebraska, but had given up his quest and turned back somewhere in Kansas. But Charley Harling and I had a strong belief that he had been along this very river. A farmer in the county north of ours, when he was breaking sod had turned up a metal stirrup of fine workmanship, and a sword with a Spanish inscription on the blade. He lent these relics to Mr. Harling, who brought them home with him. Charley and I scoured them, and they were on exhibition in the Harling office all summer. Father Kelly, the priest, had found the name of the Spanish maker on the sword, and an abbreviation that stood for the city of Cordova.

"And that I saw with my own eyes," Ántonia put in triumphantly. "So Jim and Charley were right, and the teachers were wrong!" (235–36)

As in the definitive judgment he forms upon his strained first "sight" of the prairie landscape, Jim denies the thinking that conflicts with his own "strong belief[s]" by telling his eager listeners of a Spanish stirrup and a sword unearthed by a local farmer and explaining—again, despite teachings to the contrary—that the sixteenth-century expedition of the Spanish conquistador Francisco Vasquez de Coronado had come as far north as present-day Nebraska in his search for fabled riches.[13] In a manner echoing Virgil's tracing Roman civilization to the Trojan refugee Aeneas, Cather has Jim weave a tale recognizing Coronado as the mythological father of Nebraska.

To lend credence to his interpretation of history, Jim refers to the assistance he receives restoring and interpreting the artifacts from Father Kelly and his friend Charley Harling. Mentioning these two figures lends more than an air of authenticity to his tale; it invokes the long and convoluted history of cultural imperialism. In a strategy Cather would employ later in *The Professor's House*, she uses a Roman Catholic priest—a living tribute to Western civilization and Christianity—to make sense of the archeological finds. Father Kelly's facility with Latin reinforces the preeminence of European culture, especially the legacy of the Roman Empire as well as the global reach of the Roman Catholic Church and, more importantly, establishes the United States as a European state culturally.

By naming Charley Harling, who entered the U.S. Naval Academy and would have been a junior officer during the Spanish-American War, Cather evokes the U.S. Navy, the deciding factor in America's 1898 defeat of Spain and its inheritance of former Spanish colonies.[14] As Cather would have been intimately familiar with from her days as telegraph editor for the *Pittsburgh Leader* during the Spanish-American War, George Dewey's naval victories in the Philippines were far more instrumental in winning the war than the battles won by land forces in Cuba. Cather shapes Jim's Eurocentric sense of national and cultural identity through his association with Father Kelly and Charley Harling, champions of cultural and martial imperialism, as well as his interest in the recovered Spanish antiquities that point to a once-great European empire's former presence in Nebraska—an empire, no less, that America has now largely relieved of its colonial holdings.

My Ántonia invokes the popularity of archaeology in turn-of-the-century America and uses the recovered artifacts to suggest Spanish occupation of the West predating European contact with the native inhabitants. By doing so, Cather effectively frees Jim from concern about military and political actions during the Plains Indian Wars, including the breaking of the 1851 and 1868 Treaties of Fort Laramie and Colonel Chivington's notorious attack on unarmed Cheyennes at Sand Creek in November 1864. Jim's account can be read, therefore, as an intricate piece of sophistry ascribing intermediate possession of the American West to the Spanish. The only interpreted artifacts suggest a prima facie case for Spanish claim to Nebraska by right of discovery. America's problematic relations with the indigenous civilizations of the West can be dismissed then as historically immaterial since the December 1898 Treaty of Paris (ratified in February 1899) concluding the Spanish-American War grants to the United States possession of Spain's territories in the Western Hemisphere and the Pacific.

Immediately after Jim finishes relating the legend about Coronado, he and the girls witness a curious phenomenon: a plough framed by the "molten red" of the setting sun (237). The timely vision of the silhouetted piece of farm equipment figuratively turns the swords of the conquistadors into ploughshares and triumphantly punctuates Jim's account of the wandering Spaniard, effectively reinforcing European "discovery," immigration, settlement, and agrarian development of North America with no mention of the dispossession or genocide of the indigenous population.

Alongside passages of archeological and anthropological import in *My Ántonia*, Cather makes several allusions to epic reinforcing the celebratory tone of this novel. Book II ("The Hired Girls") opens with a description of Jim's preparations for college, including his solitary reading of Virgil's *Aeneid*, Cather's hint that conventions, motifs, or formal elements of epic will be used to link late-nineteenth-century settlement to a mythic past.[15] Cather's invocation of mythic elements is particularly effective but hardly unique among American writers in the late nineteenth and early twentieth centuries. Virgil, especially in his *Aeneid* as Sollors notes, "shaped the form of American epics" by "lending itself to a sanctioning of the further transporting west of empires" (*Be-*

yond Ethnicity 239), so it is hardly surprising that his verse appears frequently in Jim's account, strategically invoked in reverse-chronological order. The last of Virgil's poems, the *Aeneid*, figures most prominently in relation to Jim Burden's college preparation, while the earlier-composed *Georgics* are mentioned later, during Jim's first year at college. As these two texts are brought together, so are the ideas informing them: the *Aeneid* and its epic concern with the westward migration of empire (from Ilium to Latium) and the *Georgics*, with its pastoral focus on "patria," which Jim is informed by his classics professor, Gaston Cleric, should be interpreted locally, "not [as] a nation or even a province, but the little rural neighborhood on the Mincio where the poet was born" (256).

In his lessons on Virgil's *Georgics*, Cleric emphasizes the significance of the local communities and landscapes subsumed by the Roman Empire; Virgil was less concerned with empire than a localized setting and culture contained within the larger state. As Jim puts it, by writing the *Georgics*, Virgil brought the muse to his country along the Mincio River (256). Though it seems natural that *My Ántonia* is Jim's attempt to do the same, he does not. Rather than bringing the muse to his country, he very literally extracts her (Ántonia and the land she personifies) like the resources and profits he draws from his interests in mines, timber, and oil. Jim's concern in *My Ántonia* is with nation in a global age. Cather cleverly has Jim invert Cleric's lesson by merging his patria — the farmland surrounding Black Hawk — into the "world's cornfields" that his grandfather foresaw: "It took a clear, meditative eye like my grandfather's to foresee that they would enlarge and multiply until they would be, not the Shimerda's cornfields, or Mr. Bushy's, but the world's cornfields; that their yield would be one of the great economic facts, like the wheat crop of Russia, which underlie all the activities of men, in peace or war" (132). Jim celebrates the political power reflected in the economic fact of the American West. Like the ledgers kept for his various enterprises, *My Ántonia* charts the nation's realization of its economic and political potential.

CONCLUSION: NEBRASKA IN
THE TIME OF NATIONS

In the passage about the "world's cornfields" Jim comments on his grandfather's ability to collapse history and see the farmland generations later. Although regarded as an uncommon ability, this destinarian vision was not peculiar to Grandfather Burden. At a fundamental level, it is the most American of capacities. As essential a contribution to success as investment capital, this prescience provides the psychological impetus and comfort necessary to undertake any new venture in peace and war, especially homesteading. Only because Jim inherited this disposition from his grandfather can he tell the story of *My Ántonia*.

In fashioning Jim Burden Cather renders a sophisticated performance of rurality meant to embody the contradictions of the age in which he lives. As such, the narrator of *My Ántonia* resembles no American more than Theodore Roosevelt, a figure deeply associated with America's territorial expansion at home and abroad. Roosevelt took office in the greatest age of American imperialism, shortly after the United States assumed possession of Spanish territories in the Caribbean and the Pacific—an event he ardently participated in, first as undersecretary of the navy in Washington DC, and finally as lieutenant colonel in the First U.S. Volunteer Cavalry serving in Cuba. As he was inaugurated twenty-sixth president of the United States, American troops engaged guerrillas in the Philippines, who were happily rid of Spain but resented America's presence. Roosevelt would make no apologies for these activities, as is evident in the foreword he wrote for the presidential edition of *The Winning of the West*:

> Many decades went by after Spain had lost her foothold on the American continent, and she still held her West Indian empire. She misgoverned the continent; and in the islands, as once upon the continent, her own children became her deadliest foes. . . . At last, at the close of one of the bloodiest and most brutal wars that even Spain ever waged with her own colonists, the United States intervened, and in a brief summer campaign destroyed the last vestiges of the mediaeval Span-

ish domain in the tropic seas alike of the West and the remote
East.

We of this generation were but carrying to completion the
work of our fathers' fathers. (ix)

In this statement, Roosevelt presents U.S. participation in the
Spanish-American War as the logical conclusion to generations
of westward migration and cultural conflict initiated by the first
Dutch and English settlers in North America. By preceding a history of American migration and settlement with an argument defending U.S. involvement in the Spanish-American War, Roosevelt
merges domestic and international concerns, continental expansion and overseas colonialism. So too does *My Ántonia*. Cather
uses Jim to frame an account of America's rise to world power,
which he describes literally in realizing the vision of his "father's
father," Josiah Burden.

It takes a person with a "clear, meditative eye" and "big Western
dreams" to make sense of the contradictions implicit in American
imperialism. Cather created Jim Burden to reconcile the nation's
global mandate and its pastoral pose. The imagery and language
employed throughout *My Ántonia* draw powerfully on the legacy
of nineteenth-century American imperialism and forecast its twentieth-century consequences. Attentive readings reveal compelling
figurative parallels to American treatment of Plains tribes and U.S.
participation in the Spanish-American War. The snake episode,
for example, parodies Theodore Roosevelt's "Big Stick Policy," his
warning to powers threatening American interests in the Western
Hemisphere. Jim's elimination of the aged serpent with a spade
reenacts the United States' displacement of American Indians and
Spaniards in the New World. Similarly, Josiah Burden's predic-
tion of the United States becoming the "world's cornfields" reflects
America's global economic and political status on the eve of the
Great War—a reality the United States will eventually enter World
War I to defend when unlimited German submarine warfare makes
feeding the world impossible.

In *Imagined Communities: Reflections on the Origin and Spread
of Nationalism* (1991), Benedict Anderson asserts, "All profound
changes in [a nation's] consciousness bring with them characteris-

Fig. 1. *Victim of Fate*. Oil on Canvas. 1898. Henry H. Cross. Library of Congress, Prints and Photographs Division. LC-USZ62-19801.

tic amnesias. Out of such oblivions, in specific historical circumstances, spring narratives" (204). The period from the end of the Plains Indian Wars to the beginning of World War I marks one such oblivion in American history. The United States changed drastically between Wounded Knee (December 1890) and the assassination of Archduke Ferdinand (June 1914). Clearly, new cultural and mythological "maps" would have to be drafted to address the changes brought about by America's acquisition of overseas territories. Cather's *My Ántonia* is one such map or mythology. From references to the political reasons for the Bohemians "natural distrust" of Austrians (*My Ántonia* 20) to the violence reflecting the war consciousness at the time of the novel's composition (Stout 165), the Great War asserts its presence in this narrative. But more than that, *My Ántonia* charts the course of American empire, from its occupation of the Central Plains in the nineteenth century to its twentieth-century obligations as a world power.

NOTES

I am grateful to Susan J. Rosowski, Kyoko Matsunaga, and James Kelley for reading and commenting upon earlier drafts of this article.

1. Written between 1912 and 1913, *Pygmalion* was first performed in England on April 11, 1914, at His Majesty's Theatre in London and in the United States on October 12, 1914, at the Park Theatre in New York while Cather lived there. Based on her favorable reviews of Shaw's earlier plays —Cather reviewed *The Devil's Disciple* (1897) and *A Perfect Wagnerite* (1898) (Woodress 134, 236, 260; Lee 53, 132)—it is possible that Cather saw or read *Pygmalion* (published in New York by Brentano in 1916) before completing *My Ántonia*.

2. For detailed discussions of this motif before and up to the nineteenth century, see Lepore, *The Name of War* (1998). For its invocation in the nineteenth century, see Sollors, *Beyond Ethnicity* (1986), and Berkhofer, "White Conceptions of Indians" (1988). For discussion of this motif in relation to the twentieth century, see Michaels, *Our America* (1994) and Berkhofer. While Sollors calls the popularity of this image "the cult of the vanishing Indian," Michaels refers to it as the "Vanishing American," a phrase taken from Zane Grey's 1925 novel of the same name. It is likely that Grey was inspired by other art such as *The Vanishing Race* (1904), one of Edward Curtis's famous photographs of his Native American subjects.

3. Ojibwa, Ojibway, Ojibwe, and Chippewa (variants of the Algonquian term "puckered moccasin"—a feature distinguishing its wearers from their neighboring tribes) all refer to the same Algonquian-speaking people, who refer to themselves as Anishinabe.

4. Although considerable debate exists as to the original meaning of the name today, most current academic resources, including *Red Cloud:*

54

MICHAEL GORMAN

Warrior-Statesman of the Lakota Sioux (Larson 1997) and the *Atlas of the North American Indian* (1985, 2000), maintain "Sioux" to be derived from the Ojibwa word for adder or snake (9; 177). Some scholars insist Naddowessioux first meant "lesser enemy" before being applied to snakes, while others believe it originally designated the Eastern Massasauga rattlesnake. Douglas R. Parks and Raymond J. DeMallie (2001) in "The Sioux" (Vol 13, pt. 2 of *The Handbook of North American Indians* 749) and Guy Gibbon in *The Sioux* (2002) are among current scholars who do not accept "Sioux" as an abbreviated synonym for snake. However, both sources rely upon the research of Ives Goddard, who based his study on Ottawa rather than Ojibwa (Chippewa). Ottawa and Ojibwa are closely related, but distinct, Algonquian dialects.

    5. In *Beyond Ethnicity,* Sollors recognizes that "many names . . . originated in frozen curses" (193). I am indebted to him for this term.

    6. According to Anders Stephanson, this famous phrase was initially coined in 1845 by John O'Sullivan, the editor of the *Democratic Review;* he defined it as America's mission "to overspread the continent allotted by Providence for the free development of our yearly multiplying millions" (xi).

    7. Slotkin notes that this nickname was given by the New York Herald (*The Fatal Environment* 390). The number of U.S. soldiers believed killed at the Battle of the Little Bighorn varies considerably. Nies claims 211 to 225 soldiers died alongside Custer (282, 283).

    8. Such images pervaded drama, fiction, history, poetry, painting, sculpture, and song throughout the nineteenth century. The titles of antebellum works treating this subject are instructive, if not very imaginative. In drama and fiction, "last of the" was an extremely popular modifying phrase, invoked in 1823 by Joseph Doddridge for his play *Logan: The Last of the Race of Shikellemus, Chief of the Cayuga Nation* and later (1829) by John Augustus Stone in his award-winning drama *Metamora; or, The Last of the Wampanoags,* and perhaps most famously in 1826 by James Fennimore Cooper in *The Last of the Mohicans,* the most popular of his *Leatherstocking Tales.* In antebellum sculpture—at least in 1856—"dying" was the modifier of choice, employed both by Thomas Crawford in his marble *The Dying Indian Chief* and somewhat more specifically by Ferdinand Pettrich in *The Dying Tecumseh,* his neo-classical interpretation of the great Shawnee leader's final moments.

    9. In *Manifest Manners: Narratives on Postindian Survivance* (1994, 1996), Gerald Vizenor argues convincingly that the name "Indian" has always implied what Sollors and Michaels see as "vanished." For Vizenor, "*indians* are immovable simulations, the tragic archives of dominance and victimry" (ix–x). In other words, "Indian" is a misnomer applied by Euro-

peans to the peoples of the New World; shaped by misinformed European notions (and Orientalizing discourse), this term can never represent a dynamic and evolving civilization. Vizenor uses the term "postindian" to connote the viability of Native American cultures.

10. In an interview for the *Philadelphia Record* (August 10, 1913), Cather described Red Cloud as "still wild enough and bleak enough when we got there. My grandfather's homestead was about eighteen miles from Red Cloud—a little town on the Burlington, named after the old Indian Chief who used to come hunting in that country, and who buried his daughter on the top of one of the river bluffs south of the town. Her grave had been looted for her rich furs and beadwork long before my family went West, but we children used to find arrowheads there and some of the bones of her pony that had been strangled above her grave" (Bohlke 9).

11. Archeology is also used to interesting effect in *The Professor's House.* Although in *The Professor's House* the relics are Ancestral Puebloan (Anasazi), they are interpreted Eurocentrically.

12. At the time Jim told "the girls" this tale, Charley was a midshipman at the U.S. Naval academy (*My Ántonia* 166).

13. Cather has used the legend of Coronado similarly in other texts. In "The Enchanted Bluff" (1909), Cather invokes the same legend, having Arthur Adams, the oldest boy in the story, inform the other Nebraskan boys that Coronado and his men "were all over this country [central Nebraska] once" (73).

14. In the 1890s the U.S. Navy was revitalized in part because of the convincing argument of Naval War College instructor Alfred Thayer Mahan, who recommended a large navy and overseas bases and coal stations to protect American interests (Brands 294). The popular reception of Mahan's *The Influence of Sea Power upon History, 1660-1783* (1890) in expansionist circles during the last decade of the nineteenth century directly contributed to assembling a respectable navy, which proved decisive in defeating the Spanish in 1898. Mahan's influential text and its recommendations for a revitalized navy were preceded in 1882 by similar recommendations made by a youthful Theodore Roosevelt in his influential history *The Naval War of 1812*, which he wrote while studying law at Columbia University. Roosevelt's study became required reading on all naval vessels shortly after its publication (Morris 599). In view of their similar interests, it is little surprise that Roosevelt and Mahan became friends, correspondents, and political confidants.

15. For a detailed discussion of Cather's employment of Virgil, see chapter 3 of Guy Reynolds' book, *Willa Cather in Context: Progress, Race, Empire* (1996). In it, Reynolds discusses Cather's use of Virgil in relation to *O Pioneers!*

WORKS CITED

Anderson, Benedict. *Imagined Communities: Reflections on the Origin and Spread of Nationalism*, revised ed. New York: Verso, 1991.

Berkhofer, Robert F., Jr. "White Conceptions of Indians." *Handbook of North American Indians*. Ed. William C. Sturtevant. Vol. 4: *Indian-White Relations*. Ed. Wilcomb E. Washburn. Washington DC: Smithsonian, 1988. 522–47.

Bohlke, L. Brent, ed. *Willa Cather in Person: Interviews, Speeches, and Letters*. Lincoln: U of Nebraska P, 1986.

Brands, H. W. *The Reckless Decade: American in the 1890s*. New York: St. Martin's, 1995.

Cather, Willa. "The Enchanted Bluff." *Harper's* April 1909: 774–78, 780–81.

———. *My Ántonia*. 1918. Willa Cather Scholarly Edition. Ed. Charles Mignon and James Woodress. Lincoln: U of Nebraska P, 1994.

Fischer, Mike. "Pastoralism and Its Discontents: Willa Cather and the Burden of Imperialism." *Mosaic* 23.1 (1990): 31–45.

Gibbon, Guy E. *The Sioux: The Dakota and Lakota Nations*. New York: Blackwell, 2002.

Hodge, Frederick Webb, ed. Preface. *Handbook of American Indians North of Mexico*. Bureau of American Ethnology. Bulletin 30. Washington DC: GPO, 1907. v–ix.

Horwitz, Howard. "Selling Relics, Preserving Antiquities: *The Professor's House* and the Narrative of American Anthropology." *Configurations* 3.3 (1995): 349–89.

Hunt, Michael. "American Ideology: Visions of National Greatness and Racism." *Imperial Surge: The United States Abroad, the 1890s-Early 1900s*. Ed. Thomas G. Paterson and Stephen G. Rabe. Lexington: Heath, 1992. 14–31.

Karush, Deborah. "Innocent Voyages: Fictions of United States Expansion in Cather, Stevens and Hurston." Diss. Yale University, 1997.

Larson, Robert W. *Red Cloud: Warrior-Statesman of the Lakota Sioux*. Norman: U of Oklahoma P, 1997.

Lepore, Jill. *The Name of War: King Philip's War and the Origins of American Identity*. 1998. New York: Vintage, 1999.

Limerick, Patricia Nelson. *The Legacy of Conquest: The Unbroken Past of the American West*. New York: Norton, 1987.

Michaels, Walter Benn. *Our America: Nativism, Modernism, and Pluralism*. Durham: Duke UP, 1995.

Milton, John. *Paradise Lost*. New ed. Ed. Merritt Y. Hughes. New York: Macmillan, 1986.

Jim Burden and the White Man's Burden

Morris, Edmund. *The Rise of Theodore Roosevelt.* 1979. Revised ed.
New York: Modern Library, 2001.

Nies, Judith. *Native American History: A Chronology of a Culture's Vast Achievements and Their Links to World Events.* New York: Ballantine, 1996.

Parks, Douglas R. Synonymy. "Sioux until 1850." Raymond J. DeMallie. *Handbook of North American Indians.* Ed. William C. Sturtevant. Vol. 13: Plains. Part 2. Ed. Raymond J. DeMallie. Washington DC: Smithsonian, 2001. 718–60.

Reynolds, Guy. *Willa Cather in Context: Progress, Race, Empire.* New York: St. Martin's, 1996.

Roosevelt, Theodore. Foreword. 1900. *The Winning of the West.* Vol. 1. 1889. Presidential ed. New York: Putnam's, 1900.

Rosowski, Susan J. *The Voyage Perilous: Willa Cather's Romanticism.* Lincoln: U of Nebraska P, 1986.

Slotkin, Richard. *The Fatal Environment: The Myth of the Frontier in the Age of Industrialization.* New York: Atheneum, 1985.

Sollors, Werner. *Beyond Ethnicity: Consent and Descent in American Culture.* New York: Oxford UP, 1986.

Stephanson, Anders. *Manifest Destiny.* New York: Hill & Wang, 1995.

Stout, Janis P. *Willa Cather: The Writer and Her World.* Charlottesville: UP of Virginia, 2000.

Urgo, Joseph. *Willa Cather and the Myth of American Migration.* Urbana: U of Illinois P, 1995.

Vizenor, Gerald. *Manifest Manners: Narratives on Postindian Survivance.* 1994. Lincoln: U of Nebraska P, 1999.

The Not-So-Great War
Cather Family Letters and the
Spanish-American War

MARGARET ANNE O'CONNOR

"The splendid little war" is the phrase Secretary of State John Hay used to refer to the altercation with Spain occurring during his term of office. Since then the name and the war have both undergone reappraisal. In 1996 historian Thomas G. Paterson writes of "the Spanish-American-Cuban-Filipino War" and another more recent revisionist historian, Louis A. Perez Jr., prefers to discuss the just as inclusive but less cumbersome appellation of "War of 1898." For U.S. combatants and the nation that sent them, this conflict was known simply—and perhaps imperialistically—as the Spanish-American War. From a perspective of a century later, the war appears to be a brief rehearsal for conflicts to come. In the Spanish-American War, four thousand U.S. military personnel lost their lives: four hundred in combat and thirty-six hundred to infections, disease, food contamination, and unsafe, unsanitary health conditions. Another four thousand American troops died during the Philippine insurrection that began as a direct result of the official Treaty of Paris signed December 10, 1898. In the Philippines Americans really fought two separate wars. After the treaty in which Spain ceded the Philippine Islands to the United States, U.S. forces found themselves fighting the Filipino forces of their previous ally—rebel leader Emilio Aguinaldo—who had been so instrumental in defeating Spain only months earlier.

The Spanish-American War was in many ways a modern war, with several innovations that changed the battlefield forever. A hot air balloon was used for reconnaissance before the battles of San

Juan Heights and San Juan Hill; for the first time film footage recorded action on ships and in land battles; Gatling guns peppered approaching forces. Yet it was also the last of the old battle styles as well. Cavalry was central to combat, but horses were more decorative than strategic in the great wars to come in the twentieth century (Lynch interview).

War came to Webster County, Nebraska, in the spring of 1898, and young men left farms to scatter as far away as Cuba and the Philippines in answer to the call for volunteers. Grosvenor (G. P.) Cather was a fifteen-year-old farm boy when the Spanish-American War broke out. He and his twelve-year-old twin brothers, Frank and Oscar, kept up a correspondence with three young men from their community who joined the Nebraska Volunteer Infantry. Two of the men were sent to Florida and Cuba and one to the Philippines; the letters they wrote back home to the teenaged sons of George P. Cather helped shape the boys' expectations of battle scenes on land and sea.[1]

In terms of military history, the small cache of letters is unremarkable. The three men writing are enlisted men, not the decision makers that military historians traditionally chronicle. The men rarely hold a vantage point on the battlefield; instead they write of everyday life at stateside camps, on troopships, or in foreign camps. As for news of the war, they rarely have more than rumors to pass on. The anonymity of the source of news about the war efforts, however, brings home universal complaints of any enlisted man in any war. He is a player on a game board—at best moved by some shrewd officers into strategic locations and put into a position of affecting the outcome of the wargame, at worst a forgotten game piece stacked beside the board, to be held in abeyance until some turn of events forces his participation. Perhaps he will not have a significant part to play at all, he fears.

Willa Cather was only twenty-five and writing with the *Pittsburgh Leader* for the few months of the war in 1898. Among her other responsibilities, she handled war dispatches from Cuba (Stout 53). Her job kept war news before her, and she was probably speaking from personal experience when she wrote her friend Frances Gere that newspapers were puffing up the war news to create reader interest (qtd. in Woodress 94). As was her cousins' in Nebraska, Cather's role was vicarious, but it offered her—and them—"war experience" before the Lost Generation writers of the next war sailed for their European conflict. Twenty years later Cather's oldest cousin, G. P., would be Webster County's first casualty in the Great War. As reported in the *Blue Hill (NE) Leader* and reprinted in the *Red Cloud (NE) Argus*, "Lieutenant Cather was the first Webster County man to enter overseas service, the first one from the county to give up his life in the war against Prussianism and the first officer from Nebraska to fall on the western front in France" (Ray Collection, June 20, 1918). Cather's 1922 novel *One of Ours* would be a tribute to him and to all those who lost their lives. In a real sense, it would be a tribute to all who fought in the war and all who fought for what her hero fought for—personal freedom. Claude Wheeler has some of Cather's own longings in his persona—great hopes for the future, a desire to escape reminiscent of the Revolt from the Village school of the era, a love of France, and a sense of the stifling effects of family and home country on personal dreams.

Janis P. Stout discusses the parallels between Claude and Willa Cather in her biography of Cather (169–71). Even in the choice of a name for her protagonist, Cather aligns herself with Claude Wheeler by reversing her own initials. Claude is a self-conscious young man on the threshold of adulthood. He tries hard to be a face in the crowd, to be the son his parents want him to be, to marry the girl from a neighboring farm, and to live a life similar to those of family and friends around him. His hopes for such a world fall apart before the coming of World War I offers him a way out. Like a deus ex machina, war in Europe lifts him from the Nebraska plains, leaving home problems unresolved.

The prototype for Claude Wheeler, Cather's cousin G. P., greeted departure for the war with the same sense of release as did Claude. Fifteen years older than his fictional counterpart, however, G. P. knew more about war and the military. Meant to typify the thousands of young soldiers innocently leaving the farms for the excitement of military adventure, Claude is more like the youthful G. P. who received letters from soldiers in 1898 than he is to the thirty-five-year-old man who went off to war in 1917.

None of the letters written to the three soldiers by G. P. or his brothers survives; only the responses to questions asked or to information provided and advice offered in the soldiers' letters give us the images of three young men at home learning about the war and the manly activity of war. The three soldiers were all from Bladen, Nebraska, and the surrounding farmlands. Though they knew one another, the three were not close friends and kept track of one another in their travels more through information in letters from home than from crossing paths with one another.

Two of the three young men writing to the Cathers were farmhands who regularly worked for the boys' father. Unused to the niceties of letter writing, their concerns are elemental: food, health, weather, news from home and about each other. Oley Iverson first writes from Camp Omaha, only a few hours by buggy from the farm where he grew up. Iverson's experiences in camp altered his views. For one, he had assumed that the big and brawny recruits are the most likely to pass the physical examinations for entrance into the regiment; instead, he writes, "It seems as if the largest and the stoutest men have more trouble passing than the little fellers have. There's lots of big stout looking [men] . . . rejected every day. All the men that we thought was sure to pass in our company was rejected" (Ray Collection, July 11, 1898).

There was no rationing at stateside camps, according to Iverson's catalog: "Each man is allowed one pound of beef a day and bread, beans, potatoes, coffee and sugar and sometime we get tomatoes" (Ray Collection, July 18, 1898). After moving on to Jacksonville, Florida, he writes, "We have dried fruit three times a day—fresh meat once, plenty of potatoes, tomatoes, onions, rice and lots of good bread. It is true that it is not cooked as good as it might be, but we have no fancy cook stoves to cook on or it would be better. But when everything has to be cooked outdoor, it makes lots of difference" (Ray Collection, October 14, 1898).

The next exotic clime on Iverson's tour of duty is Savannah, Georgia. Writing October 29, 1898, he says Company I, Third Regiment of the Nebraska Volunteer Infantry are bivouacked "two miles southeast of town. The streetcars run out to the camp so it makes it quite handy when we want to go to town. I was down one day this week and took in the city. It's a nice place. It beats Grand Island [Nebraska] all to pieces. We are camped where the rebels were camped at the time when Sherman captured the city. There is still a lot of old breastwork left to mark the place. I like Georgia ever so much better than I did Florida" (Ray Collection). A staunch Republican, as were the Cathers, Iverson mentions the most illustrious member of the regiment, Nebraska's favorite son, Col. William Jennings Bryan, who was the unsuccessful Democratic candidate against William McKinley for president in 1896. "I must tell you that I like Col. Bryan very much," he writes. "I think he is a mighty fine fellow. He is just as common as any of the boys" (Ray Collection, July 11, 1898). A week later he suggests facetiously that even Bryan might be changed by his war experiences: "Bryan is all right but his politics need fixing and we will have that fixed when we get back from war. I think he will be a Republican then" (Ray Collection, July 18, 1898).

H. C. Gress sticks with the unvarnished truth as he sees it in his first letter after arriving at Camp Cuba Libra, near Panama Park, Florida: "We left Omaha last Monday a week ago for Jacksonville, Florida, which we reached Friday morning at 8:00 o'clock. We had a long ride and a good time. We all like it pretty well here now, but we didn't like it at first. I like it fine. The Army is all right. I have good health. I feel better than I have felt in the last two years. It is awful hot down here though" (Ray Collection, July 27, 1898).

Gress spent the rest of his four months of service in Florida. In October he wrote to G. P. that he hadn't written because he was sick: "I am in the hospital now and I have been here two weeks today." No doubt largely because of his unspecified malady, Gress's view of the state of Florida had changed: "I don't like it in Florida very well. I would rather be in old Nebraska where I was raised. The climate agrees with my health better. Florida doesn't agree with my health at all but I guess I will have to stand it till they see fit to send me home. I hope it will be soon for I know if I get back to Nebraska I will be all right. I will get my health again" (Ray Collection, October 2, 1898).

Furloughed and discharged less than a month later, Gress was back in Bladen, Nebraska, in early November and wrote about his return to G. P., who had gone off to a junior college: "Everybody is husking corn and I hafto sit around and watch them. I am not able to work this fall. I don't expect I will be able to work any all fall. I get awful tired of sitting around doing nothing. I only wish I could get out and work." He ends with a sad lament of the world weary soldier: "Oh yes I received a letter from my old chum [Oley]. He said they was getting along fine now they are practicing shooting. I suppose they have a hot time alright—they can have all the fun they want to, but I have had my fun down there—all I care about anyhow" (Ray Collection, November 4, 1898).

The third correspondent, Bruce Payne, was a student from the university in Lincoln and a distant family member. He wrote G. P. from San Francisco telling him of the wonders to be experienced even in the far reaches of the United States: "My tentmates and I were over to the sea chasing waves and picking up shells," wonders indeed to a landlocked Nebraskan (Ray Collection, June 4, 1898). The troop transport crossing from Oakland to San Francisco (the Bay Bridge hadn't been built in 1898) is the *Merino*, which Payne describes as "the largest transport in the world." A hint of danger haunted the exotic, unfamiliar world, particularly since in a declared war, "the enemy" is identified: "There are many Spanish people living here in Frisco," Payne goes on. "We are careful about eating things that people give us. The people give us oranges, throw them at us, great large ones big as your two fists. They cost only 5 cts a dozen here." Golden Gate Park becomes an exotic wild animal preserve—"lions, buffalo, deer, elk, birds and many beautiful tropical flowers" as well as "a grizzly bear there that weighed over 1000 pounds." Such exotic sights could only make the young man receiving the letters envious. Seasickness, missed promotions, boredom, and waiting come up in subsequent letters, but the bright promise of exotic locales overwhelms such dull and vaguely prosaic topics.

Since he was the most educated of the three correspondents, Payne's letters are the most literate; they connect the exotic world with the known world of G. P. and his brothers: on the voyage to the Philippines, for instance, he saw a whale "as long as your barn is wide." Flying fish have wings that "look just like locust's wings." Miraculously, the Pacific Ocean is rendered in the images familiar to the Nebraska farm boys. In his second letter Payne takes G. P. on a tour of his troop ship, the uss *Senator*. Again, he emphasizes the gigantic proportions of the ship, with room for one thousand troops. "The bunks in the lower deck are not very pleasant places," he finally admits. "It is a pretty hard place to 'Remember the Maine' as one fellow put it" (June 21, 1898). The ironic reference to the most famous battle cry of the war takes on a double irony in terms of the stationery Payne uses (see fig. 1). The stars and stripes wave in color in the top left corner on both the envelope and page. Superimposed on the flag is the outline of a calling card printed by D Company, First Nebraska Infantry, United States Volunteers. The card reads, "Remember the Maine," a triumph of advertising and jingoism since the sinking of the *Maine* in Havana Harbor occurred February 15, 1898, less than four months before Payne's first letter.

Responding to questions from G. P. and his brothers, the correspondents describe their rifles: "You wanted to know what size my rifle was," writes Gress. "It is a 45 single shot Springfield. It is just a dandy" (Ray Collection, July 27, 1898). The Springfield was standard issue among state militia and was the oldest and least effective weapon in widespread use (Lynch interview). The young boys clearly want to hear more about guns and rifles, because Gress adds in a later letter: "No, we haven't done any shooting with our guns yet. We don't shoot with them when we drill." Not wanting to disappoint G. P. and his brothers, however, Gress adds all the excitement he can muster as he goes on: "The noncommissioned officers had a sham battle this morning. They had a hot time for a little while. One of our men got one of his teeth knocked out but didn't hurt him[self] very bad" (Ray Collection, August 13, 1898). R. B. Payne seems aware of the advantages and disadvantages of the rifles in use on both sides when he writes magisterially from Camp Dewey "near Manila": "The Spanish have the Mauser rifles. They repeat five times, and [are] not a deadly weapon as they fire small steel bullets. The Krag-Jogensen rifle which the regulars have shoots the same kind of a ball. They say that these balls will wound a man but [are] not likely to kill him, so it will take two men to carry off the wounded man whereas if he had been killed, no one would drop out to care for him. In this lies the advantage of the steel ball" (Ray Collection, August 8, 1898).

Payne does not go so far as to question the firepower of the rifles he and his fellow Nebraska volunteers have been issued, however:

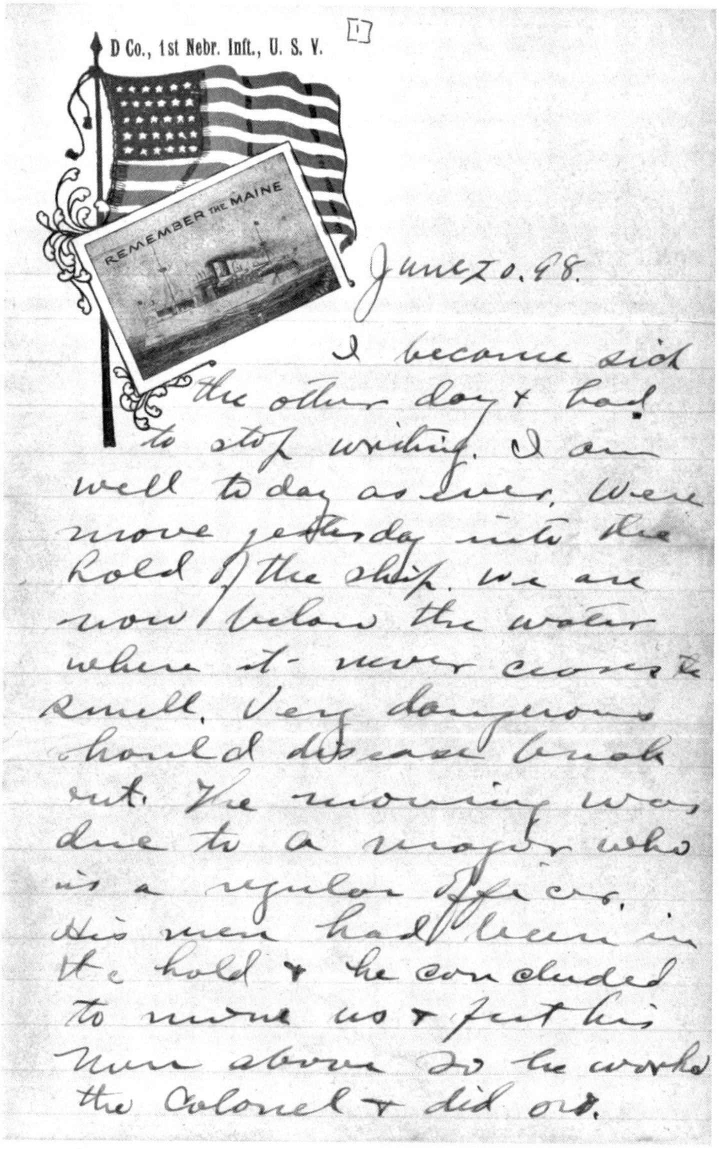
D Co., 1st Nebr. Inft., U. S. V.

REMEMBER THE MAINE

June 20. 98.

I became sick the other day & had to stop writing. I am well to day as ever. Were move yesterday into the hold of the ship. We are now below the water where it never ceases to smell. Very dangerous should disease break out. The moving was due to a major who is a regular officer. His men had been in the hold & he concluded to move us & put his men above. So he worked the Colonel & did so.

Fig. 1. Letter from Bruce Payne to G. P. Cather. George Cather Ray Collection, Archives and Special Collections, University of Nebraska–Lincoln Libraries.

"The Springfield shoots a lead ball which flattens when it strikes a man and makes a ghastly wound" (Ray Collection, August 8, 1898).

In May 1899 in the Philippines—three months after the identity of "the enemy" had changed from the Spanish imperialists to the homegrown Philippine insurgents—Payne writes of an armed encounter with the enemy: "A tree back of our lines had 11 bullet holes in it up as high as a man and in all there were 26 bullet holes in the tree. It seemed a miracle that so few of us were killed. This pencil that I am writing with was taken from one of the dead enemy. I was the first man in the trenches so I got a Mauser there, could have got another but could not carry it. In this fight my best friend in the army was wounded. The colonel was killed" (Ray Collection, May 2, 1899).

Now the possessor of a Mauser, Payne brags: "A friend and I were up to the 1st Brigade firing line. We had some nice shooting there. I proved to him that a Mauser was better than a Krag-Jorgensen" (Ray Collection, May 2, 1898). The Mauser and the pencil are both war trophies.

The few skirmishes with "the enemy," the images of rifle fire, and the tales of battle make exciting reading back home. A closer look reveals the boredom, the loneliness, an awareness of lost opportunities—friends marrying, farms flourishing, holdings growing larger. No doubt the Cather boys were more interested in Philippine battle stories and the antics of the pet monkeys in camp than in R. B. Payne's decision to study Spanish to fill his time or the illnesses that plagued him and the bugs that attacked him in his bed. What would the three Cather boys have gleaned from Oley Iverson's adventure in Havana after the treaty?

On Thursday I and another feller went to Havana and we took a boat and went over to Mossy and Cabanas Castles and went all through them. The soldiers are not allowed to go there on account of the yellow fever. There are guards all around them but we got in anyway. . . . the small pox did not get started in the Third but a good [many] of the boys in the 161st Indiana Regiment have died with it. The Third Nebraska has been healthier since we arrived in Cuba than we were before. We have only lost two men: one of them was the man that I told you of that got drunk and the other one died from vaccination. (Ray Collection, February 28, 1899)

Iverson reports that even Col. Bryan "is sick a good share of the time." Iverson's loyalties to the Republican Party do not prevent him from defending the "Great Commoner" from a question assuming partisanship: "And you also wanted to know if he did any speaking to the boys about parties. He has not got a word to say about that on either side" (Ray Collection, October 21, 1898).

The three soldiers and their young correspondents back in Nebraska are all learning from the experience of war and that experience is valued highly. After the announcement of Willa Cather's Pulitzer Prize in 1923, Ernest Hemingway chastised the woman novelist for the audacity of writing a war novel without having firsthand experience of war: "Look at *One of Ours*. Prize, big sale, people taking it seriously. You were in the war weren't you? Wasn't that last scene in the lines wonderful? Do you know where it came from? The battle scene in *Birth of a Nation* [Griffith 1915]. I identified episode after episode. Catherized. Poor woman she had to get her war experience somewhere" (letter to Edmund Wilson, November 23, 1923, qtd. in Baker 105).

Willa Cather used the letters her cousin G. P. sent home from France for a major source of the soldier's life sections of *One of Ours* (Ray Collection, G. P. Cather letters to wife, Myrtle, and parents, George P. and Frances Smith Cather, January 1916 to May 1918). She even used a senior officer's description of G. P.'s death—which was sent to his parents—in describing the death of her protagonist Claude Wheeler (Ray Collection, letter from M. Morris Andrews, July 5, 1918).

Indeed "she had to get her war experience somewhere," but her sources have more validity than Hemingway gives her credit for. She transcribed war dispatches in Pittsburgh while her cousins studied war in the letters of three Nebraskan volunteers. Such knowledge did not protect G. P. in "the Great War," but then protection is not what he sought. Many reviewers agree with Hemingway and accuse Willa Cather of glorifying war in her picture of Claude's heroic death. Such a reading ignores the final pages of

MARGARET ANNE O'CONNOR

the novel, in which Claude's mother "reads Claude's letters over again and reassures herself; for him the call was clear, the cause was glorious. Never a doubt stained his bright faith. She divines so much that he did not write. She knows what to read into those short flashes of enthusiasm; how fully he must have found his life before he could let himself go so far—he, who was so afraid of being fooled! He died believing his own country better than it is, and France better than any country can ever be. And those were beautiful beliefs to die with" (389-90).

If Claude is under the spell of the glamour of war, his mother is not. She has learned much from his letters. There was just as much information about the nature of any war to be gleaned by youthful G. P. and his brothers in their letters from the war zones. H. C. Gress, the first of this group to be mustered out said it best: "[T]hey can have all the fun they want to, but I have had my fun down there—all I care about anyhow" (Ray Collection, October 15, 1898).

NOTE

1. The George Cather Ray Collection of letters and memorabilia at the University of Nebraska Love Library offers a multitude of insights into the life of first- and second-generation settlers of Nebraska. While the letters reviewed here are only a small part of the collection, they give much insight into Nebraskans in their time and into the timeless concerns of men and war.

More than twenty of the three men's letters home were preserved, first by the young Cather brothers and later by their mother, Frances Smith Cather.

WORKS CITED

Baker, Carlos, ed. *Ernest Hemingway: Selected Letters, 1917-1961*. New York: Scribners, 1981.

Cather, Willa. *One of Ours*. 1922. New York: Vintage, 1971.

Lynch, Col. John M., U.S. Army, Ret. Personal Interviews. Great Falls VA, September 25 and 27, 1998.

O'Connor, Margaret Anne, ed. *Willa Cather: The Contemporary Reviews*. New York: Cambridge UP, 2001.

Paterson, Thomas G. "United States Intervention in Cuba, 1898: Interpretations of the Spanish-American-Cuban-Filipino War." *History Teacher* 29 (May 1996): 341–61.

Perez, Louis A., Jr. *The War of 1898: The United States and Cuba in History and Historiography.* Chapel Hill: U of North Carolina P, 1998.

The George Cather Ray Collection, 1873–1919. Love Library, University of Nebraska, Lincoln.

The Spanish American War. http://www.spanamwar.com. [1998–2003]. Some Basic Information/ War in Cuba/ War in Philippines/ Medicine in the War/ Weapons Profiles.

Stout, Janis P. *Willa Cather: The Writer and Her World.* Charlottesville: UP of Virginia, 2000.

Woodress, James. *Willa Cather: A Literary Life.* Lincoln: U of Nebraska P, 1987.

Between Two Wars in a Breaking World
Willa Cather and the Persistence of War Consciousness

JANIS P. STOUT

Was it at the Marne? At Versailles, when a new geography
was being made on paper?
— Willa Cather, *"148 Charles Street"*

In 1947 Willa Cather's fellow modernist Katherine Anne Porter—a writer of whom Cather left no signs of awareness but who was keenly aware of Cather—wrote an aggressively humorous essay about Gertrude Stein in which she characterized the "literary young" who gathered around Stein in Paris in the 1920s as children stranded "between two wars in a falling world."[1] Porter's metaphoric adjective for the interwar period—"falling"—is evocative, if ambiguous, summoning echoes both of the "fallen" on the battlefield and of the "fall" from innocence in Eden, as well as the common phrase about the bottom dropping out from under one. Cather's metaphor for the postwar period (it could not yet be called interwar at the time she was writing) was, of course, a different one—a metaphor of brokenness. In the preface to *Not Under Forty* (1936) she famously declared that the world "broke in two" in 1922 "or thereabouts" (812).

Cather was scarcely alone in feeling this sense of rupture. The very year she alluded to (in so strangely evasive a way), 1922, was indeed the year of T. S. Eliot's *The Waste Land*, with its insistent images of brokenness. Michael North and others have pointed out that brokenness was a metaphor invoked not only by Eliot but by many writers struggling, during the postwar years, to convey their sense of how thoroughly their lives and life in general had been disrupted. Europeans and Americans alike, perhaps people all around the world, were haunted by a feeling of having been severed from any intelligible past. They were haunted, that is, by the Great War — by a sense that, as Cather put it, the literary as well as geopolitical world had been so thoroughly sundered at the Marne or at Versailles that the present could no longer connect to the past. Many of them were troubled too by the sense that another war was impending. In that respect, Porter's metaphor, though unusual and elusive, is perhaps a richer and more satisfying one than Cather's. In using the progressive form "falling," rather than "fallen," she captured the sense of an ongoing process—as it most assuredly was. Cather's phrase "broke in two" implies, instead, a one-time event, an action already complete.

Writing in 1947, more than a decade after Cather affixed her preface to *Not Under Forty,* Porter (and everyone else) could easily see in retrospect that the years 1918 to 1939 were a time "between two wars." It was by then a self-evident historical fact. But she had already been foreseeing the second war and thus implicitly defining the 1920s and 1930s as a period between two wars as early as 1931. Several of Porter's letters written in that year, as well as on through the rest of the decade, show that she was seized by a troubled apprehension of what was ahead.[2] Not that her sense of foreboding was terribly unusual. She herself said that "everyone" was talking about the likelihood of war—a characteristically hyberbolic statement but one verified, to some extent, when we note that John Dos Passos (to cite just one example) was equally prescient in his view of the international situation by 1931. Various characters in his momentous 1932 novel *1919* characterize the Treaty of Versailles as a false peace and expect a renewal of war. Such fears were well founded. Though neither Porter nor Dos Passos nor the many others apprehensive about a return of war could have known it, the Nazi leaders who were seizing power in Germany in 1931 and 1932 (Adolf Hitler was named chancellor on January 30, 1933) fervently believed "the war did not end in 1918." To think it did, declared one, was "a laugh."[3]

Cather made no such pronouncements on the Versailles Treaty

(though she did indicate, during the Conference, that she wondered what Europeans thought of Woodrow Wilson). Nor, to my knowledge, did she make any such predictions of renewed war—except one, far in advance. In a letter of December 21, 1914, to Ferris Greenslet, her editor at Houghton Mifflin and a correspondent who would regularly tie his own letters to the events of both the Great War and the next, she made a statement that is significant not so much as an indicator of some kind of uncanny prescience (though it is that and perhaps even more so than Porter's statements in the 1930s) but as a demonstration of her emotional involvement in the great calamity of the time. Here, of course, I must paraphrase, and thereby lose the emotional overtones of her language. At this early point in the war she wrote that not only was there no possibility of pleasantness in the world as long as the war went on, but she supposed that after some sort of cobbled together peace treaty at some point "they" would repeat the process in another twenty-five years.[4] Twenty-five years from 1914 would be 1939. Hitler's armies invaded Poland on September 1, 1939, and France and England declared war two days later. An uncanny prescience indeed, based as it was not on information and observation, as Porter's was in 1931, but solely on a disheartened emotional apperception of how the world seemed to be going.

It is that emotional apperception that is my subject here. We can see the keenness of Cather's awareness not only of news of the war but of what Wilfred Owen called "the pity of war" (his phrase for what he hoped his war poems would put before the faces of his readers) in her many letters written during the World War I years. She speaks of the war as a disturbing and engrossing worry, an intrusion on her mental vision that would not go away. As early as September 28, 1914—less than two months after the outbreak of hostilities—she was reporting that the news of the terrible battles going on had interrupted her enjoyment of the summer's visit to northern New Mexico, and in November of that year she lamented to her Aunt Franc (who was to be a centrally important figure in Cather's war consciousness by 1918, leading to the writing of *One of Ours*) that she could think of little else but the war and the suffering of the Belgians (*Calendar* #287 and #289). Her distress arose, then, with the fall 1914 battles on the Marne (later referred to in her pained question about the disruption of civilization, "Was it at the Marne?"), and it would stay with her well beyond the November 1918 armistice and Versailles.[5] According to Elizabeth Shepley Sergeant, when Cather was first conceiving *My Ántonia*, in 1916, she could not "forget that, in these war days, the youth of Europe, its finest flower, was dying," and shared Sergeant's own fear that "American youth" was also doomed to make that sacrifice (Sergeant 148). It was in the following spring, of course, that American youth would in fact be summoned into the conflict, with the U.S. declaration of war on April 15, 1917.

My purpose here is to demonstrate that all through the next two decades, the 1920s and 1930s, Cather was still not "able to forget" the pity of the Great War. Like many others of her generation, she was haunted by it for years afterward—indeed, in my judgment, for the rest of her life. To be sure, the persistence of that haunting is not so easy to trace as her distress during the war itself. As we would expect from this writer who sought "not to hold the note, not to use an incident for all there is in it—but to touch and pass on" (*On Writing* 9), the traces of the war in Cather's fiction are, with the exception of *One of Ours*, fleeting and relatively subtle. Nor did she persist in lamenting the war in her letters (so far as they survive). Nevertheless, and even though she did not, as Porter did, regularly and explicitly express a sense of foreboding about a renewal of war in Europe, it is demonstrable that Cather fully participated in the Janus-faced sensibility of the interwar years—a sensibility of gloomy expectation of another war to come as well as a fixation on the Great War experience. Despite her metaphor of a *broken* world, she experienced an ongoing process of *breaking* throughout the interwar years and on through World War II.

As both her letters and her fiction demonstrate, Cather's response to the First World War was an intensely emotional one. She referred to the war at various times as "terrible" and "unjust" and repeatedly asserted that it had unleashed a general misery infecting every aspect of life so that no one could have any true happiness as long as it went on. In part, these feelings sprang from her reading about the sufferings of civilians in the war zone (as we see, for example, in her letter to her aunt about the hardships endured by the Belgians) and from firsthand reports by people who had been there. Toward the end of the war, however, the intensity of her emotional engagement can be attributed more directly to the fact that her first cousin, Grosvenor P. Cather, enlisted in the American Expeditionary Forces and was killed in action on May 28, 1918.

Why the death of a cousin would have affected her so deeply is an important question, though one for which we may not find very clear answers. Yes, she seems to have known him well; according to a letter to Dorothy Canfield Fisher that was written during the final stages of work on *One of Ours,* she had helped care for him when he was a baby or small child (March 8, 1922; *Calendar* #595). But that fact in itself would not seem to account for the strength of emotion she expressed in her various letters touching on Grosvenor's (or as she usually called him, G. P.'s) story. There was also the fact that she was strongly devoted to his mother, her Aunt Franc. She seems to have felt her aunt's grief very keenly and may have wished to magnify his status as hero in the hope of easing that grief. But the emotional dynamic was yet more complex. Grosvenor had been—as Cather shows her hero Claude Wheeler to have been—perpetually dissatisfied with his life before going into the military. In the real life, as opposed to the fictional version, that dissatisfaction had expressed itself in illicit sexual relations that apparently even led to the death of his pregnant lover.[6] Misdeeds of this kind would undoubtedly have been gravely distressing to Franc Cather. When he was killed in action at Cantigny, however, his story could be constructed as one of redemption to a kind of secular sainthood, since, as Cather told her aunt in a letter of June 12, 1918 (*Calendar* #419), the label "killed in action" set such men apart from others.

It was after his death that Cather came to regard her cousin as having been, in some mysterious or even mystical way, bound up with herself so that, as she claimed, part of her was buried in his grave (*Calendar* #589). To speculate that she was in some way reading her own life story to that point as being also a story of redemption would not be implausible, though it goes far beyond the purposes of this essay to do so. Yet some such process of self-dramatization through identification with Grosvenor seems to have been at work and would account for the persistence of her fixation on him. Four years after his death she would still insist that he had become so deeply a part of her that she might never be the same and could absolutely not have written anything else until she wrote his story (*Calendar* #589). She declared that his presence kept returning and seizing her while she was reading proofs of *One of Ours* (*Calendar* #590).[7] The intensity of her fixation on Grosvenor hints at an obsessional quality, for instance, when she expresses a sense that she may never be able to shake off the concern that drove *One of Ours* (*Calendar* #595).

This intensity of emotion over Grosvenor's death was restoked, of course, as Cather continued to have interactions with her aunt and especially when she went to France in 1920. There, on July 4, she watched a parade of war orphans and shortly afterward located her cousin's grave. One wonders, indeed, if her feelings about his death would not have been revived simply by name association when, from 1928 to 1933, she lived in the Hotel Grosvenor whenever she was in New York.

As we have noted, though, besides the complex emotional dimensions of this personal association, Cather's keen awareness of the unfolding of the war would have been fed by what we know to have been her avid reading of newspapers, especially the New York papers. The evidence that she was an avid newspaper reader is scattered throughout her letters. In addition to the information about the war that we know she devoured, including casualty lists (she first learned of her cousin's death from such a casualty list), the print media would have provided her a keen visual sense of the war. The *New York Times*, for example, regularly published whole pages of pictures from the Western Front. She may also have seen pictorial images of "dead Boches" as well as Allied casualties on postcards or cards for use in stereoscopic viewers, since, according to Niall Ferguson in *The Pity of War*, these were widely distributed. "The horror of war," Ferguson concludes, "was concealed from the public less than is sometimes thought" (180–81). The effects of such images on a sensitive and imaginative person —as Cather most certainly was—do not have to be conjectured; they are evident in *One of Ours*. She may have insisted that the story was entirely centered in Claude Wheeler's perceptions and that he didn't see things as pictures (*Calendar* #589), but she did.[8]

Brief as the battlefield sections of the novel are, they offer several pictorial images of devastation, wounding, death, and dismemberment. To be sure, Cather would have gleaned some of the elements of these pictures from her reading and from conversations with the wounded soldiers she visited in hospitals in New York (as she told Canfield Fisher she did during the winter of 1918, in an undated letter written in 1922 [*Calendar* #588]), but the grimness and the specificity of the verbal pictures she produced may well reflect the fact of her having seen such pictures in newspapers or other media.[9]

I would argue, then, that visual shock played a significant part in the persistence of Cather's wartime awareness of suffering, destruction, and battlefield horrors well after the time she encountered such reports—a persistence demonstrated by *One of Ours*. But *One of Ours* is a notoriously ambiguous piece of evidence of war consciousness. Not only is the novel's account of combat lacking in realism, in some ways—though, it seems to me, not so lacking as contemporaries such as Ernest Hemingway would have us believe—but its publication came so soon after the end of the war that, after all, it can scarcely in itself demonstrate a very lengthy persistence. Published in 1922, it preceded by several years such postwar cultural products as the 1926 movies *What Price Glory?*, *The Big Parade*, and *Wings* and the 1926 hit song "My Dream of the Big Parade," in which a patriotic celebration turns into a parade of wounds, dismemberments, and grieving mothers, not to mention the 1929–30 "boom" of books about the war that came in the wake of Erich Maria Remarque's *All Quiet on the Western Front*.[10] Indeed, *One of Ours* might have been a considerably different book and might have had a considerably different reception if Cather had let her wartime concerns, exacerbated as they were by her awareness of her cousin Grosvenor's experiences and his letters home to his mother, ripen for a few years. Instead, she went directly into planning and work on "Claude," as she first titled the manuscript, as soon as she finished *My Ántonia*—which itself can well be seen, indirectly, as a war novel.[11] As a result, *One of Ours* has been judged by standards of sensibility that for the most part developed *after* its conception and tone were firmly set in Cather's mind—that is, by standards reflecting postwar disillusionment, whereas the novel itself reflects the more immediate impressions and emotions of wartime, particularly Cather's wish to present her cousin in a heroic light. A tone of glorification appears in letters Cather wrote to Aunt Franc on June 6 and June 12 following Grosvenor's death on May 28, 1918 (*Calendar* #418 and #419), and she called the report of his death to the attention of her editor at Houghton Mifflin on July 2 (*Calendar* #421). All of these letters were written months before the end of the war, let alone the unfolding of the Versailles Treaty and the widespread erosion of a sense that there had been any real purpose to the carnage.

It is to texts other than *One of Ours*, then, that we must turn in seeking evidence that the trauma of the First World War persisted, for Cather, long after 1918 and that all during the interwar period her world kept breaking, despite her insistence that it had broken once and for all in or about 1922. The very fact that it was in 1936 that she wrote that statement about the world's brokenness indicates—assuming one accepts the view that it refers at least in part to the war and its effects—a persistence of war consciousness.[12] Her letters during the later 1920s and the 1930s do not provide support for the idea of such persistence, however; except for perfunctory references, the war is not even mentioned after 1922 until the beginning of the Second World War. Instead, it is from traces in her fiction that we can see that the concern with the war that impelled her writing of *One of Ours* did not disappear after that work was completed.

The Professor's House provides, of course, abundant demonstration that Cather's distress over the war persisted at least until 1925, the year of its publication. Indeed, it is this novel, rather than *One of Ours*, that most clearly bears the stamp of postwar disillusionment, in its generally wearied and disheartened tone and specifically in its account of what seems to be the pointlessness of Tom Outland's death in the war. Professor St. Peter, it seems, has lived (as Cather told Canfield Fisher, in her 1922 letter already cited, they both were living) in a different world than the one he knew before, a world with less hope, less glamour, and certainly less love. Steven Trout appropriately places *The Professor's House* in the company of such novels as Virginia Woolf's *Mrs. Dalloway* (also

1925) and Ernest Hemingway's *The Sun Also Rises* (1926) in "the category of fiction devoted to the aftereffects of the Great War" (Trout 161). If *The Professor's House* is Cather's greater war novel, however—a point I will not pursue because it has been capably argued elsewhere—we must concede that its concern with the war is far more subtle, far less foregrounded, than that of *One of Ours*.[13]

I would propose, however, that another work of that same year, 1925, is equally, if even more subtly, a work about the war: the short story "Uncle Valentine."[14] A story that turns toward the turn-of-the-century past so determinedly that it all but ignores the existence of the war at all, despite its postwar perspective, "Uncle Valentine" would appear to be concerned with issues of the tension between art, or beauty of any kind, and commerce, intertwined with issues of youth and innocence doomed to sad awareness by time and its corruptions. In both respects, it is a lament for a lost world. That lost world is represented in the story by Bonnie Brae, the estate on which the composer Valentine Ramsay lives, as did his family before him. The estate is located in an enclave of such estates near a village called Greenacre that is seemingly set off from the rush of the twentieth century as represented by the nearby city of Pittsburgh and its industries.[15] At the end of the story, Bonnie Brae has been demolished—having been "pulled down," significantly enough, "during the war" (249).

Is that simple phrase identifying when it was that Bonnie Brae was "pulled down" only an insignificant marker? Hardly. If we turn back to the beginning of the story within a story that makes up the central text of "Uncle Valentine," we see the narrator's summary of her acquaintance with the musician, whom she called by the honorific "uncle" though he was in fact no relative at all: "Yes, I had known Valentine Ramsay. I knew him in a lovely place, at a lovely time, in a bygone period of American life; just at the incoming of this century which has made all the world so different" (210). With this reference to history's having "made all the world so different," the story is marked as expression of mourning for all that was lost when "the world broke in two." Cather had lamented to Canfield Fisher in 1922 that they seemed to be living in a different world than the one they used to know (as I have inadequately paraphrased the statement in her letter probably written on June 17, 1922, in *Calendar* #601). Not quite three years later, in this 1925 story, Cather again laments the loss of that familiar world destroyed (or perhaps "pulled down") by the war. In the context of the story's strategically placed reference to the changes wrought by twentieth-century history, the reference to Valentine Ramsay's song "I know a wall where red roses grow" (Cather writes it this way, without capitalization, in the story) takes on a larger resonance. Apparently written as a reference to the red roses that grew on his beloved neighbor's wall, the song becomes an emblem of the beauties of a civilization now "pulled down": "The roses of song and the roses of memory, they are the only ones that last" (249). Such roses are remembered from the other side of the break. Moreover, the association of roses and song with the war's devastation was already well established and lay ready to hand when Cather wrote "Uncle Valentine," through the tremendous popularity of the World War I song "Roses of Picardy" (1916, words by British officer Frederick Weatherley, music by Haydn Wood). Often sung by ordinary song lovers and professionals alike, "Roses of Picardy" was recorded in 1919 by the celebrated John McCormack. We know that Cather knew the song since, as John March notes (639), it is whistled by a character in *One of Ours*.

Four years later, in 1929, Cather returned to a similar thematic structure, again with the Pittsburgh setting and an emblematic rose, in "Double Birthday." Here, the oppositions of beauty and commerce, innocence and corruption are not so clearly drawn as in "Uncle Valentine." Beauty survives alongside getting and spending, the character emblematic of commerce is not altogether unbeautiful, and corruption is never a very threatening presence. Sentimental hopes exist only to be disappointed, however, and an undercurrent of concern about the war and the break separating past from present is much in evidence.

The title "Double Birthday" refers to the common birthday of the two central characters, who also share a name. Albert Engelhardt, the son of a wealthy industrialist, has been reduced to a small-salaried civil service job and residence in a shabby part of town as a result of his own and his brothers' squandering (so his father's old friend Judge Hammersley believes) of their inheritance, but he is quite content with his lot and doesn't regret a minute of his joyous youth. On the night of the birthday celebration narrated in the story, Albert is turning fifty-five. His uncle, Dr. Albert Engelhardt, long retired from a medical practice that brought him more prestige than money, is an amusingly vain old man who still enjoys good food, good wine (when someone gives it to him), and the company of beautiful women—one of whom, the judge's daughter, joins the birthday dinner. He also enjoys music of the nineteenth century and before, though emphatically not that of the twentieth. Uncle Albert is turning eighty. If we assume that the story was written in 1928, the year prior to its publication, and take its time-present to be that year, Albert the younger was born in Cather's own birth year, 1873, and his uncle in the year of her father's birth, 1848. As we will see, this is not the only trace of a personal presence in the story.[16]

The war motif enters the story inconspicuously enough when Judge Hammersley mentions to his daughter that he has seen Albert the younger. She hasn't seen him "for years," she says, "not since the war" (253). Soon, as a result of her father's offer to provide wine for the birthday dinner, she does see Albert, and the two reflect on their days in Italy some years ago. When he recalls that they were "always going to run away to Russia together, and now there is no Russia," it becomes clear that their time in Italy was before the war. "Everything has changed," he adds (267). Both parts of Albert's remark are characteristically Catherian in the brevity of their allusions—first to the Russian Revolution, then to her own conviction (not yet formulated in the familiar prefatory statement) that the world had "broken in two." As if fearful we will miss it, though, Cather repeats the message in a second reference to the fall of the dynasties during the Great War. Remembering how Pittsburgh used to seem to him when he was young, Albert thinks that "a lot of water had run under this bridge since then, and kingdoms and empires had fallen" (269). When the judge's daughter joins the birthday dinner, she reflects that the two Alberts' house is "the only spot I know in the world that is before-the-war." The war, she adds, "destroyed" all the charm young people used to enjoy (273). As in "Uncle Valentine," a rose symbolizes the beauty that is lost—or in this story, significantly, is *being lost*, because it is not a rose of the past but a rose surviving beyond its time. A young girl who comes to bid Uncle Doctor Engelhardt happy birthday is, he says, "the rose in winter," the rose that cannot last.

Once again, as in "Uncle Valentine," Cather reaches back to the sense of the world's breaking—the idea she had expressed to Canfield Fisher in 1922 and would formulate in her 1936 preface. Here, though, she adds another element: notice of a new danger rising in Europe. In response to his nephew's reminiscing about Italy, the old uncle asks, "What is Mussolini's flower, Albert? Advise your friends in Rome that a Supreme Dictator should always have a flower" (270). The story announces itself, then, as inhabiting a time "between two wars, in a falling world." Though Cather may not yet have foreseen the "fall" into the Second World War, it is clear that present events in Europe, as well as the war of the previous decade, were troubling her. We can see that there were two wars bracketing the melancholy birthday party; she could not yet see the second, only the rise of a dictator; but she could quite clearly see two worlds, with a break between. Both Alberts prefer the former, the world from which they have been separated by the war: Albert the elder drinks to "the lost Lenore," a lost ideal of female beauty, and Albert the younger drinks to his—and Cather's—"beautiful youth" (274–75).

In February 1933, four years after "Double Birthday," Cather published (in the *Atlantic Monthly*) an essay called "A Chance Meeting," in which she describes her brief acquaintance with the niece of Gustave Flaubert. Here, there is only the slightest manifestation of her persistent war consciousness; she touches the note and does not hold it but passes on. Still, it is often from such lightly touched notes in Cather's writing that we catch the theme. She did not carelessly throw in extraneous details; we know that. We take notice, then, when she mentions that this woman whose perseverance in living out her life to the fullest had been in Italy "a great deal . . . during the late war of 1914" (*Not Under Forty* 825). And indeed when Cather returned to "A Chance Meeting," using it as the basis for her story "The Old Beauty," she greatly expanded this seemingly incidental reference.

In the same year in which she rewrote "A Chance Meeting" into "The Old Beauty," 1936, she also revisited two other earlier pieces

JANIS P. STOUT

—"The House on Charles Street," from 1922, and "Katherine Mansfield," from 1925 (the year of *The Professor's House* and "Uncle Valentine"). Both were revised for inclusion in *Not Under Forty*. In all three of these revisitings she either expanded or added, and greatly emphasized, references to the war. Clearly, the Great War was weighing heavily on her mind.

In revising the essay on Katherine Mansfield, Cather chose to add a quasi-fictional introductory frame and a final section about the personal difficulties with which Mansfield had to cope. As a part of this material, she pointedly added that Mansfield's brother was killed in action in the war and that for the rest of her life (seven years) "her brother seems to have been almost constantly in her mind" (881).[17] This lost brother was indeed "the person who had freed her from the self-consciousness and affectations of the experimenting young writer, and had brought her to her realest self" —as perhaps Cather felt that Grosvenor Cather had for her.

In rewriting "A Chance Meeting" as a story rather than an essay, Cather not only greatly increased the emphasis on World War I but relocated the time frame to 1922, the year when she told Canfield Fisher that they seemed to be living in a different world than the one they used to know (*Calendar* #601). The year is specified in the story's opening sentence. "The Old Beauty" thus becomes a parable of the broken world, which like "a beautiful woman may become"—and indeed, in the wake of the war did become—"a ruin" (705). We recall that a beautiful woman, "the lost Lenore," represented the beautiful past to the elder Albert in "Double Birthday" and to the song-writing Valentine in "Uncle Valentine."

Pointers to the centrality of the war in "The Old Beauty," a story of quiet retreat to aristocratic hotels and old ways beset by the new, are peppered throughout, from the note that Gabriella Longstreet had remarried "during the war" and that her husband "was killed,—in '17" (700) to a recollection that the narrator's friend Hardwick "was killed in the war" (706). In the story's section VIII alone (712–14), a great cluster of references to the war includes the following: Gabriella Longstreet (now Madame de Coucy) and her companion are "the queerest partnership that war and desolation have made" (712); again, Madame de Coucy's French second husband "was killed in action" (713); her younger friends "were killed or disabled" in the war (713); an "old French officer, blinded in the war" comes to visit her (713); she had sold her place in England "before the war" (713); Mrs. Allison, her companion, served on a committee with her "during the war" (713); and "after the war broke out and everybody was all mixed up" (714). It could scarcely be more clear that in 1936, eighteen years after the Armistice, Cather was still thinking about the event that Seabury, the narrator of "The Old Beauty," calls "a storm to which the French Revolution, which used to be our standard of horrors, was merely a breeze" (715).[18]

The theme of the world's breaking accompanies these reminders of the war throughout the story. Seabury's remark that "long ago" he had liked the grand hotel where they are staying (707) expresses his wish for continuity, for the survival rather than the destruction of the past. But the story will not allow that continuity. Mrs. Allison explicitly states that Madame de Coucy "thought, once the war was over, the world would be just as it used to be" but that "of course it isn't . . . it's all very different . . . everything" (714, 720). The signs of difference are scattered throughout, and all—or almost all—are differences of deterioration if not ruin. Seabury himself has noticed that Madame de Coucy seems "a little antagonistic to the present order" (711). That antagonism, as well as his own, is evident over and over. When they seek to visit a very old monastery that represents "the world of the past," it is guarded by "a one-armed guard in uniform" (723)—presumably a war veteran. The impossibility of a return to the world represented by the monastery is made clear when, on their return drive, they have a near-collision with a newfangled sports car driven by brash American women of uncertain gender. The point is clear that the Old Beauty, Seabury, and apparently the author herself belong on the far side of the break guarded by the veteran.

Still, two small details in the story give reason to think that perhaps the postwar world is not altogether bad: Young people at a dance in Seabury's hotel are not rude or irritable when he interrupts the playing of modern music to request a waltz, which leaves the floor empty for himself and Gabrielle; they respectfully applaud. And Mrs. Allison, recalling how one Nurse Ames arranged her introduction to Madame de Coucy, comments that the war

JANIS P. STOUT

"made a lot of wise nurses" (713). There may be some survivals of courtesy, then, and some small benefits of the disaster – fragments to shore up against ruin.

The third essay that Cather revised and expanded in 1936, "The House on Charles Street," became "148 Charles Street" in *Not Under Forty*. The original essay (or review) was an "appreciation" of a volume of collected extracts from the diaries of Annie Adams Fields, widow of the publisher whose name was half of Tichnor and Fields and herself a celebrated hostess to the literary world for, as Cather says, sixty years. It was at Annie Fields's house on Charles Street in Boston that Cather first met Sarah Orne Jewett. The house represented, then, a beautiful and highly cultured past now lost; and its representation of that past was charged, for her, with strong emotion. Just as she grieved the deaths of Jewett and later of Mrs. Fields, she now, in revising the essay, seems to have grieved afresh the loss of the house and all it meant. Its loss takes a place in her vision of the brokenness of the world, with beauty such as that centered in 148 Charles Street stranded on the other side of the break.

On March 9, 1936, while she was preparing *Not Under Forty*, Cather wrote to Ferris Greenslet (whose office was, of course, in Boston) asking if it was true that a garage had been built on the site of the Fields house (*Calendar* #1301). Greenslet's confirmation of the fact two days later allowed her to begin the closing section that she was now adding to her essay with this passage that so compactly sums up her theme of the break "in 1922 or thereabouts" and all that it meant: "Today, in 1936, a garage stands on the site of 148 Charles Street. Only in memory exists the long, green-carpeted, softly lighted drawing-room, and the dining-table where Learning and Talent met, enjoying good food and good wit and rare vintages, looking confidently forward to the growth of their country in the finer amenities of life. Perhaps the garage and all it stands for represent the only real development, and have altogether taken the place of things formerly cherished on that spot" (*Not Under Forty* 847). Two paragraphs later she makes the link with World War I that I have used as an epigraph. Here is the passage quoted more fully: "Just how did this change come about, one wonders. When and where were the Arnolds overthrown and the Brownings devaluated? Was it at the Marne? At Versailles, when a new geography was being made on paper? Certainly the literary world which emerged from the war used a new coinage" (848). How powerfully this passage demonstrates the persistence of Cather's war memories! She is writing about literary history and the depredations of a modernism of which she herself was, of course, a part, and she expresses her sense of that subject in terms of the war. We can see here how her consciousness of the Great War lay always ready, just below the surface of her mind, available to be drawn on whatever the topic.

Cather's association of a sense of loss (here, of the Fields house and all it meant) with the losses of the war was characteristic. In much the same way, she had earlier, in 1927, manifested her continuing war consciousness by speaking of the past—again, a lost past—in terms of the war even though the war was unrelated to the subject at hand. In a public letter to the editor of *The Commonweal* giving an account of how she came to write *Death Comes for the Archbishop*, she recalled a Belgian missionary priest named Father Haltermann whom she had known in or around 1912, whose driving from mission to far-flung mission had entered into her depiction of Father Vaillant. In the course of this brief reference, she added a point totally unrelated to the novel except insofar as it may be reflected in the sense of loss evident toward the book's end: "He went home during the war to serve as a chaplain in the French army, and when I last heard of him he was an invalid" (*On Writing* 4).

Cather's return to such a keenness of war consciousness in 1936, as she prepared *Not Under Forty*—the poignant addition to "148 Charles Street," her prefatory statement about the world's having broken in two, her revision of "Katherine Mansfield" by adding a paragraph about the brother who died in the war, her revision of "A Chance Meeting" into a story laden with markers of the war—is tantalizing. Why then? What made 1936 such a watershed of remembrance? Her correspondence gives no clue. Her letters do, throughout the 1930s, show clear evidence of her dismay over the widespread sufferings brought by the Great Depression—itself an aftermath of the Great War. Whether she saw the Depression in that way or not (and I know of no evidence that she did), it was a continuation of the spectacle of breakage that she had been witnessing and feeling for years. Her personalization of the economic news she read in the newspapers in terms of people she had known in Nebraska and the letters she received from farm people there telling her their hardships and often their fear of losing their farms—to which she responded more than once by sending money to prevent foreclosure—must have continually borne in on her the sense of how different life had been for these same people when she first knew them. It was another aspect of the sense of loss after the break, another kind of breaking. What the letters she wrote during those hard times do *not* do, so far as I have been able to find, is talk explicitly about the war or about current international politics and tensions. The Japanese invasion of China is not mentioned. Hitler's rise to power in Germany is not mentioned. The Spanish Civil War is mentioned only a single time, and quite indirectly— though, to be sure, in a very significant way, because it demonstrates her fear of the coming war. In an unclearly dated letter to Yaltah Menuhin, probably written on September 3, 1938, Cather expresses her gratification that Yehudi was able to see Spain before it went crazy and urges Yaltah to go to Venice before it too is bombed.[19]

Despite the near-total absence in her 1930s letters of evidence of a sense of foreboding about the impending return of war, one wonders if the resurgence in 1936 of evidence of Cather's long-ago feeling of devastation over World War I may not have been as much forward-looking as backward-looking. That is, one wonders if it was a result of increasing unrest in Europe, the now unmistakable signs of a next war looming on the horizon. It was in 1936 that the Spanish Civil War broke out, and, in the United States, debates over isolationism made it clear that a new war in Europe was so firmly expected that Americans were trying to think through what their posture toward it should be. The fact that it was also in 1936 that Cather met the eccentric British nobleman Stephen Tennant may not be coincidental; their conversations may well have included the ominous events of the day. At any rate, this cluster of expressions in 1936 of ongoing distress over the First World War seems to indicate indirectly Cather's Januslike awareness of war both behind and ahead. Only a year later, in 1937, she began work on *Sapphira and the Slave Girl*, a novel of the prewar (pre–Civil War) South that briefly looks forward to a postwar period in which positive, rather than entirely negative, changes can be seen. Perhaps this note in *Sapphira* is an indication of hope that something good might come out of what was now looking inevitable, as it had from the war that preceded Cather's birth by only a few years. After a storm of family sorrows, she took the novel back up in 1939 and completed it, so she told Canfield Fisher, as an escape from the distress of the new war (letter October 14, 1940, *Calendar* #1497).

If the parallel with the Civil War and its having made possible a better life for people like Nancy and Till does indicate, by parallel, a slim hope for some good result of the coming renewal of world war, that hope seems to have been very hard for Cather to maintain. Her correspondence during these years bears the marks of renewed war worry and grief. In October 1940, slightly over a year after the German invasion of Poland, when things were looking dark for the people of England and France, she called the war unspeakable (as she had once referred to World War I as terrible and unjust). On that same October day in 1940 she wrote to Van Wyck Brooks, telling him that she greatly admired Winston Churchill and agreed with Archibald MacLeish that the United States should enter the war in defense of democracy (*Calendar* #1496). The seeming tension between considering the war unspeakable and considering it a just cause is scarcely surprising; many people in the United States had conflicting feelings about American entry into the war. It foreshadows the conflicted feelings that would torment her for the next five years.

Cather's surviving correspondence from this late period in her life indicates that the war would seldom be out of her consciousness. Her spirits would sag and sag as she saw the devastation spread, even as she celebrated the staunchness of the British people and the resistance of her friend Sigrid Undset's fellow Danes. She especially grieved over the suffering of American soldiers in the South Pacific and over wartime separations in her own family. Why, she cried out to her old friend Viola Roseboro' in the dark days of 1944, did a single generation have to see civilization destroyed in not one war, but two? (*Calendar* #1659). Like Porter,

Cather had been caught between two wars in a world that had not simply broken but kept breaking.

NOTES

My appreciation to Dr. Patrick Lesley, who offered suggestions that greatly improved this essay.

1. Porter's essay in which this phrase appears, "The Wooden Umbrella," was first published in December 1947 in *Harper's* as "Gertrude Stein: A Self-Portrait." It was reprinted in *The Days Before,* a collection of Porter's essays, before being incorporated into her *Collected Essays and Occasional Writings.* See *Collected Essays* 257.

2. See, for example, Porter's letter to Peggy Cowley dated October 1, 1931, written from Berlin, referring to "the strain of the next war"; also, to Eugene Pressly, dated December 27, 1931, stating, "War is just over the horizon, or so it seems." Neither of these letters appears in Isabel Bayley's *Letters of Katherine Anne Porter* (1990). Both are found in the Papers of Katherine Anne Porter at the Library of the University of Maryland, College Park, Special Collections, and are quoted by permission of the University of Maryland Libraries and Porter's executor, Barbara Thompson Davis.

3. See Eksteins, *Rites of Spring,* 308–09.

4. Cather's letters are still protected by copyright, and her executor never gives permission to quote, primarily because of Cather's own explicit instructions in her will. The letter referred to here appears in *A Calendar of the Letters of Willa Cather* as #292, but the necessarily brief summary given there does not indicate the presence of this sentence about the likelihood of another war. My reference, then, is to the letter itself, which is held at Houghton Library, Harvard University. Subsequent references to the letters will provide the entry number in the *Calendar of Letters* and will indicate when the information cited does not appear in the summary given there. Locations of actual letters are given in the Works Cited.

5. It is notable that Cather's question was, "Was it at the Marne?" rather than, "Was it at the Somme?" The breaking of the world was more commonly seen to have come at the Battle of the Somme, two years later.

6. Conversation with Mary Weddle, June 2003. Ms. Weddle is the great-granddaughter of Franc Cather and has recently donated Grosvenor Cather's letters to his mother to the University of Nebraska.

7. This is the only instance I am aware of when Cather even approached a belief in Spiritualism. That it was in connection with a soldier's death that she expressed such a sense of a presence from beyond the grave aligns

her response with the far more literal and protracted beliefs of many thousands whose desire for continued contact with their war dead produced a great surge of Spiritualist activity during the war and on through the 1930s; see Cannadine, 227–31.

8. See my earlier discussions of the pictorial nature of Cather's imagination in "Willa Cather's Poetry and the Object(s) of Art" and "The Observant Eye, the Art of Illustration, and Willa Cather's *My Ántonia*."

9. For example, the hand that protrudes from the side of Claude's trench may have come from a newspaper image of a hand projecting upward from the ground. I have been unable to find the source of this particular image, but it appears in the video version of Robert Hughes's *The Shock of the New*. On the other hand, severed body parts are so often mentioned in verbal texts that she might well have composed that image from her reading alone. Eksteins reports that "in the Ypres salient at one point men being relieved all filed past an arm protruding from the side of the trench and shook hands with it" and "those effecting the relief did the same on arrival" (151). The documentation for this particular instance of the presence of body parts in the trenches is in unpublished papers that Cather could not have known, but as Eksteins points out, "Mutilation was a daily spectacle in some sectors" (152). She could have learned about such horrors from any number of poems by the "Trench Poets" (Edmund Blunden, Herbert Read, Isaac Rosenburg, Siegfried Sassoon, Wilfred Owen, and others) or from other sources.

10. See Eksteins, the chapter "Memory," 275–99.

11. For an argument that *My Ántonia* reflects the culture of war, see Stout, *Willa Cather* 155.

12. Scholars continue to debate the meaning of Cather's "broke in two" statement. It is often linked to the publication of *One of Ours* and the flood of negative reviews that so distressed Cather. However, the letter in which she first stated the idea was written in 1922, several months before the novel was published; see *Calendar* #601.

13. For an extended reading of *The Professor's House* as a novel preoccupied with war, see Trout 148–87.

14. "Uncle Valentine" was published in 1925 in *Woman's Home Companion.*

15. The fictional Greenacre is a close sound-alike for Vineacre, the family estate of the composer Ethelbert Nevin, whom Cather knew in Pittsburgh. The fictional song "I know a wall where red roses grow" is in part a reference to the frequency of roses in Nevin's songs.

16. Both Woodress and Lee also point out biographical parallels in "Double Birthday" but not those asserted here.

17. I am indebted for this information and for the dates of original pub-

lication of the essays in *Not Under Forty* to Sharon O'Brien's notes in the Library of America volume *Cather: Stories, Poems, and Other Writings*.

18. That these were indeed purposeful additions to the essay, not traces of earlier deletions that she had now decided to restore, seems to be indicated by a typescript of "A Chance Meeting" held at the New York Public Library, bearing Cather's holograph corrections. There are no struck-through elements comparable to the new phrases I have indicated.

19. Letter to Yaltah Menuhin, September 3, [1938?], Princeton. My summary of this letter in *Calendar* #1416 unfortunately does not include these references to Spain and to Venice.

WORKS CITED

Cannadine, David. "War and Death, Grief and Mourning in Modern Britain." In *Mirrors of Mortality: Studies in the Social History of Death*. Ed. T. Joachim Whaley. London: Europa, 1981. 187–242.

Cather, Willa. *A Calendar of the Letters of Willa Cather*. Ed. Janis P. Stout. Lincoln: U of Nebraska P, 2002.

———. "A Chance Meeting." Typescript. New York Public Library.

———. "Double Birthday." 1929. Rpt. *Willa Cather: Stories, Poems, and Other Writings*. With notes by Sharon O'Brien. New York: The Library of America, 1992.

———. Letters to:

Van Wyck Brooks, October 14, 1940. Van Pelt-Dietrich Library, U of Pennsylvania.

Dorothy Canfield Fisher, March 8, 1922; April 1922 (fragment); April 26, 1922 [?]; [April 28, 1922?]; [May 8, 1922]; June 17, 1922; October 14, 1940. Bailey-Howe Library, U of Vermont.

Mrs. George P. Cather (Aunt Franc), November 17, 1914; June 6, 1918; June 12, 1918. Love Library, U of Nebraska.

Ferris Greenslet, December 21, 1914; July 2, 1918; March 9, 1936. Houghton Library, Harvard U.

Yaltah Menuhin, September 3, [1938?]. Princeton U.

Viola Roseboro', February 12, 1944. U of Virginia.

Elizabeth Shepley Sergeant, pm. November 13, 1914, Pierpont Morgan Library, New York.

———. *Not Under Forty*. 1936. Rpt. *Willa Cather: Stories, Poems, and Other Writings*. With notes by Sharon O'Brien. New York: The Library of America, 1992.

———. "The Old Beauty." *The Old Beauty and Others*. 1948. *Willa Cather: Stories, Poems, and Other Writings*. New York: The Library of America, 1992.

91

Between Two Wars in a Breaking World

———. *On Writing*. Lincoln: University of Nebraska Press, 1988.

———. "Uncle Valentine." 1925. *Willa Cather: Stories, Poems, and Other Writings*. New York: The Library of America, 1992.

Eksteins, Modris. *Rites of Spring: The Great War and the Birth of the Modern Age*. Boston: Houghton Mifflin, 1989.

Ferguson, Niall. *The Pity of War*. New York: Basic Books, 1999.

Lee, Hermione. *Willa Cather: Double Lives*. New York: Pantheon, 1989.

March, John. *A Reader's Companion to the Fiction of Willa Cather*. Ed. Marilyn Arnold, with Debra Lynn Thornton. Westport CT: Greenwood P, 1993.

North, Michael. *Reading 1922: A Return to the Scene of the Modern*. New York: Oxford UP, 1999.

Porter, Katherine Anne. *Collected Essays and Occasional Writings*. Boston: Houghton Mifflin/Seymour Lawrence, 1970.

———. Letters to Peggy Cowley, October 1, 1931, and to Eugene Pressly, December 27, 1931. Papers of Katherine Anne Porter, Special Collections, University of Maryland Libraries, College Park MD.

Stout, Janis P. "The Observant Eye, the Art of Illustration, and Willa Cather's *My Ántonia*." *Cather Studies 5: Willa Cather's Ecological Imagination*. Ed. Susan J. Rosowski. Lincoln: U of Nebraska P, 2003. 128–52.

———. *Willa Cather: The Writer and Her World*. Charlottesville: UP of Virginia, 2000.

———. "Willa Cather's Poetry and the Object(s) of Art." *American Literary Realism* 35 (2003): 159–74.

Trout, Steven. *Memorial Fictions: Willa Cather and the First World War*. Lincoln: U of Nebraska P, 2002.

Woodress, James. *Willa Cather: A Literary Life*. Lincoln: U of Nebraska P, 1987.

The "Enid Problem"
Dangerous Modernity in *One of Ours*

PEARL JAMES

Woman, German woman or American woman, or every other sort of woman, in the last war, was something frightening.

The very women who are most busy saving the bodies of men: . . . these women-doctors, these nurses, these educationalists, these public-spirited women, these female saviours: they are all, from the inside, sending out waves of destructive malevolence which eat out the inner life of a man, like a cancer.

—*D. H. Lawrence*, Studies in Classic American Literature

In the epigraph, D. H. Lawrence redraws the battle lines of World War I as a war between the sexes rather than a war between nations. He describes the war as an occasion upon which women exerted a "destructive malevolence" toward men, rather than as a conflict during which armies of men wounded and killed each other. In his account, the war's most damaging wounds were (and still "are") inflicted by a monstrous New Woman.[1]

Lawrence's misogyny comes as no surprise. But it is surprising that a similar misogyny also structures postwar writing produced by women writers such as Willa Cather. Cather herself was something of a New Woman, who had challenged professional and literary notions of women's proper sphere. She had herself been an "educationalist," had once had ambition of becoming a "woman-doctor," and had, in print, advocated nursing as a profession for women ("Nursing" 319-23). Her status as an independent and professional woman, famously discontented with traditional gender roles, makes her recourse to the same vituperative antifeminist logic that we hear from Lawrence curious.[2] Yet, her war novel, *One of Ours* (1922), traces the damage suffered by its male protagonist to female monstrosity—a monstrosity symbolized, by Cather as by Lawrence, by female action and independence called up by the war effort.

One of Ours narrates the experience of its protagonist, Claude Wheeler, who experiences a masculine crisis. Claude's crisis is both vague and overdetermined, and it provides the precondition for a war experience that enables him to come into his own as a man. Rather than depicting the war as traumatic for men, Cather traces its modern wounds to women—particularly to Claude's wife, Enid—and then jettisons them from the novel. Marilee Lindemann notes that both war and misogyny play a role in the recuperation of Claude's masculinity (74). What has not been appreciated, though, is the relationship between the war, particularly its modernity, and Enid's unnatural femininity. Cather characterizes Enid through a series of tropes that pervaded representations of women's roles in the war: practicing home economy, nursing, and driving. Through these tropes, Enid comes to stand for a paradigmatic New Woman, whose bids for independence threaten men. Why do both Cather's and Lawrence's postwar writings express dismay, not at the violence done by men nor at women who stayed at home as if content to let men suffer but by "nurses," "doctors," "educationalists"—women "saviours"?

One of Ours has invited perpetual controversy for its depiction of World War I. It won a Pulitzer Prize and was a commercial success, but its critical reception records the mixed feelings that the war inspired in Americans in 1922. The novel provided an occasion for a debate about the war, its representation, and its place in recent memory.[3] Scholars have continued to disagree about the novel's attitude toward the war.[4] For many readers, then and now, Cather's depiction of the war seems too romantic because it provides an opportunity for traditional and heroic masculine achievement. Before the war, Claude Wheeler is tormented by vague desires: he wants a more "splendid" life (52). The war fulfills this desire by giving him a chance to act heroically. To many, Cather's depiction of Claude's "clean" wounds and glorious battlefield death sanitizes the horror of trench warfare (453). Yet, other critics note the ironic tone at the novel's conclusion, in which Claude's mother reflects on her son's naïve illusions.

I would argue that Cather's direct representation of the war is actually rather well balanced. She incorporates evidence of the war's destruction as well as its excitement. Claude loves being a soldier. Cather describes the strange—even repulsive—elation that the death of others inspires in him. As letters, diaries, and other records of combatant testimony—including those from her cousin G. P. Cather, on whom Claude is based—attest, this perspective is not universal, but it is authentic.[5] Claude's heroic notions (shared by some actual soldiers) were authorized and invited by propaganda that pictured Pershing's American Expeditionary Forces as heroes. Cather remains faithful to the perspective through which her protagonist viewed the war, but she also frames it as such.

I would like to shift the debate over the novel's depiction of the war back to the Nebraska section of the novel and to what Sinclair Lewis dubbed the "Enid problem." The novel's real interest, Lewis argued in his review, was the problem posed by Claude's wife, who refuses to consummate their marriage: "Here is young Claude Wheeler, for all his indecisiveness a person of fine perceptions, valiant desires, and a thoroughly normal body, married to an evangelical prig who very much knows what she doesn't want" (O'Connor 128). Having created this interesting conflict, Lewis argues, Cather didn't know how to finish her story. She "throws it away," he says, by arbitrarily sending Claude off to war: "She might as well have pushed him down a well" (O'Connor 129). In lamenting the novel's turn to the war, Lewis underestimates the pathos that it was still capable of evoking in many readers (as many reviews attest). He also oversimplifies the novel's central problem, which centers not just in Enid but in Claude. In pronouncing that Claude has a "thoroughly normal body," Lewis ignores his dread of sexual encounters with women and his "sharp disgust for sensuality" (56). The "Enid problem" makes this easy for Lewis—and many readers—to forget. Enid's refusal to consummate their marriage takes the focus away from Claude's ambivalent sexuality and leaves the reader to assume, as Lewis does, that Claude has a "normal" body, with normative desires. But before Enid refuses him, Claude seems less normal, even "queer," as his friend Ernest puts it (138). In his reading of the novel, Lewis accepts and reiterates its scapegoat structure, remaining blind to the ideological work done by Cather's pejorative picture of the New Woman.

Cather invites Lewis's reading by making Enid extremely unsympathetic. She portrays Enid's refusal of Claude on their wedding night in a way that forbids sympathy: Enid locks him out of their stateroom on the train with a complaint so trivial it cuts ("Claude, would you mind getting a berth somewhere out in the car tonight? . . . I think the dressing on the chicken salad must have been too rich" [195]). The next morning, after Claude's humiliation has been compounded by a "long, dirty, uncomfortable ride," Enid greets him with a "fresh smiling face" and the (cruelly?) ironic observation that "[she] never lose[s] things on the train" (198)—including her virginity. Enid's portrayal plays a crucial role in the novel's economy of sympathy. As if in accord with a law of constants that governs the distribution of the reader's finite amount of sympathy, Cather demonizes Enid so that the reader will begin to favor Claude. The explicitness of the "Enid problem" compensates for and adumbrates the "thing not named" in *One of Ours:* Claude's "problem" (Cather, "The Novel Démeublé" 41).

This more latent conflict remains cloaked in obscurity. Claude is simply, as his mother describes it, "on the wrong side" of his differences with and from the men around him (53). The vagueness of this phrase reflects not only a mother's desire to shield a beloved son but the imprecision that characterizes this conflict within the text at large. Cather equivocates about whether Claude's differences reflect his own inadequacies or those of his society. Vague descriptions of Claude's "problem" pervade the first section of the novel: he harbors unreasonable fears; his attempts to be valiant fail; he is easy to manipulate; and he pleases himself best by "impos[ing] physical tests and penances upon himself" (29). Cather's portrait emerges: weak, at the mercy of his emotions, and vulnerable to others' manipulations, Claude develops masochistic tendencies. Claude's masochism shapes the reader's response;

his impatience with himself exhausts our patience in turn, which is worn thin by the repetitious, and repetitiously superficial, accounts of what's "wrong" with him (53).

Claude's problem provokes continual speculation:

> Claude knew, and everybody else knew, seemingly, that there was something wrong with him. . . . Mr. Wheeler was afraid he was one of those visionary fellows who make unnecessary difficulties for themselves and other people. Mrs. Wheeler thought the trouble with her son was that he had not yet found his Saviour. Bayliss was convinced that his brother was a moral rebel, that behind his reticence and his guarded manner he concealed the most dangerous opinions. . . . Claude was aware that his energy, instead of accomplishing something, was spent in resisting unalterable conditions, and in unavailing efforts to subdue his own nature. When he thought he had at last got himself in hand, a moment would undo the work of days; in a flash he would be transformed from a wooden post into a living boy. He would spring to his feet . . . because the old belief flashed up in him with an intense kind of hope, an intense kind of pain, — the conviction that there was something splendid about life, if he could but find it! (103)

Cather introduces a series of codes to describe what's "queer about that boy," each inflected by a different ideological perspective and anxiety: his father fears he's a "visionary fellow" (a Greenwich Village "artistic" type); his mother fears he's a sinner; his brother fears he's a secretive radical. The characters who attempt to name what is "wrong" with Claude fall short—a warning for later generations of readers and critics. For although Cather's lack of specificity invites interpretation, it also defies it.[6] That said, a certain gender trouble seems undeniable: Claude fails to express a maleness that is often assumed to be natural and struggles with "his own nature." Not surprisingly, recent critics have read Claude's problem as that other unnamable, the love that dare not speak its name. Echoing Cather's own account of her aesthetic practice of withholding information in "The Novel Démeublé," Timothy Cramer glosses Claude's mysterious problem as a counterpart of her lesbianism: "The thing not named in Cather's life, of course, is her homosexuality, and its presence is divined throughout much of her work" (151).[7] According to this line of thinking, the war provides a solution to Claude's crisis by giving him a chance to work and live not just in a homosocial relationship to other men but in an explicitly homosexual one.[8] Once in France, Claude meets David Gerhardt, and their relationship eventually inspires confidence in Claude. But reading their relationship as "openly gay," as Cramer does, overstates matters. Army life does consolidate Claude's masculinity, but we need to think more broadly about the malaise it cures.

Claude's problem resembles a condition identified in 1919 as "American Nervousness," an ephemeral neurosis blamed for sapping American manhood. "Our whole continent has been growing nervous. Everywhere we have had a steady increase in all forces making for neuroticism," Frederick E. Pierce worried in the *North American Review* (81). Modern life was corroding the virile traditions of American life. Claude echoes this diagnosis when he later refers to his "enervated" boyhood (419). Cather's diction and imagery suggest that Claude's problem is his lack of masculinity—the fact that he is a "sissie," as Claude thinks his name sounds. As Susan J. Rosowski argues, "[Claude's] best moments are those in which he assumes conventionally female roles. . . . Conversely, he is most miserable—and violent—when doing what is expected of him as a man" (111). Cather figures what's "wrong" with Claude through a series of sexually and gender-coded keywords, including "nervous" and "queer," that, as Lindemann puts it, "snap crackle and pop" with the tensions of "acute anxiety and ideological work" (12). It is tempting, but too simple, to read such terms as referring only to Claude's sexual orientation. The regime of normative masculinity requires more than heterosexuality. Claude's gender trouble signifies his resistance to, or failure to meet, multiple social expectations.

In some moments, for instance, Claude's inadequacy surfaces as a lack of vocation. He chafes at the question of money and profession: "I don't believe I can ever settle down to anything," he tells a friend (52); he feels "a childish contempt for money-values," a phrase that traces his failure to come of age to his attitudes towards modern, consumer society (101). This failure to fit in to existing economic structures seems odd in a novel about a western farmer. Claude's economic and social standing locate him within a producer class of yeoman farmers rarely associated with effeminacy or "nervousness." Claude will inherit a farm; he is neither at leisure nor alienated from his labor (as are his father's hired men). Instead, the strength he exerts with his male body on what will be his own land would seem to offer a solid material basis on which to build a coherent identity. But it doesn't because, in Cather's novel, the West—so long imagined as an escape from the degenerate, modern world—has been infiltrated by machines and what Anthony Giddens describes as "disembedding mechanisms," or new technologies that reorganize space and time and uproot individuals from their cultural and vocational traditions (10–34). Unlike most of his community, Claude responds to these changes with hostility. "With prosperity came a kind of callousness," he muses (101); "the people themselves had changed" (102). Cather figures this callousness as a new relationship to modern machinery, particularly the automobile: "The orchards . . . were now left to die out of neglect. It was less trouble to run into town in an automobile and buy fruit than it was to raise it" (102).

These reflections of Claude's resonate with more narrative authority and eloquence than is usual. His thoughts in this passage might easily have been lifted from one of Cather's other novels or essays.[9] Visions of the lost Eden of a fruit orchard appear throughout her fiction; she repeatedly figures encroaching modernity as an assault on such a pastoral setting. This signature topos appears most memorably in O Pioneers! (1913), where an orchard provides the setting for the novel's climactic murder scene. In One of Ours, it is embedded in a lost past, when Claude recalls his father's murder of a cherry tree: "The beautiful, round-topped cherry tree, full of green leaves and red fruit,—his father had sawed it through! It lay on the ground beside its bleeding stump" (27). Claude identifies the "bleeding stump" of the cherry tree with himself and his future. The scene and its memory leave Claude feeling angry and paralyzed; his father's power to cut down the fruitful tree turns the pastoral landscape of childhood into a site of castration. This episode constitutes the novel's primal scene—the original, mythic conflict that structures Claude's problem and its narration in the novel. The whole novel seems to be an attempt to reverse this action.

With the vision of the murdered cherry tree, Cather suggests a cultural loss of innocence and a fall into modernity that have particularly difficult consequences for men. The details of Claude's castration anxiety seem inspired less by Freud than by American myth, in which cherry trees have an archetypal significance in the relationship between fathers and sons. In the tale of George Washington and his father's cherry tree, the father's law stands for right, honesty, and forbearance. Young George breaks that law by cutting the tree down. But when questioned, he finds that he "cannot tell a lie." Thus in breaking the father's law, he learns to respect and abide by it. Once chastened, Washington grows to embody and enforce the law himself, taking his place in a patriarchal line and ultimately becoming the "father" of the nation. Cather evokes this myth so as to show its degeneration. In the Wheeler family, Mr. Wheeler does not teach Claude respect for the past, since he chops down the tree he himself had cultivated for years; nor does he teach Claude to respect the future, since the tree will never bear fruit again. Mr. Wheeler commits an act of violence that destroys, rather than enforces, the law of rightful rule as it is passed from one generation of American men to the next. In Claude's fall from innocence, the father's will seems capricious, unpredictable, impossible to learn and despicable to imitate, leaving the son ambivalent about becoming a man in his own right. Not wanting to be like his father, Claude is bereft of male models to emulate.

This primal scene deidealizes the West as a masculine space free both of women and domestic entanglement. The Wheeler farm is no longer virgin land; it has been claimed and violated in a scene of implicitly sexual violence. The adventure of settlement over, the only masculine way to engage in the frontier is to fight to preserve it—to fight a battle that has been, always-already, lost.

Claude's nostalgia for the past and rejection of modernity isolates him from other men: Mr. Wheeler speculates in land and chops down the tree; Bayliss wants to tear down the oldest home in town, built (complete with the traditionally masculine retreat, the billiard room) by two "carousing" "boys" back when the town was "still a tough little frontier settlement" (109); and Ralph buys an endless series of modern "labour-saving devices" that are too difficult to use (19). In contrast, Claude shares his mother's respect for the past. When their neighbor, Mr. Royce, converts his mill to electric power, he thinks, "There's just one fellow in the county will be sorry to see the old wheel go, and that's Claude Wheeler" (148). Seen from this perspective, Claude's "problem" stems from his location in time. The frontier used to be a space where carousing boys could be men. It was a site of adventure, beauty, and drama: rugged Nature *made* men. All that has passed Claude by. Machines and the matrix of consumer culture that accompany them have made western life too easy, too mundane, not "splendid." His quest in "a modern wasteland" against "the foes of materialism" (though difficult, as Rosowski notes) does not seem to be enough to bring Claude's masculinity into being (Rosowski 97). Paradoxically, Claude's respect for the past does not assure his masculinity, despite its resonance with Theodore Roosevelt's call to "strenuous life" and the masculinity of an earlier generation of "tough" settlers. Encroaching modernity makes Claude's masculinity seem vulnerable, anachronistic, and effeminate.

Cather crystallizes the threat modernity poses to Claude's masculinity in the scene of an accident, which connects mechanical violence to the male body with a debilitating dependence on women. This scene acts as a lynchpin for the novel's ideological conflicts:

Have you heard Claude Wheeler got hurt yesterday? . . . It was the queerest thing I ever saw. He was out with the team of mules and a heavy plough, working the road in that deep cut between their place and mine. The gasoline motor-truck came along, making more noise than usual, maybe. But those mules know a motor truck, and what they did was pure cussedness. They begun to rear and plunge in that deep cut. I was working my corn over in the field and shouted to the gasoline man to stop, but he didn't hear me. Claude jumped for the critters' heads and got 'em by the bits, but by that time he was all tangled up in the lines. . . . They carried him right along,

swinging in the air, and finally ran him into the barb-wire
fence and cut his face and neck up. (137–38)

Modernity has already marked the family farm: Claude works
in a "deep cut" that evokes both a primordial wound and the
land's division into pieces of private property. This "cut" evokes
the wound of birth that will be repeated in death. Claude is
dragged from the cleft in the earth, as he is into life, to struggle
amidst the entangling (umbilical-like) reigns and barbed wires that
tie him to others and to their doom. The mutual labor of man
and beast has been interrupted by machines—a motor-truck—
with terrible consequences. Man's curse—labor—has been per-
verted and made more difficult by the conditions of modernity,
despite the fact that machines supposedly save labor. Cather's
"picture making" of Claude's accident evokes archetypal expressions of masculine anxiety about dependence, lack of agency, and
the entanglements of fate that seem to deprive men of their power
and autonomy.[10] "It was the queerest thing I ever saw": it resembles a fantasy in which all men's traditional subjects rise up
against Claude—the machine, the earth, the beasts of burden, and
even inanimate tools (plough and wire) conspire against their master and inventor. Yet this scene pictures modernity's wound in
terms that are both primordial and historically particular: the
image of a man tangled in barbed wire alludes to the closing and
domestication of the American frontier and to the apocalyptic
landscape of No Man's Land on the Western Front.

Having emphasized the fragility of male bodies in an industrialized world, Cather goes on to suggest that the traditional masculine response—stoicism—further endangers them. Claude attempts to deny his wound, resuming his work the day after his
accident and so becoming seriously ill. There is no particular glory
to be gained by working in the hot sun the day after his accident, but Claude does it anyway, acting out a masochistic martyr-
fantasy and displaying his ability to endure physical trials. Cather
suggests that, in the absence of meaningful opportunities to demonstrate heroism, the performance of masculinity has degenerated
into a series of futile and self-destructive gestures.

In the scene of Claude's accident and the plot developments that lead from it, Cather begins to change keys. The paired themes of castrating modernity and Claude's "queer" inner conflict mingle with and give way to a leitmotif that announces the New Woman. At the level of plot what happens is simple: Claude is nursed by Enid, and he falls in love with her. He imagines that marrying her will solve his "problem," as if playing opposite a woman in a marriage plot will bring his manhood to the fore. In the most literal sense, Claude is disappointed in this hope. Enid refuses to play the feminine role that he casts her in. But at another level, marrying Enid *does* have the effect Claude wants: she does make him seem "thoroughly normal," as Lewis puts it, both to characters within the novel and to readers. Suddenly, Claude's struggle deserves sympathy; rather than a fool, a misfit, or "queer," he seems more like a tragic hero. After this point in the narrative, Claude's crisis becomes the "Enid problem"—the problem of *her* rejection of traditional femininity. Enid's lack of femininity acts as a magnet, binding Claude's inadequacies to it and liberating him from their taint.

At this point the novel turns toward resolution by demonizing Enid on the one hand and celebrating Claude's experience of fighting in World War I on the other. Cather's novel wishfully splits Claude's problem—modernity, his place in history—in two. Enid comes to embody the threatening aspects of modernity and machine culture, while the war comes to stand for an ironically antiquated, antimodern crusade carried out in the name of "history." The drive for narrative resolution outweighs the imperatives of realism (and, we might add, feminism).

Claude imagines himself fighting not just the Germans but an attitude toward modernity that exists in the United States as well: "No battlefield or shattered country he had seen was as ugly as this world would be if men like his brother Bayliss controlled it altogether. Until the war broke out, he had supposed that they did control it; his boyhood had been clouded and enervated by that belief. The Prussians had believed that too, apparently. But the event had shown that there were a great many people left who cared about something else" (419). Claude's anachronistic fantasy enables him to filter out awareness not just of the war's ugliness but of its modernity: "The intervals of the distant artillery fire grew shorter, as if the big guns were tuning up, choking to get something out. . . . The sound of the guns had from the first been pleasant to him, had given him a feeling of confidence and safety; tonight he knew why. What they said was, that men could still die for an idea; and would burn all they had made to keep their dreams. He knew the future of the world was safe" (419). "Safe," the phrase goes, "for democracy." In the way it echoes Wilson's famous declaration, Cather's text registers ideology's power to shape point of view and experience far beyond the limits one might imagine. To most who heard them, the sounds of the "big guns" meant something else altogether: not that the "world was safe" but that machines had facilitated a new level of danger. In 1918 (when this scene is set), the German army was using the biggest guns yet manufactured to send an altogether different message to the civilians of Paris: that *nothing* was "safe"; that the front lines of the battle extended to what seemed like almost infinite distances. The "big guns" metonymically evoke the range of innovative technologies used in World War I—including not just artillery but also submarines, airplanes, chemical weapons, and so on—and so mark the modernization and mechanization of war, the very thing against which Claude imagines he's fighting. Yet ironically, Claude hears the sounds of bombardment—the voice of mechanized war, pure and untranslated—as evidence that he's winning a war against modernity. In moments such as these, Cather's novel strains against a difficult contradiction.

The war's destructive violence does find its way into the novel—but not where it is most often sought, in the final third set in France. Instead, the most dystopic elements of the war and its modernity surface and disappear in the Nebraska part of the novel. Enid embodies what is to Claude—and to Cather, I think—the most frightening aspect of the war: its modernity. And here, Cather's narrative *does* harbor and structure romantic sentiments; Cather too is fighting Claude's fight. What is most curious, though, is that her narrative frames the fight against modernity as a war between the sexes, as a fight for sympathy between Claude and the New Woman. *One of Ours* conflates a nostalgia for "natural" preindustrial frontier life with a nostalgia for traditional femininity and a traditionally heterosexual union and division of labor.

PEARL JAMES

THE "ENID PROBLEM" REVISITED

In Book II ("Enid"), Cather's novel turns away from what's "wrong" with Claude to what's "not natura[l]" (131) about Enid's femininity. Enid comes to stand for the war's dystopic aspects through her association with a series of visual and verbal tropes that present women in relation to the war effort. Cather specifically refers to popular media and the powerful ways gender had been displayed in images designed to generate consent for the war. Perhaps because of the United States' relative distance from the theater of war, its shorter period of official engagement, and its comparatively few—though still substantial (over fifty thousand combat mortalities)—casualties, the cultural impact of the war has been under-appreciated. Reading Cather's novel requires a deeper understanding of how close the war seemed to Americans. Cather refers specifically to a range of visual references, particularly recruiting posters, which brought the war home to Americans.[11] Walter Rawls reports that "America printed more than twenty million copies of perhaps twenty five hundred posters, more posters than all the other belligerents combined" (12). Cather's novel corroborates his claim that "it was on the main streets of Home Front America that these posters did their job so effectively" (12).

In *One of Ours*, Cather alludes to recruiting images in a variety of ways. Claude's fight against modernity echoes pictures of the American forces as "Pershing's Crusaders," a band of chivalric knights. Before that, when Claude tells his neighbor, Leonard, that he plans to enlist, Leonard responds,

"Better wait a few weeks and I'll go with you. I'm going to try for the Marines. They take my eye."

Claude, standing at the edge of the tank, almost fell backward. "Why, what—what for?"

Leonard looked him over. "Good Lord, Claude, you ain't the only fellow around here that wears pants! What for? Well, I'll tell you what for," he held up three red fingers threateningly, "Belgium, the *Lusitania*, Edith Cavell. That dirt's got under my skin. I'll get my corn planted, and then Father'll look after Susie till I come back." (236)

Leonard lists the highlights of the Allied propaganda war: "Belgium, the *Lusitania*, Edith Cavell." All three were pictured in propaganda posters that appealed particularly to men by presenting the war as assaults on vulnerable women. Cather draws our attention to visual mediation: the Marines "take [Leonard's] eye"; "he looked Claude over" before suggesting they both "[wear] pants" (a visual trope for manhood); his words are accompanied by a striking physical pose ("he held up three red fingers threateningly"). Visual tropes of female vulnerability in need of male defense have reinforced Leonard's sense of his role as a man in the family (he "wears pants") and of his wife's vulnerability ("Father'll look after Susie").

Cather alludes to the impact of visual propaganda even more explicitly in her depiction of Mahailey, a character who takes graphic representations of the war as pictures of reality. Mahailey feels as if she has direct access to the war through these images. Her distance from the war is overcome by the immediacy of the graphic images, and she feels herself to be at war. Though Mahailey is simpleminded, her response to propaganda alerts the reader to the reach of visual propaganda. Historians describe World War I as the first "total war," and a primary aspect of its totalization is the militarization and mobilization of civilian life. Even by staying at home and within a traditionally feminine domestic sphere, women such as Mahailey were invited to think of themselves as combatants on the "home front." "Total war" was a byproduct not only of an industrialized economy but also of new modes of mass communication, including newspapers, film, and war posters.

Alerted by Cather to the effectiveness of visual propaganda and the extent to which it reached Americans even in rural areas, I suggest that we attend to the ways in which Enid reflects and condenses images of a certain kind of active and modern femininity that appeared in war posters. Unlike the images of women in need of male defense that seem to motivate Leonard, many posters figured women as contributing to the war effort in a variety of ways:

by doing either "women's work" or more masculine kinds of labor on the home front and by working abroad near the front.[12] On the face of things, these representations seem to advance feminist ideals. They suggest the war sparked a reevaluation of the notion of female passivity and fragility and offered a new range of actions to women.

Cather portrays Enid in both ways. At times she seems reassuringly traditional, as when she sews her trousseau. Yet even such traditional female labor was frequently recruited for the war effort, as it is in W. T. Benda's "You can help" (fig. 1).[13] Even this modest activity, its legend suggest, can help win the war. Such images left women in the home but placed the home on the front line. In other words, they strike a fragile balance between traditional and new roles for women. Even as they assert women's place in the domestic sphere, these images covertly modernize, nationalize, and professionalize women's roles. Despite their traditional imagery, they contribute to an ultimately radical change in the way women's work could be understood. Such images were central to the processes of national incorporation that Claude finds so alienating and of which Cather's narrative at large seems so disapproving. Most negative in Cather's account is the extent to which such images covertly modernize traditional labor. Enid's execution of traditional women's work is problematically but surreptitiously modern. This makes her faults as a wife hard to see: "She managed a house easily and systematically. On Monday morning Claude turned on the washing machine before he went to work, and by nine o'clock the clothes were on the line. Enid liked to iron, and Claude had never before in his life worn so many clean shirts, or worn them with such satisfaction. She told him he need not economize in working shirts; it was as easy to iron six as three" (209). Enid's domestic labor is both mechanized and rationalized according to clock-time. Moreover, as if benefiting from the work place efficiency innovations of Fordism and Taylorism, more work simply makes Enid more efficient: it is "as easy to iron six shirts as three." But although Claude wears his shirts "with satisfaction," Cather portrays that pleasure as a poor substitute for the fulfillment of more primal desires.

Fig. 1. "You can help." Wladyslaw Theodore Benda. U.S.A. Black and White, 20 × 30 inches. Circa 1918. War Poster Collection. Manuscripts and Archives, Yale University Library.

PEARL JAMES

The scientific domestic economy that defines Enid's housekeeping and cooking reflects the discourse used to mobilize women on the home front, in their kitchens, parlors, and gardens. One of Enid's most unsympathetic moments emerges directly from wartime educational propaganda aimed at women. The U.S. Food Administration used a series of posters to indoctrinate a primarily female audience into a new science of domestic economy. One poster in this series informs its viewer that unfertilized poultry eggs "last longer"[14]—a piece of scientific information that Enid puts to use by keeping her hens separate from the rooster. The neighbors, who prefer to do things the "natural" and "old-fashioned" way, disapprove of Enid's "fanatic" enforcement of sexual discipline and condemn her modern methods (203, 204). Through their remarks, Cather frames an essentially positive and empowering wartime script for women as one that makes them monstrous and unfeminine. Both Enid's scientific farming and her vegetarianism emerge directly from publicity disseminated as part of the war effort ("Eat Less Meat" and "Eat Less Wheat" were popular commands). In *One of Ours,* such traits take on negative connotations as the symptoms of Enid's retreat from sexuality and the body, which leaves Claude feeling sexually frustrated and underfed.

But Cather grounds Enid's lack of sympathy in other, less traditional wartime images of women as well. In addition to collecting money and goods, knitting for soldiers and refugees, and growing and conserving food, women also participated in the war in less "feminine" ways. Not long after the United States declared war in 1917, the navy began enlisting women as a way of coping with an intense demand for personnel (Gavin 1–24). In addition to those who enlisted in the armed forces, many women were mobilized by volunteer organizations such as the Red Cross, the Salvation Army, and the YMCA and YWCA. According to historian Susan Zeiger, "Women's work at the front was much more than a simple extension of their participation in the civilian labor force. It was also military or quasi-military service and therefore had profound implications for a society grappling with questions about the nature of women and their place in the public life of the nation, in war and peacetime" (3–4). Questions about women's proper

Fig. 2. "If You Want to Fight! Join the Marines." Howard Chandler Christy. U.S.A. Color, 27 × 40. 1917. War Poster Collection. Manuscripts and Archives, Yale University Library.

sphere repeatedly find their way into war posters, many of which provide far from simplistic messages. Howard Chandler Christy would repeatedly harness such questions in his poster illustrations (see fig. 2, "If You Want to Fight!"). Christy clearly plays with the possibility of women taking military roles. The image invites a male viewer to assert his difference from the female figure, whose male impersonation visibly fails. But the failure, I would argue, is not absolute: Christy's female figure flirts with androgyny. Christy's posters work primarily through an erotic charge generated by woman-as-object, but they also allude to female independence.[15] This contradiction generates the posters' success. Posted as a challenge, female ambition incites a male viewer to assert his difference by doing things she cannot, such as enlisting. That women ultimately were admitted to the navy and marines only heightened the effectiveness of such images.[16] If the spectacle of women simply contemplating men's work was an energizing one, then their actually doing it could be pictured as an even more effective challenge to men.

As women began to work near the front, this visual flirtation with the possibility of women taking traditionally male roles in the war effort became an increasingly dominant motif. Playful and eroticized cross-dressing gives way to a more serious depiction of women laboring in unfeminine circumstances. We catch of glimpse of this in "The Salvation Army Lassie" (fig. 3). This poster plays with the possibility of similarity between men and women, with the possibility that women can replace or work as men. Part of the pleasure of looking emerges as an interpretive game of comparing and differentiating masculinity from femininity. "The Salvation Army Lassie" ostensibly exemplifies a traditional version of gender roles in wartime (since the "lassie" serves refreshments to the men). She is in the poster's background, literally the girl *behind* the man who fights the war. The male soldier stands in the foreground and speaks for her. But the poster plays verbally and visually with their similarity. Its text, "Oh, Boy! *that's* the Girl!," demonstrates the arbitrary signification of words like "boy" and "girl." The visual similarity between the figures—their khaki uniforms, steel helmets, and youthful smiles—emphasize their likeness and exchangeability. This poster gives visual shape to an actual gender confusion surrounding the mobilization of women in France. The presence of Salvation Army "lassies" was predicated on male dependence on women and on a notion that women could contribute in a fundamental way to the AEF's strength. Male soldiers, it was argued, would naturally be homesick; and American women could comfort them in a way French women, imagined as inherently more sexual, could (or should) not. The Salvation Army,

Fig. 3. "The Salvation Army Lassie. Oh Boy! That's the Girl!" Anonymous. U.S.A. Color, 30 × 40. 1918. War Poster Collection. Manuscripts and Archives, Yale University Library.

the Red Cross, and the hospitality services of the armed forces took a good deal of care to supervise and desexualize the interactions of American soldiers and their female support corps. The kind of bond Salvation Army "lassies" like this one were supposedly able to offer male soldiers was continually figured as a sibling

112

PEARL JAMES

or maternal one. "American women . . . were expected to provide the troops with a wholesome but winning distraction from French prostitutes or lovers"; by their presence, American women could comfort soldiers and help them observe the AEF's "policy of sexual continence" against venereal disease (Zeiger 56). In other words, women working at the front had to walk a thin line between being feminine (comforting) but not too feminine (alluring) —they had to enact their difference from soldiers while still being their "chums."

Such imagery inflects Cather's portrait of Enid's asexuality. Enid refuses her husband as a sexual partner and often thinks of him as a brother or even a son. Cather's portrait recalls the deliberate desexualization of women war workers in France, who "were envoys of the American home front, representatives of the mothers, wives, and sisters left behind" but as such were represented in imagery that emphasized "sentimentality and homey comfort" over sexuality (Zeiger 57). Policies governing the recruitment of women (in the armed forces and in relief agencies) largely "excluded those with husbands in the war. . . . Organizations were looking for a special type of volunteer," who would not be "preoccupied with finding their loved ones" and who were "independent of familial and marital ties" (Chuppa-Cornell 469). In direct correlation, Enid describes herself as "not naturally drawn to people" and "free" to move abroad (131).

The official and conscious intent of assuring sisterly or maternal roles for women was to contain and discipline the threat of female sexuality, particularly the threat of its free expression outside the bounds of marriage. But this campaign to desexualize women's presence had an ironic result in that it gave form and coherence to a new kind of female independence that was equally, or perhaps even more, threatening. Certainly, Enid's lack of sexual desire is her most threatening quality, the one which makes her most unsympathetic to readers and critics—that is what exercises Sinclair Lewis in his review. The "Enid problem" is that Claude needs Enid but Enid doesn't want Claude: he needs a wife to make him the man of the house; he needs her care and her domestic labor as a grounding contrast to his masculinity; he needs their sexual relationship to bring his body's normative desires to the fore. But the very things that make Enid useful and necessary to Claude also make her strangely independent and unnaturally asexual.

Cather's description of this lack of traditional reciprocity evoke the new gender relations established during the war. Claude's need for Enid originally surfaces as a need for nursing. After Claude's accident in the barbed wire, she visits him every day, brings him flowers—reversing the traditional courtship ritual, as Rosowski notes (111)—and helps him pass the time while he convalesces. Enid's nursing activity conflates traditional femininity (providing support to men) with New Womanhood (lack of concern for decorum). If this conflation causes confusion to Mrs. Wheeler and to Claude—blinding them to Enid's lack of physical attraction to him and to her sexual unavailability—this too alludes to a constellation of fascination and anxiety that coalesced around the figure of the nurse during the war. The image of the nurse merged both feminine roles (nurturing) and masculine roles (being a new kind of soldier). We can see this in the ethical confusion provoked by the murder of Edith Cavell: Was she a civilian (a woman) or a soldier (a man)?[17] In killing her, did the Germans commit an atrocity on an innocent civilian woman or a justifiable act of war on the body of an enemy? "Total war" confused the gendered categories that war had traditionally enforced and made visible. Enid's role as a nurse invites us to see her as powerful and to see Claude, by contrast, as weak and ill, making it easy to read him (as Lewis does) as her victim. Cather makes Enid's nursing duplicitous and anxiety-provoking rather than admirable or courageous.

In this, Cather's novel resembles largely anxiety-ridden male-authored representations of nurses, rather than female-authored ones. Although she treats nursing rather briefly, her portrait predicts the nurse's popularity as a signal figure in the mediation of postwar gender anxiety. As I have argued elsewhere, several texts deflect anxiety about masculinity onto a sinister nurse figure, who heals wounded men only to entrap them in a painful and compromised life.[18] This trope of the dangerous nurse—a version of Lawrence's threatening "woman-saviour"—threads through fiction by male American modernists, notably William Faulkner and Ernest Hemingway. In *A Farewell to Arms*, Hemingway negotiates a war-triggered crisis of male autonomy through the body of a nurse.

Hemingway takes the most feminizing aspects of male war experience (being a "little crazy" and dying a bloody death) and assigns them to Catherine Barkley. His narrative reinscribes the male body's vulnerability in wartime onto the otherwise powerful body of the nurse. The danger of professional independence that female nurses seem to pose is contained, or negated, by an old-fashioned lack of control over their bodies' reproductive capacities. Hemingway reembeds "nursing" in the biological context that the word's origin implies: female anatomy is destiny.

During the war, the profession of female nursing confounded gender difference by merging categories of soldiers and civilians and by reversing its opposite, the other popular plotline in propaganda: women in need of male rescue. Female nursing also raised questions of sexuality and propriety by bringing upper- and middle-class women into unsupervised, physical contact with soldiers. But if the nurse was a locus of anxiety about women's new independence in the hands of some postwar writers, the sexuality of female nurses also provided the means of restoring gender difference: feminine sexual weakness foils male independence. Cather's narrative does not provide the same comfort. She portrays the nurse as desexualized and, in consequence, dangerous.

Cather figures Enid's monstrously independent femininity most deliberately through another trope: the figure of the woman driver. This, the most explicitly negative sign of Enid's independence, is also the one that ties her most consistently to the war and to modernity. The figure of Enid at the wheel condenses these various aspects of Cather's narrative. Enid's skill as a driver first appears in a dramatic storm scene. After taking a day trip in the car, Claude and Enid find themselves seventy miles away from home with a storm coming up on the prairie. Claude suggests that they wait until the next day to drive home, but Enid refuses. This episode allows Cather to showcase Enid's "quiet"—and ominous— "determination": she "could not bear to have her plans changed by people or circumstances" (133). She exhibits a fearlessness that embarrasses Claude into acquiescence. But his unmanly caution seems justified when the storm arrives and he loses control of the car. He reiterates his suggestion that they seek shelter until the storm is over. Enid refuses, again, complaining that the nearby

farm is "not very clean" and too crowded with children (134)—
foreshadowing her "unfeminine" attitude toward domesticity. At
that point, Enid herself takes the wheel. She insists that Claude is
"nervous" (a watchword for effeminacy and for unmanly response
to the pressures of war) and that she has more experience driving:
"[Claude] was chafed by her stubbornness, but he had to admire
her resourcefulness in handling the car. At the bottom of one of the
worst hills was a new cement culvert, overlaid with liquid mud,
where there was nothing for the chains to grip. The car slid to the
edge of the culvert and stopped on the very brink. While they were
ploughing up the other side of the hill, Enid remarked, 'It's a good
thing your starter works well; a little jar would have thrown us
over'" (134). Although Enid gets them home safely, Claude's manhood sustains some injury. On the very next page, Claude's accident occurs. The danger of injury, once averted, quickly returns,
again tied to driving machines. Claude's accident with the truck
and the mules in a sense reiterates the symbolic castration of his
drive with Enid. His accident, along with his frustrated response
to it, triggers his effeminizing illness and leads directly to his need
for Enid's nursing—which leads, in turn, to the ultimate castration of their unconsummated marriage. Although Claude keeps
Enid's sexual refusal a secret from his family and friends, her driving makes her physical abs(tin)ence visible to everyone: "Having
a wife with a car of her own is next to having no wife at all,"
Leonard exclaims. "How they do like to roll around! I've been
mighty blamed careful to see that Susie never learned to drive a
car" (202). The scene of Enid's driving condenses everything unsympathetic about her: her determination, her inflexibility, her independence from Claude, her flight from domesticity and sexuality.

Embedded in a landscape of treacherous mud, Cather's portrayal of Enid's driving emerges directly from representations of
women drivers for the war. Enid's driving establishes the fact that
steely nerves and determination reside within an otherwise feminine and supposedly fragile body. Cather's portrayal seems indebted to images of war because it differs from the other dominant
trends in the way that women's access to cars was pictured by the
automobile industry and in other popular representations.[19] For in-

stance, although most car advertisements before the 1920s picture women as passengers, Cather insists that Enid is the better driver. Contrary to other popular beliefs about how women would experience cars, Enid is not interested in the car as an accessory nor as a sign of status nor yet as a vehicle for unchaperoned sexual adventure (which is the fantasy implicitly keeping Leonard from letting his wife learn to drive—"How they do like to roll around!"). While most car advertisers imagined that women would want to drive short distances and that power and speed would be far less important to them than features of comfort and aesthetic appeal, Enid values the car for how it works, rather than for how it looks or feels to ride in. (Enid's appreciation of the car's self-starting mechanism suggests her technical understanding.) Finally, the episode underscores that Enid's primary interest in the car is as a vehicle for getting somewhere rather than as a pretense for being unchaperoned with her beau. The secluded and mobile privacy that the car made possible alarmed parents and others concerned with the morals of American youth; its speed and danger became a symbol, early on, for both sexual desire and female availability.

In all these particulars, Enid's driving resembles the professional attitude of women who served during the war under the auspices of various motor corps. Hélène Jones's "Motor Corps of America" (fig. 4) and Edward Penfield's "'Yes Sir—I am Here!' Recruits Wanted Motor Corps of America" (fig. 5) show women working in uniform as agents in their own right. Rather than serving male soldiers who pose in front of them and speak for them, these female figures are pictured working independently or with other women. They handle machinery; they answer for themselves; they seem serious and professional rather than friendly and hospitable. Women who drove in France worked hard hours on bad roads, did their own maintenance, and worked alone close to the front.[20] These posters feature female figures with ambition, independence, and responsibility—all characteristics of Enid, who has a strong sense of her own personal mission for demanding labor in an international setting.

The femininity of these figures is ambivalent and hard to interpret: we cannot tell if they have short cropped hair or the more traditional long hair pulled back in a cap. While their uniforms

Fig. 4. "The Motor Corps of America." Hélène Jones. U.S.A. Color, 30 × 40 inches. Circa 1918. War Poster Collection. Manuscripts and Archives, Yale University Library.

mostly obscure their femininity, the Sam Browne belt—visible in both images—accentuates both their feminine, narrow waists *and* the fact that they are serving, like men, at the front (these belts could only be worn abroad).[21] Their sex appeal is similarly ambivalent: it emerges primarily from the challenge that their lack of traditional femininity provokes. It is precisely this kind of chal-

Fig. 5. "'Yes Sir—I am Here!' Recruits Wanted. Motor Corps of America." Edward Penfield. U.S.A. Color, 27 × 40. Circa 1918. War Poster Collection. Manuscripts and Archives, Yale University Library.

lenge that makes Enid such a treacherous figure. Enid's body both
draws and resists Claude's sexualizing gaze: "He wonder[s] why
she ha[s] no shades of feeling to correspond to her natural grace
. . . to the gentle, almost wistful attitudes of her body" (211).
Though she looks "wistful" to Claude, what she longs for is not
the reassuringly "natural" desires he imagines. For, Cather writes,
"Everything about a man's embrace was distasteful to Enid. . . .
[S]he disliked ardour of any kind" (210). Cather depicts Enid's
body—like the female figures in these posters—as wistfully feminine but also efficient, Taylorized, even machinelike. Enid's body
works rather than reproduces. Enid has exactly what Claude feels
that he lacks as a man: she wholly identifies with a mission larger
than herself. Unlike Claude, and in a reversal of traditional gender stereotypes, Enid does not need her raison d'être to be embodied by another person. In contrast to the notion that women
develop strong social bonds and define their identity in social terms
rather than abstract ones, Cather describes Enid as "not naturally
much drawn to people," as perpetually "free" from intimate bonds
(131). Enid's ministrations to Claude after his accident, ostensibly
the sign of female service to men, signify precisely the opposite.
She cares for him because his accident gives her an opportunity
to enact, in a small way, her professional ambition of becoming
a missionary. Missionary work ultimately takes her, as it had her
sister Carrie (a name that evokes the dangers of female mobility in
early-twentieth-century fiction) to China.

What makes Enid so monstrous is her lack of need for a man.
She does not need a masculine partner against whom her own
femininity can cohere in contrast. Enid never seems as tormented
by her lack of traditional femininity as Claude is by his failure to
be a "normal" man. Her lack of sexuality aligns her with Claude's
castrating father because she withholds and forbids what Claude
imagines he needs to make his manhood real in the world. It would
be possible to read this as lesbianism, and yet Cather figures the
danger the New Woman poses not as undisciplined desire but as
erotophobia.[22] Enid's monstrosity exists not in her appetites but
in her lack of them: she's a virgin, a teetotaler, and a vegetarian.
She's not pictured as overly or voraciously feminine but instead

as androgynous and autotelic. Like one of Lawrence's "women saviours," Enid drives herself to save the world. That drive makes her an unfit wife, one who wounds her husband and who is perceived as posing a general threat to men and male homosociality: "Within a few months Enid's car traveled more than two thousand miles for the Prohibitionist cause" — a cause which leaves Claude home alone and alienates him from his male friends (209).

Having depicted this dangerous New Woman, Cather banishes her from the novel. Enid takes the dangers posed by modernity with her and makes the war "safe." Before Claude goes off to war, Enid goes off to China, and his masculine crisis disappears with her. Once she's gone, machines no longer seem to pose the same threat. Treacherous mud and lacerating barbed wire only seem to threaten Claude when Enid is nearby. In comparison with the "queer," disfiguring, and infection-prone wounds Claude receives at home, Cather describes his war wounds as "clean" (453).

Indeed, even the automobile — which Cather describes elsewhere as "misshapen and sullen, like an ugly threat in a stream of things that were bright and beautiful and alive"[23] — can be recuperated once Enid is no longer at the wheel. Toward the end of the novel, Cather suggests that the automobile will provide postwar consolation to men: "What Hicks had wanted most in this world was to run a garage and repair shop with his old chum, Dell Able. Beaufort ended all that. He means to conduct a sort of memorial shop, anyhow, with 'Hicks and Able' over the door. He wants to roll up his sleeves and look at the *logical and beautiful inwards of automobiles* for the rest of his life" (456–57, italics added). If cars had once been vehicles of castration, Cather associates them here with healing, and with male agency ("Able"). Similarly, while Enid's driving isolates Claude, postwar driving will bring men together: "Though Bert lives on the Platte and Hicks on the Big Blue, the automobile roads between these two rivers are excellent" (456).

The negative aspects of modernity disappear with Enid. Interestingly, Cather suspends her portrayal and judgment of the character at that point in the narrative. She never disciplines Enid within the plot itself, which may be why critics like Lewis felt the need to condemn the character so vociferously. The fact that Enid disappears does not, of course, mitigate the misogyny of Cather's portrait. Instead, Cather's suspension of discipline makes itself felt as the "thing not named" in the text, and in turn engenders the tradition of name calling (Enid is "an evangelical prig who very much knows what she doesn't want") that so many critics have relished.

In an ironic way, then, the novel authorizes the misogyny that has marked its critical reception, in its own time and in later decades. Cather's novel received criticism when it was published not only because it offered a heroic version of the war but because Cather was a woman writer. H. L. Mencken broaches this criticism in a rather subtle way, by comparing her novel, to its detriment, with John Dos Passos's "bold realism" in *Three Soldiers* (1921):

> What spoils [Cather's] story is simply that a year or so ago a young soldier named John Dos Passos printed a novel called *Three Soldiers*. Until *Three Soldiers* is forgotten and fancy achieves its inevitable victory over fact, no war story can be written in the United States without challenging comparison with it. . . . At one blast it disposed of oceans of romance and blather. It changed the whole tone of American opinion about the war; it even changed the recollections of actual veterans of the war. They saw, no doubt, substantially what Dos Passos saw, but it took his bold realism to disentangle their recollection from the prevailing buncombe and sentimentality. . . . The war [Miss Cather] depicts has its thrills and even its touches of plausibility, but at bottom it is fought out, not in France, but on a Hollywood movie-lot. (O'Connor 142)

The opposition Mencken sets up between the "young soldier's" view of the war and that offered by "Miss Cather" hinges on their gender and the access that gender supposedly provided to the war. He offers this critique in literary terms but in literary terms that inscribe gender: a "blast" of "bold realism" versus "fancy," "oceans of romance and blather," "buncombe and sentimentality." Hemingway, famously, offered a much more explicit attack on Cather as a woman who dared to write about male experience.[24]

The same kind of identity politics that characterize these early criticisms long continued to define the parameters of discussions of *One of Ours*. In his 1967 *World War I and the American Novel*,

Stanley Cooperman's analysis of *One of Ours* and the war fiction of Edith Wharton justifies his conclusion that women cannot represent war. Both authors earn Cooperman's disapproval for "sentimentality and intrusive rhetoric"—for being too propagandistic and for offering a romantic view of the war (129). He reiterates what Hemingway had written and assumes that, as a woman, Cather "knew very little about the war she was describing" (136). But if *One of Ours* seems spurious to some for being a female-authored war novel, it has also proven somewhat intractable to feminist reevaluations of Cather and her work. The novel's misogyny disrupts the neatness of Sharon O'Brien's description of Cather's progress as a woman writer in *Willa Cather: The Emerging Voice*. Cather published it years after having, as O'Brien articulates so well, replaced an early identification with men and male authors with a feminine aesthetic. In other words, in *One of Ours* Cather expresses what seems like an atavistic doubt and dread about femininity. This contributes, I think, to the comparatively little attention the novel has received among Cather scholars. Too "womanly" for some, not "womanly" enough for others, the novel long continued both to provoke and to betray a desire for coherent and predictable differences between masculinity and femininity.

Rather than offering a psychological account of the sexual and gender conflicts Cather as an individual may have been working out in *One of Ours*, I want to conclude by considering the novel's use of gender to organize what was an extremely confusing and painful cultural experience. The deepest insight of Mencken's review of the novel comes in the form of his admission that people needed help ordering their "memories" of the war and in the ongoing postwar process of determining what it had meant: "[Dos Passos's novel] changed the whole tone of American opinion about the war; it *even changed the recollections of actual veterans of the war*," he writes (142, italics added). If "actual" witnesses of the war could change their "recollections" of what happened there, then the mutability of visions of more distant observers is hardly surprising. Recollections and fictions about the war, then, continued to be the vehicle for the negotiation of conflict. Telling the story of the war offered individuals and the culture at large ways to debate how to value the violence suffered and inflicted in the name of manhood and the nation and how to judge the nation that had demanded such sacrifice in such terms.

Misogynistic representations of the war testify, then, not simply to cultural (or personal) attitudes about women but to the depth of anger and resentment that followed the experience of war, even among the so-called victors. The need to find a scapegoat overwhelmed many level-headed and well-meaning attempts to account for and remember the war. Coming to terms with its costs —particularly the human costs—was difficult. The unprecedented losses of World War I provoked a crisis in cultural mourning practices, which in turn triggered a variety of postwar rituals and narratives, both innovative and traditional. Holding women responsible for the war was only one of several responses. The difficulty of telling the story of the war made that story porous: it repeatedly absorbed and was used to formulate other anxieties and conflicts. Cather's war novel encodes a melancholic and nostalgic desire for the past, for a time before the war, and a for a time when some, including Cather and her character Claude, had "hoped extravagantly" to win a fight against modernity (459).

NOTES

I received helpful suggestions from several participants at Great Passions and Great Aspirations: Willa Cather and World War I, a conference at the University of Nebraska–Lincoln in April 2002. I thank the organizers and participants, particularly Susan Rosowski, Margie Rine, Steven Trout, and Richard Harris.

1. On the figure of the New Woman, see especially Smith-Rosenberg.

2. Marilee Lindemann points out that elsewhere Cather "responded directly and resistantly to the all-male pantheon . . . erected by her acquaintance D. H. Lawrence in his controversial *Studies in Classic American Literature*" (85).

3. See O'Connor.

4. Recent critical opinion runs the gamut: Patricia Lee Yongue calls it an "an anti-war novel and a woman's novel"; most others have followed in the footsteps of early critics and interpreted its attitude toward the war as "romantic." The debate turns on the recognition of the distance between Cather, her narrator, and Claude. See Lindemann 69–78; Yongue 141; Boxwell; Stout; Schwind; Arnold; Wilson; and Ryan. Most recently,

Steven Trout has argued that Cather does not romanticize the war, pointing to her inclusion of certain details: dead bodies, wounded soldiers, a hand sticking out of the trench wall that refuses to be buried, and so on (see *Memorial Fictions*).

5. It has long been known that Cather based her portrait of Claude on her cousin, George P. ("G. P.") Cather, who served as an officer in the AEF and died at Cantigny in 1918. She spent time with him before he left for France, when they renewed a lapsed childhood bond. Her letters attest to her interest and investment in G. P.'s life as he fought and died in France. She attributed her strong desire to write the novel to wanting to tell her cousin's story. On a trip back to Nebraska after G. P.'s death, Cather read his wartime letters to his parents. These letters have recently been donated to the University of Nebraska.

6. Blanche H. Gelfant makes this point but then can't resist filling in what it is that Claude is searching for: the happiness of family life (see "What Was It . . . ?").

7. As mentioned above, the phrase "the thing not named" comes from Cather's account of her own style in the essay "The Novel Démeublé."

8. Cramer argues that "the experience of war itself . . . makes it possible for Claude and David to experience their intense relationship. . . . Far from the constraints of society, Claude is finally able to confront and accept his homosexuality, and, by doing so, he can love David without reservations" (158).

9. Cather's first book-length biographer, E. K. Brown, makes this point in his analysis of the "cult of machinery" in the novel, which he compares to Cather's descriptions of the automobile elsewhere. In her story "Coming, Aphrodite!" (1920), she describes the sight of "an automobile, misshapen and sullen, like an ugly threat in a stream of things that were bright and beautiful and alive" (8). Similarly, in her essay "Nebraska" (published in *The Nation* in 1923), she writes, "The generation now in the driver's seat hates to make anything, wants to live and die in an automobile, scudding past those acres where the old men used to follow the long corn-rows up and down. They want to buy everything ready-made: clothes, food, education, music, pleasure" (see Brown 219–21).

10. Rosowski explains that although Cather described her usual writing method as "scene" making—"When a writer has a strong or revelatory experience with his characters, he unconsciously creates a scene; gets a depth of picture, and writes, as it were, in three dimensions instead of two" (Cather, "Defoe's" 80)—in the case of *One of Ours*, she claimed that she "cut out all picture making because that boy [Claude] does not see pictures" (96–97). This scene is a crucial exception.

11. Martha Banta isolates posters as "the single most important visual means for promoting national values during the war of 1917–18" (560).

12. For a more developed account of the way women were figured in World War I posters, see Knutson.

13. Apparently an admirer of Benda's war posters, Cather had him do the illustrations for *My Ántonia* in 1918, which included a strikingly similar image of the same model, knitting again, though on the prairie (see *My Ántonia* 188).

14. "Help Feed Yourself," an anonymous poster (16 × 24 inches) published by the U.S. Food Administration. War Poster Collection, Sterling Memorial Library Manuscripts and Archive Collection, Yale University, MS #671, YUS 0163.

15. "Sexual provocation was the essence of the 'Christy girl' recruiting posters" (Paret, Lewis, and Paret 56).

16. The marines admitted women in August 1918 for work that would, according to their publicity motto, "Free a Man to Fight." For more information, see Gavin, chapter 2, "Women Marines."

17. Edith Cavell was a nurse in the British Red Cross. While in charge of a hospital in occupied Belgium, she was arrested by the German army and accused of helping wounded Allied soldiers escape to the Dutch border. Despite international protest, she was executed by firing squad in October 1915 and became a martyr of German "atrocity." Her image was a centerpiece in anti-German propaganda campaigns throughout the war. Klaus Theweileit offers a provocative psychoanalytic account of why nurses arouse so much anxiety (particularly in Germany) during the First World War: The nurse is a woman who wields a knife, and she is also "a castrated doctor"—male fantasies of castration, therefore, become cathected to the figure of the nurse (132).

18. See James, "From Trench to Trope."

19. For a history of images of the woman driver, see Scharf.

20. "The typical driver was a woman of culture and means who was familiar with both the French language and the intricacies of auto mechanics. Drivers usually performed their own maintenance work, including oil changes, small repairs, and cleaning. Since the essence of the unit's work was its deliveries, maintaining a reliable vehicle was a top priority" (Chuppa-Cornell 468). For more on the realities of women drivers for the war, see Zeiger, chapter 6, "Serving Uncle Sam"; Gavin, chapter 9; and Scharf 94.

21. I thank Richard Harris and Steven Trout for bringing this to my attention.

22. Enid is an atypical illustration of the New Woman, primarily because the New Woman was more often associated with liberal sexuality.

PEARL JAMES

Caroll Smith-Rosenberg argues that the New Woman's sexuality seemed a betrayal of the previous generations of feminists, and that to young women, older feminists seem to have betrayed them. She suggests that members of the older generation—i.e., Cather's—were not discursively equipped to think of themselves as "sexual subjects," and sexuality was simply avoided (as it is in Enid's case). But the younger generation, coming of age when sexuality was discussed (by sexologists, doctors, and in the popular media), were able to think of themselves as sexual subjects but, at the same time, had difficulty forming alliances with older feminists. The generation gap between women formed a more forbidding obstacle than the political gap between men and women seemed to. Cather's illustration of the New Woman runs counter to these general patterns: Enid is both politically active for Prohibition (a descendant of the classic nineteenth-century feminist cause, Temperance) and avoids all sexuality.

23. This quote comes from Cather's story "Coming, Aphrodite!" and is cited by E. K. Brown as an example of Cather's negative depictions of modernity. See previous note.

24. For a discussion of Hemingway's response to Cather's novel, see Boxwell 290-91.

WORKS CITED

Arnold, Marilyn. "*One of Ours:* Willa Cather's Losing Battle." *Western American Literature* 13.3 (1978): 259-66.

Banta, Martha. *Imaging American Women: Idea and Ideals in Cultural History.* New York: Columbia UP, 1987.

Boxwell, D. A. "In Formation: Male Homosocial Desire in Willa Cather's *One of Ours.*" *Eroticism and Containment: Notes from the Flood Plain.* Ed. Carol Siegel and Ann Kibbey. New York: New York UP, 1994. 285-310.

Brown, E. K. *Willa Cather: A Critical Biography.* New York: Knopf, 1953.

Cather, Willa. "Coming, Aphrodite!" *Youth and the Bright Medusa.* 1920. Boston: Houghton Mifflin, 1937.

———. "Defoe's *The Fortunate Mistress.*" 1920. *Willa Cather on Writing: Critical Studies on Writing as an Art.* Lincoln: U of Nebraska P, 1988. 75-88.

———. *My Ántonia.* Boston: Houghton Mifflin, 1918.

———. "The Novel Démeublé." 1922. *Willa Cather on Writing: Critical Studies on Writing as an Art.* Lincoln: U of Nebraska P, 1988. 33-44.

———. "Nursing as a Profession for Women" 1879. *The World and the*

Parish: Willa Cather's Articles and Reviews. Ed. William M. Curtin. 2 vols. Lincoln: U of Nebraska P, 1970. 1:319–23.

———. *One of Ours.* New York: Knopf, 1922.

Chuppa-Cornell, Kimberly. "The U.S. Women's Motor Corps in France." *Historian* 56.3 (1994): 465–76.

Cooperman, Stanley. *World War I and the American Novel.* Baltimore MD: Johns Hopkins UP, 1967.

Cramer, Timothy R. "Claude's Case: A Study of Homosexual Temperament in Willa Cather's *One of Ours.*" *South Dakota Review* 31 (Fall 1993): 151.

Gavin, Lettie. *American Women in World War I: They Also Served.* Niwot: U of Colorado, 1997.

Gelfant, Blanche H. "'What Was It . . . ?' The Secret of Family Accord in *One of Ours.*" *Modern Fiction Studies* 36.1 (1990): 61–78.

Giddens, Anthony. *Modernity and Self-Identity: Self and Society in the Later Modern Age.* Stanford: Stanford UP, 1991.

Hemingway, Ernest. *A Farewell to Arms.* New York: Charles Scribner's Sons, 1929.

James, Pearl. "From Trench to Trope: Narrating American Masculinity after World War I." PhD diss. Yale U, 2002.

Knutson, Anne Classen. "Breasts, Brawn, and Selling a War: American World War I Propaganda Posters 1917–1918." PhD diss. U of Pittsburgh, 1997.

Lindemann, Marilee. *Willa Cather: Queering America.* New York: Columbia UP, 1999. 85.

O'Brien, Sharon. *Willa Cather: The Emerging Voice.* Oxford: Oxford UP, 1987.

O'Connor, Margaret Anne, ed. *Willa Cather: The Contemporary Reviews.* New York: Cambridge UP, 2001.

Paret, Peter, Beth Irwon, and Paul Paret, eds. *Persuasive Images: Posters of the War and Revolution from the Hoover Institution Archives.* Princeton: Princeton UP, 1992.

Pierce, Frederick E. "Nervous New England." *North American Review* 210.764 (1919): 81–85.

Rawls, Walton. *Wake Up, America! World War I and the American Poster.* New York: Abbeville P, 1988.

Rosowski, Susan J. *The Voyage Perilous: Willa Cather's Romanticism.* Lincoln: U of Nebraska P, 1986.

Ryan, Maureen. "No Woman's Land: Gender in Willa Cather's *One of Ours.*" *Studies in American Fiction* 18.1 (1990): 65–76.

Scharf, Virginia. *Taking the Wheel: Women and the Coming of the Motor Age.* New York: Free P, 1991.

Schwind, Jean. "The 'Beautiful' War in *One of Ours.*" *Modern Fiction Studies* 30.1 (1984): 53–72.

Smith-Rosenberg, Carroll. "Discourses of Sexuality and Subjectivity: The New Woman, 1870–1936." *Hidden from History: Reclaiming the Gay and Lesbian Past.* Ed. Martin Bauml Duberman, Martha Vicinus, and George Chauncey Jr. New York: Penguin, 1989. 264–80.

Stout, Janis P. "The Making of Willa Cather's *One of Ours:* The Role of Dorothy Canfield Fisher." *War, Literature and the Arts* 11.2 (1999): 48–59.

Theweileit, Klaus. *Male Fantasies Volume 1: Women, Floods, Bodies, History.* Minneapolis: U of Minnesota P, 1987.

Trout, Steven. *Memorial Fictions: Willa Cather and the First World War.* Lincoln: U of Nebraska P, 2002.

Wilson, Raymond J., III. "Willa Cather's *One of Ours:* A Novel of the Great Plains and the Great War." *Midamerica* 11 (1984): 20–33.

Yongue, Patricia Lee. "For Better and for Worse: At Home and at War in *One of Ours.*" *Willa Cather: Family, Community, and History.* Ed. John J. Murphy. Provo UT: Brigham Young U Humanities Publications, 1990.

Zeiger, Susan. *In Uncle Sam's Service: Women Workers with the American Expeditionary Force, 1917–1919.* Ithaca NY: Cornell UP, 1999.

"Squeezed into an Unnatural Shape"
Bayliss Wheeler and the Element of Control in *One of Ours*

CELIA M. KINGSBURY

In his 1987 biography *Willa Cather: A Literary Life*, James Woodress compares *One of Ours* to T. S. Eliot's *The Waste Land*. Thematically and structurally, according to Woodress, the works, conceived on opposite sides of the Atlantic, address the question of social disintegration; in his words, both works open "with a panorama of society's failures, followed by views of personal failure . . . and [end] with a promise of spiritual rebirth" (329). Woodress's assertion that the novel deals with social and personal failure is a virtual given. Claude Wheeler cannot negotiate the spiritual void he finds in the materialistic world of his brothers, Ralph and Bayliss, and therein lies much of the conflict that sends Claude to war. But Woodress's suggestion that the novel demonstrates "a promise of spiritual rebirth" plays down the cynicism, ironically that of the religious Evangeline Wheeler, that closes the novel in a place far from *The Waste Land*'s optimistic cultural and spiritual synthesis. Nothing about Lovely Creek changes as a result of Claude's sacrifice. While the enemy abroad is ultimately defeated, the enemy at home survives with a vengeance.

One of Ours was a difficult novel for Cather to write.[1] She suffered through several periods of illness as well as the psychological trauma of revisiting the life and death of her cousin G. P. Cather, who served as her model for Claude Wheeler. Cather also renewed her friendship with Dorothy Canfield Fisher during the composition of the novel because Cather needed Canfield Fisher's expertise to complete the sections of the novel set in France. Cather and Canfield Fisher had traveled together to France in 1902, and at the time, Cather had been painfully aware of her own provincialism and envied Canfield Fisher's sophistication. When Claude Wheeler arrives in France, he is equally aware of his shortcomings and becomes, in fact, resentful. Janis P. Stout argues that these sections of the novel, and Cather's reliance on Canfield Fisher's help in developing them, reveal Claude's sense of insufficiency as well as Cather's own. According to Stout, Cather's reliance on Canfield Fisher "demonstrates how central, in Cather's conception of the novel, was Claude's sense of cultural deprivation" (49). Like Edith Wharton's *A Son at the Front* and Rebecca West's *The Return of the Soldier, One of Ours* is a novel of the home front, a largely corrupt home front from which escape is desirable. If the novel seems in places to glorify war, to see war as a noble endeavor that finally gives purpose to Claude Wheeler's life, it does so with a sense of bitterness and betrayal and with a strong sense of irony.

Claude Wheeler never loses sight of the spiritually blighted world that produced him. Frankfort, Nebraska, stands for all that is wrong with American culture—its materialism and its religious fanaticism. Steven Trout calls Frankfort "a place of cultural conformity, big business, and the emergence of everything associated with the appropriately constrictive term 'Bible belt'" ("Iconography" 195). Trout's association of big business with the rural Frankfort rings truer than we might imagine. Cather produces in the figure of Claude's brother Bayliss a far more sinister model of American acquisitiveness and coercion than the image of Frankfort alone can achieve.

In the early decades of the twentieth century as science and technology triumphed, the entrepreneurs who made their fortunes researching and manufacturing the new products to fuel American consumerism became important figures in the public eye. Two in particular, Henry Ford and John Harvey Kellogg, promoted their products with a religious zeal, and in doing so, dramatically changed American culture. Both men were evangelical in their approach to business; like Bayliss Wheeler, both believed they knew what was best for American consumers. Business, religion, science, and technology all were to work together to create utopian worlds where everyone drove a basic black Model-T Ford and "learned to live on nuts and toasted cereals" as Enid Royce and her mother do (103). The worlds Ford and Kellogg sought to create were indeed worlds of frightening conformity and little artistic beauty and little pleasure—the same kind of world Bayliss Wheeler and Enid Royce inhabit and, ironically, the same kind of world Americans and the British believed would result from a German victory in the war. And of course by the mid 1930s, Henry Ford had become an icon in what was rapidly becoming Nazi Germany.

Henry Ford perfected the assembly line, paid an astonishing five dollars a day to his workers, and made the Model-T affordable so all his employees could buy one. Ford also published anti-Semitic articles in the *Dearborn (MI) Independent* and employed former boxers to discourage union activity in his plants. Because Ford did not trust the decision-making capabilities of his workers, he officially discouraged drinking and smoking on the part of his employees. Reputed to have said, "History is more or less bunk," Ford remains one of history's most controversial figures. In 1915 Ford financed a trip to Europe, his Peace Ship, in an effort to stop the war, an endeavor that clearly did not succeed and, once the United States entered the war, turned popular opinion against him. An article concerning Ford's unsuccessful bid for a Senate seat in Michigan in the July 1918 issue of *Leslie's Illustrated Weekly Newspaper* endorses Ford's opponent, Truman Newberry, in terms that make Ford out to be manipulative and clownish. Before naming Ford as the subject of his diatribe, Edwin Ralph Estep, author of the piece, raises the rhetorical question whether or not it is "politically practicable to slip an anti-detection suit over a man's past and rush him to the capitol in the guise of a tongue-tied angel with a blue-eyed baby stare" (79). Estep names Ford and goes on to call him, among other things, "the demon propagandist and ship leaser, . . . who put forth a harrowing belch because the United States wanted to loan France and England a few honest dollars that didn't belong to him" (79). Part of Estep's attack involves linking Ford with "an Austrian adventuress," undoubtedly Rosika Schwimmer, who came to the United States on a peace mission and enlisted Ford's help. Schwimmer was one of the "couple of hundred homogomphs" Ford provided with "a free trip to Europe"

(79). Ironically, Schwimmer, a feminist and a Jew, was forced to leave Europe years later when Hitler came to power. The year of her death, she was also nominated for a Nobel Peace Prize, hardly the accomplishment of an adventuress (Flowers and Lahutsky 366). Two things are notable here. First, by 1918, in spite of his successes in the automotive industry, Ford was despised for his opposition to the war; the veiled reference in the *Leslie's* article implies that his connection to Austria motivated Ford's desire for peace. While this article is clearly jingoistic, Ford was also undeniably a Nazi sympathizer before the United States entered World War II. Ford was one of Adolf Hitler's idols. According to John Betton and Thomas J. Hench, Hitler had photos of Ford in his office, and Ford's German plant, Ford Werke, employed slave labor during World War II at the same time his American plants manufactured war planes (533-34). Propaganda of all sorts aside, it would appear that Ford's opportunism—he was after all a major entrepreneur—informed his decisions. When his antiwar efforts failed in 1915, Ford returned to the United States and converted his automobile plants to munitions plants, although Frank Wicks's laudatory article in *Mechanical Engineering* claims he refused to take any profits from the plants.[2] These details are pertinent because they reveal the same kind of amorality reflected in Bayliss Wheeler. Ford ran his plants with the same kind of paternalism, the same kind of interference, and the same kind of spying, as it were, that Bayliss employs against Claude, against Gladys, and even against his mother. Appropriately, Henry Ford becomes a deity in Aldous Huxley's futuristic novel *Brave New World,* which was written while Ford was still alive. Our Ford, as he is called, encourages his followers to remain childlike and to enjoy the art of consumption, to believe, as one of the clichés of the day dictates, that "ending is better than mending." Consumerism and social control join forces here to create a world Bayliss Wheeler would undoubtedly understand. Bayliss is a small-town version of Ford in all his negative glory.

Like Henry Ford, John Harvey Kellogg changed the face of American culture. More than merely the father of Corn Flakes, Kellogg promoted dietary and lifestyle restrictions at his Battle Creek Sanitarium in Michigan. A Seventh-Day Adventist, Kellogg began his medical career at a religious institution and pursued his career with religious enthusiasm. A short filler article published in the journal *Pediatrics* describes some of the outlandish treatments prescribed for patients at the Kellogg sanitarium. Underweight patients were subjected to treatments similar to those used by S. Weir Mitchell to cure "hysteria." Patients often consumed over twenty meals a day and had sandbags placed on their abdomens and their teeth brushed by attendants to avoid burning calories (528). Elizabeth Fee and Theodore M. Brown also point out that one of the Kellogg foundations, the Race Betterment Foundation, was devoted to the "science" of eugenics, a parallel to Ford's anti-Semitism and his connection to the Nazis.

World War I propaganda consistently portrays German *Kultur* as a monster that seeks to control, convert, and destroy. Within this context, Bayliss reflects many of the characteristics of Kultur. Once in France, Claude realizes that Bayliss's world is one to which he does not wish to return. The world Bayliss has created, the world he forces others to inhabit, is no different from the regulated and mechanistic enemy machine. Claude believes, "No battlefield or shattered country he had seen was as ugly as this world would be if men like his brother Bayliss controlled it altogether" (339); that is, Bayliss and the enemy are indistinguishable. In fighting a vague and largely unseen enemy, Claude is fighting the "careful planners" like Bayliss and, by extension his wife, Enid, who are trying to "put [the world] into a straight-jacket" (339). Ironically, while the war frees Claude personally and gives him a sense of purpose, he is helpless against the enemy at home. Bayliss is a force of nature and, like Enid, a force to be reckoned with. The war Claude faces at home is as ugly as the one he faces at the front.

Frankfort is a prison to Claude. Most prominent among his jailers are Bayliss and his father, Nat. Both men keep an eye on Claude, judging and belittling as opportunities arise, but Bayliss instigates much of Claude's torture. Early in the novel when the circus comes to town, Claude thinks about inviting his friend Ernest Havel to eat at the local hotel but does not because he knows Bayliss and his father believe dining out is a form of "putting on airs," a transgression for which he would be criticized. If the two found out—and Claude insists, "Bayliss heard everything"—they would, Claude believes, "get back at him" (11).

This system of surveillance and punishment creates of Frankfort a panopiticonlike model, what Foucault refers to in *Discipline and Punish* as a "disciplinary society" (209), with Bayliss in place as enforcer and executioner. Before the war, Bayliss as well as Enid focus their attention on their "virulent Prohibition[ism]," both literally and figuratively. Bayliss wants to "regulate everybody's diet by his own feeble constitution" (9), and Enid, who goes on yearly pilgrimages to Battle Creek with her mother, is bent on both dietary and religious conversion and sexual repression. Enid has no roosters among the hens on their farm, what neighbor Leonard Dawson refers to as doing "missionary work among [her] chickens" (168). Bayliss is also acquisitive. He buys the old Trevor place, a mansion and local landmark, with the intention of tearing it down rather than restoring it. And always, Bayliss is controlling. He has most likely given the unconventional Gladys Farmer her fur coat with the intention of marrying and thus controlling her. Gladys herself believes that "her own little life was squeezed into an unnatural shape" because of Bayliss (129).

On the surface at least, Bayliss backs up his evangelical beliefs by declaring himself a pacifist when the war breaks out. But Bayliss's pacifism is only an extension of his desire to acquire and control. As he argues against the war in his hardware store, Bayliss repeats not a peaceful philosophy but a cynical one that wants to control the world. America should remain out of the war and, in his words, "gather up what Europe was wasting," at which time, "she would be in actual possession of the capital of the world" (190). Like a vulture, Bayliss would let the two powers fight it out and then scavenge the battlefield for its spoil, a plan unparalleled in its ability to ignore pain and bloodshed, a plan unparalleled in its amorality.

Bayliss's desire for personal and national acquisition mirrors the Allied perception of Germany's desire for world dominance. Before the outbreak of war, however, Americans admired the qualities of hard work and orderliness attributed to Germans and the German "national character." Based on what he has seen of his German neighbors, Claude believes "the German people were pre-eminent in the virtues Americans most admire; a month [before the outbreak of war] he would have said they had all the ideals a decent American boy would fight for" (136). Reflected here, of course, is Cather's own admiration for the immigrant vitality celebrated in *My Ántonia* and elsewhere. But the question of German nationalism is foreign to Claude, and he is surprised at the German invasion of Belgium. In England and the rest of Europe, German militarism was widely distrusted and feared. Rudyard Kipling, for instance, hated Germans with a vengeance and did so long before his son Jack was killed in the war. The poem "For All We Have and Are" makes use of the pejorative term "Hun," as do earlier poems as well. In a letter to Herbert Baillie in January of 1916, after Jack went missing at the battle of the Somme, Kipling declares, "the German is typhoid or plague—Pestis teutonicus, if you like" (355–56). Kipling aside, Germany's preparation for a European war was no secret to many associated with German Emperor Wilhelm II, or Kaiser Bill, as Americans became fond of calling him. James W. Gerard, ambassador to Germany from 1913 to 1917, reports, second hand, a conversation between "a beautiful American woman of [his] acquaintance," (96) and the Crown Prince, son of Wilhelm II, in which the Crown Prince is reported to have said that if his father didn't start a war with the rest of Europe and American, he would. According to Gerard's "acquaintance" the war would be "just for the fun of it" (96). This conversation, which took place during the winter before the war, expresses a prevalent understanding of German military philosophy, albeit an oversimplified one linked to the concept of "Kultur," a word that came to stand for all that was wrong with Germany and German society and that became the focus for the demonization of Germany in both British and American propaganda.

In 1915, two years before American involvement in the war, Funk and Wagnalls published a tiny dictionary of war-words, "A key to the Spelling, Pronunciation and Meaning of many terms brought into public notice by the War." This dictionary defines the word "Kultur" as "Progress, advancement, and achievement in all forms of theory and practice, whether political, economic, scientific, social, or artistic, including the processes involved and the results attained, both mental and material; civilization" (17). This definition, of course, describes all the virtues Claude Wheeler refers to in his assessment of German character, but when the concept is demonized in propaganda, it becomes "That Monstrous Thing Called Kultur" alluded to in an advertisement for Liberty Bonds in the August 1918 issue of *The National Geographic Magazine*. According to the ad copy, Americans are too clean and upright to understand the consequences of Kultur but must, even so, buy war bonds to defeat it. Since the definition of Kultur includes economic endeavor, propaganda published during the war also points to German manufacturing as a facet of German militarism and the evils represented by Kultur. American propaganda leaflets, many published by the American Defense Society, a patriotic organization that lists Theodore Roosevelt as its honorary president, allude to a so-called deal between German manufacturers and the German government. Struck during a series of meetings beginning as early as 1912, the deal promised money and land to German manufacturers who supported the Kaiser's war efforts. The details of the agreement were supposedly revealed in a pamphlet written by August Thyssen, who was promised mining land in Australia and a loan with which to develop it. One American pamphlet entitled *The Most Damning Revelation of Germany's Turpitude Ever Published* tells the Thyssen's story and concludes, "Thyssen's revelations show that Germany's business men definitely entered upon this war to loot the world for their own enrichment," (13) an assessment that similarly could be made of Bayliss Wheeler. Another pamphlet urging an American boycott of German products quotes Thyssen and then goes on to declare "In other words, . . . these infernal scoundrels, the leading business men of Germany, on the confession of one of them, agreed to help their Government to destroy Governments, steal lands, rob banks and individuals, murder unoffending people by wholesale, and when the whole nameless job was done to (in thieves parlance) 'divide up the swag'!" (*Remember*). Minus the murdering, the values attributed to these German manufacturers parallel the policy of acquisition Bayliss Wheeler advocates.

Bayliss's desire to acquire and control is evident from the beginning of the novel. Mary R. Ryder suggests that Bayliss is "insensitive to non-material needs and entertains only the hard facts of interest, debits, and expenditures in running his implement dealership" (156). But his material needs extend to the nonmaterial because they involve so deeply his need to control. When Claude sees Bayliss on the day of the circus, Bayliss has a black eye. Claude does not inquire about it, but later in the day as Leonard Dawson, the Wheelers' neighbor, is driving Claude home, Leonard admits to having hit Bayliss. Leonard explains that he hit Bayliss because Bayliss has made derogatory remarks against Susie Gray, soon to become Susie Dawson. Susie and her friend had cajoled the front man for the circus into buying tickets to the firemen's dinner, and Bayliss doesn't approve of Susie's manner. Bayliss sees himself here as the arbiter of correct behavior and, as such, does not care whose reputation he tarnishes. In a town as small as Frankfort, where gossip is a force, Bayliss and his talk can ruin Susie, but Bayliss does not care as long as he is in control. His presence every day in his farm implement store, where he sees everything, facilitates Bayliss's control; the store becomes the center of the panopticon, and Bayliss, although he remains highly visible, functions as the inspector, the enforcer, the eyes that see all. He makes of Frankfort, in Foucault's words, "a cruel ingenious cage" (205).

Beyond his desire to control, Bayliss has no interest in Susie Gray. But his pursuit of Gladys Farmer reflects both a desire to control and a desire to acquire. Like Claude, Gladys is a free spirit, and in fact, Claude misses an opportunity for happiness when he chooses Enid over Gladys. A talented musician, Gladys loves the finer things in life: clothes, shoes, and trips to Omaha to the opera. While Bayliss acquiesces to some of these desires—Gladys's fur coat, which Enid tells Claude she "suspect[s]" Bayliss of, for example—he does so to establish ownership, a ploy not lost on Claude. The fur also puts Gladys in jeopardy because the coat arouses gossip. Gladys's mother is always behind on her property taxes, and Gladys's clothes garner disapproval. Enid, who is almost a Doppelganger of Bayliss, laughs about the gossip, but for a single woman who must earn her own living teaching school, public disapproval is a real danger. Enid tells Claude, "All the old ladies are so terribly puzzled about [the furs]; they can't find out whether your brother really gave them to her for Christmas or not. If they were sure she bought them for herself, I believe they'd hold a public meeting" (88). This public scrutiny later forces Gladys to abandon her trip to the opera in Omaha because "such an extravagance would have aroused a corrective spirit in all her friends, and in the school-board as well; they would probably have decided not to give her the little increase in salary she counted upon having next year" (129). The desire here on the part of the old ladies and the school board is to squelch any perceived independence on Gladys's part. As long as she is connected to Bayliss, she, perhaps grudgingly, earns Frankfort's approval, but she loses something of herself in the process. Like the destructive force of Kultur, Bayliss makes life bleak, perfunctory, utilitarian.

Even his own mother falls prey to Bayliss's vigilance. At the Wheeler farm for Christmas dinner, Bayliss chides his mother for drinking a second cup of coffee after her meal. In what Cather describes as a "gentle grieved tone," a suggestion of Bayliss's smug self-righteousness, Bayliss tells Evangeline, "I'm sorry to see you taking two [cups], Mother" (76). In response to her assertion that coffee does her no harm, Bayliss replies, "Of course it does; it's a stimulant" (76). To her credit, Mrs. Wheeler ignores Bayliss and has the second cup of coffee. But Gladys understands that her relationship with Bayliss is most likely the source of her doom; she also knows that Claude will "become one of those dead people that moved about the streets of Frankfort" if he marries Enid (128). Correctly assessing the power of the inquisitive eye, Gladys "believe[s] that all things which might make the world beautiful—love and kindness, leisure and art—were shut up in prison, and that successful men like Bayliss Wheeler held the keys" (129). When Gladys finds out that Bayliss has bought the Trevor place, the two couples have embarked on a sleigh ride in newly fallen snow, a moment that should be full of romance. But the moment is far from pleasant for any of the four. Claude is angry because Gladys allows Bayliss to court her, and Gladys is furious with Bayliss for buying a landmark she has for so long wanted. She knows Bayliss will never remodel the house—he resents the whiskey bottles in the cellar—and so she concedes that the house is "spoiled" for her. When Claude angrily asserts that he wants to see the world before he builds a house, Gladys, "in a tone of sudden weariness," asks him to take her with him. Enid, who knows Gladys's true feelings about Bayliss, believes that Bayliss "must have captured Gladys' hand under the buffalo robe" (93). The use of the word capture here underscores Bayliss's goal and Gladys's sense of defeat at his accomplishment of it.

In addition to being Prohibitionists, Bayliss and Enid are both vegetarians; their prescriptive religion and their dietary habits overlap. All of their pursuits take on an evangelical quality. Here again, Bayliss and also Enid reflect an American fixation, not only with materialism and mechanical objects but with food. Just as Henry Ford changed American life with the mass production of the Model-T, John Harvey Kellogg changed American diets with Corn Flakes. The end of the nineteenth century, in fact, saw a number of food fads, among them the revolution in Battle Creek and the evolution of the domestic science movement, a movement designed to apply scientific scrutiny to homemaking, including the art of cooking.[3] Both "movements" appear in *One of Ours*. Cather herself disapproved of the domestic science movement because it encouraged the use of commercially canned and otherwise prepackaged foods at the expense of quality, and it interfered with the idea of immigrant vitality that Cather valued so highly. In a speech to the Fine Art Society in Omaha, Cather raised the issue of standardization, the subject of her address, and said, among other things, "The Americanization committee worker who persuades an old Bohemian housewife that it is better for her to feed her family out of tin cans instead of cooking them a steaming goose for dinner is committing a crime against art" (qtd. in Woodress, *Literary Life* 320). According to Woodress, the Omaha ladies, who undoubtedly used canned foods themselves or had their servants use them, laughed at this assertion. But Cather was correct in her notion that cooking was becoming standardized, and the domestic science movement was the culprit.

Domestic science also promoted the use of labor-saving devices, a notion reflected in Ralph Wheeler's desire to see his mother and Mahailey use the separator he has bought for them to separate milk from cream. Of course, the machine is not practical — it takes much longer to disassemble and scald than hand skimming — but Ralph insists they use it because it is "up-to-date" (17). Claude defends his mother's resistance to the machine and offers to scald it on a Sunday morning so she can get to church on time. But the machine becomes part of the materialistic culture Claude's brothers endorse. Bayliss, of course, sells machinery and thus becomes a source of this standardization at the same time his eating habits promote it. We might also note here that the evangelical zeal of the domestic science movement fed into the war effort in U.S. Food Administration propaganda that encouraged food conservation. Susie Dawson alludes to Enid's practice of domestic science when she tells Leonard that Claude's meals are most likely better when Brother Weldon, the hypocritical minister Claude detests, is visiting than when Enid and Claude are alone. Perplexed at Enid's habits, Susie declares, "Preachers won't be fed on calories, or whatever it is Enid calls 'em, . . . Claude's wife keeps a wonderful kitchen; but so could I, if I never cooked any more than she does" (168). Calories had just become part of new information the modern cook must master, and Enid's knowledge of them makes her as up-to-date as the cream separator.

Enid also uses books on raising chickens, an idea that infuriates Leonard, who rightfully connects her chickens and her religion. After hearing Claude's explanation that their only rooster is cooped because Enid believes unfertilized eggs keep better, Leonard goes home virtually speechless. He tells Susie, "in an awful temper," that Enid "ain't content with practicing prohibition on humankind; she's begun now on the hens" (167). In addition to the chickens, what has put Leonard in a dither is walking in on Claude's supper, which Enid has left for him before heading into town on Prohibition business. The meal most definitely reflects both domestic science and the efforts of food conservation that later came into force under the auspices of the U.S. Food Administration. More suitable for a ladies' tea luncheon, the dinner consists of "a dish of canned salmon with a white sauce; hardboiled eggs, peeled and lying in a nest of lettuce leaves; a bowl of ripe tomatoes, a bit of cold rice pudding; cream and butter" (165). To this feast, Claude adds bread and a newspaper for the war news. We might acknowledge that the new prepared foods present an opportunity for women to get out of the kitchen. But here, Cather is examining what Enid is doing with her free time, not the fact that she has it. In a sentiment similar to the one Gladys expresses, Claude admits that he "suffer[s] . . . in his ideals, in his vague sense of what was beautiful. Enid could make his life hideous to him without ever knowing it. At such times he hated himself for accepting at all her grudging hospitality. He was wronging something in himself" (173).

Ironically, Enid and Bayliss are perfect for each other. Like Ford and Kellogg, the two reformers are intent on promoting what is for them a utopian way of life. Bayliss visits often, and Claude observes that "Enid's vegetarian suppers suited him and . . . they always had [Prohibition] business to discuss" (173). Cather juxtaposes religion, Prohibition, and vegetarianism here, as well as the desire to control, to enforce behavior—in this case on humans, not chickens. Like the coffee his mother drinks after Christmas dinner, alcohol becomes for Bayliss a thing to fear. Claude believes that "Bayliss had a social as well as a hygienic prejudice against alcohol, and he hated it less for the harm it did than for the pleasure it gave" (173). Since Bayliss is a destroyer of pleasure in everyone he touches, with the exception of Enid, Claude is correct to fear and reject his world. While Claude fights on foreign soil, he is indeed fighting an enemy closer to home. After thinking how lost the world would be if men like Bayliss controlled it, Claude concludes in a rare moment of optimism that "until the war broke out, he had supposed they did control it; his boyhood had been clouded and enervated by that belief. The Prussians had believed it, too, apparently. But the event had shown that there were a great many people left who cared about something else" (339). Once again, Claude links Bayliss with Kultur but believes he can defeat them both. His optimism allows him to overlook the reality that Enid is in China doing missionary work, and Bayliss is still entrenched in his hardware store as the eyes of Frankfort, still waiting for the end of war when he can scavenge the ruins of civilization.

By 1922, the year she completed *One of Ours*, Cather had observed four years of postwar cynicism, which color the end of the novel in the response of Claude's sincerely religious mother, who believes Claude is better dead in battle than faced with the disillusionment that caused so many veterans to commit suicide.

After she received the news of Claude's death, Evangeline Wheeler continues to receive Claude's letters and the consoling letters of his comrades and commanding officers. This is a time for Mrs. Wheeler when "human nature looked to her uglier than it had ever done before" (369). Cather's narrative suggests that Mrs. Wheeler no longer accepts those "beautiful beliefs" Claude died with, that she "would have dreaded [his] awakening" (370). Describing the despair and suicide of returning veterans, Mrs. Wheeler understands the need for idealism as a motivation for self-sacrifice, but she also understands the illusory nature of that idealism. Soldiers like Claude had "hoped and believed too much" (370), and their return to civilian life had dashed those hopes. Mrs. Wheeler and Mahailey may believe they feel Claude's presence on the farm, but they do not glory in his death as propaganda demanded of the mothers of fallen heroes.

Elizabeth Shepley Sergeant, Cather's friend for many years, was one of the few of her friends who did not speak favorably of *One of Ours*. Sergeant spent a large part of the war in Paris and was wounded as she toured a battlefield that had not yet been cleared of explosives, an experience she writes of in *Shadow-Shapes: The Journal of a Wounded Woman*. As might be expected, Sergeant viewed the war as a combatant and resists the cleaned up version of war Cather depicts at the end of the novel. But even Sergeant admits that the novel "suffers no disillusion, till [its] last pages" (*Willa Cather* 181). To compare *One of Ours* to Eliot's *The Waste Land* is to miss the irony of its conclusion. In contrast to all the religious hypocrites in the novel, Evangeline Wheeler's religion is personal and unobtrusive. For her to be the one character who understands the force of postwar despair is telling. *The Waste Land* concludes with the speaker declaring, "These fragments I have shored against my ruins" (line 431). *One of Ours* concludes with Mrs. Wheeler's faith intact, and yet in contrast to the more primitive Mahailey's belief, God is perhaps light years away. The synthesis we might wish for eludes us. Claude has died for an illusion, and the "careful planners" (339) are still conducting business as usual.

NOTES

1. For a concise discussion of the critical responses to *One of Ours* as well as a thorough discussion of Cather's contribution to the immense body of World War I literature, see Trout, *Memorial Fictions*.

2. Two letters to the editor in the November 2003 issue of *Mechanical Engineering* take Wicks to task for ignoring Ford's link to Hitler, thereby whitewashing Ford's image as an American business man. Ivan G. Most writes, "Recording history is an awesome task. If we are not accurate, and show both the shine and the smudges, we will propagate myths that do not teach, but confuse" (8). Ford, it might seem, was more smudges than shine. Aldous Huxley's elevation of Ford to a god in *Brave New World* illustrates well the idea of the confusing, or confused, myth.

3. For a further discussion of domestic science in *One of Ours*, see Kingsbury, *The Peculiar Sanity of War*. For an examination of the U.S. Food Administration and its employment of domestic science in World War I propaganda, see Kingsbury, "In Close Touch with Her Government."

WORKS CITED

Betton, John, and Thomas J. Hench. "'Any Color as Long as It's Black': Henry Ford and the Ethics of Business." *Journal of Genocide Research* 4.4 (2002): 533–41.

Cather, Willa. *One of Ours*. 1922. New York: Vintage, 1991.

Eliot, T. S. *The Wasteland and Other Poems*. New York: Harcourt, 1934.

Estep, Edwin Ralph. "How Fickle Is the Public?" *Leslie's Illustrated Weekly Newspaper*. July 20, 1918: 79.

Fee, Elizabeth, and Theodore M. Brown. "John Harvey Kellogg, M.D.: Health Reformer and Antismoking Crusader." *American Journal of Public Health* 92.6 (2002): 935.

Flowers, Ronald B., and Nadia M. Lahutsky. "The Naturalization of Rosika Schwimmer." *A Journal of Church and State* 32.2 (1990): 343–66.

Foucault, Michel. *Discipline and Punish: The Birth of the Prison*. Trans. Alan Sheridan. New York: Vintage, 1991.

Gerard, James W. *My Four Years in Germany*. New York: George H. Doran, 1917.

Glant, Tibor. "Against All Odds: Vira B. Whitehouse and Rosika Schwimmer in Switzerland, 1918." *American Studies International* 40.1 (2002): 34–51.

144

"Kellogg's Flakery." *Pediatrics* 97.4 (1996): 528.

Kingsbury, Celia M. " 'In Close Touch with Her Government': Women and the Domestic Science Movement in World War One Propaganda." *The Recipe Reader: Narratives—Contexts—Traditions.* Ed. Janet Floyd and Laurel Forster. Aldershot: Ashgate, 2003. 88–101.

————. *The Peculiar Sanity of War: Hysteria in the Literature of World War One.* Lubbock: Texas Tech UP, 2002.

Kipling, Rudyard. *The Letters of Rudyard Kipling.* Ed. Thomas Pinney. Vol. 4. Iowa City: U of Iowa P, 1999.

Most, Ivan G. "The Darker Side of Henry Ford." *Mechanical Engineering* 125.11 (2003): 8.

The Most Damning Revelation of Germany's Turpitude Ever Published. Baltimore: Manufacturers Record Publishing, 1918.

Remember—Use Nothing German. New York: American Defense Society, 1918.

Ryder, Mary R. "Sinclair Lewis and Willa Cather: The Intersection of Main Street with One of Ours." *Sinclair Lewis: New Essays in Criticism.* Ed. James M. Hutchisson. Troy NY: Whitston, 1997. 147–61.

Sergeant, Elizabeth Shepley. *Shadow-Shapes: The Journal of a Wounded Woman.* Boston: Houghton Mifflin, 1920.

————. *Willa Cather: A Memoir.* Lincoln: U of Nebraska P, 1963.

Stout, Janis P. "The Making of Willa Cather's *One of Ours.*" *War, Literature, and the Arts: An International Journal of the Humanities* 11.2 (1999): 48–59.

"That Monstrous Thing Called Kultur." Advertisement for U.S. Government Bonds of the Fourth Liberty Loan. *The National Geographic Magazine* 34.2 (1918).

Trout, Steven. *Memorial Fictions: Willa Cather and the First World War.* Lincoln: U of Nebraska P, 2002.

————. "Willa Cather's *One of Ours* and the Iconography of Remembrance." *Cather Studies 4: Willa Cather's Canadian and Old World Connections.* Ed. Robert Thacker and Michael A. Peterman. Lincoln: U of Nebraska P, 1999. 187–204.

War-Words. New York: Funk & Wagnalls, 1915.

Wicks, Frank. "The Remarkable Henry Ford." *Mechanical Engineering* 125.5 (2003): 50–55.

Woodress, James. *Willa Cather: Her Life and Art.* New York: Pegasus, 1970.

————. *Willa Cather: A Literary Life.* Lincoln: U of Nebraska P, 1987.

"As Green as Their Money"
The Doughboy Naïfs in *One of Ours*

MARY R. RYDER

In *The Music Man,* a musical comedy set in the early 1900s, the conman and boys' band salesman Harold Hill, who is aboard a train bound for central Iowa, answers the question "How far are you going, friend?" with the quip "Wherever the people are as green as the money, friend." This answer, though comic, conveys a perception of the people of Middle America that Cather undoubtedly recognized and, to some degree, embraced. The American doughboys she pictures in *One of Ours,* and not just Claude Wheeler, are representatives of this American type and of what her friend Dorothy Canfield Fisher called "dear, tender-hearted, uncomprehending America" (241). While Claude has rightfully been described and criticized as a romantic quester and idealist whose beautiful beliefs make his character unbelievable in the face of the realities of war, what has gone largely unrecognized is that Claude and his compatriots are cut from the same cloth. They are all, or once were, as green as their money, and if Claude is innocent in the extreme, his fellow doughboys are equally naïfs, bumbling young Adams before the Fall.

That these young soldiers come from the center of the nation —largely Kansas and Nebraska—is more than an indication of Cather's personal roots. They are sons of the not undefiled but less contaminated frontier of the Middle West. Like Ellen Boardman in Canfield Fisher's war story "A Little Kansas Leaven," they empathize greatly, dream largely, and strut innocently. Their simple idealism is America's lost heritage, revived for her salvation.

While the last third of *One of Ours* focuses on Claude and his perceptions of war and of his fellow soldiers, Cather's narrative voice—not to be confused with Claude's—introduces more than one green doughboy whose entrenched values are unassailable and who embraces his mission as "God's errand into the wilderness." To keep clear the distinction between Claude's vision and Cather's is tantamount in understanding this text. As Jean Schwind points out in her article "The 'Beautiful' War in *One of Ours,*" Claude's "romantic vision of war" (56) and "the romantic sensibility" of the novel are "part of Cather's fiction, and not the unintentional by-product of her authorial naïveté" (57). When Schwind asserts that Claude's "beautiful beliefs in *One of Ours* are exclusively Claude's" (56), she distinguishes between the narrative and authorial viewpoints, but Claude's view is not singular among those offered by other characters of the novel. It belongs to Claude's compatriots as well. Claude is not the only romantic boy who goes off to war.

In the first chapters of "The Voyage of the Anchises," Cather repeatedly refers to the recruits as "boys," using "men" almost exclusively when they act in concert and under command. As boys, they "moan and shout" (267) when their train makes an unexpected stop, they crowd to the windows to discover the cause, and they come running back to leap aboard the train as it, "like an old turkey-hen," recalls its brood (269). The "boys were disappointed," Cather writes (272), when a misty morning obscures the New York skyline and ruins their "vacation" vista. For the "twenty-five hundred boys, as for Claude" (273), their first glimpse of Lady Liberty inspires a fierce patriotism, and they sail forth "like nothing but a crowd of American boys going to a football game somewhere" (272). They wear looks of "fine candour, . . . cheerful expectancy and confident goodwill" (280–81). In Claude's estimation a "modelled" face like that of the marine Albert Usher stands out as more manly. His regrets and reminiscences seem filled with experiential meaning that is lacking in the Swedish "boys" whose rendition of "Long, Long Ago" entertains the troops (283).

The "open, credulous face" of Claude, whom Victor Morse recognizes as a "novice" (288–89), is replicated in the troops who

have made homage to their Goddess Liberty. Their naïveté begins
to erode, though, as the flu epidemic sweeps the ship. "The boys
lay in heaps on the deck, trying to keep warm by hugging each
other close," and Cather writes tellingly that "excepting those who
were sick, the *boys* turned out to a *man*" for the first burial at sea
(293, italics added). Even the big German-American Fritz Tann-
hauser dies "in perfect dignity . . . like a brave boy giving back
what was not his to keep." Like the others, he was "one of those
farmer boys" who "only wanted to serve" (300). During the height
of the epidemic, Claude, as naïve as his companions, sees one of
his "men misconducting himself, snivelling and crying like a baby
—a fine husky boy of eighteen who had never given any trouble"
(294). Claude's success in bringing the boy back to a manly pose
is due largely to his identification with the youth. They are both
Nebraska boys, whose towns, Claude reminds him, thought they
were sending off men and fine soldiers (295).

That Cather chose the term "boy" to characterize these raw recruits is hardly accidental. As Steven Trout notes in his work on
Cather and the iconography of the war, "Cather relied in part on
the kind of imagery used by organizations such as the American
Legion, the Red Cross, and the Society of the First Division" (66)
in writing *One of Ours* as a kind of memorial fiction to her lost
cousin, and to those Nebraska boys so like him. Surrounded by
the greatest propaganda campaign in history in support of a war,
Cather realistically described the naïve enthusiasm of her culture
in recruiting its boys for what would be the greatest slaughter
of the modern era. In *Words That Won the War,* James R. Mock
and Cedric Larson summarize the power of that campaign on the
nation as a whole: "The Committee on Public Information had
done its work so well that there was a burning eagerness to believe, to conform, to feel the exaltation of joining in a great and
selfless enterprise" (6). The campaign reached into even the re-
motest areas and targeted specifically those rugged youths of rural
America whose strength and stamina would offer the best hope for
"bleeding France." So effective was the dissemination of this propaganda that when a "simple, uneducated family, far from urban
centers of information and five thousand miles across the sea and
land from the battlefields of France, sat down to a threshers' sup-

148

MARY R. RYDER

per in the summer of 1918 they were more conscious of the World War than many more literate people had been of any war since fighting began" (Mock and Larson 6).

That vast appeal to the nation to give up its sons, its boys, was reinforced by a barrage of war posters, which Cather undoubtedly saw.[1] To secure family support for the doughboys, the Victory Boys organization, for example, launched its poster campaign with phrases such as "A million boys behind a million fighters" and "Every American Boy should Enroll in the Victory Boys." For the brothers who were left out of the great adventure because they were too young, here was the opportunity to support the older "boys." One Victory Boys poster showed a little farm boy in overalls with his hand on the shoulder of a soldier who thrusts his bayonet forward. Even if they were too young to serve, boys were not too young to help the war effort. Likewise, the YMCA campaign touted, "Help Us Help Our Boys." In these posters, youth like Claude and his compatriots are pictured as uniformed boys who are little different than they were back home. The YMCA lass pours coffee "For Your Boy"; the Red Cross is "Our Boys' Big Brother," ushering them toward a cozy, lighted home on a hillside in France. Numerous posters call for socks and books for "our boys," and the Salvation Army, picturing an all-American maid with doughnuts and coffee, assures that they "get it to the boys in the trenches over there."[2] Parents are pictured encouraging others to buy liberty bonds for their boys. "You Help My Boy Win the War," pleads one mother whose soldier son's arm encircles her. Even industry is targeted through the U.S. Fuel Administration poster to "Stand by the Boys in the Trenches: Mine More Coal."

Even living in Frankfort, Nebraska, Claude too would have been inundated by such images and influenced by their sophistries. Like his companions, Claude is, to a large degree, "the provincial American midwesterner [who] was not accustomed to dealing with words and abstractions" (Cooperman 52–53). Embracing the war rhetoric that described not only himself but also the bestial Hun, Claude is forced to reconsider his preconceived notions of self-identity and of otherness. The idea of the German Menace, as depicted in war posters, is foreign to his experience. He has only known hard-working German farm neighbors and the well-educated, gracious Erlich brothers, all of whom he admires. Claude muses, "a month ago he would have said they had all the ideals a decent American *boy* would fight for. . . . He still cherished the hope that there had been some great mistake; that this splendid people would apologize and right itself with the world" (166, italics added). To justify his enlistment, Claude can embrace the war rhetoric, even if never fully convinced of its truth, and he remains, as Stanley Cooperman writes, "a good boy, a pure adolescent," and he will be "a brave soldier, an effective officer" (130).

When he then finds himself part of the AEF, Claude is neither still a boy, though perhaps he longs to be, nor yet fully a man. The iconography of the war confirms that he must, though, play a double role in the national imagination. The posters refer to the men in uniform when the troops are wounded or at a military disadvantage: "Our men need drugs and bandages," proclaims one war bond poster; "Our men need first aid kits," reads another. "Shoot Ships to Germany and help American Win," claims a 1917 poster, for without ships, "our men will not have an equal chance to fight." As Cooperman argues, then, "It was still possible for the young men setting out on their bold journey in 1916 or 1917, backed by rhetoric and traditional ideas of what was involved with fighting, to think of war in terms of traditional heroism and a chance for a free visit to a Europe they knew largely from novels" (46). Anxious to escape the narrow experiences of small-town Middle America, they could envision themselves joining "the *men* of history books, the brave soldiers of destiny, doing something more vital than putting in a crop and wondering what the prices would be next harvest time" (Cooperman 52, italics added).

Like Claude, the doughboys thus were destined to live "a double life" (303). They are men on the outside but unflagging boys on the inside. Not having yet developed the "wisdom of the serpent" (as has Victor Morse) or the cultural sophistication of David Gerhardt, the doughboys arrive in France starved for homegrown food and for affection. The "boys" fall like wolves upon the cheesemaker's stock (325) and, like Canfield Fisher's characters, throw American greenbacks at everything in a kind of apology for their behaviors. The shopkeeper sees them as "grown men" (327) with "large, well-shaped hands" (325); simultaneously, they are little boys who cannot even count money and care not if they are cheated. They bumble about on ungainly adolescent legs, stubbing their toes and then examining with keen interest the sunken step, the perpetrating cause of their accident (327). Their "good humour" is unabashed by any situation, and they cannot recognize the flimsiness of the "fictitious values" that they believe will protect them from harm (326). They wear their innocence like a shield, convinced that they will make the world safe. They explore churches because in their minds it was an inescapable duty to do so. Like little boys—Cather's word choice—they express astonishment that fields actually host poppies and that alfalfa grows anyplace beyond the American prairies (339). Every doughboy has his plans to visit Paris, each with a different and confused mental picture of what he will find there. They associate with the famous city "only attributes they [have] been taught to admire"—immensity, vastness, hugeness (341).

Convinced that they harbor secret knowledge that could repair and restore "bleeding France," these boys vow to return after the war and to establish an American Eden, themselves acting as young Adams who will install waterworks and teach the French peasant how to farm. This singular self-assuredness of youth is a cultural bluster that disguises an innocence both attractive in its idealism and repulsive in its arrogance. Claude reminds his "boys" about Americans' bad reputation for "butting in on things" (343), but they laugh off the idea as ludicrous. In their naïveté they are confident that they best model all that is great and good in life, and they cling to time-honored beliefs, one even stoutly arguing that cherubim still guard the Garden of Eden.

All in all, the young Americans, who believe themselves progressive and knowing, mimic the Pal Battalions of "fresh-faced school boys" that they encounter (377). Like the British youth battalions, who, as Claude observes, were "a giggly lot," the American doughboys too are "very young" (374), Cather writes. But Claude doesn't believe that "American boys ever seem as young as that" (378). Claude implicitly makes the distinction between his American boys and British lads, a linguistic variant that underscores the kind of relationship Claude would later develop with the troops under his command. Members of the Pal Battalions are the endearing lads of the Victorian aesthetic movement: fair-haired, "especially beautiful, brave, pure, and vulnerable," the "bright boy knights" (Fussell 275). Cather, an admirer of A. E. Housman's work, was surely aware that the *Shropshire Lad* (1896) had essentially given to the war the image of the "beautiful brave doomed boy" (Fussell 282). In British diction, though, the designation "brave boys" is an homoerotic extension of the term "men" but connotes less sexual attachment than the term "lad" (Fussell 282). Claude, who embraces the American idiom, does not perceive of these "fresh-faced schoolboys" in such terms. Rather than potential lovers, they are pathetic sacrifices to a god of war. He dismisses them as unlike his own doughboys, who were true soldiers, the rightful subjects of patriotic song: "Turn the dark cloud inside out, / Till the boys come home" ("Keep the Home Fires Burning"). Claude would separate the men from the boys, but for Americans back home, the men of the AEF were their boys.

Terribly afraid of "being disliked" and even more afraid of being duped (380), the naïve doughboys are cheered by anything that reminds them of home and the strength of the America that lay behind them—American goods boxes, binders, and even field flowers. Taking to heart the French perception of them as heaven-sent saviors, "men of destiny" (390), these naïve doughboys would, like "new men, just created in a new world" (433), re-create in Beaufort the prairie Edens they have left behind.

That Cather intended Claude as the prototype of the young and naïve American soldiers is without question. Drawing upon the character of her cousin G. P. Cather, who was killed at Cantigny in 1918, Cather made clear that her protagonist was "just a redheaded prairie boy" whom she came to know better than herself. While she found it hard to "cut out all picture making" in this novel because, as she noted, "that boy does not see pictures," she was willing "to pay the price" for conveying an accurate portrait of "this boy" (qtd. in Mahoney 39). Cather allowed to Claude, even on the battlefield, a more culturally enlightened companion, like the Erlich brothers, who could introduce him to "many human and cultural pleasures and realizations" (Sergeant 183), uncolored by the rosy hues of naïve idealism. This "man" appears as David Gerhardt.

MARY R. RYDER

Gerhardt's character was, Cather admitted, inspired by her acquaintance with David Hochstein, the young violinist whom she had first met in 1916. In writing to friends about her three brief encounters with Hochstein, Cather notably refers to him as a "man," never a boy, although he was at age twenty-four approximately the age of Claude. He inculcated the "something splendid" that Claude would seek, and Cather uses that very word, first to describe Hochstein's playing and later in recording his attitude toward his comrades in camp: the men were "splendid," "fine fellows," and he was "learning a great deal" from them, he remarked ("Fiction Recalls" 54). On her first encounter with Hochstein, Cather noted his youthfulness—"very young and fresh among the older men"—but she carefully avoids referring to him as boyish. He is, instead, "a very thoughtful young man" who kept his opinions to himself and didn't draw "rash and comforting conclusions" about the war (53). Like Gerhardt, this man did not accept that "any war could end war" or that this war would make the world safe for democracy (53). Later meeting Hochstein after he had been in camp for a few weeks, Cather saw "a much discouraged young man" and writes that "It was soldiers of his kind, who hadn't any simple, joyful faith or any feeling of being out for a lark, who gave up most, certainly" (54). Like G. P. Cather, Hochstein died in France in 1918, and Cather later found herself recalling the violinist when she was searching for a character who could provide for Claude that "splendid friendship" with someone he could admire. Hochstein's figure "walked into my study," she said, and became that friend, David Gerhardt. She writes, "I had not known him very well, but neither would Claude Wheeler know him very well; the farmer boy hadn't the background, the sophistication to get very far with a man like Hochstein" (qtd. in Bohlke 56–57). In this statement alone, Cather confirms her intent to separate the men from the boys and sets the stage for the encounter of naïve idealism with mature realism in her so-called war novel.

Cather introduces Gerhardt to her narrative through Lieutenant Colonel Scott's viewpoint. He tells Captain Maxey, who needs a replacement officer, "I think I've got a man here . . . a New York man . . . who [has] some experience" (346). While Claude finds nothing patronizing in Gerhardt's manner, he is "ill at ease" with the young officer, perhaps because, as Cather writes, "he did not look boyish" (347). Claude's later assessment of "a man like Gerhardt" as belonging over here in the war because he "had always lived in a more or less rose-coloured world" (375) not only smacks of irony but also reveals Claude's limited understanding of the complex man with whom he billets. By contrast, Claude views the dead Victor Morse as heroic, a kind of "debauched baby," a "little fellow from a little town" for whom the war provided a cinematic backdrop to die like a rebel angel (375). Cather believed that it was men like Gerhardt and Hochstein, not the Victor Morses, who would give up the most in a war like this one, but the boyish Claude is incredulous when Gerhardt asserts that he's lost "much more than time" and can "never go back to the violin" (407). Like Hochstein, Gerhardt explains that he sought no exemption from service: "I didn't feel I was a good enough violinist to admit that I wasn't a man" (407). Almost replicating her own comments on Hochstein, Cather has Gerhardt remark that he doesn't know what the war is for, but it is "certainly not to make the world safe for Democracy, or any rhetoric of that sort" (409).

In his subsequent admission that he now believes in immortality, something about which Claude is confused and unsure, Gerhardt separates himself from the boys philosophically, much as he is separated from them socially. Echoing the Biblical passage "When I was a child, I spoke like a child, I thought like a child; . . . when I became a man, I gave up childish ways" (I Corinthians 13:11), Gerhardt comments that such "ideas used to seem childish to me" but recognizes how befuddling these ideas are still to a boy like Claude. "Oh, don't bother about it!" he advises Claude. "If it comes to you, it comes" (410). Claude, now twenty-five, is "having his youth in France" (410–11); David is concluding his manhood. What seems "childish" to Claude is not the troubling ideas of life, death, and immortality but the absurd tensions he had felt as a prairie youth when he thought he was "going to miss everything" (411). Now part of the "big show" (358), as the war was called, he sees as destiny his meeting with "a man like Gerhardt" whom "he could envy, emulate, wish to be" (411).

Like so many of his fellow doughboys, though, Claude, with his romantic idealism, is destined to remain a boy, never to become the man he wishes to be. After hearing David play his violin for Madame Fleury, Claude has a brief epiphany about his own inadequacies. He is "torn between generous admiration and bitter, bitter envy" (418). Cather writes: "He felt that a man might have been made of him, but nobody had taken the trouble to do it" (418). But, like the boys he commands, Claude lapses into a romantic illusion that the beautiful things in life are recoverable. He tells Gerhardt, "It's men like you that get the worst of it. . . . But as for me, I never knew there was anything worth living for, till this war came on" (419). Claude refuses to believe that the war "has killed everything" (418); in fact, he asserts, "I don't believe it has killed anything. It has only scattered things" (419). The distinct gulf between Claude's voice and Cather's is evident here. Her affection for this "inarticulate" youth "butting his way through the world" (Cather qtd. in Merrill 78) is as genuine as is her respect for the man who realizes that no one is ever going back to anything (409). Cather implies that indeed men could "still die for an idea" (419), but boys like Claude would only die for the wrong idea.

In their advance to the front, Claude, who is deeply committed to his "own adventure" and to "the bright face of danger" (420), goes to find a place for his men to sleep (421), and in response to Captain Maxey's directive, "Come along, *boys*," Claude counters, "The *men* are pretty well beat out, Captain Maxey" (425–26, italics added). Believing that he now knows about life and war, Claude promotes his troop of weary boys to heroic status as splendid men. They take the road as haggard men (426) but begin "squaring their shoulders and throwing out their chests" (428) in a show of childlike bravado before the residents of Beaufort. Later when treated almost like gods for having driven out the Germans, Claude's company revels in the attention they receive, and "the boys [lose] all their bashfulness" (436). Only after observing the troops' relationships with the village women does Claude feel that he must lecture "his men" (436). But, just as in the incident of discovering the dead German officer's photograph of his male lover, Claude does not admit that his men's philandering is anything more than harmless flirtation that merits scolding. For Claude, his splendid men are wonderful boys too, and adult sexual behavior and its consequences are not something he wishes to acknowledge. Claude's admiration for the boy-men under his command follows what Paul Fussell describes as a "standard experience during the war," that is, an "officer's discovery that his attitude toward his men, beginning in anxiety and formality, [turns] into something close to devotion" (164). He cannot chastise them, for they have become a part of himself; together they form a true *comitatus*. Together as men they have embarked on the "great adventure," sanctioned by a shared, boyish idealism.

Interestingly, in the penultimate chapter of the novel, as Company B attempts to hold the Boar's Snout and the Moltke Trench, Cather interchangeably refers to the troops as men and boys, Claude's very perception. They are boys when they are wilted with fatigue or frightened and repulsed by the escaping gases from decaying bodies. They are men when they relieve the exhausted Texas contingent, "dying men" when their trenches explode beneath them, and men who "had become like rock" as they hold the position (451–52). Blind to taking any action except by express command, these doughboys become at once the objects of Cather's respect and of her regret.

Biographers of Cather recount with what interest and compassion she talked with returning men of the American Expeditionary Forces, even having groups of them visit at her Bank Street apartment. She visited sick ones at the hospital and was "moved by these encounters" (Woodress 305). Elizabeth Shepley Sergeant records that Cather "wanted to know" about the war, but as Cather wrote in a letter to Sergeant, many of the thousands of returning doughboys were reluctant to tell all, sure that "they did *not* win the war," and they "hid their decorations . . . under their greatcoats" (155, 154). Still, Cather wrote, they were "so surprisingly endearing, vital!" (qtd. in Sergeant 154). Her simultaneous attraction to these youths and repugnance for the sacrifice they had been asked to make underscore her narrative stance, which appears at times "unstable and shifting," as Sharon O'Brien has pointed out (191). Cather clearly found the "results of this roll call on the prairies" both "terrible" and "wonderful" (qtd. in O'Brien 192). She knew the slim chance such prairie youths had of returning from a war that took eight million lives, but if some vestige of that lost simplicity might endure, she was ready to welcome it.

Cather's vision, however, is not Claude's limited vision. Raymond Wilson correctly asserts that "the person who created the cynical realism of David Gerhardt could not have had Claude's naïveté" (30). Cather is not Claude, but Claude is "meant to be a representative foot soldier" (Skaggs 41). He is one of our boys, in all his innocence, as some early reviewers realized. "Miss Cather intended Claude to be not an exceptional type but a thoroughly representative American soldier," writes Heywood Broun in his *New York World* review of 1922 (133). "His companions in the regiment were like him, American boys never more American than in foreign surroundings and in circumstances unforeseen, inexplicable and appalling," writes another contemporary reviewer (Lovett 146).

If Cather overidealized the American doughboy and the war, as John H. Randall III claims (170), many of her contemporaries did not see it. Rather, they saw in Cather's doughboys their own boys. But that such naïfs should survive the war was problematic, except for their natural vigor and physical stamina. Cather describes the returning transports' decks covered not with boys but "with brown *men*" (455, italics added). "They are not the same men who went away"; they are melancholy, indifferent, and thoughtful (455). A "slightly cynical expression" lies on some faces, and their expressions are likely to "puzzle [their] friends when [they] get home" (456, 457). These returning soldiers are no longer naïve boys. They are men who "square their shoulders and smile knowingly at one another" (457). Only the few return, though, for, like Claude, "Most of the boys who fell in [the] war were unknown, even to themselves. They were too young" (394). Mrs. Wheeler realizes this fact and thinks that "the flood of meanness and greed had been held back just long enough for the *boys* to go over" but that "one by one the heroes of that war, the *men* of dazzling soldiership, leave prematurely the world they have come back to" (458, italics added). The slow-witted but compassionate Mahailey knows instinctively these facts and offers the final characterization of Claude and what he represents: "You'll see your boy up yonder," she tells Mrs. Wheeler (459).

In 1915 Henry James wrote that the war had "used up words . . . and we are now confronted with a depreciation of all our terms, or, otherwise speaking, with a loss of expression" (qtd. in Buitenhuis 61). Through the experience and propaganda of war, language had changed, had even been devalued. Claude, as a representative of his time and of his peers, struggles to find the words that will suffice. He is the doughboy, and they, he. But, in the final analysis, these boys are expected to perform as men, to shed their naïveté and to make the world safe. Cather's war novel thus offers more than the portrait of a singular, disillusioned youth whose high ideals go unmolested by a convenient death. Claude's comrades in arms are as important to Cather's purpose as is her protagonist. If Claude is proud of his "wonderful men" (453), as he perceives them to be, Cather has great affection for her "American boys who had a right to fight for a civilization they knew" (312). They were as green as their money, but they were "dear, tender-hearted," and fully American.

NOTES

1. Cather's acquaintance with such posters is assumed since their national distribution and ubiquitous presence would assure her exposure to them. Images of these posters, including those cited in this text, can be found at a number of Web sites, such as those of the special collections at Georgetown University and Colorado College. The most comprehensive collection to date, providing available information on title, artist, publisher, and approximate date of release, is available from the national archival collection at http://www.lcweb2.loc.gov/pp/wwiposquery.html.

2. Interestingly, Wladyslaw T. Benda, whom Cather chose to illustrate *My Àntonia* (1918), produced war posters as well. One of particular interest he designed in 1918 for the Red Cross. Picturing a young woman knitting socks for the "boys," its appeal is "You Can Help: American Red Cross." The figure is strikingly similar in features to that of Lena Lingard in *My Àntonia*, who stands in a field knitting stockings for her brothers and sisters. (See http://memory.loc.gov/pp/wwiposhtml/wwiposAuthors 01.html.)

WORKS CITED

Bohlke, L. Brent, ed. *Willa Cather in Person: Interviews, Speeches, and Letters.* Lincoln: University of Nebraska Press, 1986.

Broun, Heywood. "It Seems to Me." Rev. of *One of Ours*, by Willa Cather. *New York World*, September 20, 1922: 11. Rpt. in O'Connor, *Willa Cather*, 132–33.

Buitenhuis, Peter. *The Great War of Words: British, American and Canadian Propaganda and Fiction, 1914–1933*. Vancouver: U of British Columbia P, 1987.

Cather, Willa. Interview. "Fiction Recalls Violinist Lost in War." *New York Herald*, December 24, 1922, section 8. Rpt. in Bohlke, *Willa Cather in Person*, 51–57.

———. *One of Ours*. New York: Knopf, 1922.

Cooperman, Stanley. *World War I and the American Novel*. Baltimore: Johns Hopkins P, 1967.

Fisher, Dorothy Canfield. *Home Fires in France*. New York: Holt, 1918.

Fussell, Paul. *The Great War and Modern Memory*. New York: Oxford UP, 1975.

Lovett, Robert Morse. "Americana." Rev. of *One of Ours*, by Willa Cather. *New Republic* 32 (October 11, 1922): 177–78. Rpt. in O'Connor, *Willa Cather*, 145–46.

Mahoney, Eva. "How Willa Cather Found Herself." *Omaha World-Herald*, November 27, 1921. Rpt. in Bohlke, *Willa Cather in Person*, 33–39.

Merrill, Flora. "A Short Story Course Can Only Delay." *New York World*, April 19, 1925, 3:1, 6. Rpt. in Bohlke, *Willa Cather in Person*, 73–80.

Mock, James R., and Cedric Larson. *Words That Won the War: The Story of the Committee on Public Information 1917–1919*. Princeton: Princeton UP, 1939.

O'Brien, Sharon. "Combat Envy and Survivor Guilt: Willa Cather's 'Manly Battle Yarn.'" *Arms and the Woman: War, Gender, and Literary Representation*. Ed. Helen M. Cooper, Adrienne Auslander Munich, and Susan Merrill Squier. Chapel Hill: U of North Carolina P, 1989. 184–204.

O'Connor, Margaret Anne, ed. *Willa Cather: The Contemporary Reviews*. Cambridge: Cambridge UP, 2001.

Randall, John H., III. *The Landscape and the Looking Glass: Willa Cather's Search for Value*. Boston: Houghton Mifflin, 1960.

Schwind, Jean. "The 'Beautiful' War in *One of Ours*." *Modern Fiction Studies* 30 (1984): 53–71.

Sergeant, Elizabeth Shepley. *Willa Cather: A Memoir*. Lincoln: U of Nebraska P, 1953.

Skaggs, Merrill Maguire. *After the World Broke in Two: The Later Novels of Willa Cather*. Charlottesville: UP of Virginia, 1990.

Trout, Steven. *Memorial Fictions: Willa Cather and the First World War.* Lincoln: U of Nebraska P, 2002.

Wilson, Raymond J., III. "Willa Cather's *One of Ours:* A Novel of the Great Plains and the Great War." *Midamerica: The Yearbook of the Society for the Study of Midwestern Literature* (1984): 20–33.

Woodress, James. *Willa Cather: A Literary Life.* Lincoln: U of Nebraska P, 1987.

Recreation in World War I and the Practice of Play in *One of Ours*

MARK A. ROBISON

Thumbing through photo pages in biographies and other books about Willa Cather, one encounters captivating images of an active author posing before natural backdrops. Photographs show Cather propelling a railroad handcar across the high plains of Wyoming and pausing momentarily in the summer woods of New Hampshire, walking staff in hand.

Among my favorite photographs of Cather is a snapshot taken at Mesa Verde, Colorado, in 1915 (see fig. 1). One gloved hand grasping a twisted pine post, Cather gazes steadily at the camera from the shade of a broad-brimmed Stetson. Her white blouse collar flares above her trail outfit as she stands in front of Cliff Palace, the epitome of robust adventuring. Cather, a lifelong practitioner of recreation, knew the benefits of remaining playful. She consistently reinvigorated her work by regulating the conditions under which she labored: by getting away from it all to Nebraska or the desert Southwest, by regularly changing her work setting throughout the calendar year from New York to Jaffrey or Grand Manan and back, and often by moving outdoors to compose and revise.

In the summer of 1919 one of Cather's concerns involved shipping a new tent to Jaffrey, New Hampshire (Stout 73–74), and pitching it in a meadow near the Shattuck Inn, allowing her to work *al fresco* on the manuscript that was to become her Pulitzer Prize–winning novel *One of Ours* (Woodress 309). The novel that emerged features a protagonist who discovers self most clearly in outdoor settings. Reclining in the Wheeler timber claim, gazing at the sea from the rolling deck of the *Anchises*, strolling through

Fig. 1. Cather, seen here at Cliff Palace on Mesa Verde in 1915, made several recreational excursions to the American Southwest. Archives and Special Collections, University of Nebraska–Lincoln Libraries.

the woods and fields of rural France, Claude Wheeler lives most completely—physically, mentally, spiritually—in these moments. Bernard Mergen, in his essay "From Play to Recreation: The Acceptance of Leisure in the United States, 1890–1930," states, "Play, and later recreation and leisure, were symbols of a whole complex of values and attitudes about opportunity, creativity, and self-fulfillment" (55). Both Cather and her protagonist embody what Mergen identifies as core beliefs of the early-twentieth-century play movement: that interaction with nature has the power to restore and that "a separate area for recreation" ought to be established in people's lives (55).

In *One of Ours* Cather traverses the curious intersection between American war efforts and the ideas emerging in the new field of recreation. Within the prairie setting of the first three sections of the novel, Cather weaves playful activities (the very activities promoted by the recreation movement) into the fabric of her plot: picnics, circus outings, ice skating, sleigh riding, walking, athletics, attending concerts and plays. As her characters watch their nation edge into war, however, they experience the increased burdens imposed by wartime conditions on western U.S. farm communities, a situation that not only demonstrates rural families' close connections to the prosecution of warfare in Europe but also points to the need for recreation and its restorative power. What is surprising in Cather's depiction of play, however, is the degree to which recreational activities pervade the novel's war sections. As Cather constructs Claude Wheeler's journey toward war and fashions his experience in the war zone, she continues to surround her protagonist with recreational events: playing music, playing games, reading, singing, dancing, sight-seeing. Indeed, Cather employs the mechanisms of play in showing how Claude's war experience leads the young Nebraskan to begin intellectually and spiritually to reconstruct his life. Just as one would expect a week's holiday to restore vigor to a farm or factory worker, Claude's contact with the war environment elevates his mental, physical, social, and spiritual well-being.

THE RECREATION MOVEMENT

In 1922, the same year that *One of Ours* appeared, the University of Chicago Press published Clarence Rainwater's landmark study of burgeoning recreation trends titled *The Play Movement in the United States*. The recreation movement sought to shape leisure time, employing it for civic and national purposes as well as personal benefits. Rainwater and other authors touted recreational theories, facilities, and programs that encouraged people to spend their leisure hours playfully in physical and social activities because, in so doing, people became socially, spiritually, and physically whole, ultimately returning to their work more efficient and productive. As the United States moved toward engaging in the European conflict in 1917, recreation proponents asserted the benefits provided by recreation in the military training of soldiers.

Rainwater traces the play movement's origins to the sand gardens provided for the children of Boston in 1885 (44) and shows the emergence of recreation centers around 1905 (91). These two features were only the beginning. A growing recognition that recreation would benefit not only children but adults led to an expansion in the number of recreation facilities, their hours of availability, and a widening of the kinds of activities promoted as recreational. Lee Hanmer and Howard Knight's 1915 bibliography *Sources of Information on Play and Recreation* lists twenty-four categories of recreation, including athletics, dramatics, sports, entertainments and socials, motion pictures, rural recreation, and home recreation.

The recreation movement in its various forms emerged in response to, among other factors, a relatively sudden abundance of leisure time for working class persons.[1] Frederic C. Howe reiterates this central concern in a 1914 article: "Leisure for millions is a new factor in the world. It is one of the most significant facts of present-day democracy. What shall we do with this leisure? . . . for the way a people use its leisure determines its civilization almost as much as the way a people works" (415). As the number of hours in the average work day declined and as more child labor laws took effect, people of all ages acquired time for themselves—significant amounts of time. Howe indicates that typical work days shortened from ten and twelve hours in length to eight or nine hours. Howe cites "a recent report of the Department of Labor in Washington [that] shows that in seven years' time working hours have been reduced from 5 to 20 percent in certain trades" (415). To use this newly acquired leisure time profitably became the goal.

Writers extolled recreation's power to restore people to mental, spiritual, and social wholeness, reasoning that reinvigorated workers would be more productive in their jobs. In a 1913 article appearing in a civic planning magazine, *The American City*, H. S. Braucher refers to families whose "need for financial aid might have been avoided had the breadwinners who had worked hour after hour, day after day, year after year, in monotonous factory work, had a chance to play in their leisure hours" (369). Braucher expresses concern for the spiritual well-being of hard-pressed workers for whom "life had ceased to be vital, their spirit had been taken away, efficiency had disappeared, because there was no adequate provision for wholesome pleasure" (369, 371). Many articles of the time recommend specific activities to boost morale. A 1906 *Harper's Weekly* urges its readers to "keep some little side issue, where they turn from time to time, for sheer joy," suggesting stamp collecting, gardening, seeing a good play, walking, playing golf or tennis, boating, listening to music, poetry—the author stipulates "reading, not writing it" ("Relaxation" 1667).

Notice how closely this list corresponds to the recreational activities of Cather's characters in *One of Ours*. During her vacation time, Gladys Farmer walks "out to the mill in the cool of the morning," meeting Enid in the Royce garden, where the two stop "to smell the heliotrope" (151). David Gerhardt enjoys a game of tennis with Claire Fleury between stints in the trenches. Music infiltrates the trenches where the soldiers listen to "Meditations from Thaïs" on a phonograph (370–71). Claude and his mother read together—novels such as *Bleak House* (95) and *Kidnapped* (354) but also the poetry of Longfellow (96)—and later on they read news reports and encyclopedia articles as they attempt to understand the progress of the war. The author of the *Harper's Weekly* article would nod in recognition at Claude's practice of languidly isolating himself "in the deep grass" within the Wheeler timber claim (210) because he is keeping—as the article exhorts—"a little spot solely for the heart's delight . . . a spot whereinto no one enters, so that we are independent of all mischances and changes of mood other than our own" ("Relaxation" 1667). Whenever Claude chooses to walk—whether to campus rather than "sit bumping in a street car" (63) or through the big woods near the Jouberts' home (352–53)—he participates in an activity that the *Harper's* article commends because "it is wholesome for the body, sends blood to the brain and gives it pleasant thoughts, and by reason of the wide and spacious universe we enter . . . it is a recreation replete with spiritual elevation" ("Relaxation" 1667).

Proponents believed that personal benefits resulting from recreation could also contribute to civic and national well-being. A 1916 report on an International Recreation Congress held at Grand Rapids, Michigan, calls for "an American renaissance" based on "the invigoration of American life through wholesome use of leisure hours of all the people." The conference focused on the availability of an estimated three billion leisure hours per week in the United States: "Any great advances in civilization must be developed out of this margin, this slack, this unworked mine. Recreation changes leisure hours from liabilities to assets." A congress speaker queried, "What right have we to hold a recreation congress when Europe is aflame?" One answer that emerges in the report is that recreation provides military benefits. The essentials of military training "are best developed, not by gun drill, but by games, athletics, [and] physical education, . . . [which are] the best means of building character and efficiency—whether for peace or war" ("Play Makes Men"). What appears to be zealous rhetoric became established military policy for American troops deployed in Europe, assuming especial urgency in the months of occupation following the Armistice.

RECREATION FOR THE AMERICAN EXPEDITIONARY FORCES

By early 1919 athletics had superceded other forms of physical training for the American Expeditionary Forces in France.[2] Army bulletins issued after the Armistice give increasing

166

MARK A. ROBISON

attention to athletic events such as tennis tournaments (U.S. Army,
Bulletins 153), golf (239), and horse shows "both as a source of
recreation and entertainment and as a means of stimulating interest in the proper care and treatment of animals and their equipment" (154). A training bulletin published in February 1919 out-
lines plans for an American Expeditionary Forces Championships
in athletic events such as boxing and wrestling, track and field,
baseball, football, basketball, and tennis (162–70). Subsequent
bulletins add events in soccer and swimming (250). The AEF's final
bulletin, issued on June 6, 1919, contains an official baseball schedule listing dates and places for games to be played in cities throughout France and western Germany and authorizes all "travel necessary to carry out the above schedule" (267). Such promotion of
athletic contests addressed a letdown in troop morale that accompanied the cessation of combat.

In his book *Over There: The United States in the Great War, 1917–
1918,* Byron Farwell emphasizes the critical place of recreational
activities in combating low morale after the Armistice:

Morale fell to such an extent that some at [General John J.]
Pershing's headquarters feared soldiers would "go Bolshe-
vist." With the end of hostilities there was a natural relaxation of responsibility and the number of men going AWOL
increased. Fifty-one additional companies of military police
failed to stem the tide. A "morale conference" was called in
Paris and from this sprang the American Legion. Pershing
substituted sports for the hated drill, and on 24 January 1919
Liberty trucks pulled away from the YMCA Paris warehouses
loaded with thirty-four tons of athletic equipment, including
10,000 baseballs, 2,000 footballs, 1,800 soccer balls, nearly
1,500 basketballs, and 600 sets of boxing gloves. (270)

Pershing's pride in the army's implementation of recreational
sports is revealed in his final report to Secretary of War Newton
Baker: "The athletic program in the spring of 1919 culminated in
the Inter-Allied games in June, held in the concrete stadium erected
by our Engineers near Paris, the necessary funds being contributed by the YMCA. In number of participants and quality of entry,
these games probably surpassed any of the past Olympic contests"

(68). In addition to furnishing athletic facilities and equipment, the army in collaboration with the YMCA provided education and amusement to boost troop morale.

Before the Armistice the YMCA offered voluntary educational classes, while afterward the army itself instigated "a systematic organization of nonmilitary educational training," which Pershing deemed "of undoubted value, not only in improving morale, but in concrete benefit to the individual officer and soldier" (69). A pair of army bulletins issued in March 1919 describe nine courses in business education and another thirty courses dealing with mechanical and industrial trade (U.S. Army, *Bulletins* 213–37). Provisions for amusement, most already in place during hostilities, were stepped up after the Armistice. An AEF bulletin published in February 1919 establishes the intent to "provide, so far as possible, suitable entertainment each night in every important center occupied by American troops" (195). In order to accomplish this ambitious scheme, the army appointed entertainment officers in every unit, while the YMCA (which in August of 1917 had been officially designated to provide amusement and recreation to the AEF) supplied professional entertainers and "acted as a training and booking agency for soldier talent." Pershing reported to Secretary Baker that around "650 soldier shows were developed, which entertained hundreds of thousands of soldiers, who will remember this as one of the pleasant and unique enterprises of the American Expeditionary Forces" (68). Of course, the AEF provisions for building morale owe much to the British and French, whose practices of establishing regular leave and providing sports and entertainment for their soldiers were already firmly in place by the time the American forces began arriving in the late spring of 1917.[3] Yet, even before leaving for Europe, troops in U.S. training camps found themselves cared for solicitously.

In 1917 the U.S. government established the Commission on Training Camp Activities (CTCA) "to link together in a comprehensive organization, under official sanction, all the agencies, private and public, which could be utilized to surround our troops with a healthy and cheerful environment" (Wilson vii). At the behest of the CTCA the YMCA, the YWCA, the Knights of Columbus, the Jewish Welfare Board, the Salvation Army, and the American Library Association (ALA) worked to supply recreational services. Headed by Raymond D. Fosdick, the "CTCA promoted the wholesome use of leisure time" (Durham, "Commission" 160), but Fosdick's vision went beyond invigorating individuals and increasing physical and mental efficiency through recreation.[4] According to Weldon B. Durham, military training was seen by President Woodrow Wilson and his advisors as an avenue to "promote progressive social ideas and sustain middle class virtues," and the Commission on Training Camp Activities was a means for achieving "progressive social reform" ("Commission" 160). In the training camps, an environment in which Claude Wheeler spent significant time as an instructor, athletic directors supervised team and individual sports activities while song leaders encouraged "recreational singing" (160). When American troops left U.S. training camps to sail for Europe, the YMCA came along too, continuing to promote CTCA activities and ideals: "In France the YMCA constructed 'Y huts,' each in charge of a 'Y secretary' charged with providing athletic, religious, educational, recreational, and social programs, including motion pictures, organized sports, talent contests, plays, recreational singing, and vaudeville shows as well as pool tables, pianos, and victrolas with records, offering hundreds of thousands of men from lower economic classes unprecedented access to middle class culture" (Farwell 137). Such provision for the well-being of soldiers serving in the AEF prompted President Wilson to remark, "I do not believe it an exaggeration to say that no army ever before assembled has had more conscientious and painstaking thought given to the protection and stimulation of its mental, moral and physical manhood" (vii).

In *One of Ours* Cather refers to AEF recreational opportunities ranging from an impromptu boxing match that Sergeant Hicks sets up on a rainy afternoon in training camp (352) to the availability of entertainment Claude finds at headquarters, where although the major complains, "There's not much to do here, by way of amusement," he nevertheless reveals to Claude that there is a "movie show tonight" (379). Recreational music entertains Claude and his fellow troops aboard the *Anchises*, where fifteen soldiers from small-town Kansas, members of "the town band, [who] had enlisted in a body, had gone into training together, and had never been separated" (276), play afternoon and evening concerts. The U.S. Army actively supported AEF bands, even providing band music in "sets of 78 selections" to "each authorized band in France" (*Bulletins* 239). Soldiers who had talent for music or other entertainments were valued by the army. Although Claude's fellow officer David Gerhardt "came over in the band and got transferred to infantry" (346), he "could have had a soft job . . . as an organizer of camp entertainments" (357) because of his musical abilities. After the Armistice, talented soldiers could opt "to remain in France for entertainment duty" rather than returning stateside with their regular units (U.S. Army, *Bulletins* 198). Singing was encouraged among the soldiers for its "distinct military value" (Allen 68). A 1918 book, *Keeping Our Fighters Fit for War and After*, fairly chirps, "A singing army is a cheerful one, and, other things being equal, a cheerful army is invincible" (Allen 67).[5] Cather's soldiers demonstrate their own version of cheerful invincibility. As they sail past the Statue of Liberty, "the Kansas band in the bow began playing 'Over There.' Two thousand voices took it up, booming out over the water the gay, indomitable resolution of that jaunty air" (273).

Reading as a pastime was supported by the American Library Association, which was authorized to supply "book collections directly to military units and [to loan] books directly to members of the AEF" (U.S. Army, *Bulletins* 137). Donated books were collected by the ALA, who sent them to be read in training camps, on troop ships, and in combat zones. A Charles Buckles Falls poster depicts a uniformed doughboy with rifle and pack slung on his back, carrying a stack of books that rises above his head. The poster's slogan reads: "Books Wanted for Our Men in Camp and 'Over There'; Take Your Gifts to the Public Library" (Kate). Later the ALA provided "a weekly magazine service to every unit whose commanding officer will ask for it" (U.S. Army, *Bulletins* 258). The army itself provided reading matter by initiating the publication of *Stars and Stripes*, "an A.E.F. newspaper, bringing its members regularly every week the news which up to now it has received at best irregularly and in an unsatisfactory manner" (*Bulletins* 39). Men in Claude's unit would agree that news arrives irregularly and unsatisfactorily. Instead of "a little war news" from France they must content themselves by listening to Dell Able read "a clipping from the *Kansas City Star;* a long account by one of the British war correspondents in Mesopotamia" (367).

Beyond the recreation found in reading and making music, the soldiers in *One of Ours* find their greatest renewal through going on leave. The ten-day leave given to B Company after their first combat sortie (401) is three days longer than those normally granted by the AEF. Seven-day leaves were granted every four months to provide extra respite (Pershing 68). The army recognized early on that "the need of relaxation was much greater" for those stationed overseas "because of the constant physical and mental strain . . . [and] isolation from their homes." A system of leaves would help "to protect the morale as well as the health of officers and soldiers" (U.S. Army, *Reports* 218). The army eventually established more than twenty-five leave areas for members of the AEF to experience rejuvenation (Farwell 146), and soldiers on leave found themselves well provided for. General Pershing reported to War Secretary Baker that "in the leave areas free board and lodging at first class hotels were provided for soldiers, and the YMCA furnished recreational and amusement facilities" (68). The army selected leave areas judiciously, preferring locales isolated from population centers, places where soldiers were less likely to contract a venereal disease.

Venereal disease threatened to erode Wilsonian notions of moral and physical manhood. The army made it clear that "sexual continence is the plain duty of members of the AEF, both for the vigorous conduct of the war and for the clean health of the American people after the war (U.S. Army, *Bulletins* 82). According to Farwell, General Pershing was especially vigilant in combating this disease among his troops: "As the venereal rate climbed, Pershing watched it carefully. Reducing it became almost an obsession. James Harbord, Pershing's chief of staff, later remembered: 'There was no subject on which more emphasis was laid, throughout the existence of the American Expeditionary Forces.' In his first six months in France Pershing issued three general orders on the subject. Unit commanders were held responsible for the rate in their units, and at inspections Pershing's first question always addressed the number of venereal cases" (143).[6] Pershing, labeling prostitution as "this menace to the young manhood of the army forces and the health and future well-being of our peoples," battled its presence by declaring all houses of prostitution off-limits to troops, and the army worked with French authorities to make certain that "every effort [would] be made to repress clandestine prostitution and street walkers" (U.S. Army, *Bulletins* 83). In taking such action, Pershing was mirroring vigorous antiprostitution campaigns already encircling army training camps back in the United States, where "women arrested for prostitution in camp zones were confined in CTCA detention houses before trial (their right of habeus corpus thereby suspended) and given medical treatment for venereal disease" (Durham, "Commission" 160). In the army's fight to reduce the incidence of venereal disease, night and weekend leaves were discouraged because they provided "a fertile source of infection, multiplying contacts and delaying prophylaxis" (U.S. Army, *Bulletins* 82). Prophylaxis stations were made readily available and "regular inspections of penises, known as 'short arm inspections'" were carried out (Farwell 142). Soldiers and officers who contracted a venereal disease were subject to courts-martial "sufficiently severe . . . to deter men from willful exposure" (U.S. Army, *Bulletins* 83). If the consequences for having a disease seem high, the treatment for preventing disease was perhaps even more disagreeable: "The procedure to be followed at the prophylaxis stations was set forth by Major Deane C. Howard of the Army Medical Corps in 1912: the external genital organs were first to be thoroughly washed with a solution of bichloride of mercury and then 4 cc. of argyrol was injected into the urethra with 'an ordinary penis syringe,' the solution to remain 'for *full five* minutes'; finally, the entire penis was smeared with two grams of calomel ointment and 'allowed to remain undisturbed'" (Farwell 142). Is it any wonder then that Victor Morse, Claude's cabin mate on the *Anchises* tries to avoid official notice of his symptoms by treating his venereal disease on the sly?

Cather's characters in *One of Ours* dramatize the tussle over morals that was being played out within the American Expeditionary Forces. Victor Morse, whose inebriation and womanizing lead Claude to think of him as "a sort of debauched baby" (375), could serve as poster boy for bad behavior, while Claude

MARK A. ROBISON

more closely represents the official ideal, and one can evaluate each man's moral stance by judging his recreational habits, particularly those involving women. Though he listens to Victor's instruction on "dodging the guard, [and] getting into scrapes with women and getting out again" (289), Claude remains untainted, refusing Victor's invitation to accompany him "in quest of amorous adventure" (332). Instead, Claude prefers the chaste intimacy of visiting Mademoiselle Olive de Courcy of the French Red Cross in a convent garden: "Two people could hardly give each other more if they were together for years, he thought" (391–92). Claude is not an asexual prude. When Cather limns out her protagonist, she inscribes a balanced account of Claude's sexuality. Cather tells readers that Claude is "a boy with strong impulses," yet he retains "a sharp disgust for sensuality" (56). Claude desires females and is desired by them, and as an officer, he does not impose inordinate moral rectitude on the men in his command although he is aware of their having transgressed army demands for sexual forbearance. Army orders stated, "Commanding officers will urge continence on all men of their commands as their duty as soldiers" and, as lieutenant of his company, Claude was obligated to compel "sexual abstinence at the front" (U.S. Army, *Bulletins* 82). While occupying the French town of Beaufort, Claude's men encounter a willing female populace, and although Claude realizes that "a good deal was going on," he deliberately refrains from interfering beyond lecturing "his men at parade" (436). Though Cather shows the degree of vexation that his decision to turn a blind eye toward his men's amorous sprees causes Claude, his willingness to wink at his men's behavior places Claude on middle ground between the licentiousness of Victor Morse and the straightlaced moral rectitude of official army policy. At other times the author's droll tone indicates that Cather did not fully share Pershing's preoccupation with sexual probity. For instance, as Claude travels home on leave from training camp, he peruses "a French phrase-book (made up of sentences chosen for their usefulness to soldiers,—such as; 'Non, jamais je ne regarde les femmes')" (244). The laughably absolute chastity implied by the phrase suggests that Cather considered the extent of army concern over soldiers' sex lives a little silly.

In substituting wholesome activities for other, morally suspect forms of recreation, the army appropriated the practices of the recreation movement to focus on the troublesome problem of venereal disease: "Athletics and amusements [were to] be used to the fullest extent in furthering the practice of continence" in addition to instruction and drill (U.S. Army, *Bulletins* 82). This is not to say, however, that combating sexually transmitted diseases was the only boon that the army saw in employing recreation. Soldiers needed rest and relaxation to restore fighting vigor. The pragmatic employment of play and recreation to maintain troop efficiency contributed to military effectiveness, with life and death consequences. Army officers were urged: "Keep track of the prevalence of colds, sore throats and of depressed health or spirits of any kind among your men. Use every endeavor to prevent exhaustion in marching, drilling and labor of all kinds by judicious use of rest and amusement" (118). Such uses of recreation by the AEF align with recreation movement notions of the power of play to effect "the invigoration of American life through the wholesome use of leisure hours" ("Play Makes Men"). In turn, the wholehearted adoption of recreational practices by the military provided two benefits to the recreation movement. First, the incorporation of recreation and amusement into the army's day-to-day operation offered a unique opportunity to verify the value of play in a wide-ranging, if unscientifically monitored, laboratory. Second, to accustom thousands of young American troops with the frequent and systematic practice of play within an officially sanctioned occupation must have gone far toward expanding the demand for recreational experiences upon their return to civilian America.

If in writing *One of Ours* Cather privileges private and impromptu recreational moments over officially organized activities, she may do so because her protagonist remains suspicious of army attempts to enforce morality. Cather is mostly silent about YMCA activities, but when she does name the organization in *One of Ours*, references to the YMCA are consistently unflattering. Victor Morse sneers at American soldiers in London who never see the city because "they sit in a Y hut and write to their Pollyannas" (288). Early in the novel while Claude is still in college, Cather virtually dismisses YMCA personnel. To soldiers, the quasi-official status of YMCA secretaries as uniformed "militarized civilians" was "a matter of considerable perplexity" in the war zone (U.S. Army, *Reports* 226), and the sight of these personnel must have reminded Claude of his insipid landlord in Lincoln: "Edward Chapin was a man of twenty-six, with an old, wasted face," who was "studying for the ministry" and "did secretarial work for the college and for the Young Men's Christian Association" (32). For Claude, whose dislike of the parasitic Brother Weldon and any others whose "Faith" he viewed as "a substitute for most of the manly qualities he admired" (50), the army's endorsement of YMCA "amusement and recreation by means of its usual program of social, educational, physical, and religious activities" (U.S. Army, *Reports* 226) must have been particularly irksome. Given his antipathy toward those in charge of conducting official recreation, it should come as no surprise that Claude Wheeler creates his own recreational moments. Instead of watching a boxing match, Claude prefers the solitary recreation of walking in "the big wood that had tempted him ever since his arrival" (352). Instead of watching a movie show, Claude seeks out intimate conversation with a French woman. Instead of joining his men at "the dance in the square" (437), Claude meanders through the night-shrouded Beaufort church yard. It is in these quiet moments of his own choosing that Claude finds renewal of mind, body, and spirit.

WAR MEETS RECREATION ON THE HOME FRONT

Wartime uses of recreation at home in the United States went beyond army training camp practices. During World War I the civilian population was mobilized across the home front to prosecute the war effort. The distance between battle front and home front was not as great as twenty-first-century readers might assume, and this proximity can be seen not only in Cather's fiction but also in periodical literature of the day, perhaps no place better than in the *Reclamation Record*, which was circulated throughout the American West by the U.S. Bureau of Reclamation to keep farmers apprised of bureau irrigation projects. While bureau water did not reach their farm on Lovely Creek, the Wheeler family almost certainly would have been aware of the Sweetwater project begun in 1905 on the North Platte River in Wyoming and western Nebraska ("North Platte Project").

Cather takes pains to show how important maps are to the Wheelers in visualizing the conflict in Europe, and, indeed, *Reclamation Record* readers, as early as 1914, were shown maps of the western United States with the names of European nations superimposed upon them "to illustrate the relative areas of the countries now engaged in war as compared with the size of these Western States" ("The Country of Peaceful Progress" 434). As the United States geared up in 1917 to enter the war across the Atlantic, reclamation farmers were reminded by a slogan across the top of the *Reclamation Record* cover page that "every 40-acre farm intensively cultivated will support a family and keep five men at the front" (8:209).[7] Soon after the United States entered the war, President Woodrow Wilson called for large harvests, urging men and boys to "turn in hosts to the farms." Appearing on the cover of the June 1917 *Reclamation Record*, a message from Wilson stresses the importance of food in the war effort: "Upon the farmers of this country, in large measure, rests the fate of the war and the fates of the nations" (257). Women were also called on in significant ways to join the war effort. In 1917 U.S. Interior Secretary Franklin Lane wrote: "The women of America can do no greater work at this time than to raise their own vegetables, can their own fruit, prevent waste in their homes and give impulse and enthusiasm to the men of the land. If they do this they will be doing a good 50 percent of the work of fighting the war to a finish" (qtd. in Littlepage, "Conservation Deluxe" 222). In June 1918 Reclamation Service statistician C. J. Blanchard praised farmers in the manner of a military officer exhorting his troops: "The spring drive to lick the Kaiser is in full blast on our western front. Reclamation farmers . . . are making a supreme effort to down the unspeakable Hun by producing the biggest crop ever wrung from the desert's stubborn breast" (263). In a similarly militaristic vein, Bureau Irrigation Supervisor I. D. O'Donnell refers to weeds as German troops:

June will be the time for their great drive, and, like the Huns, they will come in swarms. They will come in the open and from behind the trenches and over the trenches. . . . And when you mow them down and cut off their first advance, another horde will follow up. . . .
The weed has but one friend on earth, and that is the Kaiser. Do you want to help him? (268)

The linking of farm field to battlefront gave western farmers a new sense of purpose (in addition to anticipation of increased income). In *One of Ours*, Mr. Wheeler puts in six hundred acres of wheat because "on the other side of the world, they would need bread," and this burst of industry prompts his neighbors to remark that "nobody but the Kaiser had ever been able to get Nat Wheeler down to regular work" (171). Claude's joining the army assures that regular work will continue for Nat Wheeler because his son's absence leaves more chores for those who remain at home. Even Mr. Wheeler's request to hire one of his neighbor Gus Yoeder's sons will provide only temporary relief. In Yoeder's acerbic reply that "you can have any of my boys, — till the draft gets them" (242), Cather portends the labor shortfalls to come.

As more and more young men left for the war in Europe, the resulting shortages of labor created hardship for those left behind to carry on with farming. To offset this increasing burden, home front workers were cautioned to husband human resources through recreation.

The August 1917 issue of *Reclamation Record* (see fig. 2) features a photo of a woman on horseback in a mountain meadow; beneath, the secretary of the interior's signature endorses the following statement: "It is even more important now than in times of peace that the health and vitality of the nation's citizens be conserved. That rest and recreation must materially assist in this conservation of human tissue and energy" (353). Later in the same issue, Luella Littlepage writes:

> The strife of nations already has taken some of the men from these new homes . . . leaving the burden of farm and home on the women. In the meantime the Government has been making heavy demands for additional farm work . . . and all

Reclamation Record

ISSUED MONTHLY BY THE RECLAMATION SERVICE
DEPARTMENT OF THE INTERIOR, WASHINGTON, D. C.

Better Business : Better Farming : Better Living

KEEPING HEALTHY IS A PART OF DOING YOUR BIT.

VOLUME 8, No. 8   PRICE {NOTHING FOR OUR WATER USERS, FIFTY CENTS A YEAR FOR OTHERS.}   AUGUST, 1917

AS TO VACATIONS

IT IS EVEN MORE IMPORTANT NOW THAN IN TIMES OF PEACE THAT THE HEALTH AND VITALITY OF THE NATION'S CITIZENSHIP BE CONSERV-ED. THAT REST AND RECREATION MUST MATERIALLY ASSIST IN THIS CONSERVATION OF HUMAN TISSUE AND ENERGY.

Fig. 2. Readers of the *Reclamation Record* were urged to fulfill their role in the war effort by keeping healthy through recreation.

MARK A. ROBISON

kinds of conservation, and quietly and systematically these requests have been made. But there is one thing which we should all hasten to conserve while the conserving is good, and that is our health, for it is the very foundation of efficiency. Get away for a few days and "let go." ("Project Women" 361)

This dictum to get away and let go is illustrated by Cather in the incongruous setting of wartorn France: Claude Wheeler's journey toward war and his immersion in it are conspicuously recreational.

WAR AS RECREATIONAL ACTIVITY

Cather's descriptions of Claude's departure for Europe render the journey nearly indistinguishable from playful pastime. The train ride to Hoboken for embarkation reads like a Saturday excursion; to onlookers, the departing troop ship carries a "howling swarm of brown arms and hats and faces [that] looked like nothing but a crowd of American boys going to a football game somewhere" (274). Sailing to war is a lark. Lieutenant Fanning brings "a pair of white flannel pants," thinking that he might "be asked to a[n English] garden party!" (275–76). A band plays a three o'clock concert on deck. Cather tells us, "After long months of intensive training, the sudden drop into an idle, soothing existence was grateful to them" (278). Such scenes and their corresponding commentary work to heighten the irony that many of these eager voyagers will never return home—some will not even reach Europe—yet Cather refuses to become facilely sardonic. For Cather's protagonist, the voyage of the *Anchises* turns out to be decidedly recreational: in spite of the foul weather, contagion, and death that soon overtake the ship, this sea passage provides a setting in which Claude begins to reconstruct his life. Cather writes, "Here on the *Anchises* [Claude] seemed to begin where childhood had left off" (304). Claude has joined the army because he is searching for solace. As Claude earlier closes up his house after his wife Enid's departure for China, his accompanying soliloquy reveals a person in profound need of recreation:

The débris of human life was more worthless and ugly than the dead and decaying things in nature. Rubbish . . . junk . . . his mind could not picture anything that so exposed and condemned all the dreary, weary, ever-repeated actions by which life is continued from day to day. Actions without meaning. . . . As he looked out and saw the grey landscape through the gently falling snow, he could not help thinking how much better it would be if people could go to sleep like the fields; could be blanketed down under the snow, to wake with their hurts healed and their defeats forgotten. He wondered how he was to go through the years ahead of him, unless he could get rid of this sick feeling in his soul. (223)

Any proponent of the salutary effects of play would have prescribed recreational activity to revitalize this soul-sick man. In Claude's life it is his mother who shows the most solicitude for his well-being, acting as barometer to his mental and spiritual condition, intuitively sensing those infrequent moments when "all was well in his inner kingdom" (69), and it is she who provides an assessment of her son's ultimate situation.

Between shifts of taking care of his sick men aboard the *Anchises*, Claude savors moments of respite: "But when he had an hour to himself on deck, the tingling sense of ever-widening freedom flashed up in him again" (303–04). By describing Claude's voyage as if it involves the discovery of some hidden pleasure, Cather punctuates the incongruity of Claude's reawakening to life amidst sickness and death. When the troop doctor chides him for not missing his life back home on the farm, Claude is exposed: "It was quite true, he realized; the doctor had caught him. He was enjoying himself all the while and didn't want to be safe anywhere. . . . The discomforts and misfortunes of this voyage had not spoiled it for him. . . . Something inside him, as elastic as the grey ridges over which they were tipping, kept bounding up and saying: 'I am all here. I've left everything behind me. I am going over'" (310–11). About Claude's voyage Cather tells us, "He awoke every morning with that sense of freedom and going forward, as if the world were growing bigger each day and he were growing with it" (311), and she insists that Claude's sea voyage and the larger war itself are

MARK A. ROBISON

"miracle" and "golden chance" because they instill "the feeling of purpose, of fateful purpose" in her protagonist's breast (312). By 1922, of course, Cather could not have helped but recognize the deep levels of irony that accompany such an insistence that war achieves no less noble a purpose than revitalizing a Nebraska farm boy. It is as if the novelist herself is indulging in a guilty pleasure. And it is an indulgence in which Cather persists.[8]

With its succinctly reported combat scenes and its refusal to stay mired in the trenches, the fifth section of One of Ours is more travelogue of the French countryside than war chronicle. More significantly, Claude Wheeler's wartime experiences in the book's final chapters coalesce into a restorative tonic to which he responds in a manner that clearly shows their recreational properties at work in him. Shortly before their final battle, Claude tells David Gerhardt, "I never knew there was anything worth living for, till this war came on." Although Gerhardt reminds Claude that war is "a costly way of providing adventure for the young," Claude, transformed by his experiences in France, remains convinced that "no battlefield or shattered country he had seen was as ugly as this world would be if men like his brother Bayliss controlled it altogether." Even distant artillery fire Claude finds comforting because the sounds give him "a feeling of confidence and safety. . . . What they said was, that men could still die for an idea; and would burn all they had made to keep their dreams" (419). Claude still carries this optimistic view as he smilingly dies.

Claude's death embodies a collision between irreconcilables. On one side stands an intense optimism that manifests in the recreation movement, an optimism that commends the re-creation of Claude Wheeler, that celebrates his becoming whole. On the other side lurks a sharp pessimism that decries Claude's ironically wasteful death. As Thomas Hardy says, war is a quaint and curious thing, for, at the moment of his self-actualization, the very vehicle that brings Claude fulfillment also becomes the instrument of his death. Both literally and figuratively, Claude's stance is undermined, and his playground devolves into wasteland.

Yet, Cather's novel does not conclude with Claude's death. In the final pages of One of Ours, Cather continues to depict recreational acts. Not long after Claude is killed, Sergeant Hicks wrangles two weeks' leave to travel to Venice "because he had always heard about it," and when he returns, Bert Fuller throws a wine party to welcome him (456). As the novel closes, Mrs. Wheeler sits reading in the farmhouse when the telephone brings the news of Claude's death. Later, she continues to read the newspapers, and "when she can see nothing that has come of it all but evil, she reads Claude's letters over again and reassures herself" (458). Reassures herself of what? That Claude died before experiencing disillusionment? That "never a doubt stained his bright faith"; that "the call was clear, the cause was glorious" (458) and remained so for Claude? Perhaps.

Like a conscientious army officer keeping track of the health and spirits of one of his men, Mrs. Wheeler discerns Claude's spiritual pulse by reading between the lines. "She divines so much that he did not write. She knows what to read into those short flashes of enthusiasm; how fully he must have found his life before he could let himself go so far—he, who was so afraid of being fooled!" (458). Mrs. Wheeler's concerns for Claude disregard the politics of war. What reassures her is that her son has experienced recreation, that he has found his life, that at the moment of his death, all is well in Claude Wheeler's inner kingdom.

NOTES

1. In addition to noting an increase in leisure time, Jesse Steiner lists several factors including accelerating urbanization, increases in disposable income, a shift in the stance of religious organizations from opposing amusement to promoting recreational programs, and a trend toward governmental agencies assuming responsibility for providing recreational facilities (9–11).

2. Although he would not have experienced the culmination of AEF recreational activity because he was killed in 1918 a month before the Armistice, Claude Wheeler would have witnessed most forms of recreation that were encouraged by the army throughout American involvement in World War I.

3. For a thorough discussion of British use of sports, concert parties, and cinema to raise morale, see Fuller, *Troop Morale*.

4. Fosdick subscribed to Woodrow Wilson's "belief in the perfectability of a morally ordered society," a conviction acquired while he was a

student at Princeton at the same time Wilson was president of that university. Fosdick worked for John D. Rockefeller Jr. as a Bureau of Social Hygiene investigator and later studied the problems of alcoholism and venereal disease among U.S. troops in Mexico for the Wilson administration before being appointed chair of the Commission on Training Camp Activities (Durham, "Fosdick" 234–35).

5. Although the book was written by Edward Frank Allen, the cover bears only the name of the CTCA chairman, Raymond B. Fosdick.

6. Pershing knew firsthand the discomforts of venereal disease. Farwell reports that Pershing "had himself contracted gonorrhea in his youth" (141).

7. Information and quotes from unsigned or untitled materials that appear in the U.S. Reclamation Service's *Reclamation Record* from 1917 and 1918 are cited within the text and are not listed among the works cited.

8. Cather may very well have paid dearly for her insistence on this recreational theme by losing the support of critics looking for a more pessimistic treatment of World War I.

WORKS CITED

Allen, Edward Frank. *Keeping Our Fighters Fit for War and After.* New York: Century, 1918.

Blanchard, C. J. "Current Comments Gathered from the Project Press and People." *Reclamation Record* 9 (1918): 263–66.

Braucher, H. S. "How to Aid the Cause of Public Recreation." *The American City* 8 (1913): 367–71.

Cather, Willa. *One of Ours.* New York: Knopf, 1922.

"The Country of Peaceful Progress." *Reclamation Record* 5 (1914): 434, 436.

Durham, Weldon B. "Commission on Training Camp Activities." *The United States in the First World War: An Encyclopedia.* Ed. Anne Cipriano Venzon. New York: Garland, 1995. 159–61.

———. "Raymond Blaine Fosdick (1883–1972)." *The United States in the First World War: An Encyclopedia.* Ed. Anne Cipriano Venzon. New York: Garland, 1995. 234–35.

Farwell, Byron. *Over There: The United States in the Great War 1917–1918.* New York: Norton, 1999.

Fuller, J. G. *Troop Morale and Popular Culture in the British and Dominion Armies 1914–1918.* Oxford: Clarendon P, 1990.

Hanmer, Lee F., and Howard R. Knight. *Sources of Information on Play and Recreation.* New York: Russell Sage Foundation, 1915.

Howe, Frederic C. "Leisure." *The Survey* 31 (1914): 415–16.

Kate, Maggie, ed. *World War I Posters: 16 Art Stickers*. Mineola NY: Dover, 2000.

Littlepage, Louella. "Conservation Deluxe." *Reclamation Record* 8 (1917): 222–24.

———. "Project Women and Their Interests." *Reclamation Record* 8 (1917): 361–62.

Mergen, Bernard. "From Play to Recreation: The Acceptance of Leisure in the United States, 1890–1930." *Studies in the Anthropology of Play: Papers in Memory of Allan Tindall*. Ed. Phillips Stevens Jr. West Point NY: Leisure P, 1977.

"North Platte Project Nebraska and Wyoming." *Dams, Projects, and Powerplants*. U.S. Bureau of Reclamation. May 4, 2004. http://www.usbr.gov/dataweb/html/northplatte.html.

O'Donnell, I. D. "Hints from a Practical Farmer." *Reclamation Record* 9 (1918): 268–71.

Pershing, John J. "Final Report of General John J. Pershing." *Reports of the Commander-in-Chief, Staff Sections and Services*. U.S. Army. 1948. Washington: GPO, 1991. Vol. 12 of *United States Army in the World War 1917–1919*. 17 vols. 1988–92. 15–71.

"Play Makes Men." *The Survey* 37 (1916): 51.

Rainwater, Clarence E. *The Play Movement in the United States: A Study of Community Recreation*. Chicago: U of Chicago P, 1922.

"Relaxation." *Harper's Weekly* 50 (1906): 1666–67.

Steiner, Jesse. *Americans at Play: Recent Trends in Recreation and Leisure Time Activities*. New York: McGraw-Hill, 1933.

Stout, Janis P., ed. *A Calendar of the Letters of Willa Cather*. Lincoln: U of Nebraska P, 2002.

U.S. Army. *Bulletins, GHQ, AEF*. 1948. Washington: GPO, 1992. Vol. 17 of *United States Army in the World War 1917–1919*. 17 vols. 1988–92.

———. *Reports of the Commander-in-Chief, Staff Sections and Services*. 1948. Washington: GPO, 1991. Vol. 12 of *United States Army in the World War 1917–1919*. 17 vols. 1988–92.

Woodress, James. *Willa Cather: A Literary Life*. Lincoln: U of Nebraska P, 1987.

Wilson, Woodrow. "Special Statement." *Keeping Our Fighters Fit for War and After*. By Edward Frank Allen. New York: Century, 1918. vii–viii.

Culture and the "Cathedral"
Tourism as Potlatch in *One of Ours*

DEBRA RAE COHEN

ANTITOURISM AND CULTURAL POSITIONING

Early in the last section of Willa Cather's *One of Ours*, Claude Wheeler experiences what seems to be a transcendent moment of orientation and meaning. Sitting in what he believes is the cathedral of Rouen, he tries to commune with his surroundings by summoning up what he knows about Gothic architecture:

> Gothic . . . that was a mere word; to him it suggested something very peaked and pointed, sharp arches, steep roofs. It had nothing to do with these slim white columns that rose so straight and far, or with the window, burning up there in its vault of gloom. . . . While he was vainly trying to think about architecture, some recollection of old astronomy lessons brushed across his brain, something about stars whose light travels through space for hundreds of years before it reaches the earth and the human eye. The purple and crimson and peacock-green of this window had been shining quite as long as that before it got to him. . . . He felt distinctly that it went through him and farther still . . . as if his mother were looking over his shoulder. (343)

One of a series of blinkered epiphanies that dot the novel, enabling readers to plot the shifting distance between Cather and her protagonist (which critics of the book most often employ as the prime diagnostic measure of its political positioning),[1] this scene attests to the complex and overdetermined nature of that distance.

On one level the scene functions as a classic moment of modernist irony, with Claude's sense of almost Copernican centrality ironized by his *dis*orientation — not only the lack of fit between his internalized models of "culture" and his immediate perceptions but also the fact that he is actually in the wrong church. Claude's exaggerated reverence for the "cathedral" as exemplar of cultural authenticity — in Georges Bataille's terms, the regulatory "ideal soul" (qtd. in Hollier 47) of an idealized France — thus can be read as calling into question that idealism itself. Indeed, in the maternal oversight that permeates Claude's vision, the passage also prefigures the novel's conclusion, in which Mrs. Wheeler's disillusion leads her to treasure the dead Claude's unsullied "bright faith" (458) as an anachronized relic.

But the scene underscores as well the degree to which *any* American positioning within the war is mediated by notions of cultural belatedness to which Cather (who was capable of romanticizing an elderly Frenchwoman as "a mountain of memories" in which "lay most of one's mental past" [*Not Under Forty* 16]) was herself vulnerable.[2] By 1914 the terms of this belatedness had both shaped and been shaped by the conventions of tourism; indeed, the rhetoric of tourist practice governed much of the discourse surrounding American entry into the war.[3] As Christopher Endy has shown, arguments in favor of intervention, particularly those invoked by women, who had become the target consumers for cultural tourism, raised the specter of "the destruction of the traveler's conception of the Old World as a museum showcasing refinement and civilization" (592). Noted traveler Edith Wharton marshaled her credentials of connoisseurship for the purposes of propaganda, invoking and transmuting the stylized conventions of her own earlier travel chronicles.[4]

Key to this discourse was the mobilization of the exclusionary rhetorical distinction between "tourist" and "real traveler" that Jonathan Culler has identified as itself "integral to [tourism] rather than outside it or beyond it" (156). By the end of the nineteenth century antitourism had become a reflexive mechanism for the construction of cultural distinctions and the testing of cultural representations, a tool for scripting the meanings of what Judith Adler has called "travel performance." As adapted for propaganda, the

discourses of antitourism aligned the insensitive traveler by implication with the Germans, depicted by journalist and popular novelist Clara E. Laughlin—soon to launch her own postwar travel-
guide empire—as harboring "a long-cherished determination to
supersede French civilization and to consign it to oblivion" (*Martyred* vi).

Such antitouristic distinctions help shape much American fiction of the First World War, particularly that by women. Key moments of epistemological crisis in such works are often rendered
in terms of touristic spatiality; rather than the maps of the generals, as so often in British novels of the war,[5] it's Baedeker and
Murray whose representations prove inadequate to a newly chaotic world. Within a particular subset of popular war novels published between 1915 and the writing of *One of Ours*—most of them
propagandistic, preemptively or retrospectively justifying American intervention—the quality of their prior touristic practice functions as a predictor of characters' ability to negotiate the epistemological minefields of wartime France; the discourses of antitourism
are mobilized to distinguish those sensitive enough to endorse war
in defense of "culture" from those "mere tourists" for whom it
represents a collapse of that rationality and logistical control they
associate with America itself.

To read *One of Ours* in the context of such novels is to illumi-
nate not only Cather's attitudes toward such "rational" control as
manifested in the processes of homogenization and accumulation
that mark the novel, processes often identified by critics with the
"birth of [American] empire" (Urgo 144), but also her relationship
to her protagonist. The relevance of tourist practice to *One of Ours*
has not been ignored: Steven Trout, drawing on the research of
Mark Meigs, has recently elucidated the importance for the novel
of the historical motivation-building exercises of the AEF, and in
particular the training of doughboys in the ways of tourism and
consumption. Trout argues convincingly that Cather ties Claude's
growing identification with his fellow Americans to his internal-
ization of the AEF cultural agenda. Yet in doing so Trout natural-
izes the tourist/traveler dichotomy, which mediated Cather's own
travel experiences and those of her contemporaries and thus underlies *One of Ours* as much as do the actual practices of the AEF: in-

deed, in Cather's self-conscious modernist reworking of the popular propaganda form, the complex relations between Claude and Cather are negotiated along the fault line of the tourist/traveler divide.[6]

COLLAPSING THE ITINERARY

Recapitulating the "self-exemptive self-fashioning" (Buzard 336) of nineteenth- and early-twentieth-century travel writing, the popular war novels of writers like Anna Robeson Burr, Clara E. Laughlin, and Mary Hastings Bradley manipulate the antitouristic dialectic of self-distinction and solidarity—setting oneself apart from the "herd," appealing to the like-minded—to support their interventionist message. These novels exploit persistent exclusionary distinctions between "tourist" and "traveler" to link survival in disrupted wartime space to sensitivity toward the French war effort; those characters most wedded to the rigid predictors of itinerary and schedule—those unable to adapt effectively to wartime fracturing, fluidity, and unpredictability—also prove impervious to the emotional appeal of the war and of service. The initial moment of trial in these novels—the moment of testing and fracture—invariably depicts American tourists in Europe, usually France, overtaken by the onrush of war. This moment of crisis when tour turns to war, when the itinerary, the "map" of time, collapses into meaninglessness, distinguishes a moral hierarchy of travelers: those passively wedded to a predictable, well-worn and, implicitly, Americanized version of touristic space, for whom the collapse of tourist routine renders that space unprecedentedly and terrifyingly "foreign" (for whom, in other words, foreignness *equals* chaos); those logistically and rationally adept—usually planners of their own travel itineraries—who are capable of negotiating escape from a chaoticized environment that they assume results from a dearth of American pragmatism (for whom, in other words, American neutrality is the only rational stance); and finally, those anointed by the text as a special class of sensitives, able to intuit their proper path in a world without tourist markers (those, in other words, who choose to stay on in Europe).

The key point here is not simply that these models depict the inevitable disruption of prewar models of touristic practice but that they exploit and echo the hierarchical discourses of tourism itself to suggest a new ontological map for wartime behavior. American pragmatism, within the propaganda fictions, is not sufficient to "remap" the wartime world properly but must be tied to a spiritualized affinity with France, the attribute of the "authentic" traveler. In Anna Robeson Burr's 1921 *The House on Charles Street*, for example, two young women caught by the war while on holiday in the Alps stand apart from the panic-stricken and hysterically abusive crowds who "linger in tears" (20) around the landmarks of American Europe—banks, telegraph offices, the lobbies of luxury hotels—and whose lumpen-tourist status is reflected in the "herd impulse" that now "stampede[s] them to their homes" (7). But the two also stand in contrast to one another. Elizabeth, the pragmatist, who has briskly negotiated the "chief business" (21) of European travel, "moving on well-laid rails of training and purpose toward definite ends" (17), while wrapped in an aura of efficiency that "enfold[s] her as completely as a diver's helmet" (15), now finds herself to be "the spectator of a universal madness, which must pass; or the dreamer of a dream too hateful and too vivid to last" (5). She considers that "the whole continent had suddenly turned itself into an assemblage of dangerous lunatics and the sensible thing to do was to get back as quickly as possible to the only country where people were still sane" (22). For her more sensitive and imaginative friend Sydney, meanwhile, the withdrawal of logistical certainty is in and of itself unimportant—"What does it matter if the Americans get home comfortably or not?" she asks Elizabeth (20). Rather, it prompts the reawakening of buried, intuitive, modes of perception, "certain stirrings in her own soul—movements which, while new, are yet very old. . . . These had as yet no vocabulary, but one was forming fast" (5). The image of Mont Blanc, the tourist destination that looms over these reflections, serves as the touchstone for the women's differing responses. For Elizabeth, Mont Blanc, in its aloof inaccessibility, is emblematic of her displacement from logistical and perceptual centrality, her disorientation by forces that "did not seem to have taken account of her at all" (7), while for Sydney the mountain's iconic self-sufficiency—the very existence of that different, distinct, per-spective—is somehow comforting.

Sydney's response to the crisis is prefigured in her own previous approach to travel. Sydney is "thrilled to the soul," thinks Eliza-beth indignantly, not by certified monuments and masterpieces but by "trifles merely curious. . . . A skylark, which, springing up from her feet, had lost itself, singing in the blue; a London policeman standing impassive in the evening mist; a Savoyard woman, knit-ting, as she walked behind her cattle—these had been the sights which had brought delight into Sydney's eyes" (21–22). Burr ranges Sydney's idiosyncratic, synecdochal "map" of European sights in opposition to guidebook travel, whether active or passive, and implicitly to the American version, in which, as Terry Caesar puts it, "the American travels, first, as an American, and second, in order to have a more encompassing experience of the world that never ceases to be a deeper experience of America itself" (73).

The moral hierarchy thus established is allowed to persist throughout these war novels to distinguish, as Jean Méral has noted, between come-first and come-lately Francophiles; those with the empathetic sensitivity to navigate a disrupted Paris resent the reimposition of, in effect, an American spatial grid. Late in *The House on Charles Street*, Elizabeth's return to Europe, as now "the most aggressive of pro-Allies" (248), carries the epistemological arrogance and discipline of the encyclopedic guidebook: "There was nothing apparently in the soul of France concealed from her. . . . She knew all about the beauty of French family life; the cus-tom of the *dot;* the advisability of light wines; and 'our obligations to Lafayette.' . . . Her soul seemed to have put on uniform as well as her body" (249).

By contrast, Sydney's "map"—subjective, nonhierarchical, fem-inized—prefigures a kind of wartime orientation by affinity that marks her and similar protagonists of these fictions. In Mary Hast-ings Bradley's *The Splendid Chance*, published in 1915, for example, the heroine Katherine's status as "the real thing" (17)—an Ameri-can traveling to Paris to be an artist, not a tourist—is confirmed by her perception of Paris as a discontinuous "bright and shift-ing spectacle" (35) experienced as vignettes or "purple and gold masses" (34) rather than a series of tourist views or historic sites.

190

Indeed, although Katherine continually (and typically) refers to tourists in order to reconfirm her own distinct status—chiding a fellow artist for not condescending to allow a group of old ladies to tour his studio with the words "It would have given them the feeling that they were really seeing Paris" (99)—not until the second, wartime, section of the book does she list tourist "sights," and then only as a collection of vulnerabilities. Even as the enumeration of French cultural sites serves the arguments for American intervention, that enumeration is depicted here as analogous to enemy targeting, the "mapping" of Paris through gunsights.

Katherine's own mode of orientation, once she has proved immune to the touristic "contagion for flight" (177), is foreshadowed by Bradley in an image of Katherine's Parisian concierge, "whose wrinkled face was a map of shrewd experience" (41–42). Katherine's spiritual union with the French in their suffering—her ability to read that emotive, idiosyncratic "map"—allows her to perform feats of associative orienteering, such as winding up in the very village in which her lover's company is beset by German troops or wandering across No Man's Land to end up at his dying side. Similarly, in Clara E. Laughlin's *The Keys of Heaven* (1918), a visionary businessman flees the materialist demands of his superficial wife and, while the world thinks him dead, achieves apotheosis and pure love in France as an elevated anti-Baedeker species of travel courier, rejoicing in a sense of spiritual heirship that prefigures, of course, his further transfiguration into a comrade-in-arms. In these works the "map" of emotive experience proves more reliable than those wielded by invaders—whether American tourists or German military—bent on acquisitive remapping in their own images.

ARMY OF TOURISTS

Cather, in *One of Ours*, alludes to the key elements of these novels' design, especially the separation into categories of American travelers. The panoply of touristic alternatives presented by the propaganda novels is recapitulated here as what Trout has identified as an array of case studies of the "cross-cultural impulse" (76) populating the later sections of the book. But categorical distinctions that equate tourists with invaders are necessarily problematized when the invading army is one's own. The presence of tourist rhetoric in *One of Ours* foregrounds the contradictions by which tourism becomes war's metaphorical opposite and double:[7] a war to "preserve culture," which confirms its status as such by the touristic enumneration of "important sites," nevertheless participates in the erosion of that culture in the very process of "saving" it,[8] by the imperial intrusion of what Joseph R. Urgo calls "the idea of made things" (151).[9] As Trout and Urgo have both noted, the scene of the "invasion" of the French cheese shop by Sergeant Hicks and his men is key in this regard, with its interpolation of the shopowner's voice bemoaning the substitution of "fictitious values" (326) for the real in the wake of the arrival of American money and American goods, "shiploads of useless things" (327).

Yet what is Claude's relation to this process? If Hicks and his men are meant to appear as "an especially amusing band of ugly Americans" (Trout 88), then, by analogy with the propaganda novels, Claude, whose touristic mode seems so distinctly different, would seem to represent the "authentic" sensitive. Indeed, Cather's presentation of Claude can be and has been read in ways that unproblematically preserve the tourist/traveler divide — as John N. Swift and Joseph R. Urgo do, for example, when they class Claude among Cather's "good tourists" as opposed to her "bad" ones (1). Claude's attempt to embrace culture, his Francophilia, his desire to learn the language and know the "real" French, all seem to locate him within the standard scripting of cultural tourism, undertaken, says Adler, as a means of "bestowing meaning on the self" (1368) through the antitouristic mechanism of "self-exemptive self-fashioning" (Buzard 336). Whereas, as Trout points out, Sergeant Hicks and his merry band conduct themselves according to an AEF-derived checklist model, set on gleaning "touristy facts and figures . . . for the future edification of the folks back home" (86–87), Claude's own impulse is to measure himself against a model of an "authentically" sensitive relation to France — in other words, to think of himself as traveler, not tourist, in keeping with the rhetoric of antitouristic othering. Though he does not despise his men, he does not form part of their touristic army:

DEBRA RAE COHEN

he facilitates but does not participate in the consumerist gutting of the cheese shop; in Rouen, he follows, or so it appears, his own cultural star, breaking a trail apart from the Hicksian beaten path. In the "cathedral," for example, as Claude positions himself for self-authenticating revelation, to receive "the superlatives toward which his mind had always been groping" (342), he mentally distinguishes himself from the Americans who have earned opprobrium by "slouching all over the place and butting in on things" (343). And the "guidebook" against which he measures himself is an internalized model of culture that can confirm his ontological distinction.[10] But whereas Burr uses the Europe-inspired new-ancient "stirrings" of her heroine Sydney to endorse the notion of a distinction she can then employ in turn to endorse the American war effort, Cather allows Claude to appeal to such distinctions to bootstrap doubtful revelation—thus fueling uncertainty about the distinctions themselves as well as any propaganda purposes for which they might be used. Indeed, Claude's "self-exemptive self-fashioning," like his need to distinguish himself from the Frankfort culture of waste, is defensive and self-exculpatory (he clears the decks for his musings on gothic architecture by practicing—in French—the excuse he will give if his presence is challenged), reflecting a touristic status that is itself far from stable. If to Hicks and his crew Claude represents the authentic traveler who can "speak French like a native," in the presence of David Gerhardt he himself is the hick, absolved of the responsibilities of courtesy to his French hosts by his assumed linguistic incompetence (327, 415) and filled, in his recognition of his own inauthenticity, with self-loathing. Listening to Gerhardt play the violin, he condemns himself as a "wooden thing amongst living people" (418)—implicitly too insensitive to appreciate, let alone create, culture. He sees himself doomed only to "paw and upset things," to "break and destroy"—conflating himself by implication in the first clause with the class of intrusive Americans from whom he was so anxious, in the "cathedral," to be recognized as distinct, and in the second with the Germans. If, in terms of Claude's own psychology, we can read these blurred boundaries of identification as equating to anxieties and longings related to both class and sexuality, they function in Cather's larger project as implicit commentary on the inherent contradictions of the position of the military "traveler," deliberately unsettling the expectations—the "itinerary"—of readers seeking a secure position.

Even the "cathedral" scene itself not only renders ambiguous Claude's relation to the homogenizing tourism of the AEF but also implicates readers in that ambiguity. Claude, in pursuing a touristic path seemingly distinct from that of his men, is nevertheless actually attempting the same pilgrimage—to follow in the steps of Joan of Arc.

As Trout points out, the Maid of Orleans is central to Claude's early romantic vision of France (49); she floats surrounded in his imagination by a vague haze of ancillary images ("the banner with lilies . . . a great church . . . cities with walls" [62]) that prefigure their later reacquisition as tourist views. Cather shows us Claude marveling at the ability of such "essential facts"—"a picture, a word, a phrase"—to move the minds of children, signaling to readers the sheer typicality of Claude's romantic imaginings (as well as proleptically ironizing the iconographic use of Joan of Arc in the war effort).[11] Claude's academic study of Joan—though it is at the time "quite the most important thing in his life" (61)—also involves the naïve retracing of well-worn paths, visiting evidence previously "pawed over" (61) (a verb the text associates with the touristic invasion).

Indeed, the annexation of Joan of Arc for the purposes of American self-improvement formed a vital part of the prewar conventions of tourism. Laughlin's 1914 novel *Everybody's Birthright: A Vision of Jeanne d'Arc,* for example, uses the framework of a travel narrative as sentimental conduct-fiction, in which girls are urged to be "imbued with the spirit of the Maid" (101) through visits to the "holy" sites of her history (136)—a prescription that enacts what Judith Adler sees as a characteristic trope of travel performance: "In a double movement of projection and reinternalization, values are emblematically fixed in landscape and then reappropriated through encounter with literal geography" (1376). Such "reappropriation" of sites associated with Joan of Arc was, by the war, already so much a touristic cliché that Cather alludes to it by omission: "Everybody knew what had happened at Rouen— if any one didn't, his neighbors were only too eager to inform him!

It had happened in the market-place, and the market-place was what they were going to find" (341). Cather collapses distinction between modes of tourism here; Claude's difference disappears. Readers too are rendered part of the touristic herd by virtue of their assumed familiarity with the site of Joan's execution, eroding their distance from implication in wartime depredations just as Claude's assertions of "culture" are eroded.

The "cathedral" scene, in which Claude "[finds] himself alone" (341),[12] follows a long sequence detailing the responses of the "boys" to the French countryside and their expectations for the city—a sequence that continually unsettles Claude's relation to the "boys" and their perceptions, in another example of the destabilizing effect of what Guy Reynolds identifies as Cather's use of free indirect discourse.[13] Perceptions credited specifically to Claude and clearly characteristic of his own impulses toward "culture" ("Deeper and deeper into flowery France! That was the sentence Claude kept saying over to himself." [339]) are juxtaposed with perceptions even more naïve that seem just as clearly not his ("There seemed to be a good deal of France that wasn't the war." [340]). At other times, as in the "boys'" astonishment at finding cottonwoods in France, their perceptions overlap and merge. This unsettling sequence ends with the characterization of the "boys'" suppositions about Paris—a scene that does not locate Claude either within or without:

> Only a little way up that river was Paris, the place where every doughboy meant to go; and as they leaned on the rail and looked down at the slow-flowing water, each one had in his mind a confused picture of what it would be like. The Seine, they felt sure, must be very much wider there, and it was spanned by many bridges, all longer than the bridge over the Missouri at Omaha. There would be spires and golden domes past counting, all the buildings higher than anything in Chicago, and brilliant—dazzlingly brilliant, nothing grey and shabby about it like this old Rouen. They attributed to the city of their desire incalculable immensity, bewildering vastness, Babylonian hugeness and heaviness—the only attributes they had been taught to admire. (341)

The end of this passage is particularly significant in its conflation of the mechanics of tourist practice with the culture of grandiosity and waste that Claude has spent the novel fleeing. One is tempted to see Cather's characterization of the soldiers' expectations, in its evocation of these cultural ideals, as excluding Claude, but once again this is left deliberately ambiguous—setting up readers for the difference-that-is-no-difference, the revelation-that-is-no-revelation, of the "cathedral" scene itself. The "Paris" passage suggests not just the structural contiguity of tourism and waste (as does the scene in the cheese shop) but also the illusory nature of the immunity from this contiguity that the tourist/traveler distinction provides.

PARIS IS BURNING

The degree to which, in *One of Ours,* the self-exemptive self-fashioning of antitouristic rhetoric is collapsed back onto itself, revealed to be structurally part of the system (in an anticipation of the arguments of contemporary theorists of tourism)[14] clearly marks the book's divergence from the model of antitourism utilized in the popular novels. So too does Cather's important metaphoric linkage between tourism and waste, an equation that's structurally disguised in practice by what Caesar calls the "imperative of usefulness" inherent in American cultural tourism (61). Travel, one might say, entails the wasting of capital through leisure display in a way that "purchases" not only cultural distinction but also a sense of coherent American identity and an "authenticity" only obtainable, due to cultural belatedness, from abroad. What's being described here is the mechanism of potlatch, the deceptive mechanism of competitive "wastage" of capital central to the theories of Georges Bataille; the centrality of the potlatch mechanism in both the Nebraskan and European sections of *One of Ours* underscores the structural identity of the experiences that Claude mistakenly reads as distinct—the way that one is metaphorically "mapped" onto the other—and thus Claude's own implication in the processes from which he tries, both literally and metaphorically, to distance himself.[15]

DEBRA RAE COHEN

Bataille's notion of the "general economy" hinges on the inas-similable nature of excess and the need for "catastrophic expenditure" to eliminate surplus wealth. Capitalism, he maintains, has replaced the transcendent, erotic expenditure of unproductive sacrifice with the self-deception of potlatch, the competitive giving of gifts or destruction of capital—the acquisition, through expenditure, of the rank and prestige that attaches to the capacity to lose. The potlatch mechanism, and the self-deception attached to it, underlies both the Frankfort culture of waste and the expenditure of cultural tourism and links both to the "wastage" of war.[16]

Bataille claims that it is only single beings or discrete groups who are plagued by the problem of necessity; systems as a whole must deal with "the general movement of exudation (of waste)" (*Accursed Share* 23). Societies define themselves by the choices that they make in relation to this problem of expenditure. "Unproductive works" (25) break the lockstep reproductive cycle of growth in which all expenditure is fed back into a closed system until an explosion—such as war—results; Bataille blames just such "industrial plethora" for the outbreak of both world wars.

Early societies, says Bataille, to relieve the blockage of excess, relied on festivals, the building of useless monuments, and especially on sacrifice, for Bataille the epitome of transcendent expenditure, the blind spot in the rational economy, in which sacrificers and victim fuse in a public sundering of taboos. Sacrifice represents the return to the sacred of that which has been made into merely a thing (55–61). In *One of Ours*, the judgmental bourgeois society of Frankfort suppresses such useless expenditure, condemning what it terms "waste" in favor of relentless accumulation.[17] To Frankfort, "waste" connotes inappropriate spending, spending, as Claude says of the Erlichs, "on [oneself] instead of on machines" (43); thus Gladys Farmer's extravagance is spoken of almost as a sexual sin—one that can only be "cured" by marriage. The very word "waste" takes on an erotic charge in the text by its relationship to thwarted desire; Claude wishes that Enid "would ask for something unreasonable and extravagant" (176) with a secret, almost voyeuristic longing. Bemoaning his lot on the steps of the State House in Denver, Claude rails against the "waste of power" involved in his interior "storm" (118), conjuring up for readers a vision of onanistic profusion to which he himself—in another blinkered epiphany—seems blind. The discipline involved in thwarting useless expenditure threatens to turn Claude, thinks Gladys, into yet another "thing"—"a big machine with the springs broken inside" (156).

The potentially transformative energies of unproductive expenditure are harnessed, in the production economy, says Bataille, into the deceptive practice of potlatch, expenditure that purchases not material goods but the markers of status that come with the capacity to squander.[18] In *One of Ours* the potlatch mechanism is first and most clearly demonstrated in the person of Nat Wheeler, who gives "liberally to churches and charities" (7) and is known for his open hand to his neighbor, which serves to emphasize his own well-being; he has the power to "waste" the cherry tree as a visible demonstration of how much (and whom) else he owns. With his seemingly unproductive spending, he purchases his status in the community. At the same time, Nat's continued acquisition of land seems self-evident to him as a course of action: as he expostulates to his wife, "You might as well ask me why I want to make more money when I haven't spent all I've got" (66).

Potlatch, then, represents a masking of the impulse to acquire that actually facilitates continued accumulation; it lies behind not only commerce but charity, leisure spending, and warfare as well: it is the willingness to expend vital resources in war that yields a return in terms of empire and "glory" (Bataille, *Accursed Share* 71). Elaine Scarry describes war as "a contest" in which "the goal is to out-injure the opponent" (63). Since to "out-injure" means to bring the opponent to its own "perceived level of intolerable injury" before one's own is reached (89), this is obviously a potlatch competition; the willingness to expend resources unprofitably becomes a path to the status of "victor." The ties here to touristic display, largesse, and consumption, to the "legend of waste and prodigality" (326) that the cheese shop owner identifies with Sergeant Hicks and his touristic army, are clear. The owner's condemnation of "fictitious values" spills over onto all the values acquired through potlatch—rank, status, hierarchy, glory—rendering empty Claude's special pleading for the integrity of war and the transformative powers of culture. The reoccurring mecha-

198

DEBRA RAE COHEN

nism of potlatch emphasizes for readers a contiguity between Nebraska and France to which Claude allows himself to be blind
(even though he first heard the war discussed in terms of its effects
on wheat prices); the "martyred trees" on the battlefield, (403)
whose destruction Claude reads as glorious sacrifice, are simply
cognates of the one cut down by Nat Wheeler. Claude's need to
isolate a romantic realm of sacrifice and glory doesn't allow him
to recognize the operation of war as a homogenizing process—one
in which French ruins come to look like American dump-heaps
(waste imitating waste).

In fact, the elimination of alternative modes of unprofitable expenditure in favor of potlatch leads to the repression of difference. If the standardized touristic program of the AEF is linked
to the cycle of production and the expansion of American empire through the wasting of excess through largesse and display
—"open palms full of crumpled notes" (325)—Claude's mode of
travelership is only illusorily distinct from this process. Indeed, as
Endy points out, the mobilization of connoisseurship for propaganda purposes—as in the novels of Laughlin, Burr, and Bradley—
only underscores the extent to which by the early 1900s "culture
and 'taste' had become elements of the national interest" (592).

Claude's own first comment on Paris signals his unconscious
subsumption into the cycle of production by its link to the mechanism of potlatch: upon hearing that the French have moved the
functions of government to Bordeaux, he expostulates that they
should burn Paris behind them—"They can do better than that
now, they can dynamite it!" (169). In other words, the French
should "waste" cultural and economic capital in a spectacular display that will win them a "victory" of prestige. Like the destruction of David Gerhardt's Stradivarius, this is potential potlatch
that Claude misreads as authentic sacrifice, just as he misreads
the colonization of France by American goods, the exportation
of the panoply of paraphernalia, like the broken machines that
clog the Wheeler basement—signaled in the use of American shipping crates to shore up temporary shelters—as a species of reclamation of the authentic, the kind of mending he practiced on
Mahailey's tools.[19]

The last section of *One of Ours* emphasizes the extent to which

Claude's idealism is coopted by, in Bataille's terms, the debased practices that have replaced the sacrifice. A romantic in a material world, Claude embraces a dream of culture that is contiguous with and determined by the very world of waste he rejects. Cather uses Gerhardt himself to point up this contiguity. In a key scene, Claude argues for the war as, implicitly, a broadening experience, one that performs and extends the designated function of "authentic" travelership, to serve, in Chris Rojek's terms, "as a resource in the task of self-making," yielding "an intensified, heightened experience of oneself" (175). "As for me," he bursts out, "I never knew there was anything worth living for, till this war came on. Before that, the world seemed like a business proposition." Gerhardt responds with "You'll admit it's a costly way of providing adventure for the young" (419)—a line that recognizes the war as a potlatch operation implicated in that very world of "business" to which Claude opposes it.

Claude's reactions to France, however, like his blinkered epiphanies, betray a kind of tunnel vision, a kind of wishful myopia, as he grooms himself for the martyrdom that has fascinated him all along (as an alternative to becoming one of "those dead people that [move] about the streets of Frankfort" [154] or, in Bataille's terms, one who "los[es] the meaning of life to stay alive" [qtd. in Hollier 97]).[20] He remains implacably oblivious to the implications of that self-sacrifice, the degree to which the romantic protest it represents feeds the very world of business he rejects.[21]

Claude's apotheosis in death is rendered by Cather as one final blinkered epiphany, his own idealistic vision supplanted by a meta-perspective that locates him firmly within the system. "The . . . unconsciousness of the warrior," says Bataille, "mainly works in favor of a predominance of the real order. The sacred prestige he arrogates to himself [as a potential sacrifice] is the false weight of a world brought down to the weight of utility" (*Theory of Religion* 59). The "glory" of the dead soldier, then, is recuperated by the rational economy, just as the ruins of war swell the itineraries of postwar tourism; each colonizes and absorbs what appears to be its opposite. That Cather ends the novel with Mrs. Wheeler's musings, in which she recognizes that Claude's "sacrifice" is preserved as "glorious" only in his own dead imagination, that in actuality his death is only fodder for continued "meanness and greed" (458), foregrounds this process for readers of *One of Ours*. As in the "cathedral," the maternal viewpoint at novel's end locates Claude in astronomical perspective. But whereas Claude's "cathedral" epiphany placed him as the "authentic," privileged receptor of an accumulated cultural inheritance summed up in one image of "purple and crimson and peacock-green," the novel's final pages point up the fallacy of that image. They locate him "beyond everything else, at the farthest edge of consciousness, like the evening sun on the horizon" (457), immutably peripheral and immutably past, his status as traveler ironized into that of souvenir.

NOTES

1. See Steven Trout's useful overview in *Memorial Fictions* (3–6).
2. As Janis P. Stout has pointed out, Claude's Francophilia is Cather's own: "The complex movement between irony and a desperate idealism in *One of Ours*," she says, "does not . . . vitiate its picture of the American's longing for a Europe that is taken to represent cultural maturity, beauty, and enlightenment" (181).
3. See Levenstein, *Seductive Journey*, for a salient overview of American tourism in France at the period.
4. A great deal of work has been done on Wharton's particular cast (or perhaps caste) of travelership, and its bearing on her war writing. See in particular Mary Suzanne Schriber's reading of Wharton's *Fighting France* (201–09) and Caesar, *Forgiving the Boundaries* chapter 3; Alan Price contributes useful contextualization in *The End of the Age of Innocence*. Sarah Bird Wright's structuralist reading of Wharton's travel texts, while it emphasizes the elitist nature of Wharton's "connoisseurship," if anything obscures the rhetorical and historical contexts for her self-positioning.
5. See on this subject Eve Sorum's work on Ford Madox Ford, "Mapping No Man's Land," and the arguments of Allyson Booth in *Postcards from the Trenches*, chapter 4. One flaw in Booth's fascinating study is that she generalizes observations about Britain to other countries, eliding the differences between and within national spatializings of the war to assume a unitary "modernist" effect. In particular, American stances in relation to the conflict were shaped by a quite different set of cultural and spatial relationships, with the very "over thereness" of "Over There" mediated by assumptions derived from touristic models.
6. It's important to recognize that, like the war memorials and unit histories Trout cites, these novels made up an important part of the "now

forgotten contexts" (8) for the writing of *One of Ours*. Like Rebecca West's use of the women's magazine romance in *The Return of the Soldier*, Cather's relation to these novels is both knowing and ironic.

7. See Loselle 28–32 on the degree to which the equation between war and tourism has pervaded the theorizing of the latter.

8. The touristic avidity of Sergeant Hicks and his men bodes as ill for France as for the German army: "It was in their minds that they must not let a church escape, any more than they would let a Boche escape" (327).

9. Bataille terms this the "unreserved surrender to *things*" (*Accursed Share* 136); see my argument below.

10. As such the passage provides an interesting variation on what Pericles Lewis has recently identified as a classic modernist topos, in which "lone male wanderers, often with touristic inclinations" (670) visit churches in search of a spiritual solace that organized religion can no longer provide. Lewis sees in these scenes a tension between the role of seeker and that of tourist, which he reads as "an outsider, a sort of amateur anthropologist" (684); I would argue that in this scene Claude's ontological self-distinction conflates the two roles, that it is exactly in his self-definition as "traveler" that the church is found to yield meaning.

11. Ian Ousby has stressed the way the figure of Joan of Arc represented a site of contestation, of varying and contradictory meanings that merged in her wartime elevation by the French as the supreme national symbol; the "essential facts" of her history, in fact, were used as support for mutually exclusive ideas. It's telling in connection with her inspirational significance for Claude to remember too Marina Warner's blunt observation that "it is astonishing how many of Joan's apologists like her dead" (268).

12. And it's worth noting here how often Cather employs this phrase with regard to Claude—the first chapter of the section begins the same way—as if to emphasize the hapless passivity of Claude's travels even as it refers back to the mission of the cultural tourist to "discover" himself in Europe. Once again, Cather's locutions are deliberately Janus-faced.

13. Reynolds confines his analysis of Cather's use of such interpositional narration to the way it mediates her treatment of Claude's idealism; I'd argue that it also governs the depiction of his unstable subsumption into the AEF community.

14. See not only Culler in this context but also the work of John Urry and Dean MacCannell.

15. The salience of the potlatch mechanism to the patterns of *One of Ours* renders Bataille's theories of waste far more useful for interpreting the novel than alternative models derived from psychoanalytic or Bakhtinian theory—as does the importance of the Great War itself to Bataille's theoretical development. See Irwin 127–29.

16. It's important, in this context, to distinguish "waste" in Batail-

lean terms—the predictable outcome of systemic overproduction—from "mess," the formless and often alluring product of chance. David Trotter, who has contributed brilliantly to the theorization of the latter, describes it as "what contingency's signature would look like, if contingency *had* a signature" (15); it is therefore an uncanny category, ripe, as sign and symptom of modernity, for both rejection and embrace. Whereas Trotter's analysis acknowledges as emblematic of literary responses to capitalism bifurcated responses to "good mess" and "bad mess," Bataille's diagnosis is that "good mess" is rendered, in the capitalist economy, accessible only in the debased and illusionary form of potlatch. Reading the novel through the latter model gives added irony to the expression of the nostalgic gap between transcendence and cooptation that so pervades Cather's text. Too, Bataille's cultural pessimism resonates with Veblenian notions of conspicuous consumption current early in the American century.

17. The degree to which waste dominates the negative metaphorics of the Nebraska sections of *One of Ours* was identified long ago by Susan J. Rosowski, Blanche Gelfant, and others. Gelfant stresses, in particular, the association of waste with the Wheeler family basement, as if to identify it as the family's "foundational secret" (90). Though Hermione Lee discerns beneath the relentless depiction of "a country that has been pasted over with a layer of philistinism and materialism" (174) perhaps "just a hint . . . that junk, once it starts ageing into antiques, might be seductive" (175), she's just about the only critic to do so, and she quickly abandons that suggestion to emphasize that Claude "has been living in a civilization . . . which has not needed a war to turn itself into rubbish."

18. "[Man] must waste the excess, but he remains eager to acquire even when he does the opposite, and so he makes waste itself an object of acquisition. Once the resources are dissipated, there remains the prestige *acquired* by the one who wastes. The waste is an ostentatious squandering to this end, with a view to a superiority over others that he attributes to himself by this means" (Bataille, *Accursed Share* 72–73).

19. In Elaine Scarry's terms, Claude is mistaking an act of "unmaking" —the homogenization of culture through the wastage of war—for an act of making that confers "humane awareness" (305).

20. This includes a willing participation in the process of euphemism that Scarry sees as inherent in the apparatus of war. Though, as Sharon O'Brien points out, the margins of the text teem with mutilated soldiers (194), they are far more visible to readers than they are to Claude, for whom as Jean Schwind has detailed, the realities of bodies give way to an idealized traveler's landscape.

21. The degree to which one feeds the other is signaled in Bayliss's comment that that the war's "waste" will leave America "in actual possession of the capital of the world" (232).

WORKS CITED

Adler, Judith. "Travel as Performed Art." *American Journal of Sociology* 94 (1989): 1366-91.

Bataille, Georges. *The Accursed Share: An Essay on General Economy.* Vol. 1. Trans. Robert Hurley. 1967. New York: Zone, 1991.

———. *Theory of Religion.* Trans. Robert Hurley. New York: Zone, 1989.

Booth, Allyson. *Postcards from the Trenches: Negotiating the Space between Modernism and the First World War.* New York: Oxford UP, 1996.

Bradley, Mary Hastings. *The Splendid Chance.* New York: Appleton, 1915.

Burr, Anna Robeson. *The House on Charles Street.* New York: Duffield, 1921.

Buzard, James. *The Beaten Track: European Tourism, Literature, and the Ways to Culture 1800-1918.* Oxford: Clarendon, 1993.

Caesar, Terry. *Forgiving the Boundaries: Home as Abroad in American Travel Writing.* Athens: U of Georgia P, 1995.

Cather, Willa. *Not Under Forty.* New York: Knopf, 1936.

———. *One of Ours.* New York: Knopf, 1923.

Culler, Jonathan. "The Semiotics of Tourism." *Framing the Sign: Criticism and Its Institutions.* Norman: U of Oklahoma P, 1988. 153-67.

Endy, Christopher. "Travel and World Power: Americans in Europe 1890-1917." *Diplomatic History* 22.4 (1998): 565-94.

Gelfant, Blanche. "'What Was It . . . ?': The Secret of Family Accord in *One of Ours.*" *Willa Cather: Family, Community and History.* Ed. John J. Murphy. Provo UT: BYU Humanities Publications Center, 1990. 85-102.

Hollier, Denis. *Against Architecture: The Writings of Georges Bataille.* Cambridge: MIT Press, 1989.

Irwin, Alexander. *Saints of the Impossible: Bataille, Weil, and the Politics of the Sacred.* Minneapolis: U of Minnesota P, 2002.

Laughlin, Clara E. *Everybody's Birthright: A Vision of Jeanne d'Arc.* New York: Fleming H. Revell, 1914.

———. *The Keys of Heaven.* New York: Doran, 1918.

———. *The Martyred Towns of France.* New York: Putnam, 1919.

Lee, Hermione. *Willa Cather: Double Lives.* New York: Pantheon, 1989.

Levenstein, Harvey. *Seductive Journey: American Tourists in France from Jefferson to the Jazz Age.* Chicago: U of Chicago P, 1998.

Lewis, Pericles. "Churchgoing in the Modern Novel." *Modernism/Modernity* 11.4 (2004): 669-94.

Loselle, Andrea. *History's Double: Cultural Tourism in Twentieth-Century French Writing*. New York: St. Martin's, 1997.

Méral, Jean. *Paris in American Literature*. Chapel Hill: U of North Carolina P, 1989.

O'Brien, Sharon. "Combat Envy and Survivor Guilt: Willa Cather's Manly Battle Yarn. *Arms and the Woman: War, Gender and Literary Representation*. Ed. Helen M. Cooper, Adrienne Auslander Munich, and Susan Merrill Squier. Chapel Hill: U of North Carolina P, 1989. 184–204.

Ousby, Ian. *The Road to Verdun: World War I's Most Momentous Battle and the Folly of Nationalism*. New York: Doubleday, 2002.

Price, Alan. *The End of the Age of Innocence: Edith Wharton and the First World War*. New York: St. Martin's, 1996.

Reynolds, Guy. *Willa Cather in Context: Progress, Race, Empire*. New York: St. Martin's, 1996.

Rojek, Chris. *Ways of Escape: Modern Transformations in Leisure and Travel*. Lanham MD: Rowman & Littlefield, 1994.

Scarry, Elaine. *The Body in Pain: The Making and Unmaking of the World*. New York: Oxford UP, 1985.

Schriber, Mary Suzanne. *Writing Home: American Women Abroad, 1830-1920*. Charlottesville: UP of Virginia, 1997.

Schwind, Jean. "The 'Beautiful' War in *One of Ours*." *Modern Fiction Studies* 30 (1984): 53–71.

Sorum, Eve. "Mapping No Man's Land: Ordering the War in Ford Madox Ford's *Parade's End*." MSA Convention. Birmingham, UK, September 28, 2003.

Stout, Janis P. *Willa Cather: The Writer and Her World*. Charlottesville: UP of Virginia, 2000.

Swift, John N., and Joseph R. Urgo. "Introduction: Literate Tourism and Cather's Southwest." *Willa Cather and the American Southwest*. Lincoln: U of Nebraska P, 2002.

Trotter, David. Cooking with Mud: The Idea of Mess in Nineteenth-Century Art and Fiction. New York: Oxford UP, 2000.

Trout, Steven. *Memorial Fictions: Willa Cather and the First World War*. Lincoln: U of Nebraska P, 2002.

Urgo, Joseph R. *Willa Cather and the Myth of American Migration*. Urbana: U of Illinois P, 1995.

Warner, Marina. *Joan of Arc: The Image of Female Heroism*.1981. Berkeley: U of California P, 2000.

Wright, Sarah Bird. *Edith Wharton's Travel Writing: The Making of a Connoisseur*. New York: St. Martin's, 1997.

On the Front and at Home
Wharton, Cather, the Jews,
and the First World War

SUSAN MEYER

When Professor St. Peter walks home one October afternoon, at the beginning of chapter 6 of Willa Cather's *The Professor's House* (1925), he admires from outside the house the vivid
autumn foliage his wife has brought into the drawing room. He
muses over the way it is selection and placement that create art:
"The hand, fastidious and bold, which selected and placed—it was
that which made the difference" (75). Through the open French
window, St. Peter also glimpses his wife and his Jewish son-in-law,
Louie Marsellus, "a little lacquer table between them, bending, it
seemed, over casket of jewels" (75). Framed by the window, the
two also seem transformed into a picture, suspended in the sta-
sis of art. And Louie's pose is a familiar one in which to find a
Jew in the Western aesthetic tradition. Behind him are figures like
Dickens's Fagin, pulling a box of jewels in secret from beneath the
floorboards of his decrepit house, trickling gems through his fingers, and gloating that dead men tell no tales.

But as St. Peter approaches and Lillian and Louie begin to speak,
the meaning of the scene deepens and changes: the two are no
longer "selected and placed" (75) in a picture so easily read
through anti-Semitic archetypes. It is, after all, St. Peter himself
who has framed the two figures in this way. By ending the immediately preceding chapter with an account of St. Peter as an artist of
living pictures, Cather emphasizes St. Peter's agency in the picture-
making. As chapter 5 ends, St. Peter remembers once posing his
two sons-in-law in a living picture for a historical pageant for

his students. Though St. Peter believed the picture "quite fair" to Louie and Scott, Lillian's critical response to that picture implies that it was a reductive oversimplification of the two young men — and that this picture is a similarly reductive vision of her and Louie. Yet, it is also Cather herself, complicitous with St. Peter, who has, at least initially, framed Lillian and Louie in this pose over the jewel casket for the reader. Throughout the novel, Cather certainly evokes many familiar anti-Semitic resonances with the character of Louie Marsellus. But she just as certainly suggests the limitations of those stereotypes and humanizes and deepens the character who inhabits them.

Wealthy though he is, Louie is not the simple materialist the framed picture of him with Lillian suggests. As soon as St. Peter enters the room, swinging himself over the window rail, Louie begins to speak with enthusiasm about the Professor's lectures. In the world of St. Peter's state university, in which the interests of athletics, commerce, and agriculture are crowding out the liberal arts, St. Peter's own avid pursuit of historical understanding finds little appreciative audience. But Louie is *not* driven (as the university seems to be) only by materialistic concerns. He is hungry to hear St. Peter talk about his work: Louie immediately begins to speak of his regret at never having had the opportunity to study with St. Peter. And as the chapter ends, after Louie has left, St. Peter and his wife discuss Louie's attempt to join the "Arts and Letters." The Professor urges Lillian to persuade Louie not to let his name come up, lest he be blackballed by someone in the group. As St. Peter explains, although Louie has been allowed into the country club, "the Arts and Letters is a little group of fellows, and . . . fussy" (79). Louie *is* subsequently blackballed and kept out of this fussy little club, but there is surely something suggestive in Cather's story of a Jew being excluded from the Arts and Letters. If at first she frames her Jewish character in familiar anti-Semitic terms, her novel also invites the reader to meditate on the way the arts and letters have blackballed and excluded Jews, and in the process dwindled into a fussy little social club. But why this apparent contradiction? On what terms does Cather's own art, in *The Professor's House*, allow the Jew admittance?

The representation of Louie Marsellus has long puzzled — and sometimes disturbed—critics of *The Professor's House*. The two critics who most strongly make the case that Louie's is an anti-Semitic portrait are James Schroeter (in 1964) and Walter Benn Michaels (in 1995). Schroeter, noting the antithesis in the novel between Tom Outland and Louie Marsellus, comments that as Cather represents the Jew, he is "a moneymaker rather than a creator, a traditionless aggressor who invades from the outside; he threatens and destroys the past; and he symbolizes what is wrong with the present" (503). Through Louie's prosperity Cather suggests, Schroeter writes, "that America is falling into the hands of the Jews" (503). The Jews are represented in her novel as "unworthy inheritors of that tradition and wealth which they had no share in making" (504). Michaels discusses Cather as one of a number of novelists in the 1920s who was concerned with defining American identity against invasive outsiders. In marrying Rosamond, Louie is the "nativist's nightmare Jew . . . the one who wants to marry his daughter" (69). The novel's anti-Semitism, for Michaels, functions in the service of its redefinition of a pure, archetypal American identity, located in the feeling Tom has for the vanished Indians of the mesa, whom he views as his ancestors (Michaels 151n54). In order to affirm this archetype and yet suggest the way it is threatened, Cather creates in Louie Marsellus, Michaels contends, the "nightmare Jew."

But other Cather critics either counter the claim that the representation of Louie is anti-Semitic (Wasserman, Woodress, Lee) or see a duality in Cather's attitude toward him. Janis P. Stout observes that Louie "is painfully . . . stigmatized by stereotypical personal associations with moneymaking, showy spending, and . . . social climbing" but has "an attractive personal generosity" (226–27). Ann Fisher-Wirth similarly sees the representation of Louie in the first half of the novel as characterized by a typical modernist anti-Semitism (he is, she writes, "a 'mackerel-tinted' materialist" [23]); but as the novel proceeds, "Louie gradually surpasses the categories that contain him" (23).

That this character can be interpreted in such diametrically opposing ways grows, I believe, out of contradictory impulses in the novel itself. Like Stout and Fisher-Wirth, I see this novel as deeply ambivalent in its representation of the Professor's emphatically

208

SUSAN MEYER

Jewish son-in-law. The ambivalence with which Cather represents the Jewish Marsellus makes most sense, I will contend here, when *The Professor's House* is thought of as a postwar novel, a novel reflecting Cather's deeply troubled and conflicted reaction to the Great War. Her representation of Jews in this novel is intricately involved with her reaction to the war. During the war years, and in the early twenties, a pervasive popular discourse accused the Jews of an unpatriotic, self-interested response to the war. Edith Wharton's novel of the war, *A Son at the Front* (1923), published just two years before *The Professor's House*, represents Jews in a way very congruent with the way they were being represented in popular discourse; in Wharton's war novel the figure of the Jew serves to emphasize, by contrast, the nobility of self-sacrifice for the war. When Cather's *The Professor's House* is considered in the context of contemporary discourse about Jews and war, what is most striking about her representation of the Jewish Marsellus is its relative subtlety and complexity. I will contend that, like Wharton, Cather uses the Jew to represent the antithesis of noble self-sacrifice in war, but her ambivalence about what constitutes the most appropriate human response to that "great catastrophe" (236) is reflected in a more conflicted, and ultimately more sympathetic, representation of the Jew.

Widespread, angry criticism of Jews in the United States, alleging their lack of patriotism and inclination toward draft evasion, filled the summer of 1917.[1] In April 1917 the United States had entered the war, and in May Congress passed the Selective Service Act, which required all men from aged twenty-one to thirty to register for the draft on June 5. The irate rhetoric against Jews beginning in the summer of 1917 did spring in part from what can be seen as a legitimate grievance, due to peculiarities of the draft law, though it was hardly fair to hold Jews and other recent immigrants responsible for the effects of these peculiarities. Although all men ages twenty-one to thirty were obligated to register on Registration Day, June 5, 1917, immigrants who had not yet begun the official process of naturalization were, as citizens of other countries, exempt from the draft. Yet each district had to provide a certain quota of men based on its total population, a population count in which these "non-declarant aliens" were included. As a result, American citizens (as well as immigrants who had begun the process of naturalization) who lived in districts with high percentages of recent immigrants were conscripted at significantly higher rates than in other areas of the country. In one such case, 25 percent of the men who registered in one Brooklyn district were nondeclarant Russian Jewish immigrants (Chambers, *To Raise an Army* 226–27; Sterba 73). Senator Henry Cabot Lodge claimed in September of 1917 that 70 percent of the registered men in one Chicago district were foreign citizens and therefore draft-exempt and that so many men in one Brooklyn district were nondeclarant aliens that "every eligible American" citizen in that district was drafted (qtd. in Chambers, *To Raise an Army* 227). Unsurprisingly, this situation fomented a great deal of anger against immigrants.

The public perception of this situation was not helped by the fact that many prominent Jewish socialists and liberals did oppose the war. The Jewish population in the United States numbered two million: one and a half million of them were living in New York City, and one and a half million were recent arrivals from Russia and Poland (Vital 664). These Russian and Polish Jews had come to the United States in order to escape the oppressive treatment they suffered under the Russian czar (violent pogroms, forcible relocation, overcrowding and starvation in the Pale of Settlement, as well as conscription into the most dangerous positions in the army). Before the United States entered the war, from 1914 to 1917, most Russian Jewish immigrants, fearing that the czar would come to dominate new regions in which Jews lived, hoped for a German triumph over Russia (Sterba 63; Vital 658). But in the year following the abdication of Czar Nicholas II in March of 1917, Jewish opinion in the United States largely turned in favor of the Allies and in support of the war effort (Sterba 64).

Despite their draft-exempt status, between 1917 and 1918, hundreds of thousands of undeclared immigrants voluntarily joined the armed services: by September 1918, they numbered 191,000 (Chambers, *To Raise an Army* 228–29). Statistics show that approximately 20 percent of United States draftees were foreign born and that 9 percent of the men who ultimately served in the U.S. armed services during World War I were not citizens of the United

States (Chambers, *To Raise an Army* 229). Jews were a particular target of the anti-immigrant hostility. Yet, largely because of volunteerism, some 200,000 Jews became soldiers for the United States (Sterba 29). A considerably *higher* proportion of the Jewish than the non-Jewish population served in the United States military during World War I (Vital 650). But the perception of injustice caused by the terms of the draft law (and by the vocal opposition of some prominent Jews to the war) inflamed public anger against the Jews. Anger against Jews was widely expressed by public speakers and in the press. In New York City, anti-Semitic soapbox orators drew large crowds. One Russell Dunne (who had also spoken at recruitment events) delivered an anti-Semitic tirade in Madison Square Garden on August 25, 1917, that got particularly ugly. He described Jews as "long-nosed greasy vermin," and he urged his audience to boycott Jewish businesses. Denouncing the Jews as "slackers," he encouraged his listeners to recreate the violence of the pogroms the Jews had fled in coming to the United States: "Teach the foreigners the lesson they were taught in Russia," he proclaimed (qtd. in Sterba 28–29). Violence erupted, although the police were called in, and Jewish merchants in Brooklyn later felt the effects of the called-for boycott (Sterba 28–29).

Discontent over the perceived inequities of the draft was so pervasive that most prominent newspapers ran editorials taking the position that immigrants who had not yet declared their intent to become citizens should be eligible for the draft (Chambers, *To Raise an Army* 227–28).[2] Some newspapers were more inflammatory: in August 1917 the *New York World* claimed that the Jews were working in league with German agents to oppose the war (Sterba 73). One draft board in Brooklyn sent a much-reprinted telegram to Woodrow Wilson in which they protested that tremendous numbers of exemption claims were being made by the Russian Jewish men in their district: "The flower of our neighborhood is being torn from home . . . to fight for these miserable specimens of humanity, who under the law may remain smugly at home" (qtd. in Sterba 73). Medical advisory boards who examined candidates for military service were informed by the *Army Manual of Instruction* in 1917: "The foreign born, and especially Jews, are more apt to malinger than the native born" (Wallace 105). Even Jewish attorney Louis Marshall, president of the American Jewish Committee, commented that he saw a "slacker spirit on the part of our people" (Sterba 69). The *American Jewish Chronicle* reported the particularly scurrilous comment made by a member of a Brooklyn draft board at a pro-war rally: "There are three epochs in the life of the Jewish boy: first, at birth, circumcision; second, at 13, confirmation; third, at 21, exemption" (qtd. in Sterba 74).

When Jews did enter the military, they experienced discrimination. In 1914 the American Jewish Committee complained about the discriminatory treatment of Jews in the armed services in a letter to the War Department. In response, the War Department internally circulated a memo that included the comment, "The Jew never was and never will be a soldier" (Wallace 105). One Jewish lieutenant, Jacob Rader Marcus, kept a diary during the First World War in which he recorded occurrences of anti-Semitic discrimination in the armed services, noting instances of Jews being unjustly kept from promotion, denied the opportunity for religious observance, and singled out for disciplinary treatment (Sterba 194–95).

Jews were accused of being slackers and malingerers and of being unpatriotic; when they were in the military, they were accused of being poor soldiers. During the war years and in the twenties, Jews were also blamed for causing or for profiting from the war (see McCall 165). These accusations may have arisen in part from the fact that some prominent Jewish figures tried to use their influence to improve the situation of Jews in Russia. Jacob Schiff, the Jewish head of Kuhn, Loeb, and Company and of other investment banks in New York, disturbed by the treatment of Jews in Russia, advocated a position of neutrality in 1915. When in the summer of 1915 J. P. Morgan asked Schiff to have his firm join in issuing a loan of $500 million to the Allies, Schiff was only willing to do so if he could be assured that none of the money would go to Russia. But his condition was not met, and Schiff withdrew from the loan (Vital 659). The American Jewish Committee, a group of prominent Jews, hoped that the governments of Britain and France would use their influence with Russia, and the president of the American Jewish Committee wrote to a Russian mediator about the willingness of Schiff and other Jewish bankers to join in offering Russia a loan if certain conditions were met by Russia: Russia must agree to abolish the Pale of Settlement and recognize the right to expatriation as well as the equality of Jews with all Russian citizens. But once again the terms were not met (Vital 660–61). In response to such efforts, the British ambassador wrote in a letter to the Foreign Office: "German Jewish bankers are toiling in a solid phalanx to compass our destruction" (Vital 659). During the negotiations between the British and French governments and U.S. bankers, the myth that Jews formed a coherent international group, self-interested and unpatriotic, garnered strength. "I do not think it is easy to exaggerate the international power of the Jews," wrote Lord Robert Cecil (qtd. in Vital 662).

These accusations of international Jewish conspiracy, warmongering, and profiteering did not die out after the war was over. A motion was introduced in the Senate in March 1923 by Robert La Follette of Wisconsin in which World War I was blamed on international bankers and in particular the Jewish Rothschilds (Wallace 28). Henry Ford's *The International Jew*, a collection of anti-Semitic articles initially published in his newspaper, the *Dearborn Independent*, disseminated such accusations around the world in the early 1920s (Wallace 43–44). In 1922, Hilaire Belloc, a well-known, French-born British writer, published a popular book entitled *The Jews*, which promoted the belief that Jews were capable of no loyalty or patriotism to the countries they were living in.

Samuel Walker McCall, former member of the House of Representatives and then Governor of Massachusetts, was so disturbed by the rise in hostility toward the Jews during and after World War I, and in particular by what was said about Jews' lack of patriotism and nonengagement in the war, that he wrote an entire book titled *Patriotism of the American Jew* (1924). The book is devoted to countering the claim that Jews have no capacity for national loyalty or patriotism.[3] In it, McCall traces and celebrates the history of the participation by Jews in all American armed conflicts and points out that statistics demonstrate that Jews served in the armed services during the Great War at an exceptionally high rate. Given the percentage of the population that was Jewish, one would have expected the percentage of Jews in the military to have been 3 percent, but in fact it was one third higher, at 4 percent, because of the large numbers of Jewish volunteers (McCall 128). McCall quotes prominent Jews who spoke in favor of U.S. participation and who urged Jews to volunteer, recounts the relief work done by Jews, and narrates incidents of heroic action by Jews serving in the U.S. military during the war. That McCall felt the need in 1924 to write an entire book arguing for the *Patriotism of the American Jew* reveals how much his views on that topic were at odds with the prevailing sentiments of the time. What was said on the street and in popular publications during the war years and afterward was that Jews were slackers and cowards, who evaded military service out of self-interest and who had profited from and caused the war.

Both Edith Wharton's war novel *A Son at the Front* (1923) and Willa Cather's *The Professor's House* (1925) were written in this wartime and postwar climate. Wharton wrote *A Son at the Front* while she was living in France and doing relief work between the spring of 1918 and 1922. In this novel of World War I, Wharton uses race metaphorically, and in doing so, she invokes familiar stereotypes of the Jews. At one point in the novel, George Campton, a young American serving in the French military, whom Wharton celebrates as heroic in his wartime self-sacrifice, says in a fury of the Germans after they have invaded Belgium, "They're not fit to live with white people" (51). In Wharton's other war novel, *The Marne* (1918), a silly young American woman who has come to France with the ridiculous ambition of teaching the French to value home and family as Americans do, uses similar language a year later to describe her startled recognition that the French are civilized too: "I tell you, they're *white!*" Miss Warlick exclaims (99). Wharton's point in this passage in *The Marne* is to mock the young American woman for her belated recognition: for Wharton the French are the epitome of civilization, the epitome of "whiteness." Being "white," for Wharton, signifies decency, humanity, culture; it means being willing to sacrifice everything to defend France against Germany, to defend civilization against barbarism.[4] But if being white for Wharton signifies being fully attuned to the values of humanity, culture, and civilization, being Jewish signifies the opposite. Wharton uses Jews in *A Son at the Front* to repre-

214

sent an ignoble wartime failure to rise to self-sacrifice in defense
of civilization.

A Son at the Front focuses on the experiences of John Campton,
an American painter living in Paris, and on his relationship with
his son, George. George, though an American with two American parents, was accidentally born in France (of a father also born
in France) and is therefore subject to mobilization in the French
army. Campton at first schemes with his former wife and her influential banker husband to keep George from being mobilized and
then to keep him from being sent to the front. But as the months go
by Campton comes to feel ashamed of his efforts to keep George
out of active fighting. Campton comes to believe that no "civilized man could afford to stand aside from such a conflict" (102).
France, he realizes, has always been not only her people but "an
Idea" in "the story of civilization; a luminous point about which
striving visions and purposes could rally" (192). "If France went,"
Campton thinks, "western civilization went with her; and then all
they had believed in and been guided by would perish" (192). At
the heart of this novel is Campton's delicately rendered struggle to
let his one child, his deeply loved son, go to risk death at the front.
His agonizing internal struggle is heart-rendingly represented in
the novel.

But to depict the antithesis of the sacrifice Campton learns he
must make, and allow his son to make, for the war, Wharton uses
the Jews. As Campton comes to realize that he must let George go,
he comes to despise those around him who advocate neutrality for
the United States or who scheme to protect their loved ones from
active service. Wharton makes Jewish characters the most repulsive examples of wartime selfishness, and it is by seeing the similarity between his own actions and those of these Jewish figures
that Campton grows to realize that protecting his son is dishonorable. Campton is viscerally disgusted by the fat, red, international
banker Jorgenstein, a figure in Wharton's novel who clearly reflects and derives from the popular wartime and postwar condemnation of Jewish bankers. Jorgenstein, with what Wharton terms
his "air of bloated satisfaction" (124), thrives during the war at
his "vile . . . money-making," (14) growing ever richer and fatter
and achieving unearned honors from France and Britain for his

putative patriotism. Léonce Black, the dealer who handles the sale of Campton's art, is a younger Semitic figure who has similarly remained fleshy and prosperous during the war, discussing with Campton the effect of the war on business while gazing at him under "plump eyelids" and stroking "his Assyrian nose as though its handsome curve followed the pure Delphic line" (89). Black, who "loung[es] in a glossy War Office uniform" (88) has also managed to secure himself a safe military post and avoid being sent into active fighting.

But what most appalls Campton, and finally causes him to re-evaluate his efforts to keep George from being sent to the front, is hearing those efforts on behalf of George invoked by a woman whose lover is a Jew, Mme de Dolmetsch. Mme de Dolmetsch is the lover of Ladislas Isador, whom Campton thinks of as that "fat middle-aged philanderer with his Jewish eyes, his Slav eloquence, his Levantine gift for getting on, and for getting out from under" (97). Believing Campton to have been successful in protecting George, Mme de Dolmetsch implores Campton's aid in keeping Isador at a safe office position in Paris. Campton's "gorge r[ises] at the thought that people should associate in their minds cases as different as those of his son and Mme. de Dolmetsch's lover" (97); he feels "everything . . . dearest to him, the thought of George . . . defiled by this monstrous coupling of [his] name . . . with that of the supple middle-aged adventurer safe in his spotless uniform at the War Office" (85). After this encounter, Campton tells his former wife for the first time that there are some steps that he will not take to keep George safe: "It's no use," he says. "I can't do the sort of thing to keep my son safe that Mme. de Dolmetsch would do for her lover" (97). It is in this moment when he comes to see himself as behaving like a Jew—scheming, dishonorable, staying safe at all costs, avoiding wartime sacrifice—that Campton begins to realize that he must let George go. As was the case in the U.S. armed forces, the percentage of the Jewish population in the French army in the First World War was higher than the percentage of the non-Jewish population: 35,000 Jews, some 20 percent of France's Jewish population, fought for France (Vital 650). But Wharton uses the figure of the Jew to represent the dishonorable evasion of military service. The novel follows Campton's struggle not to be like a Jew, his agonizing internal struggle to accept George's desire for active duty and to allow his one beloved son to die in the war. The sacrifice Campton learns to make during the war involves not only the loss of the one person he loves but almost the loss of art itself. Campton stops painting at the beginning of the war, feeling that "the world in which men lived at present was one in which the word 'art' had lost its meaning" (71). George himself has been throughout his life the subject of Campton's greatest work, so when he dies, it seems for a while as if Campton's art has come to an end. He cannot bear to look at his old sketches of his son or to touch "paint or pencil" (216). Only when he can see aspects of George in the first young American soldiers who come marching into Paris is he able to begin to draw again, as he begins sketching their faces. As the novel ends, Campton, who has angrily resisted helping to design the memorial statue to his son that his former wife and her husband want, has, with a tremendous emotional effort, pulled out his sketches and begun work on the model for the statue. By the novel's end, the war has not quite put its threatened end to art itself, but Campton's art has become a memorial for what he has lost. In the end *A Son at the Front* is a somber celebration of the art of losing, of accepting intolerable loss and pain, because keeping oneself from loss is ultimately more unthinkable —it is to be like a Jew.

Wharton's representation of Jews in *A Son at the Front* is painful. Somehow she cannot extend her probing and generous understanding of humanity to Jews but flattens them into caricatures of wartime attitudes she found repugnant. The novel contains other caricatures—of pacifists, of wealthy Americans who cannot give up amusement, who advocate the "new morality," or who espouse a shallow nonconventionality in art—but her satire of these characters, though not an artistic strength of the novel, is expressive of distaste for particular social or aesthetic views and not for an entire people. The hostility toward Jews often feels disturbingly arbitrary, unmotivated. In one passage in *Fighting France* (1915), Wharton's best-selling collection of nonfiction essays about her experiences visiting various parts of France's front line, Wharton, without any clear motivation or reason, suddenly associates Jews with the worst of German cruelty toward the French. In an account of her visit to Gerbérviller, known as "the martyr town," site of German atrocities carried out on a civilian population, she writes of one particularly devastated house that it was "so calcined and convulsed that, for epithets dire enough to fit it, one would have to borrow from a Hebrew prophet gloating over the fall of a city of idolaters" (93). But why suddenly evoke gloating Jews in connection with the savagery of the invading German army? It is evident that for Wharton Jews were deeply associated with the opposite of the values she felt the war was being fought to defend, the values of humanity and culture most dear to her.

To consider Cather's Louie Marsellus in the context of what was said in America and Europe about the Jews during the war and the postwar years is to see both the ways in which Cather's representation of her Jewish character is continuous with that popular discourse and the ways in which it is not. Cather's description of Louie's nose ("it grew out of his face with masterful strength" [45]) certainly derives from a tradition of anti-Semitic representation, as does her rather more original use of the term "mackerel-tinted" (44) to describe him. (The term links Louie unflatteringly with his origins, evoking Jewish fish-mongers in New York City haggling over the price of items on their pushcarts.) In discussing *The Professor's House* as a postwar novel, Steven Trout describes Louie as "a generous and likable character whose wartime actions can nevertheless be described as outright profiteering" (188). To represent a Jew as profiteering during the war was consistent with the anti-Semitic rhetoric of the time. In these ways Cather's portrayal of Jews during the war years derives from what was being widely said at the time about the Jews in relation to the war.

But unlike Wharton's *A Son at the Front*, Cather's *The Professor's House* does not particularly encourage the reader to ask how her Jewish character, Louie Marsellus, has managed not to serve in the military during the war—although, once the question is posed, a reader might wonder. As I note earlier, all American men from ages twenty-one to thirty were required to register on June 5, 1917. Those called to military service were then randomly selected by lottery: approximately one in four of those registrants were drafted (Chambers, "Selective Service" 541). Later, in September 1918, the range was broadened to include all men from ages eighteen to forty-five. Twenty percent of all American men aged eighteen to forty-five served in the military during the First World War (Chambers, *To Raise an Army* 200). Louie Marsellus, who has married Tom Outland's fiancée, seems to be about Tom's age. Tom was approximately twenty-nine when he met his death in 1915, the second year of the war, so he would have been about thirty-one in 1917.[5] Louie is apparently within a few years of Tom's age, probably younger, as Tom began college late, so he would likely have had to register for the draft in June 1917, or, if not, he definitely would have had to do so in September 1918.

Does Cather mean for us to infer that her Jewish character has pulled strings to keep himself out of the war? Possibly. Louie arrived in town just around the time of Outland's death in 1915 (133), and fairly soon afterward, Mrs. Crane suggests, was engaged to Rosamond (134). If Louie and Rosamond were engaged in 1916, they were probably married some time before Congress approved the Selective Service Act, which Wilson signed on May 18, 1917. Rosamond and Louie have evidently become engaged rather soon after Tom's death, too soon, some seem to think. Kathleen's sudden, irrevocable rejection of her sister on hearing the news of her engagement suggests that she feels that Rosamond has moved on with her life too quickly. And that the rapidity with which Rosamond has transferred her affections to Louie has become a topic of conversation between Kathleen and Scott is suggested by Scott's sotto voce joke to his wife, hinting that though Rosamond may have been, as Louie says, Tom's "virtual widow," she was not his "virtuous widow" but the "reverseous" (46). It was relatively easy for married men with dependent wives or dependent wives and children to receive an exemption from the draft, unless they had rushed to the altar in an obvious last-minute attempt to evade conscription, as many did when rumors began circulating that single men would be taken first (Chambers, *To Raise an Army* 189, 191, 185). It is just possible that the novel may be hinting that Louie and Rosamond have hurried into an engagement and into marriage out of a fear that the United States would soon enter the war. Louie, however, is also an electrical engineer, who comes to Hamilton in 1915 to put in the Edison power plant, so he could probably also have gotten himself a draft exemption on the grounds that he was essential to the economy, although such an exemption was harder to obtain than the exemption for married men (see Chambers, *To Raise an Army* 189, 191). Cather may be suggesting, to readers as conscious of the recent terms of conscription as hers were in 1925, that Louie has behaved in a vaguely dubious way in order to evade the draft.

But if the Jewish Louie has gotten himself exempted from the draft based on a "dependency hardship," so, probably, has Scott McGregor, who also, as Tom's college classmate, is most likely a few years younger than Tom and thus of draftable age even in 1917. Kathleen and Scott were engaged shortly after Rosamond and Tom were (66), and Rosamond and Tom must have been engaged before August 1914, when Tom joined the Foreign Legion. Soon after Kathleen and Scott were engaged, Scott began earning enough for the two to marry, so they were probably married by 1915, well before June 5, 1917. Although the two have been married long enough for there to be no suspicion that theirs is a hasty marriage conceived with the intent of avoiding the draft, married men were not required to claim a "dependency hardship," as it seems Scott may have done.

To think about the draft in relation to the novel is to realize how strangely untouched the populations of the university town of Hamilton and of the university itself seem to have been by conscription. Louie and Scott would have been required to register for the draft, even if they had been able to obtain exemptions, and so would many young men in the town and from the university. But there is no mention in the novel of *anyone* who has been in the war except Tom Outland and Sir Edgar Spilling, the fifty-year-old Englishman visiting the St. Peters who has been in the British Air Service during the war, "in the construction department" (43), and only Tom has seen active service. If Louie and Scott have managed not to be in the war, so it seems have all the male population of Hamilton and of the university, as the novel includes no mention of men with war injuries, of other people in the town mourning dead sons, or of memorials to students dead in the war. Although

20 percent of American men aged eighteen to forty-five were in the armed services during the war, nearly three-fifths of them conscripted, and although conscription meant that they were plucked randomly out of the population, the novel mentions no one but Tom lost in the war and no one mutilated or traumatized by it, no other lost or harmed sons or brothers or fiancées or husbands or fathers or neighbors or former students or friends.

Cather is representing her Jewish character, who has stayed out of the war and prospered while it was going on, in a significantly different light than is Wharton. Everyone else around Louie, with the tremendous exception of Tom Outland, has evidently done the same sort of thing he has during the war years. It seems to me that Cather is not so much representing Louie as having in a shady way evaded the draft as she is rewriting the history of the war, in this novel, as one without conscription. By omitting the fact of conscription, Cather's novel makes participation in the war voluntary, noble. Tom functions as the symbol of all young American men tragically dead in the war. But those deaths are rewritten as willing sacrifices. Rather than evoking the deaths of men in an American army, nearly three-fifths of whom were conscripts, that belatedly, in Cather's view, entered the war in 1917, Cather rewrites those deaths, through the figure of Tom Outland, as the willing sacrifices of men who rushed voluntarily into battle as soon as Germany invaded Belgium in 1914 and the war began. Cather thus simultaneously idealizes the war dead and represents the Americans left at home as more untouched by the war than the universality of conscription had in fact made them.

The Jewish Louie Marsellus, then, cheerfully continuing with his life during the war years and indeed making a tremendous amount of money during the war (by transforming Tom's gas into the Outland engine, an engine used in war planes that killed other men), is not depicted as exceptional in Cather's text. Instead, he is *representative* of most of the American population. His extraordinary prosperity during the war years may make him epitomize a morally obtuse American population, but it does not set him apart as an exceptional "slacker."

In *Memorial Fictions*, Trout tellingly observes that although *The Professor's House* makes very little mention of the war, the novel is haunted by the "thing not named," the First World War. One way in which we feel the haunting presence of the war, I believe, is in St. Peter's description of his students: one senses his distaste for this prosperous, postwar crop of young men. Early on in the novel St. Peter comments to Professor Langtry on the "great difference" he feels now in the students, the decline "in the all-embracing respect of quality" (55). As St. Peter later tells Rosamond that in all his years of teaching he has encountered "just one remarkable mind," that of Tom Outland (62), he cannot mean primarily that the students are less intelligent now but that they are inferior in spirit. Lillian St. Peter's description of the Professor's current students as "fat-faced boys" (70), and St. Peter's acceptance of that description, suggests that he (and, surprisingly, she too) feels disdain for the current prosperous generation, not rendered chiseled and gaunt, through loss, pain, and suffering, like the boys-turned-men who went to war.

The cheerful, highly colored, Jewish Louie Marsellus functions in the novel to represent a postwar generation oblivious to what the war has cost and blithely going on with life. The impending "advent of a young Marsellus" (273) mentioned at the end of the novel is one way in which Louie is characterized as, perhaps in a morally obtuse fashion, carrying on with life. St. Peter does not receive the news of his coming grandchild with the slightest enthusiasm. For him, as for Tom, with the war "almost Time itself" (261) has been swept away. But for Louie time has not stopped, and the fertility of this Jewish character suggests that he has been little effected by the war. In Ernest Hemingway's *The Sun Also Rises*, published in 1926, a year after *The Professor's House*, the inability of the hero, Jake Barnes, to consummate a sexual relationship or to procreate, due to a war wound, is evocative of a generation emotionally shattered by the war. Hemingway's novel is populated by the young and alienated, unable to form stable bonds with one another. The despicable Jewish character in the novel, Robert Cohn, is the only one of the main characters who has children, and that fact sets him apart (damningly to Hemingway) as less sensitive and therefore less damaged than the others. The actual birth rate in the United States dropped in 1919, just after the war, rose close to prewar levels in 1920 and 1921, and then declined steadily during the

1920s (Klein 156–57). This real decline in the birth rate may lie behind the use of childlessness in novels of the 1920s (consider also F. Scott Fitzgerald's *The Great Gatsby*) as a representation of postwar anomie. Kathleen and Scott interestingly have had no children, though they have been married for at least six years, if the date of the events at the end of *The Professor's House* is 1921 (and longer if it is closer to 1925), but by ending the novel as the St. Peters and the Marselluses anticipate the upcoming birth of Louie and Rosamond's child, Cather links her Jewish character with a cheerful, oblivious, postwar continuation of life.[6]

In *The Professor's House*, then, Cather is associating her Jewish character with nonparticipation in the war, with personally prospering in a morally suspect way during those years, and with continuing on with life apparently untouched by the war. Louie also is characterized by a certain vulgarity of manner and appearance. And yet, as critics have noted, Louie is good-hearted, pleasingly full of joie de vivre, and, as the Professor says, "an absolutely generous chap" (128). Cather does link the Jewish Louie with attitudes toward the war for which other writers (and public speakers) denigrated the Jews, but she is at the same time, I would contend, highly ambivalent about how to respond to the attitudes toward the war she has associated with her Jewish character. She is equally ambivalent about how to respond to the antithetical attitude toward the war that she associates with Tom Outland and with the Professor, an attitude that is noble, self-sacrificing, celebratory of loss in an ideal cause—and also cold and inhuman.

The references to the Dreyfus affair in the climactic argument between Tom Outland and Roddy Blake underline the way that Cather is aligning the cold purity of idealism (Tom's) with a hostile misapprehension of Jews and aligning a spirit emphasizing human ties and warm practicality rather than disembodied ideals (Roddy's) with a defense of Jews against false, anti-Semitic charges. Condemning Roddy for selling the artifacts from the Blue Mesa, Tom tells him, "You've gone and sold your country's secrets, like Dreyfus." "That man was innocent. It was a frame-up," Roddy murmurs (242). Alfred Dreyfus, a Jewish captain in the French army, was wrongly accused and convicted in 1894 of selling

French military secrets to the Germans. Amidst a storm of international controversy and anti-Semitic accusations, he appealed but was again convicted in 1899. In 1898 Emile Zola wrote his famous open letter to the French president, "J'accuse," in which he castigated the French government for unjustly conspiring with the military to condemn Dreyfus. Cather evidently agreed that Dreyfus had been wrongly condemned, as in 1899 she praised "the courage of the hand that penned the 'J'accuse' letter" (*World and the Parish* 2:724; Lee 251). Her belief that Tom is wrong about Dreyfus makes Tom's behavior toward Roddy, once he has sold the artifacts, all the more questionable.

Tom is associated with sacrificing friendship and human bonds for an ideal, "high and blue" (252) above human life, and with self-sacrifice in war. But he is also associated with the most extreme version of the belief, widely circulating in the teens and twenties, that the Jew is unpatriotic and disloyal. Those who were immediately ready to believe Dreyfus guilty did so because they thought of Jews as traitors, capable of betraying the country in which they lived and of aiding the enemy, Germany. For Cather, this was evidently a misconstruing of the Jew. And to see Roddy as like Marsellus—generous, practical, choosing human bonds rather than an insubstantial ideal—is to see that Roddy's implicit defense of Jews is a defense also of the attitudes toward the war that Cather has embodied in her Jewish character.

But if Louie is aligned with Roddy, St. Peter is aligned with Tom Outland. Like Tom, St. Peter chooses a life of intellectual idealism over connectedness with others, living high in his study above the "warm human house," immersing himself in the blue lake, withdrawing from his family, from life and from the future, feeling that the "great catastrophe" that was the Great War has swept away "all youth and all palms, and almost Time itself" (261). Cather suggests, not unsympathetically, that St. Peter's postwar disengagement from life and Tom's wartime idealism express one possible response to the war. But the response she embodies in her Jewish character is also possible and not despicable: indeed, Louie, in his pleasure in his own prosperity, his loving connections with others, his procreativity, and his apparent obliviousness to the implications of the war, his evident sense that time has not stopped, feels warmer and more human than the Professor does as the novel draws to a close.

Cather does represent the Jewish Louie ambivalently in this novel, linking him, in a way congruent with untrue anti-Semitic accusations widely circulating at the time, with particular choices in relation to the war. But she also makes him a warm, likable, and generous character, and she even indirectly calls anti-Semitic thought into question in this novel. The ambivalence with which she represents the Jewish Louie seems to arise out of her own struggle to come to terms with the war, to decide on the most humanly acceptable response to an unthinkable catastrophe. Using the figure of the Jew, Cather represents the possibilities of behavior in relation to the war in terms very similar to those that structure Wharton's *A Son at the Front* and in terms very similar to those circulating in popular discourse in the war years and the twenties. But, far more ambivalent than Wharton about embracing pain and loss and idealism, Cather struggles with a problem formulated in similar terms — embrace sacrifice or behave like a Jew — but comes to a different resolution, and in doing so, she represents Jews more sympathetically. In both *A Son at the Front* and *The Professor's House*, the stereotypical figure of the Jew — disengaged from the war, prosperous, commercial — serves to highlight self-sacrifice in war. Yet while Wharton uses her Jews to represent ignoble wartime selfishness, Cather ultimately uses the figure of the Jew to suggest the obverse postwar danger — that of refusing to move beyond the ecstasy of personal pain and loss.

NOTES

1. The following account of anti-Semitic rhetoric during the war, of Jews' participation in the war, and of the process of conscription, is heavily indebted to Sterba, Chambers, and Vital. Sterba describes the anti-Semitic rhetoric but does not connect it with the problem of draft quotas in districts filled with nondeclarant immigrants; he attributes it primarily to the prominent Jewish opposition to the war and to registered Jews, draft-averse because of their recent experiences in Russia, taking advantage of available exemptions. Chambers, who discusses this problem of

draft quotas and immigrants, does not link it with the particularly vehement anti-Semitic rhetoric. Neither of the two discusses McCall's book. My account of anti-Semitism and conscription during these years brings the two issues together and also adds a discussion of McCall's *Patriotism of the American Jew*.

2. Such a policy was never enacted, as to draft citizens of other countries would have caused a diplomatic crisis. Only in May 1918 did Congress revise the draft law so that quotas were thenceforth based not on the total population of a district but on the population of men in the most eligible draft category in that district (Chambers, *To Raise an Army* 227–28).

3. McCall's book is introduced by a foreword by Charles W. Eliot, then president emeritus of Harvard, who notes that "a wave of anti-Semitic feeling has lately passed over the American people . . . stimulated by an active propaganda through the Press" (9). Eliot supports McCall's agenda and agrees that Jews have voluntarily borne a proportionally greater burden of military service, but it is interesting to note that he also, perhaps unwittingly, expresses anti-Semitic sentiments of his own, noting that anti-Semitism is not an "unnatural feeling" in response to Jewish success in America, expressing gratification that this feeling is based not "on dislike of the Hebrew religion, but of some of the Jewish racial qualities," and expressing satisfaction that intermarriage between races "is generally condemned by medical, sanitary, and eugenic authorities" (12–13).

4. Edith Wharton's war writing seems to grant temporary, honorary "white" status to various races fighting on the side of the Allies. In a brief passage in *Fighting France*, she writes admiringly of the Indian troops serving under the British flag: she describes regiment after regiment passing "of slim turbaned Indians, with delicate proud faces like the faces of Princes in Persian miniatures" (178). Wharton is similarly pleased to see the Algerian zouaves serving in the French army. Her description of "that throng of dusky merry faces under their red fezes" and of a "grinning" soldier just decorated for bravery contains vestiges of racial characterization. But Wharton approaches the zouaves in an inclusive spirit, posing for a photograph with the regiment, noting that though the just-decorated zouave soldier protests, when drawn into the photograph, "Me? Why my ugly mug will smash the plate!" "But it didn't—" (169). The photograph of heroic, metaphorically white soldiers fighting in the Allied cause can expand to include the zouaves without "smash[ing] the plate." But Wharton's temporarily expanded racial acceptance in her wartime writing does not extend to the Jews, despite the many French Jews who fought and died for France during the war.

5. I calculate Tom to be about twenty-nine when he dies in 1915 because he guesses himself to be twenty the summer before he enters the univer-

sity (113), so he graduates at about twenty-four. Two years later he travels in the summer with St. Peter to the Southwest and the Blue Mesa (now age twenty-six; 259). The next summer they go to Mexico (age twenty-seven; 260), and the next summer is 1914, and Tom joins the Foreign Legion (age twenty-eight) and dies the following year at age twenty-nine. For other slightly varying discussions of dates in the novel, see Harrell; Stich.

6. I am not fully persuaded by Harrell's contention that the date of the novel's opening must be as early as 1919 or 1920 (Stich points out that it must be 1920, as Prohibition began that year) and that it ends in 1921. But it could be later (Prohibition did not end until 1933): Harrell calculates that it is early because he believes that Rosamond and Louie are recently married, as they speak of moving their wedding presents to Outland (Harrell 220). But Rosamond and Louie have been engaged since 1916 and may have been married quite a while. They have been living in a rented house, which they are now ready to give up, and they have been married long enough to choose furniture for that house carefully and to be ready (or at least, Louie is) to give it away and buy new furniture. Louie has a chiffonnier that Scott has admired for some time (164). If it is later than 1921 at the end of the novel, possibly some time between 1921 and 1925, then Kathleen and Scott have been married and childless for even longer than six years.

WORKS CITED

Belloc, Hilaire. *The Jews*. Boston: Houghton Mifflin, 1922.

Cather, Willa. *The Professor's House*. 1925. Willa Cather Scholarly Edition. Ed. Frederick M. Link, James Woodress, and Kari A. Ronning. Lincoln: U of Nebraska P, 2002.

———. *The World and the Parish: Willa Cather's Articles and Reviews 1893-1902*. Ed. William M. Curtin. 2 vols. Lincoln: U of Nebraska P, 1970.

Chambers, John Whiteclay, II. *To Raise an Army: The Draft Comes to Modern America*. New York: Macmillan, 1987.

———. "Selective Service." *The United States in the First World War: An Encyclopedia*. Ed. Anne Cipriano Venzon. New York: Garland, 1995.

Dearborn (MI) Independent. In *The International Jew, The World's Foremost Problem*. 4 vols. Dearborn MI: Dearborn Publishing, 1920-22.

Eliot, Charles W. Foreword. *Patriotism of the American Jew*. New York: Plymouth P, 1924.

Fisher-Wirth, Ann. "Anasazi Cannibalism: Eating Eden." *Willa Cather and the American Southwest*. Ed. John N. Swift and Joseph R. Urgo. Lincoln: U of Nebraska P, 2002. 22–30.

Fitzgerald, F. Scott. *The Great Gatsby*. 1925. New York: Macmillan, 1992.

Flynn, George Q. *Conscription and Democracy: France, Great Britain and the United States*. Westport: Greenwood, 2001.

Harrell, David. *From Mesa Verde to the Professor's House*. Albuquerque: U of New Mexico P, 1992.

Hemingway, Ernest. *The Sun Also Rises*. 1926. New York: Scribner, 1954.

Klein, Herbert S. *A Population History of the United States*. Cambridge: Cambridge UP, 2004.

Lee, Hermione. *Willa Cather: Double Lives*. New York: Vintage, 1989.

McCall, Samuel Walker. *Patriotism of the American Jew*. New York: Plymouth P, 1924.

Michaels, Walter Benn. *Our America: Nativism, Modernism, Pluralism*. Durham: Duke UP, 1995.

Schroeter, James. "Willa Cather and *The Professor's House*." *Yale Review* 54 (1965): 494–512.

Sterba, Christopher M. *Good Americans: Italian and Jewish Immigrants During the First World War*. New York: Oxford UP, 2003.

Stich, Klaus P. "*The Professor's House*: Prohibition, Ripe Grapes, and Euripedes." *Cather Studies 4: Willa Cather's Canadian and Old World Connections*. Ed. Robert Thacker and Michael A. Peterman. Lincoln: U of Nebraska P, 1999. 225–43.

Stout, Janis P. *Willa Cather: The Writer and Her World*. Charlottesville: UP of Virginia, 2000.

Trout, Steven. *Memorial Fictions: Willa Cather and the First World War*. Lincoln: U of Nebraska P, 2002.

Vital, David. *A People Apart: The Jews in Europe, 1789-1939*. New York: Oxford UP, 1999.

Wallace, Max. *The American Axis: Henry Ford, Charles Lindbergh, and the Rise of the Third Reich*. New York: St. Martin's P, 2003.

Wasserman, Loretta. "Cather's Semitism." *Cather Studies 2*. Ed. Susan J. Rosowski. Lincoln: U of Nebraska P, 1993. 1–22.

Wharton, Edith. *Fighting France: From Dunkerque to Belfort*. New York: Scribner's, 1915.

———. *The Marne*. New York: Appleton, 1918.

———. *A Son at the Front*. DeKalb: Northern Illinois UP, 1995.

Woodress, James. *Willa Cather: A Literary Life*. Lincoln: U of Nebraska P, 1987.

Looking at Agony
World War I in *The Professor's House*

JENNIFER HAYTOCK

I like a look of agony,
Because I know it's true—
—Emily Dickinson

In her prefatory note to *Not Under Forty* (1936), Willa Cather famously wrote that "the world broke in two in 1922 or thereabouts." Why she picked this year has not been satisfactorily explained, for she announces the split as a public event rather than the personal one that critics often understand her to mean.[1] Biographers and critics tend to point to the scathing reviews that her 1922 war novel *One of Ours* received and that caused Cather to sink into a depression as the reason she may have marked 1922 as a significant year. I believe, however, that Cather's ongoing attempt to understand World War I drove her to pick 1922 as the decisive year: at the end of *One of Ours*, the narrative indicates that Claude Wheeler died pointlessly, leaving us and Cather to wonder why the war occurred and how wars could be stopped. She tackled World War I again, less directly, in her 1925 novel *The Professor's House*, and in this novel she plays with a far more unsettling conclusion: that war is simultaneously meaningless and unavoidable.

The novel reflects a modernist postwar sense of alienation, fragmentation, and emptiness in Professor Godfrey St. Peter. But through "Tom Outland's Story," we see a different experience and understanding of society and civilization that seem to belie what we think we know about war. That is, most war novels reject war and the ideals that rationalize war; Cather's *One of Ours* distances itself from its war hero, Claude Wheeler, and from the propaganda of war through the eyes of Claude's mother and returning veterans in its last pages, all of whom understand that Claude's sacrifice has not changed the world. Tom Outland, however, is not Claude Wheeler. Claude enlists in the army in search of something bigger to compensate him for his sense of loss; Tom too has experienced loss, but the differences in what the two men have lost are profound. Claude's losses consist mainly of things he never had: a loving, supportive relationship with his father, a challenging education, a fulfilling marriage, and a society that values what he wants to give. Tom, on the other hand, has lost a true friend through his own self-righteousness, his innocence at the hands of the U.S. government bureaucracy, and an ancient society that gave him a sense of belonging. Tom Outland is not the immature, needy character that Claude Wheeler is. He is optimistic and idealistic but not naïve. So why does he join the fight, and why is Professor Godfrey St. Peter's middle-age malaise centered on Tom Outland's story?

This essay will address both questions, focusing first on "Tom Outland's Story" and then moving to the Professor. Tom's tale, which precipitates the Professor's crisis, resonates through the Professor's search for meaning. The ruling connection, I believe, is the concept of civilization, particularly ideas about the power of art and about the ideal society toward which members of the late-nineteenth- and early-twentieth-century Progressive Movement believed the United States was heading. Cather was deeply disturbed and depressed by the war, in part because she, like many other intellectuals and artists, saw Europe as her cultural home; Janis P. Stout, studying Cather's essays about her 1902 European tour, tells us that "France, in particular, she saw as a center of both natural beauty and high-art treasures" (165). The portrayal of Germans as kindly artists in *The Song of the Lark* (1915) suggests Cather also had sympathies with German culture, and the act of aggression on Germany's part must have been particularly disturbing to her. More broadly, Cather wrote amid the optimism of the Progressive Movement; Guy Reynolds, in *Willa Cather in Context*, describes the political and social motivations and programs that loosely fall under the Progressive banner and which can be seen as united in the quest to better the world: "Progressives thus formulated a Utopian imagery of a purified nation, a fervent language of renewal. Their secular heaven was squarely in the tradition of American idealism, a redeployment of the classic images of the godly city on the hill" (12). World War I did not destroy the impetus of Progressivism, but it did shatter the widely held belief that society was always improving and would one day reach a pinnacle of peace and prosperity.

The Professor's House takes the form of an almost entirely domestic plot: the St. Peters are in the process of moving to a new house, purchased with money won by the Professor's academic achievement, though the Professor himself resists leaving the old house, to which he is bound by both professional and personal memories. His once loving relationships with his daughters and wife are now worn out and painful; his daughters, Rosamond and Kitty, in particular are bitten by consumer greed distressing to their father. His wife, Lillian, sensing her husband's emotional indifference and clinging to her own youth, has shifted her attention from him to her sons-in-law. The Professor's detachment from his family culminates in his decision to remain at home while they travel to Europe for the summer. Their absence allows him time to loaf and daydream and to analyze his own life, in the process recalling the story of his protégé and Rosamond's former fiancé, Tom Outland, who before coming to Hamilton discovered the ruins of an ancient society in the American Southwest. As the Professor travels backward in his life and through Tom's, he must face what Steven Trout identifies as "the thing not named" in the novel (151): the Great War.

At first glance, the description of Tom Outland's departure for Europe in 1914 suggests the typical war story: a young man leaves for battle at the behest of an older man, one associated with ideals. At the beginning of the war, Father Duchene, the priest who helped Tom and his partner Rodney Blake in their study of the ancient civilization on the mesa, comes through Hamilton on his way to help refugees in his native Belgium. This circumstance fits with the propaganda that grew in the United States to convince Americans to go to war; in his 1996 study *Propaganda for War*, Stewart Halsey Ross shows that the British insisted the reason for the war was defense of Belgium neutrality and that British propagandists, in order to outrage Americans, exploited and even invented stories of atrocities committed against Belgians by Germans (46–47). It is not unreasonable to assume, as do the Professor's son-in-law Louie Marsellus (40) and many readers and critics, that Tom dashed off to be a hero on the wings of romanticism and idealism. This interpretation of his motives, however, does not coincide with what else we know about Tom; Louie, after all, has never met Tom, and even he notes that Tom's procurement of a patent for his invention is "curious" for "such a hot-headed fellow" (40). Critics often fail to account for growth or change in Tom, encapsulated as he is both within the text and within the Professor's view of him. But I think it quite likely that Tom learns from his experiences and his own weaknesses and that he changes as a character.

Although he is not unique in doing so, Tom does not go to war with the American military; he leaves in 1914, long before the United States publicly committed to the Allies, and fights with the Foreign Legion.[2] Having been to Washington to try to raise interest in his finds on the mesa and suffered under its bureaucracy, perhaps he knows that he cannot wait for the U.S. government to take action. In Washington he boards with a man who has "some position in the War Department. How it used to depress me to see all the hundreds of clerks come pouring out that big building at sunset! Their lives seemed to me so petty, so slavish" (232). Tom sees that war has become an institution populated and run by drones.[3] He also witnesses the man and his wife agonize over whether they will receive an invitation to a reception, and once they have been invited they both suffer over the wife's dress. Tom is disgusted with this concern for appearances and the living beyond one's means that it requires, but he must also note the link between the profit produced by war, problematic in itself, and the inability to enjoy it. An "Austrian Archduke" figures prominently in the director of the Smithsonian's self-satisfied stories "about balls and receptions, and the names and titles of all the people he had met" (231), suggesting that the assassination of Archduke Ferdinand might not strike Tom as a great loss. In general, Tom's Washington episode portrays the U.S. government as insulated and insular, symbolized by "the fence that shuts in the White House grounds" (233).

The president, in Tom's experience, is out of touch and inaccessible to his constituency and to the larger obligations of the nation; though Theodore Roosevelt would have been president when Tom was in Washington, the "shut in" White House signifies President Woodrow Wilson's isolationist stance—and, in fact, the isolationism of many Americans. Finally Tom leaves Washington, "wiser than I came" (236). This experience helps explain why, in August 1914, Tom leaves for war rather than wait for the U.S. entry in May 1917. He does not go to war for his country but rather for "civilization"—a sentimental ideal, perhaps, but not a national one.

Tom's story shows that he was, at one time, an idealistic young man, but he has seen his ideals fail not only through government bureaucracy but also through his own internal weakness. When he returns to the mesa after his failed visit to Washington, he attacks Roddy for selling the artifacts that are so precious to him and that are, to him, symbolic of the power of friendship: "There never was any question of money with me, where this mesa and its people were concerned. They were something that had been preserved through the ages by a miracle, and handed on to you and me, two poor cow-punchers, rough and ignorant, but I thought we were men enough to keep a trust" (244). His disappointment in Roddy demonstrates that even the most sacred of personal relationships can fail to live up to his standards. Nevertheless, he enjoys the quiet time of study and reflection on the mesa that follows Roddy's departure. Gradually, however, he acknowledges within himself a selfishness and impurity of motives, an inability to forgive his friend, and a self-centeredness that drives Roddy away: "The older I grow, the more I understand what it was I did that night on the mesa. Anyone who requites faith and friendship as I did, will have to pay for it. I'm not very sanguine about good fortune for myself. I'll be called to account when I least expect it" (253). By cherishing people dead and gone more than the living, he destroys his ideals about himself as a loyal friend, and he accepts any retribution he will receive as just.

Even before his Washington trip, however, Tom Outland learns a harsh lesson about civilization—one that Tom, the Professor, readers, and Cather herself may not want to learn. Father Duchene tells Tom that the civilization on the mesa was probably destroyed because its members became too rarefied, too absorbed in the "higher" calling of the arts to remember how to engage in physical violence: "With the proper variation of meat and vegetable diet, they developed physically and improved in the primitive arts. They had looms and mills, and experimented with dyes. At the same time, they possibly declined in the arts of war, in brute strength and ferocity" (220). Father Duchene speculates that they "[made] their mesa more and more worthy to be a home for man, purifying life by religious ceremonies and observances, caring respectfully for their dead, protecting the children, doubtless entertaining some feelings of affection and sentiment for this stronghold where they were at once so safe and so comfortable" (220). Ultimately, however, he suggests that this Edenistic society was "probably wiped out, utterly exterminated, by some roving Indian tribe without culture or domestic virtues, some horde that fell upon them in their summer camp and destroyed them for their hides and clothing and weapons, or from mere love of slaughter" (221). Father Duchene may not be the most reliable narrator—for one reason precisely *because* he insists on narrating, as John N. Swift points out (18–19)—but his is the version that Tom seems to accept, as he writes it into his diary (223). The ancient society becomes a model for Progressivism, as Reynolds demonstrates; by looking at "Tom Outland's Story" in light of the Progressive Movement, "the great, good places of Cather's fiction emerge as part of a larger cultural pattern, namely the Utopian idealism of progressive America and its reforming drive to recreate the nation as an earthly Eden" (15).

Reynolds further argues, however, that Cather could not sustain her belief in such societies, that "she also imagined the dream's failure" (15). The ideal of an ever-improving society is subverted by one of Tom and Roddy's most precious finds: a mummified woman they call "Mother Eve," whom they identify as the maternal source of the people and of their culture. But she died in violence: "We thought she had been murdered. . . . Her mouth was open as if she were screaming, and her face, through all those years, had kept a terrible look of agony" (214). Tom and Roddy do not and cannot know the story of this brutal death, but they ought to have recognized that her body and her "terrible look of agony" contradict Father Duchene's interpretation of the society as peaceful and "purified." Father Duchene later suggests that she was murdered for adultery (223), committing further violence against the dead woman by imposing his own interpretation onto her body and simultaneously suggesting that an ideal and peaceful society still has the right to exact lethal vengeance on its unfaithful women.

A society "too far advanced for their time and environment" (221)—the concept may have come back to Tom when Germany invaded Belgium. Western society generally was shocked at the event, believing Europe to be too far evolved for such violence to take place.[4] Practically speaking as well, the United States was unprepared, lacking a significant standing army and relying on a poorly trained National Guard. Historian Robert H. Zieger shows that as late as 1916 many Americans, though supportive of a navy, did not see the point of an army and were not properly informed as to its need: "Proponents of army enlargement . . . painted lurid pictures of massive ocean-borne attacks of forays up the Mississippi by battle-hardened, yet somehow unbloodied, enemies" (38). In *The Professor's House*, however, Tom Outland has learned through the destruction of his beloved ancient society that violence is sometimes necessary and that a culture that forgets this lesson risks total annihilation. (Not coincidentally, it is a German who buys Tom and Roddy's artifacts and a Frenchman as well as the Belgian priest who take an intelligent interest in the archeological find [235–36].)

Godfrey St. Peter studies his family and his memory of Tom Outland in an attempt to understand aging and his inevitable death. As Susan J. Rosowki argues, the Professor's self-analysis takes the form of journeying inward, past his family and Tom to his "original self." Rosowski ably discusses this journey, but I intend to pause longer over Tom and the First World War and to explore further what both mean to the Professor. The placement of Tom's story indicates that it serves as part of the process of the Professor's self-analysis and thus functions as a catalyst for the moment of laxity that amounts to an attempt at self-destruction. In the first part of the novel, we see that the Professor has suffered significant, though not unusual, losses, including his daughters' growing up, the ending of the intimate part of his marriage, the death of Tom, and the passing of the Professor's own youth. But a larger cultural loss the Professor must face is the rift that World War I created in his life and in his society. It is only through Tom's story that World War I begins to make sense to the Professor, although in a most disturbing way: wars exist because they have to be fought, not to "make the world safe for democracy" or to rescue Belgians or for any of the other reasons sold to the American public. Rather, they must be fought because people will fight them. Even brilliant, sensitive, educated Tom, who thinks of long-dead Indian women as his "grandmothers" (243) and who spends hours entertaining the Professor's daughters, participates in the horror of the Great War, presumably committing violence in the name of stopping it. Father Duchene's interpretation of the destruction of the mesa people serves as a warning: Americans must remember the arts of war or they will be annihilated. The death of "Mother Eve," however, redirects Father Duchene's didactic story from a warning to a no less frightening social comment: the mummy's "look of terrible agony" indicates that the mesa people were not so rarefied after all, and her violent and unexplained death suggests to the Professor that violence simply exists.

Though he rarely thinks of it, Professor St. Peter, like Cather and many Americans, continues to mourn the war and struggles to understand it. For him it is one of a series of disappointments in his life, "one of many lost causes" (143). But it is also a particular horror with which he must come to terms: he recognizes intellectually that it destroyed a young generation for a false ideal, but he does not feel it. Thinking of the dead Tom, he regrets the trip to Paris the two of them never had time to take, and the war becomes "chance" that "in one great catastrophe, swept away all youth and all palms, and almost Time itself" (260). He never tries to imagine the violence of war itself, including the many possible painful ways Tom may have died. For the Professor, Tom's death is minutely personalized (as in the never-taken trip) or broadly viewed (as the "great catastrophe") but has little to do with Tom himself. The clearest memory the Professor has of Tom, apart from Tom's story in which the Professor is not a participant, is the day Tom walked into the St. Peters' garden, lunched with the family, and gave the girls turquoises—a moment frozen in the Professor's mind: "'Hold them still a moment,' said the Professor, looking down, not at the turquoises, but at the hand that held them: the muscular, many-lined palm, the long, strong fingers with soft ends, the straight little finger, the flexible, beautifully shaped thumb that curved back from the rest of the hand as if it were its own master. What a hand! He could see it yet, with the blue stones lying in it" (121). The Professor fails to find a way to mourn Tom specifically, his death making even his life seem unreal. Instead of grieving, the Professor simply cuts himself off from his past.

This is not an entirely unconscious psychological step, however; the Professor knows that he has not fully mourned Tom or the war. Sharon O'Brien argues that in writing *One of Ours* Cather walked a fine line between "combat envy," a woman's desire to understand the transforming effects of battle, and "survivor guilt," the complex reaction of the woman writer to her power of narrating a dead soldier's story: "[Cather] was profiting at the soldiers' expense, deriving a release of creative energy from their suffering and death" (197). In *The Professor's House,* it is not Cather but the Professor who must face survivor guilt. He consistently resists financial gain from Tom's death, refusing Rosamond's offer to give him money from Tom's invention: "There can be no question of money between me and Tom Outland. I can't explain just how I feel about it, but it would somehow damage my recollections of him, would make that episode in my life commonplace like everything else" (62). Yet even in this passage the Professor's way of "profiting" from Tom's death becomes clear; he lives off the memories of his friendship with Tom. This in itself eats at the Professor as a form of "survival guilt," and he risks further "profit" through his idea to publish Tom's diary with an introduction—a project that seems to fall by the wayside after his near-suicide. The Professor's "survival guilt" is further complicated by the tricky problem of memory. Trout points out that none of the characters in *The Professor's House* effectively remember or memorialize Tom Outland—a problem, Trout argues, endemic to American postwar society in general. Even if the Professor could hold on to Tom's memory, he seems reluctant to do so. He tells his wife when she asks what disturbs him, "It's the feeling that I've put a great deal behind me, where I can't go back to it again—and I don't really wish to go back" (163). This sentence is often read as the Professor facing midlife and rejecting his family; it is also his recognition that he no longer wants even Tom back. During the Professor's summer daydreams while his family is away, Tom gets replaced: "Tom Outland had not come back again through the garden door (as he had so often done in dreams!), but another boy had: the boy the Professor had long ago left behind him in Kansas . . . the original unmodified Godfrey St. Peter" (263). By the end, the Professor acknowledges his inability and even unwillingness to keep Tom alive in memory, a failure for a historian equivalent to killing Tom all over again but simultaneously a way to avoid further "profit" from Tom's death.

World War I figures in the Professor's life not only as the loss of Tom and the signifier of a greater cultural loss but also as a turning point in his relationship with his daughters. The war corresponds to the coming-of-age and marriages of Rosamond and Kitty—in other words, their participation in the world of adult sexuality. For the Professor, I suggest, the latter event is just as traumatic as the horror of war in Europe and forever inextricably bound to it, sewn together like his daughters' dresses. He thinks longingly of the days when Kitty and Rosamond were children: "Sitting thus in his study, long afterward, St. Peter reflected that those first years, before Outland had done anything remarkable, were really the best of all. He liked to remember the charming groups of three he was always coming upon,—in the hammock swing between the linden-trees, in the window-seat, or before the dining-room fire" (125). The war "swept away all youth," not only Tom's but also Kitty's and Rosamond's; the house in which the Professor remains holds the ghost of young Kitty, sitting silently on the stairs with her hand swollen by bee stings until her father is ready to leave his work (88). Unexplored in the novel is the Professor's reaction to Rosamond and Tom's engagement or any details of their relationship at all. We do, however, discover a fragment about Kitty's engagement: "Kathleen had never been deaf to reasoning, deaf to her father, but once; and that was when, shortly after Rosamond's engagement to Tom, she announced that she was going to marry Scott McGregor" (65). That Kitty's one moment of defiance of her father is in her decision to marry—or in her choice of whom to marry—signals both the Professor's claim on his daughter and the defeat of that claim in the face of her status as an adult. The violent fate of Tom's "Mother Eve"—stabbed for infidelity, as Father Duchene speculates, and then lost down a cliff and abandoned as trash by the German profiteer—resonates through the novel, indicating severe penalties for female disloyalty. Rosamond's engagement to Tom may have provoked feelings of betrayal in her father, who later wonders if there is "no way but Medea's" (126) to keep hold of his daughters. Demaree C. Peck argues that the Professor "wishes to prevent his children from becoming 'owned' by others" and implies that by keeping Augusta's dress frames in his study, he attempts to hold on to his little girls (199–200). Tom Outland, ironically, is the form in which the loss of the Professor's daughters first appears, not only in his engagement to Rosamond but also in his storytelling, which made him a favorite with the girls when they were little. In fact, the earliest conflicts emerge in the Professor's exclusion from the circle of Tom, Rosamond, and Kitty; as Kitty reminds him, "You know Tom told us about [Roddy] long before he ever told you" (131).

The threat to the Professor's possession of his daughters does not end with Tom's death, for other suitors come and he still loses his girls, intellectually and physically. As adults, Kitty and especially Rosamond fail to worship their father and repeatedly submit him to their petty materialism and quarrels; they no longer have their "generous impulses" (126). The novel, in fact, is full of unfaithful women: Kitty and Rosamond betraying their father by marrying, Rosamond moving on after Tom's death, the possibility of Rosamond's continued feelings for Tom after her marriage to Louie Marsellus (109), and Lillian St. Peter's shifting of her emotional loyalties to her daughters' husbands. The Professor accepts, even welcomes, his wife's new interests: "With her sons-in-law she had begun the game of being a woman all over again. She dressed for them, planned for them, schemed in their interests. . . . It was splendid, St. Peter told himself. She wasn't going to have to face a stretch of boredom between being a young woman and being a young grandmother" (79). Happy though he may be for Lillian, her redirected attention must only remind him of his own lost youth and that he no longer needs a woman planning and scheming for him. The full impact of his daughters' marriages on the

Professor can best be seen on the day he almost gasses himself; he carries in his pockets letters that bring clear news of Rosamond's "infidelity"—that is, expectations for "the advent of a young Marsellus" (273). He can no longer hold his daughters close, childlike and sexless, as he does their dress forms, now that Rosamond is expecting her own child.

Thus Professor St. Peter must reconcile himself not only to the losses in his life but to the reality of his world. He cannot stay in his "walled-in garden" (14), and he cannot permanently escape to the freedom of swimming in the lake (30). He prefers peace and solitude, even quiet family time, but all these things rest on an underlying violence. Even a trip downstairs from his study is a "perilous journey" (27). His "civilization"—the worlds of domesticity, art, and intellectualism—exist only in balance with danger and violence. The reference to Medea links great art and culture with sexual jealousy and the slaughter of children, and the murder of "Mother Eve" shows that "civilization" rests on violence, whether it is the civilization of the ancient people or the civilization that grows out of the Judeo-Christian tradition. The Professor's great scholarly achievement, *Spanish Adventurers in North America*, pays homage to violence, for such explorers sacrificed many Native peoples in their quests—the Professor's life work, then, glorifies the type of violence that may have destroyed the ancient society of Tom Outland's mesa. Even in his personal life the Professor benefits from suffering, embodied in young Kitty's swollen hand and her refusal to disturb him despite her pain. His first name is actually Napoleon, a name kept secret from his daughters, just as the violence of Western civilization is kept secret through the illusion of social evolution. Merrill Maguire Skaggs argues that, artistically, the novel celebrates and pairs art and destruction, pointing to the Professor's lecture in which he says, "The Christian theologians went over the books of the Law, like great artists, getting splendid effect by excision" (qtd. in Skaggs 77), and that the Professor "is immensely interesting partially *because* he is so appealing and so appalling" (78). Peace and violence, comfort and loss in this novel are inextricably linked.

The only way to keep living, the Professor finds, is to disengage from his family but to root himself in its forms. In *The Professor's*

House domesticity is associated with both women and men. Tom and Roddy's domestic life on the mesa has been well documented.[5] The basis of this domestic life is companionship and cooperation; of Roddy, Tom says, "What he needed was a pal, a straight fellow to give an account to" (185). The relationship between the two men rests on this notion of accountability and responsibility to someone else. Not until their cook and housekeeper Henry arrives, however, are they described as a "happy family" (198), indicating that the housekeeper is a necessary part of domestic order. Henry's death is tragic to Tom and Roddy, and, significantly, it immediately precedes Father Duchene's interpretation of the civilization and the decision to send Tom to Washington.

The Professor, like Tom, relies heavily on the benefits of domesticity in order to create his intellectual work. He enjoys the sounds of his family in his house as he writes (101). Of course, the Professor clearly regulates his view of domestic activities; his very claim of enjoying the sounds below in the house demonstrate his requirement that household activities remain distant. He prefers the less personal link of his work to the seamstress Augusta's work. They share space during the weeks Augusta sews for the family, and when the St. Peters move to the new house the Professor insists that Augusta's frames for dressmaking be left behind. Augusta functions within the St. Peter household much as Henry does on the mesa; she establishes and maintains domestic order: "Augusta, he reflected, had always been a corrective, a remedial influence" (280). She understands impersonal domesticity; when the Professor confesses, the night he almost dies, that he feels lonely "for the first time in months," Augusta replies, "That's because your family are coming home" (279). The spinster Augusta ironically understands that one can feel more isolated in the presence of people one loves than in actually being alone. She also serves as a mediator through which the Professor understands death: "He used to say that he didn't mind hearing Augusta announce these deaths which seemed to happen so frequently along her way, because her manner of speaking about it made death seem less uncomfortable. She hadn't any of the sentimentality that comes from a fear of dying. She talked about death as she spoke of a hard winter or a rainy March, or any of the sadnesses of nature" (281). Augusta, as domesticity in embodied form, makes death, whether strangers', Tom's, or the Professor's own, part of the natural order.

Ultimately, the routine, reliable nature of housekeeping saves the Professor, and not only literally. In his deepest despair, the Professor thinks that falling out of love means "falling out of all domestic and social relations, out of his place in the human family" (275), but he discovers that domesticity is more powerful than personalities. Critic Ann Romines establishes domestic ritual as a way of ordering the world in the face of chaotic forces: "A woman who achieved faculty and made effective ritual of her house-keeping was taking on godlike status, as she pushed back confusion daily, to create her own domestic sphere" (10). Through the process of housekeeping we can understand how the Professor's world has been and will again be manageable. If "Time" is so nearly destroyed by war, Cather looks to the cyclical nature of housekeeping as a way to defy time. Both the Professor and Tom comment that they cannot and do not want to go back in time; Tom leaves his diary hidden in the canyon because he "didn't feel the need of that record. It would have been going backward" (252). Eventually, however, he does go "backward" and reclaim the diary. Augusta, who "pushes back confusion daily," represents truths that survive the war—the comforts of homemaking and of another human presence: "If [the Professor] had thought of Augusta sooner, he would have got up from the couch sooner. Her presence would have suggested the proper action" (279–80). The Professor's rescue by Augusta perhaps seems too contrived, but the inevitability of the Professor's journey shows us that Augusta's presence is in fact natural and expected, even required: "He even felt a sense of obligation toward her, instinctive, escaping definition, but real. And when you admitted that a thing was real, that was enough—now" (281). Tom Outland understood this obligation—again, "now," after Roddy leaves. Unlike Tom, who valued his dead "grandmothers" over the living, present Roddy and came to regret his priorities, the Professor has the opportunity to continue to live with his family and make good on his obligations.

In a comparison of Kate Chopin's *The Awakening* with *The Pro-*

fessor's House, Katherine Joslin notes the parallels between Edna Pontellier's and Godfrey St. Peter's attempts to reject domesticity and parenthood, and she concludes that "both novels suggest that in a sense there is no place beyond the house, no transcending the domestic world" (179). For Edna this revelation must end in suicide, but the Professor manages to make his peace with domesticity, if not with his family. In *The Professor's House* Cather looks into agony; she faces difficult, even heretical, truths: that war, though pointless, is unavoidable and that family love may wear out and die. Both of these points seem to be contrary to "civilization," but Cather suggests instead that "civilization" is created by an impersonal feeling of responsibility rather than by individual and unreliable loyalties: "There was still Augusta, however; a world full of Augustas, with whom one was outward bound" (281). Here, finally, the Professor has come to find a reason to keep living: family ties may loosen and wither, but ties among "the human family" do not.

NOTES

1. Cather also states in the prefatory note to *Not Under Forty* that "the book will have little interest for people under forty years of age." She saw World War I as a defining break not only for herself but for a whole generation.

2. Meirion and Susie Harries point out that fifteen thousand Americans volunteered for the war before the United States officially declared war (41).

3. Among other writers, John Dos Passos makes a similar charge in *Three Soldiers* (1921).

4. In Edith Wharton's *A Son at the Front* (1923), George Campton calmly dismisses the talk of impending war: "People are too healthy and well-fed now; they're not going off to die in a ditch to oblige anybody" (32).

5. See, for example, Lindemann, "Fear of a Queer Mesa?" for an extended discussion of the connection between Tom and Roddy's domesticity and the "Rooseveltian heteronormativity" that Tom finds in Washington (52).

WORKS CITED

Cather, Willa. *Not Under Forty*. New York: Knopf, 1936.
———. *One of Ours*. New York: Knopf, 1922.
———. *The Professor's House*. New York: Knopf, 1925.
Harries, Meirion, and Susie Harries. *The Last Days of Innocence: America at War, 1917-1918*. New York: Random House, 1997.
Joslin, Katherine. "Finding the Self at Home: Chopin's *The Awakening* and Cather's *The Professor's House*." *Kate Chopin Reconsidered: Beyond the Bayou*. Ed. Lynda S. Boren and Sara deSaussure Davis. Baton Rouge: Louisiana State UP, 1992. 166-79.
Lindemann, Marilee. "Fear of a Queer Mesa? Faith, Friendship, and National Sexuality in 'Tom Outland's Story.'" *Willa Cather and the American Southwest*. Ed. John N. Swift and Joseph R. Urgo. Lincoln: U of Nebraska P, 2002. 43-54.
O'Brien, Sharon. "Combat Envy and Survivor Guilt: Willa Cather's 'Manly Battle Yarn.'" *Arms and the Woman: War, Gender, and Literary Representation*. Ed. Helen M. Cooper, Adrienne Auslander Munich, and Susan Merrill Squier. Chapel Hill: U of North Carolina P, 1989. 184-204.
Peck, Demaree C. *The Imaginative Claims of the Artist in Willa Cather's Fiction*. Selinsgrove PA: Susquehanna UP, 1996.
Reynolds, Guy. *Willa Cather in Context: Progress, Race, Empire*. New York: St. Martin's, 1996.
Romines, Ann. *The Home Plot: Women, Writing and Domestic Ritual*. Amherst: U of Massachusetts P, 1992.
Rosowski, Susan J. *The Voyage Perilous: Willa Cather's Romanticism*. Lincoln: U of Nebraska P, 1986.
Skaggs, Merrill Maguire. *After the World Broke in Two: The Later Novels of Willa Cather*. Charlottesville: U of Virginia P, 1990.
Stout, Janis P. *Willa Cather: The Writer and Her World*. Charlottesville: U of Virginia P, 2000.
Swift, John N. "Unwrapping the Mummy: Cather's Mother Eve and the Business of Desire." *Willa Cather and the American Southwest*. Ed. John N. Swift and Joseph R. Urgo. Lincoln: U of Nebraska P, 2002. 13-21.
Trout, Steven. *Memorial Fictions: Willa Cather and the First World War*. Lincoln: U of Nebraska P, 2002.
Wharton, Edith. *A Son at the Front*. New York: Charles Scribner's Sons, 1923.
Zieger, Robert H. *America's Great War: World War I and the American Experience*. New York: Rowman & Littlefield, 2000.

Cather's Literary Choreography
The "Glittering Idea" of Scientific
Warfare in *The Professor's House*

WENDY K. PERRIMAN

This study examines how Willa Cather used the medium of dance to explore the "glittering idea" of scientific warfare. Inspired by the late-nineteenth-century classical Italian ballet *Excelsior* (juxtaposed against modern performances of *Faust* and *Jeux*), Cather was able to manipulate the "human story" of war with her own unique style of literary choreography. But the ballet motif is difficult to pin down. When Richard Giannone encountered a similar problem with Cather's music metaphors, he looked at the shifts in meaning from her early works to her later novels. This type of approach helps clarify her use of dance imagery too; it is possible to detect the transition from a simple experimental prose translation to a sophisticated subtext woven into the story. For example, *Alexander's Bridge* can be interpreted as a straightforward retelling of the plot from *Swan Lake*,[1] whereas a more mature novel like *The Professor's House* employs a far more subtle and complex approach—the result of a two-decade exposure to dance during which time Cather became an aficionado. As recent scholarship has highlighted the importance of many other arts in Cather's work, it is now time to consider the influence of ballet.

Cather's arrival in New York in 1906 coincided with a resurgence of interest in classical dance generated by Adeline Genée and the stars of the Russian Ballet. Elizabeth Shepley Sergeant's biography *Willa Cather: A Memoir* reveals how ballet "interested her vitally as a balanced trial of grace, poise, muscle and temperament in which a unique individual, the ballerina, could excel." Sergeant explains that the famous Anna Pavlova was a particular favorite of Cather because she was "a superlative mistress of coordination and aesthetic charm" (197). Ballet "divertissements" were traditionally performed as light relief during an opera, usually at the start of the third act. Consequently the Russian dance stars appeared on the same bill as the major opera divas of that period, including Cather's favorite performer, Olive Fremstad.[2] It is therefore reasonable to assume that the writer was exposed to the finest quality ballet from around 1910 onward; she thereafter followed the Russian dance movement with great enthusiasm, even when it was no longer connected to the opera house.

At the turn of the century pioneers of modern dance were following in Isadora Duncan's footsteps, seeking a new form of movement to free them from the staid conventions of European classical ballet. A similar transition was taking place in Russia, which culminated in an exciting program spearheaded by the Ballets Russes. So by the time Cather's enthusiasm was aroused there were three major professional schools of dance: the traditional classical ballet (Italy and France); modern dance, or "classic"/ "barefoot" dancing (Isadora Duncan et al); and modern ballet (the Ballets Russes). Cather dismissed the first type as being antiquated and the second style as being unskilled. Her artistic interest lay in the imagination, innovation, and dynamic energy of the Russian company that produced such phenomena as Vaslav Nijinsky and Anna Pavlova.

Perhaps one of the times when Cather's world "broke in two" was when she first saw Pavlova perform at the Metropolitan Opera House in 1910. From that point on dance could be categorized as being either pre-Pavlovian "entertainment," or post-Pavlovian "high art." For although there is no apparent sequential growth pattern in Cather's treatment of dance themes in her early short stories, they do reveal two very distinct *before* and *after* phases, commemorating the moment when modern ballet was accepted into the kingdom of art.[3]

In 1913 Cather wrote an eleven-page explanatory article for *McClure's* called "Training for the Ballet," featuring photographs and interviews from the fledgling Metropolitan School of Ballet Dancing. Setting herself up as expert, she educates readers to appreciate the five basic positions of classical ballet, bar exercises, "toe dancing," male elevation, and balance skills. She emphasizes the strength, power, and athleticism involved and the rigorous years of training. She also tries to restore the reputation of professional dancers, who for many years had functioned as kept sexual playthings of the European nobility. Cather's article also reveals her personal interest in this exciting discipline. As an artist herself, she appreciated the aesthetic and spiritual side of human movement, commenting on "the creature's enjoyment of its own vitality expressing itself in movement of the body," and recognizing how pure art elevates the soul to "escape from sordid things." She adds that the "great dancer is made, like any other artist, of two things: of a universal human impulse, and a very special and individual experience of it" (86).

Such ideas influence Cather's later work as she embellishes her stories with plots, themes, twists, reversals, and techniques that appear to originate in the world of ballet. By the time Cather wrote *The Professor's House* (1925), her use of the dance motif had become so sophisticated that it allowed her to deconstruct and subvert her own surface texts in fascinating ways—as skilful as a "real dancer's practice is beautiful to see, light and rapid, and characterized by a most satisfying elegance" ("Training" 95). While it is always possible that many other popular sources may have influenced her subtext, the detailed reference to ballets that we know were performed in New York during her time there (or which were so notoriously shocking she would have undoubtedly been familiar with them) is more than merely coincidental when it is sustained from the earliest novel throughout her entire oeuvre, and when so many consistent allusions to a particular dance or dances supplement a specific text.[4]

In a letter of 1940 Cather explains how *The Professor's House* is an experiment with the *Nouvelle* and the *Roman*, and she claims inspiration from the Dutch paintings showing a picture-window view of the sea from a warmly furnished room (Bohlke 125). She also describes the three-part sectioning of the novel as loosely based on the statement-development-restatement musical form of the sonata (Giannone 152–53). But Cather's tripartite structure also reflects three specific ballets: the plot resonates the subliminal homoeroticism of Nijinsky's *Jeux;* the characterization reflects the dance version of *Faust;* and the central theme is reminiscent of the magnificent Italian spectacle *Excelsior.* Together these ballets help elucidate Cather's views on patriarchal culture, scientific progress, and modern warfare. As Patrick W. Shaw explains in *Willa Cather and the Art of Conflict,* the Dutch painting image suggests that "Tom Outland's Story" "is the window in Professor St. Peter's conventional room" (113), but it also emphasizes Steven Trout's observation in *Memorial Fictions* that "the First World War stands much closer to the thematic center of this cryptic text than most critics have acknowledged" (10). The window of "Tom Outland's Story" provides a microcosmic portrait of the destruction of war on an earlier civilization, ironically still being reflected on the macrocosmic world stage centuries later.

When Tom Outland and Rodney Blake discover the Cliff City, they find remnants of a lost community that had "developed considerably the arts of peace" (219): primitive medicine, astronomy, farming, textiles, pottery, and painting. But rival warriors found the natives "in their summer camp and destroyed them for their hides and clothing and weapons, or from mere love of slaughter" (221). It can be no coincidence that the only "one of the original inhabitants—not a skeleton" on the Blue Mesa is a mummified woman, thought to have been murdered by her own husband (214). Her face is frozen in a horrific scream that reverberates across the ages, crying out against the injustices of gender. The novel suggests she was punished for being found "in improper company," and that her lover "may have escaped" leaving her to face the violent consequences (223). Even in supposedly advanced patriarchal societies it is common to find females blamed as the source of sin, which aligns them with the first "fallen woman" of our own culture—"Mother Eve" (214).[5]

So the Outland "picture" highlights Cather's observations that similar traits are apparent in the modern world: men have historically killed for the ownership of women and land; war has repeatedly wiped out the progress of civilization; and society suffers the consequences of unchecked male aggression. And Cather uses the ballet *Excelsior* to underscore these three important "window" themes.

WENDY K. PERRIMAN

Excelsior was first produced in Milan in 1881 to praise the "progress in science and accomplishments, in keeping with the era of supreme optimism" before the Great War (6).[6] It was written and choreographed by Luigi Manzotti to music composed by Romualdo Marenco. Hundreds of performances were given at La Scala between 1881 and 1916, and it was presented in many other theaters across Europe and the United States. Cather may have encountered this ballet on her trip to Italy in 1908, she may have seen it in New York, or she may have watched Luca Comerico's pioneering 1914 film version. As it contained over five hundred performers and an assortment of live circus animals, *Excelsior* was an extraordinarily popular spectacle that had a wider appeal than most ballets of the time. It is unlikely that Cather would have missed such a celebrated event.

Excelsior aimed "to present by means of a ballet all the great discoveries and achievements which had illuminated the late 19th century." It "reflects the optimism of the new classes who, with boundless confidence in progress of science and technology, saw in industry and the new discoveries the means that would lead mankind out of all its inherited troubles." *Excelsior* also promoted "brotherliness and internationalism" (6). The ballet consists of two parts and eleven scenes. Part 1 takes place during the dark era of the Spanish Inquisition, where the male Genius of Darkness struggles to keep the female Genius of Light silenced and in chains. Their battle of "ignorance" versus "progress" is sustained throughout the whole piece.

Cather uses a similar background for *The Professor's House* by having history professor Godfrey St. Peter spend two years on sabbatical in Spain researching his fifteen-year project: *Spanish Adventurers in North America*. We do not know the exact contents of this book, but references suggest that St. Peter was interested in the way that Spanish missionaries brought civilization to the New World.[7]

Scene 2 of *Excelsior* highlights the great deeds that triggered enlightenment: "science, culture, love, harmony, the arts and technology" (8), and in Cather's novel this is shown by the Cliff City dwellers on the Blue Mesa, who out of a "natural yearning for order and security" built a sanctuary "and humanized it" (221).

Although they seem to have dealt harshly with the transgressions of "Mother Eve," Tom Outland appreciates the mesa dwellers' primitive science, culture, love, harmony, art, and technology—to the extent that he transcends his modern self and becomes one with their ideology. At the end of his account he explains how "the mesa was no longer an adventure, but a religious emotion" (251). In the ballet, the dancer representing "Civilization" bears a red cross on her chest symbolizing both the House of Savoy and the influence of missionary Christianity. And in a similar way Outland's "religious emotion" is connected to an appreciation of the idea of civilization, making the mesa a sacred place for him.

The third scene of *Excelsior* reveals the "shores of the Weser near Bremen," where the inventor Denis Papin shows off the first steamboat. The Genius of Darkness encourages the unenlightened locals to attack and destroy this monstrosity until the Genius of Light "praises his new invention before the assembled crowd" (8). In *The Professor's House*, Cather changed the invention of steam to Tom Outland's "gas"—a formula that was such a success with "manufacturers and machinists" (138) that it generated a lot of wealth for the patent owners, St. Peter's daughter and son-in-law. The Outland patent apparently involved some commercial application of this gas in relation to the "Outland Vacuum"—the "construction of the bulkhead vacuum that is revolutionizing aviation" (40).[8] But Outland's invention (like Papin's), met with hostility from the local townsfolk, who rather than display ignorant aggression toward scientific progress chose instead to squabble over royalty payments.

The fourth scene in *Excelsior* highlights the magnificent engineering achievement of the Brooklyn Bridge, built in New York between 1870 and 1883. This innovation triggered a wave of similar structures, including the Manhattan Bridge, completed in 1909, at the time when Cather was living in the city. Perhaps because one of Cather's earlier inventors had been a bridge-builder (Bartley Alexander), in *The Professor's House* the chosen genius is an engineer whose inventions revolutionize the aviation industry. And certainly Cather intends us to acknowledge Outland as a personification of the light of progress, for St. Peter says, "The boy's mind had the superabundance of heat which is always present where there is rich germination. To share his thoughts was to see old perspectives transformed by the new effects of light" (258). Like the Roebling engineers who constructed the amazing Brooklyn Bridge, Bartley Alexander and Tom Outland are both representatives of modern science and technology.

Excelsior then shifts to "Signore Volta's Laboratory" in Lake Como in 1799. The Genius of Darkness is gloating over the pioneer's early experimental failures when suddenly an electric spark jumps across the stage, electricity is discovered, and once again Light triumphs over Darkness. Scene 6 then celebrates "The effect of electricity" in a grand finale to part 1, highlighting the invention of telegraphy and the way this new form of communication helped unite the international community. The ballet also draws a subtle connection between telegraphy and electric light, because although Volta discovered the theory of charging a body by induction, it was Thomas Edison (a telegrapher) who produced the first commercially successful incandescent lamp, and who set up the world's first power plant.

In *The Professor's House* Cather emphasizes the practical application of such developments. Louie Marsellus, a member of the Association of Electrical Engineers in Hamilton (111), was the man who later transformed Tom Outland's inventions into commercial propositions. Marsellus met his wife, Rosamond (formerly Tom's fiancée), when he arrived "to put in the Edison power plant, just at the time the city was stirred up about Outland's being killed at the front" (136). He is the practical "bringer of light." When Mrs. Crane challenges the Professor about Outland's legacy, St. Peter makes it clear that the gas her husband helped Tom Outland create would never have been an economic success without Marsellus's business acumen: "Crane and I together could never have raised a hundredth part of the capital that was necessary to get the thing started" (138). In this manner Cather suggests that the idea alone is insufficient; it takes a different kind of mind to turn it from a formula on paper into a commercial accomplishment. And had Outland not been killed, his inventions may never have achieved the same degree of fiscal reward. Cather's point seems to be that scientific progress is always a collaborative effort. But the irony is that although Outland's "gas" and "vacuum" could perhaps have been utilized in a variety of ways, the aviation industry's interest implies they would be developed for military purposes, uncannily predicting that the Second World War would be fought in the skies as much as in the trenches. Once the "idea" is out, the inventor has little control over its use.

Part 2 of *Excelsior* opens with a scene called "Desert Storm." [9] There has been a "remarkable backsliding" in progress, depicted by a caravan of tribes people "surrendering helplessly to a sandstorm that carries man and beast away with it and plunges everything into darkness." The Genius of Darkness revels in the destruction, but then the Genius of Light appears to show the travelers "a new way to safely reach their destination" (9). This reflects the perpetual human struggle against evil forces and ignorance—a theme Cather explores throughout *The Professor's House* that is perhaps best highlighted by her use of Faustian characterization, as will be discussed later.

Scene 8 heralds the building of the Suez Canal, and in a colorful *Pas-de-cinq* (dance for five people), "Civilization" brings together a variety of cultures from different parts of the globe. Scene 9 continues the theme of international unity by highlighting the "last detonation" of the Cenisio tunnel linking Italy and France; the invention of explosives is seen as a positive force connecting the people of the world. By the time Cather wrote *The Professor's House,* however, explosives had much more sinister uses. With the advent of the Great War, the high explosives traditionally used in construction were developed to propel ammunition and bombs. And instead of uniting the nations of Europe, this particular technology took the lives of millions. Alfred Nobel, the inventor of dynamite, was himself so horrified by the weapons his technology created that he set up the Nobel prizes in a belated attempt to promote art, medicine, science, and world peace.

Scene 10 of *Excelsior* moves to the final confrontation between Darkness and Light. The Genius of Light triumphantly shows her adversary "the brotherly re-unification of the peoples of the earth," before the ground "opens and devours the Genius of Darkness, who has lost his power forever." The ballet ends "in never ending jubilation" when "science, progress, brotherliness and love" are united in "an even greater glorification of the future." Victory is celebrated by a "big monument" that signifies "the triumph of the human genius" (9-10). In *Memorial Fictions* Steven Trout claims that Cather's novel *One of Ours* "represents, at least on one level, a war memorial in prose" (8) and suggests that in a similar way, in *The Professor's House*, "the 'great catastrophe' of 1914–18 is central—but nearly invisible." He adds: "Revealing its unnamed presence requires the most painstaking of textual archeology" (191). Yet by following the *Excelsior* clues encoded in the subtext it is possible to interpret *The Professor's House* as another of Cather's ironic reversals. *One of Ours* can be read as a positive "memorial" to war because it highlights the patriotic belief that the Americans would restore world peace through their excelsior-style bravery and genius: "In another year the Yankees will be flying over. They can't stop us" (257), while *The Professor's House* ultimately emerges as a negative "commemoration" of the same event. "Light" has resulted in postwar "Darkness" again; civilization has been "devoured" by the very technology it created.

This seems to have been Cather's second motive in assimilating the ballet *Excelsior* into *The Professor's House*—she wished to underscore her observation that throughout history war has repeatedly wiped out cultural and scientific progress.

The irony of *Excelsior*'s prewar optimism would not have escaped Cather's postwar analysis, and numerous critics have suggested that the author's own world "broke in two" as an aftereffect of the Great War. She seemed depressed not only about the devastation in Europe but also about its consequences in America. This tension is highlighted when the Professor's two sons-in-law are discussing Prohibition, and Louie challenges Scott to write a complaint for his newspaper. Scott replies, "And lose my job? Not much! This country's split in two, socially, and I don't know if it's ever coming together" (108). Not only had the world been blown apart on a global level, but the after shocks were causing fissures in every aspect of the supposedly civilized world: on a national level in a country divided by moral and philosophical differences, in bickering families like the St. Peters, and in individual minds where the trauma of war left deep psychological scars. For even though Godfrey St. Peter never experienced combat himself, he is Cather's reminder that the people left behind suffer as well. They have to mourn not only lost loved ones like Tom Outland but also the old secure way of life. Once such innocence is lost it can never be regained—the broken pieces can be glued back together, but the cracks will always remain visible. The pride and bravado of *Excelsior* must have suddenly seemed very dangerous and naïve, and Cather's insight into the brittle postwar psyche helps explain why the ballet *Excelsior* declined in popularity around 1916.

A third point Cather highlights is that in patriarchal societies women are still suffering the consequences of male aggression. In *Willa Cather: The Writer and Her World* Janice P. Stout detects the Parsifal "hero and fool" motif in *One of Ours* as an earlier critique of "masculinity's drive toward war" (175–78). Interestingly, although *Excelsior* was written by Italian men in 1881, it portrays the conflict between darkness and light, bad and good, savagery and civilization, war and peace, as a battle between the sexes. The Genius of Darkness is a male character (originally danced by Carlo Montanara), and both the Genius of Light and Civilization are female (portrayed in the debut performance by Bice Vergani and Rosina Viale). Ballet critic Cyril W. Beaumont describes the opening scene: "The Spirit of Darkness rejoices, for at his feet lies a woman, Light, in chains. Gradually she revives, breaks her chains, and informs the Spirit of Darkness that his reign is over and that the future belongs to her" (525). And although the pioneers of technology are male characters representing Papin, Volta, and various other scientists and engineers, they are each introduced by Light, who protects their work like an all-powerful fairy godmother. It may have been this strong feminist undertone that made *Excelsior* so interesting to Cather.[10]

The Professor's House offers a more traditional portrayal of gender roles. The women in Cather's book are either "brilliantly beautiful," like Rosamond, who "resembled her mother in feature" (36–37), or functional, like the "seasoned and sound" Augusta and her female sewing forms (281)—with the possible exception of Kathleen, who was so much more "plucky" and "I can-go-it alone" that St. Peter felt compelled to make her "docile" on occasions (64). Kathleen is brighter than her sister, "and very clever at water-color portrait sketches," but she was "deaf to her father" on the one occasion when she chose to marry Scott McGregor (64–

65). Godfrey St. Peter's possessiveness leads him to ask, "When a man had lovely children in his house . . . why couldn't he keep them?" (126). Like many patriarchs he sees the women as his property instead of adult people in their own right. And it is at this point, when the women have abandoned the old family home where St. Peter was in control, that his midlife crisis reaches its peak. Cather's aim is perhaps to show that although women are only allowed to make decisions in the domestic sphere, these decisions are generally sound. The girls select good marriage partners, and Lillian's insistence on moving to a new house will ultimately enrich the quality of their lives. Although Cather certainly uses these women to symbolize what Stout calls the " 'materialistic civilization' [that] was 'triumphant' in America" (194), they also underscore how women had little influence in the political sphere so were unable to prevent the escalation of male aggression into global war.

In contrast, the male characters represent men whose ideas have changed the world. As Merrill Maguire Skaggs explains in "Willa Cather's Great Emersonian Environmental Quartet," Napoleon Godfrey St. Peter is an eminent "embodiment of Emerson's 'American Scholar' " who "accomplished his professional work through conscious *design*," making an important contribution to academia as "the best of the West" (200). Louie Marsellus is the practical driving force that sees Tom Outland's ideas move from paper to production, thereby changing the course of aviation history. And Outland himself personifies the "glittering idea," which can now be equated with human scientific progress.

These characters represent the persistent pioneering quest for excellence made famous by Henry Wadsworth Longfellow's 1842 poem "Excelsior," which likely inspired the ballet title:

> The shades of night were falling fast,
> As through an Alpine village passed
> A youth, who bore, 'mid snow and ice,
> A banner with the strange device,
> Excelsior!
>
> His brow was sad; his eye beneath,
> Flashed like a falchion from its sheath,

And like a silver clarion rung
The accents of that unknown tongue,
Excelsior!

In happy homes he saw the light
Of household fires gleam warm and bright;
Above, the spectral glaciers shone,
And from his lips escaped a groan,
Excelsior!

"Try not the Pass!" the old man said;
"Dark lowers the tempest overhead,
The roaring torrent is deep and wide!"
And loud that clarion voice replied,
Excelsior!

"Oh stay," the maiden said, "and rest
Thy weary head upon this breast!"
A tear stood in his bright blue eye,
But still he answered, with a sigh,
Excelsior!

"Beware the pine-tree's withered branch!
Beware the awful avalanche!"
This was the peasant's last Good-night,
A voice replied, far up the height,
Excelsior!

At break of day, as heavenward
The pious monks of Saint Bernard
Uttered the oft-repeated prayer,
A voice cried through the startled air,
Excelsior!

A traveller, by the faithful hound,
Half-buried in the snow was found,
Still grasping in his hand of ice
That banner with the strange device,
Excelsior!

There in the twilight cold and gray,
Lifeless, but beautiful, he lay,

> And from the sky, serene and far,
> A voice fell, like a falling star,
> Excelsior! (22–23)

"Excelsior" means "yet higher," and Longfellow's theme heralds the bravery of human endeavor.[11] Its connection to the ballet and *The Professor's House* is further cemented by Cather's comment in "The Novel Démeublé" (1922) that writers should "present their scene by suggestion rather than by enumeration" (836). Therefore, whenever Cather "furnishes" her novel with a particular feature, it usually offers an important clue regarding subtext. She deliberately draws our attention to Longfellow by including his translation of the Norse poem "The Grave":

> For thee a house was built
> Ere thou wast born;
> For thee a mould was made
> Ere thou of woman camest. (272)[12]

Cather appears to be hinting that Longfellow's poems will reveal one of the ballet themes in this novel.

The excelsior men move civilization into the twentieth century, but the irony Cather proposes is that they also propel the world closer to total destruction. It was apparent in 1925 that the scientific progress so admired in the ballet did not (as the program promised) result in "brotherliness and love" and "an even greater glorification of the future" (10). Rather, it led to that other "great catastrophe" lurking behind *The Professor's House* that "swept away all youth and all palms, and almost Time itself" (260). As Shaw concludes, "Instead of saving and preserving humanity, Outland creates a device which when used maliciously can imperil humanity" (125–26). The suggestion is that masculine genius, without the feminine light of civilization to temper the way, *will* change the world—but not necessarily for the better.

To further emphasize the paradoxical nature of scientific progress, Tom Outland (the inventor who contributed to aerial warfare) is killed in the first technological war. Steven Trout explains how, "It is precisely . . . [Hiram Maxim's Machine Gun,] the creation of a fellow American, that presumably kills Tom Outland, an inventor whose own scientific discoveries inevitably spawn military hardware" (163). And by uncovering the remains of the peace-loving tribe on the Blue Mesa, Outland also ironically discovers his nation's heritage of violent death; he then continues the patriarchal legacy by inventing a newer, more effective way to deliver carnage and destruction to other civilizations.

Perhaps because St. Peter is intelligent enough to anticipate the escalation of technology toward weapons of mass destruction, he engages in a passive suicidal impulse. What is the point of striving for knowledge and civilization if humanity is doomed to wide-scale annihilation? So when St. Peter comments that he is "nearing the end of his life," he perhaps means literally because "he didn't in the least believe he would be alive during the fall term" (267) but also metaphorically in that his relations with other people "would be of short duration" (271) if everyone on the planet is potentially damned. In this manner, Cather flips the traditional reading of the ending of *The Professor's House* to move away from the optimistic conclusion that St. Peter "could now face with fortitude . . . the future" (283) and introduces a more pessimistic realization that the Professor's near-death experience underscores his realization that humanity's days are numbered.

Yet Cather often juxtaposes simultaneous ideas, and a more complex conclusion to this novel is suggested by aligning it with *Excelsior*. At the end of the ballet several dozen children sit on the stage holding signs reading "Pax." Perhaps this inspired Cather to add the "advent of a young Marsellus" (273) at the very point in the story where St. Peter decides his "daughters had outgrown any great need of him" (281) and after he had been reminiscing about his own grandfather (Old Napoleon Godfrey), finally "beginning to understand what the old man had been thinking about" (266). If St. Peter had lost interest in his family because they no longer needed him (and therefore he had lost control of them), his first grandchild might offer him a new lease on life, bringing unity to the divided family. He or she might finally bring them all "peace." Cather appears to have returned to a similar idea in one of her late stories, "Before Breakfast," where the jaded Henry Grenfell experiences an epiphany watching the geologist's daughter swimming against the tide. Grenfell acknowledges that "plucky youth" always endures, evolves, and finds a way forward in the true excelsior spirit "on a long hop" (769). And because of this suggestion, the children at the end of both Cather's novel and the ballet perhaps represent renewed hope for a world on the brink of self-destruction.

A second ballet influence that helps elucidate the plot of *The Professor's House* is Vaslav Nijinsky's unsuccessful production of *Jeux* (1913). This dance is no longer extant. It was choreographed to Debussy's music, and according to many sources it contained a strong homoerotic undertone. In *The Birth of the Ballets-Russes* Prince Peter Lieven describes how *Jeux* was set in a garden next to a tennis court. Likewise, *The Professor's House* also features a "walled-in [French] garden" (14) that Tom Outland walked into when he first entered St. Peter's life (253).[13] Lieven explains the plot of *Jeux:* a young man (Nijinsky) chases a tennis ball across the stage and is followed by two girls (Ludmila Schollar and Tamara Karsavina) who "become jealous of each other, but finally agree to share the young man's attentions, and the three form a sort of *ménage à trios*" (188–89). Millicent Hodson's and Kenneth Archer's Web site highlights the sensationalism of the piece:

> [*Jeux*] is a daring dance poem about the libertine manners and mores of the Bloomsbury artists that [Nijinsky] and designer Léon Bakst observed at a nocturnal tennis party in London's Bedford Square.[14]
>
> The ambiguous coupling and tripling Nijinsky explored in *Jeux* startled the public.[15]

This dance, the first to openly suggest homosexuality, appears to have inspired Cather's bold treatment of the more unconventional relationships in *The Professor's House*.

The Diary of Vaslav Nijinsky reveals how the bisexual dancer "composed this ballet on the subject of lust" to represent "the kind of life Diaghilev [founder of the Ballets Russes] dreamed of," with two male lovers (206–7).[16] And while there has been much speculation on the nature of Cather's own relationships with other women, whatever her sexual orientation may have been she certainly explores several ambiguous relationships throughout this novel, experimenting with the ménage à trois theme in both homosexual and heterosexual ways. Firstly, the two St. Peter daughters vie for Tom Outland's attention. At the start of their relationship Outland is around twenty years old, with a "manly, mature voice" (112) in contrast to the giggles of St. Peter's "two little girls" (117). He "would spend hours with them in the garden," telling stories of his adventures with Roddy Blake (122), and St. Peter recollects how he "enjoyed the prettiness and freshness and gaiety of the little girls as if they were flowers" (124). There is something disturbing about the relationship between a full-grown man and two children young enough to still require afternoon naps (131). Yet, for Tom, who perhaps harbored latent homosexual desires (in a time when such sexuality was considered deviant), the St. Peter girls might have provided a less threatening alternative to adult females. Even the Professor comments on the advantages Tom enjoys by dying before the possessive hand of a wife was laid on his own. And there is always the possibility that Outland may have been bisexual.

Some type of homoerotic bond seems to be suggested between Outland and St. Peter, of which "Lillian had been fiercely jealous." The Professor himself acknowledges how "sometimes a second infatuation" gradually "makes a difference" in a marriage. This revelation is juxtaposed against his comment that in "their own case it had been, curiously enough, his pupil, Tom Outland" so that the vague hint of a potentially romantic relationship between St. Peter and his protégé is implied (49). At the opera Lillian explains how "it wasn't the children who came between us," expressing "something that spoke of an old wound, healed and hardened and hopeless" (94). And Cather's speaker reveals that it was "after the Professor began to take Tom up to the study and talk over his work with him, began to make a companion of him" that Lillian "withdrew her favour" (173).

Outland may have also had a previous homoerotic relationship with Roddy Blake. In *Willa Cather and Others*, Jonathan Goldberg writes that Outland's treatment of the Anasazi artifacts is "a denial of the bond of friendship and love with Roddy" (146). In the middle section of *The Professor's House*, Tom tells how Roddy "had been unlucky in personal relationships" with women. He continues, "He surely got to think a lot of me, and I did of him" (185). When Henry Atkins joined them, Tom recalls, "The three

260

WENDY K. PERRIMAN

of us made a happy family" (198) in a newfound male-centered Eden that is ironically destroyed by a snake bite and a betrayal. After his final argument with Roddy, Tom recalls how there "was an ache in my arms to reach out and detain him, but there was something else that made me absolutely powerless to do so" (247). Next comes the erotic "religious" rush of possession—to have the mesa to himself and to atone for destroying his friendship with Roddy. He then romances the two St. Peter girls, gets engaged to Rosamond, but rushes off to war before he has to consummate their relationship. If Outland was either homosexual or bisexual, it is also possible that his desire to join the Professor's family might have come as much from a repressed sexual attachment to the athletic-looking father (Roddy's replacement), as to his childlike daughter.[17]

Cather then explores yet another unconventional dynamic in Lillian St. Peter's relationships with her daughters' husbands. On one occasion Lillian is described as wearing "the white silk crêpe dress that had been the most successful of her summer dresses" (reminding us of the white female tennis dress costumes of *Jeux*), and St. Peter is amused by her "coquetry," acknowledging that she "wouldn't have made herself look quite so well if Louie hadn't been coming" (77). She had also developed "arch and confidential relations" with her other son-in-law, Scott McGregor (78), and had "begun the game ["jeu/x"] of being a woman all over again" (79). Although her attraction to these young men is heterosexual, it is another subtly taboo portrayal of incestuous human interactions. The sexual overtones are underscored in the Professor's statement that "*Beaux-fils*, apparently, were meant by Providence to take the husband's place when husbands had ceased to be lovers" (160). There is no suggestion of any intentional misbehavior on Lillian's part, but her attempts to engage her daughters' partners perhaps comes from the psychological insecurity of failing to attract the dashing Tom Outland, who clearly had more interest in her husband and little daughters than in herself.

Just as the three dancers in *Jeux* form different homosexual, heterosexual, and bisexual flirtatious scenarios, the trios in *The Professor's House* do likewise. Outland seems to represent a dynamic Nijinsky character, who not only weaves in and out of the central relationships but who also haunts the lives of St. Peter's family long after he is dead. So although Goldberg concludes that in this novel, "Cather does not represent the homosexual per se as a minority" because "forms of desire are not assumed to be absolutely distinct," she (like Nijinsky) does seem to have been exploring this realm of the "secret self" (144). And her daring experimentation with a combination of new and taboo relationships serves to highlight the fact that homosexuals were often the *other* silenced victims of patriarchy.

As *The Professor's House* was the first novel Cather wrote after her confirmation in the Red Cloud Episcopal Church (1922), it is not surprising to find that, as well as exploring secular ideas, the novel also deals with spiritual issues. These same concerns form her response to a third ballet influence: images from the dance version of *Faust,* intermingled with Goethe's play and Gounod's operatic performance, account for much of the characterization and "scene changes" detectable in the novel. The *New York Times* reveals that the operatic version of *Faust* (1859) was frequently performed at the Metropolitan Opera House, with the accompanying (incidental) ballet *Walpurgisnacht* included in the program. But the full ballet version of *Faust* (three acts and seven scenes choreographed by Jules Perrot) was first performed in Milan in 1848. No doubt Cather would have known that the role model for the original Doctor Georg Faust had the reputation of a "great sodomite and necromancer" in sixteenth-century Germany. He was also described as a "vagabond who succeeded in arousing some belief in his powers of foretelling the future," especially among "gullible university students." Over the centuries his story was retold throughout Europe, perhaps most successfully in Johann Wolfgang Von Goethe's two-part epic *Faust* (1808 and 1833).[18] Goethe was a writer whom Cather greatly admired. Indeed, she draws a direct reference to the poet in *The Professor's House* when the St. Peters are at the opera and Lillian comments that the tenor "looks to me exactly like the pictures of Goethe in his youth," to which Godfrey agrees (93). This provides a clue that the Faustian theme lies at the heart of this novel.

A second direct connection to *Faust* appears at the start of the novel when Professor St. Peter is introduced: "His wicked-looking eyebrows made his students call him Mephistopheles—and there was no evading the searching eyes underneath them. [. . .] They had lost none of their fire" (13). This is clearly no coincidence, especially when in *The Kingdom of Art* Cather had already expressed very strong ideas about this particular character. She calls Mephistopheles "the spirit that denies," who is "always shrouded in mystery and doubt" (280).[19] This mystery and doubt is the source of his power. Cather concludes that "something must be done to convey the idea of supreme evil, of more than mortal hate. This cannot be done directly. It must be accomplished indirectly and by inference" (280).

In *The Professor's House* Cather seems to address the challenge of portraying evil "indirectly" by having a Mephistophelian Professor educating a Faustian Tom Outland. Outland is perhaps intended to reflect aspects of Goethe's Faust: according to the description in *Collier's Encyclopedia*, "Faust is introduced as a general, engineer, colonizer, man of affairs, and empire builder. He is at the height of his earthly career, but the inner conflict remains as painful as ever, for he cannot achieve human happiness without destroying human lives, nor create an earthly paradise with work and plenty for all without resorting to evil means" (11:195).[20] Unfortunately the lessons that St. Peter and his colleagues teach allow Outland to contribute to the "supreme evil" of war—an event involving "more than mortal hate" when sanctioned by a patriarchal Christian God.

The ballet version of *Faust* further reinforces Cather's characterization of St. Peter and Outland by casting Rosamond in the role of Marguerite, the young woman in the ballet whom Faust woos and wins with the help of his mentor. A central theme of *The Professor's House* is the quest for lost youth, which the Professor tries to recapture through his relationship with his student: "He loved youth . . . it kindled him" (28). He also lives in a house "painted the colour of ashes" (11), and his name suggests he is both God-free (free of God) and that he has denied Christ (like the Biblical St. Peter). Yet Cather portrays the Professor more as Twain's fallen angel Satan rather than the shape-changing demonic dancer on stage: his "close-growing black hair threw off a streak of light along the rounded ridge where the skull was fullest," resembling a halo (13). But St. Peter's "heaven" at the top of the house might easily be interpreted as "hell" when Cather describes his study as a "dark den" in a "dead, empty house" (15–16), filled with "headless, armless female torso[s]" (17). When he tells Augusta (perhaps representing Saint Augustine, the missionary who converted European pagans to Christianity) that "You'll never convert me back to the religion of my fathers now" (24), the suggestion is that, like Faust and Mephistopheles, the St. Peter character believes himself alienated from God.

The "staging" of Cather's novel also seems to have been inspired by the ballet version of *Faust*. At the start of chapter 3 Cather writes, "St. Peter awoke the next morning with the wish he could be transported on his mattress from the new house to the old" (46). This image comes directly from the ballet, where Mephistopheles takes Faust to various places via his magic cloak: "He spreads his cloak on the ground and signs to Faust to stand on it, when they both disappear" (Beaumont 272). The ballet also highlights the envy Marguerite inspires when Faust and Mephistopheles endow her with special gifts and jewels, a theme Cather develops with Rosamond over the Outland royalty payments and the new wealth it bestows on her. And as Beaumont explains in the *Complete Book of Ballets,* Marguerite has to battle the seven deadly sins of pride, gluttony, sloth, envy, anger, avarice, and lust (274), as do the central characters in the St. Peter family.[21]

The ballet version of *Faust* further explains why *The Professor's House* is so concerned with possessions. What people most possess is their spirituality (the soul), unless they are tempted by the seven deadly sins or they sell out for knowledge. In this latter instance St. Peter becomes like an "empty house." The Professor has spent a lifetime acquiring knowledge to fill the "upstairs room" (brain) and is described by his wife as "the wisest person in the world" (163), and yet he lacks the oldest knowledge of all—the religion of his fathers (Murphy 63). This character flaw helps demonstrate how the St. Peters' house becomes a metaphor for Godfrey himself. The Longfellow poem actually quoted in the text describes a coffin as the house promised "Ere thou wast born" and "Ere thou of woman camest" (272). Yet although St. Peter's body and house are old and empty (lacking soul), there is still time to seek salvation and refill the void with new life. The grave does not have to be the Professor's final home; his spirit can live in another dimension or cease its endless craving.

When Augusta successfully "saves" her employer, it can be interpreted as both literally from "accidental extinction" (282) and spiritually because there "was still Augusta . . . with whom one was outward bound" (281), if "outward bound" is interpreted as replacing the heaven of "the fathers" with the Buddhist concept of non-desire (Nirvana). Unlike Faust, who is damned by falling into despair (the unforgivable sin), St. Peter's near-death experience helps him find fortitude, which becomes his redeeming virtue.[22] He finally "felt the ground under his feet. He thought he knew where he was, and that he could face with fortitude the *Berengaria* and the future" (283). This interpretation of the conclusion accepts that the Professor has been "saved."

So in another of her clever reversals, Cather takes the damnation of Faust and reworks the traditional ballet ending so that in her version it is Mephistopheles who is redeemed instead of being damned to eternal hell and Faust who, rather than ascending into heaven with Marguerite, is doomed to the flames, the smoke, and the terrible screams of the Great War. In this instance war represents hell, and the way to redemption is either to enter Nirvana and end desire on an individual level or to unite in civilized groups to reclaim the metaphorical soul of humanity. Scientific progress has "given us a lot of ingenious toys" but no "new amazements" or "richer pleasures"—instead it "taketh away the sins of the world" which "impoverish(es)" people. The war wipes out "the mystery and importance of their own little individual lives" (68). When the belief in God dies, so does the value of the human soul; the "house" becomes vacant.

In many complex and sophisticated ways the tripartite structure of *The Professor's House* helps explain Cather's views on the postwar world, and her incorporation of ballet ideas into plot, theme, and characterization provide additional layers of texture and subtlety. Cather's reversal of *Excelsior*'s optimism highlights the battle of the sexes, suggesting that patriarchy leads to war and that women suffer the consequences of unchecked male aggression; and the dance trios of *Jeux* demonstrate how patriarchal culture has repressed the homoerotic or bisexual "secret self." Her use of the *Excelsior* theme also shows that progress and scientific knowledge inevitably end in destruction, a theme underscored by the additional use of *Faust* to demonstrate how knowledge and death are interconnected. She suggests that humanity makes its own hell on earth by creating full-scale technological warfare.

Interestingly, Cather chooses to reverse each of the traditional ballet endings. *Excelsior*'s optimism in scientific progress is turned full circle back to a time of post-war darkness. *Jeux*'s happily consensual ménage à trois situation is rewritten to display jealousy and unhappiness. And in Perrot's *Faust*, the protagonist ends up in heaven, while Cather's *Faust* is condemned to hell fire and death. Yet when synthesized together, these ballets offer an alternative ending to the usual interpretation of the novel that Godfrey St. Peter is "saved." Once these ideas are assimilated into the reading of the text, it is possible to believe the Professor is left in an "empty house," a world devoid of soul, where good and evil are no longer clearly definable. St. Peter experiences the postwar Modernist alienation from God—a position that may have been familiar enough to Cather to have prompted the author's own return to the Church in the time before writing this book. And through her skillful use of ballet themes, Cather successfully critiques patriarchal culture, modern warfare, and technological progress, highlighting how the "glittering idea" of scientific invention had suddenly lost its luster.

NOTES

1. Brief plot comparison between *Swan Lake* and *Alexander's Bridge*:

- Prince falls in love with Odette—Engineer falls in love with Hilda
- Prince pledges marriage to another (Odile)—Engineer marries another (Winifred)
- Prince returns to first love (Odette)—Engineer returns to first love (Hilda)
- Prince drowns—Engineer drowns.

2. The *New York Times* records all the major stars who danced at the New York Metropolitan Opera House. An advertisement on Sunday, De-

cember 18, 1910, announced that the following Tuesday Mme Olive Fremstad and Mme Anna Pavlova would appear together on a special program
marking the Russian dancer's "first evening appearance in America."
Fremstad was ill that Tuesday and failed to perform, but the Russians did
share the bill with her on several other occasions.

3. The 1905 story "Flavia and Her Artists" does not contain any representative dancers. But after Pavlova's performances convinced Cather of
the high artistry involved, she became an inspired supporter of modern
ballet.

4. Evelyn Haller writes that "Helen Cather Southwick spoke to me of
her aunt's mailing ballet programs to her family" (173). This provides further evidence that Cather was a regular patron.

5. In the *Malleus Maleficarum* (the fifteenth-century witch-finding
handbook endorsed by the Catholic Church) two priests explain the ratio-
nale behind original sin: "For though the devil tempted Eve to sin, yet Eve
seduced Adam. And as the sin of Eve would not have brought death to our
soul and body unless the sin had afterwards passed on to Adam, to which
he was tempted by Eve, not by the devil, therefore she is more bitter than
death" (47). Thus, female sin is associated with sexuality: "To conclude.
All witchcraft comes from carnal lust, which is in women insatiable" (47).

"Mother Eve" may also represent the murder of the *sacred feminine*
—the earth goddess suppressed by male-dominated sky god religions—
which upset the natural balance of the world and led to war. According to
Crow legend, Old Man Coyote one day met another coyote called Shirape.
Shirape urged his older brother to create "enmity" and "war" because this
gave the male warrior his battle honors. The book *The American Indians:
The Spirit World* explains how "Old Man Coyote divided the people into
tribes, giving them different languages. Then there was war, then there
was horse stealing, then there was counting coup, then there were songs of
honor" (25). In this Native American explanation, war is the direct result
of male ego. It derives from an aggressive urge to create hostile situations
that will allow warriors to win approval and admiration.

6. References are to the recent reconstruction of *Excelsior* by the Orchestra and Corps De Ballet of the Teatro Alla Scala, Milan (May 2002).
This performance is available on DVD (Tai Trade, 2002).

7. Outland and St. Peter went "down into the South-west together" following Fray Garces's diary. They covered "every mile of his trail" to locate
"the exact spot at which the missionary crossed the Rio Colorado . . . in
1775" (259).

8. Although vaguely explained in the text, this invention may have been
an early type of vacuum pump to pull fuel through the carburetor to the
engine.

According to *Collier's Encyclopedia*, "To bring about the practical flying machine, a number of parallel streams of endeavor and invention had had to be born . . . 1) the science of aerodynamics; 2) the technology of structures and aeroplane configuration; 3) fuel technology; 4) engine technology; 5) airscrew design; and 6) flight control" (3:376). Outland's contribution apparently involved fuel technology and engine technology, a conclusion strengthened by Nichole Bennett's recent discovery (as explained at the International Cather Seminar, 2005) that Cather's references to "gas" and to the "bulkheaded vacuum" have their origin in Rudyard Kipling's story of futuristic dirigibles, "With the Night Mail."

9. Ironically this title would be given to another military campaign in 1991, when allied forces liberated Kuwait from Iraq.

10. A poster in an online ballet chat room discussing the restaging of *Excelsior* in 2002 explains that dance purists generally consider this production to be "Terrible kitsche, old-fashioned, . . . you can't call this a ballet." Had it not been for the feminist "message," it would probably not have appealed to Cather's high artistic taste.

11. *British Empire University Modern English Dictionary*. London: Syndicate, 1924.

12. Cather's version is slightly incorrect. Longfellow actually wrote:

> For thee was a house built
> Ere thou wast born,
> For thee was a mould meant
> Ere thou of mother camest.

Substituting the word "made" for "meant" undermines Longfellow's suggestion that individual life is already predetermined before birth; in Cather's world individuals are responsible for their own souls. The "mother" figure (associated with the Christian figure of the passive, subservient Virgin Mary) is replaced by the more modern term "woman," which suggests a feminist rejection of the patriarchal stereotypes promoted by "the fathers."

13. The walled garden is a popular literary motif for a place of sexual encounter (probably relating back to Adam and Eve in the Garden of Eden). Stephen Daniels explains how "Gardens, especially old monastery gardens, were erotic sites in Gothic romances, settings for seductions and transgressive, moonlight trysts" (4).

14. Bedford Square is also Hilda Burgoyne's residence in *Alexander's Bridge*.

15. Hodson and Archer explain that Nijinsky utilized the "pleasure-garden themes inspired by Wagner's *Parsifal*" (*Jeux* 1). This also links *Jeux* with Cather's other war book because Janice Stout has suggested that the *Parsifal* theme is detectable in *One Of Ours* (Stout 175–78).

16. Vaslav Nijinsky and Sergei Diaghilev became lovers in 1908, and

their sexual relationship continued until 1912. Nijinsky then suddenly married Romola de Pulszky on a 1913 tour of Argentina. When Diaghilev heard of this "betrayal," he fired Nijinsky from the Ballets Russes.

17. On a surface reading it is possible to interpret Outland's relationship with both Roddy Blake and Godfrey St. Peter as replacement father figures. But once the ballet *Jeux* is superimposed on the text, a homoerotic theme is strongly suggested (as Diaghilev played the role of incestuous father to Nijinsky).

18. Information supplied by *Collier's Encyclopedia*, vols. 9 and 11.

19. As Skaggs explains, "We recall St. Peter's students call him Mephistopheles, and that he leaves behind him a smell of smoke" (*After the World* 75).

20. Cather may also have been influenced by Mark Twain's characterizations in *Connecticut Yankee* and *Papers of the Adam Family* (comment made by Merrill Maguire Skaggs, not in print).

21. Pride: "You are too severe with Scott and Louie. All young men have foolish vanities—you had plenty" (Lillian to the Professor, 35).

Gluttony: The lunch Lillian provides appears quite substantial for one person: "Chicken sandwiches with lettuce leaves, red California grapes, and two shapely, long-necked russet pears. That would do very well." But St. Peter supplements this: "From the chest he took out a round cheese, and a bottle of wine, and began to polish a sherry glass" (102). Sloth: "But for the present I don't want anything very stimulating" (St. Peter to Lillian, 164)

Envy: "I can't help it, Father. I *am* envious. I don't think I would be if she left me alone, but she comes here with her magnificence and takes the life out of all our poor little things" (Kathleen to the Professor, 84–85).

Anger: In an angry outburst, the Professor says to Lillian, "Hang it, Outland doesn't need their generosity! They've got everything he ought to have had, and the least they can do is to be quiet about it, and not convert his very bones into a personal asset" (47).

Avarice: After his trip with Rosamond, St. Peter tells his wife, "Too much is certainly worse than too little—of anything. It turned out to be rather an orgy of acquisition" (154).

Lust: When St. Peter insists on keeping his "ladies" (the sewing forms), Augusta "looked down her nose as she did at church when the dark sins were mentioned," and from "the tilt of her chin he saw that she felt the presence of some improper suggestion" (22). The skirted form apparently suggests a lady of the night or similar image.

22. Skaggs explains in "Willa Cather's Great Emersonian Environmental Quartet" that the Professor is "reduced to *acedia*, depression—that sinful condition theologians equate with spiritual sloth" (201).

WORKS CITED

The American Indians: The Spirit World. Ed. Time-Life Books. Alexandria, VA: Time-Life, 1992.

"Ballet.co Postings Pages." *Excelsior* Reviews, 2002. http://www.danze.co.uk/dcforum/happening/2424.html. January 15, 2004.

Beaumont, Cyril W. *Complete Book of Ballets.* New York: Garden City, 1941.

Bohlke, L. Brent. *Willa Cather in Person: Interviews, Speeches, and Letters.* Lincoln: U of Nebraska P, 1986.

Cather, Willa. *Alexander's Bridge.* Boston: Houghton Mifflin, 1912.

———. "Before Breakfast." *Stories, Poems, and Other Writings.* Ed. Sharon O'Brien. New York: The Library of America, 1992. 758–69.

———. "The Novel Démeublé." 1922. *Stories, Poems, and Other Writings.* Ed. Sharon O'Brien. New York: The Library of America, 1992. 834–37.

———. *One of Ours.* New York: Knopf, 1922.

———. *The Professor's House.* New York: Knopf, 1925.

———. "Training for the Ballet." *McClure's* 41.6 (1913): 85–96. Drew University Adams Lot 152 3C.

Collier's Encyclopedia. New York: Macmillan, 1974.

Daniels, Stephen. "Gothic Gallantry: Humphrey Repton, Lord Byron, and the Sexual Politics of Landscape Gardening." *Bourgeois and Aristocratic Cultural Encounters In Garden Art, 1550–1850,* vol. 23. http://www.doaks.org/etexts.html. February 25, 2004.

Giannone, Richard. *Music in Willa Cather's Fiction.* Lincoln: U of Nebraska P, 2001.

Goldberg, Jonathan. *Willa Cather and Others.* Durham: Duke UP, 2001.

Haller, Evelyn. "Willa Cather and Leon Bakst: Her Portraitist Who Was Designer to Diaghilev's Russian Ballet." *Willa Cather's New York: New Essays on Cather in the City.* Ed. Merrill Maguire Skaggs. City: Associated UP, 2000. 169–89.

Hodson, Millicent, and Kenneth Archer. *Jeux.* http://www.pendragonpress.com/whatsnew.html#bloomsbury. January 15, 2004.

Lieven, Prince Peter. *The Birth of the Ballet-Russes.* New York: Dover, 1973.

Longfellow, Henry Wadsworth. "Excelsior." *Henry Wadsworth Longfellow: Selected Poems.* New York: Bell, 1993. 22–23.

———. "The Grave." *Henry Wadsworth Longfellow: Poems and Other Writings.* Ed. J. D. McClatchy. New York: Library of America, 2000. 697–98.

Malleus Maleficarum of Heinrich Kramer and James Sprenger. Ed.
Montague Summers. New York: Dover, 1971.

Manzotti, Luigi. *Excelsior.* Orchestra and Corps De Ballet of the Teatro
Alla Scala, Milan (May 2002). Worldwide: Tai Trade DVD, 2002.

Murphy, John J. "Holy Cities, Poor Savages, and the Science Culture:
Repositioning *The Professor's House.*" *Willa Cather and the American
Southwest.* Ed. John N. Swift and Joseph R. Urgo. Lincoln: U of
Nebraska P, 2002. 55–68.

Nijinsky, Vaslav. *The Diary of Vaslav Nijinsky.* Ed. Joan Acocella. New
York: Farrar, Straus and Giroux, 1999.

Sergeant, Elizabeth Shepley. *Willa Cather: A Memoir.* Lincoln: U of
Nebraska P, 1963.

Shaw, Patrick W. *Willa Cather and the Art of Conflict: Re-Visioning Her
Creative Imagination.* New York: Whitston, 1992.

Skaggs, Merrill Maguire. *After the World Broke in Two: The Later
Novels of Willa Cather.* Charlottesville: UP of Virginia, 1990.

———. "Willa Cather's Great Emersonian Environmental Quartet."
Cather Studies 5. Ed. Susan J. Rosowski. Lincoln: U of Nebraska P,
2003. 199–215.

———, ed. *Willa Cather's New York: New Essays on Cather in the City.*
New York: Associated UP, 2000.

Slote, Bernice. *The Kingdom of Art: First Principles and Critical
Statements, 1893-1896.* Lincoln: U of Nebraska P, 1966.

Stout, Janis P. *Willa Cather: The Writer and Her World.* Charlottesville:
UP of Virginia, 2000.

Trout, Steven. *Memorial Fictions: Willa Cather and the First World War.*
Lincoln: U of Nebraska P, 2002.

Rebuilding the Outland Engine
A New Source for *The Professor's House*

STEVEN TROUT

As revealed by the Southwick typescript of *The Professor's House*,[1] Willa Cather struggled when trying to imagine the specific scientific "principle" that Tom Outland discovers and that Louis Marcellus later incorporates into a highly profitable commodity— the celebrated Outland engine. In the typescript (see fig. 1), Louis awkwardly recounts Outland's successes to Sir Edgar, the English scholar who dines with the St. Peters in chapter 2 of "The Family," as follows: "Before he dashed off to the front this youngster had discovered the principle of the Outland vacuum, worked out the construction of the bulkheaded vacuum—that is, a vacuum protected by a gas that does not fill it, the thing that is revolutionizing aviation" (26). Wisely, Cather scratched out the obfuscating phrase "that is, a vacuum protected by a gas that does not fill it" and made other significant changes to this passage (changes not indicated on the Southwick typescript) later in the revision process. Here are Louie's comments in their more familiar form, as they appear in the tenth printing of the first edition published by Knopf in 1925: "Before he dashed off to the front, this youngster had discovered the principle of the Outland vacuum, worked out the construction of the Outland engine that is revolutionizing aviation" (42). In tracing Cather's difficulties with this passage, we see that the Outland vacuum was just that—a gap within the narrative, a space or void where Cather's ordinarily sure-footed imagination could find no purchase. Thus, the more she attempted to describe it, the more obscure the vacuum became—with stylistically awkward results. In the end, her decision to condense Louie's remarks, in a way that leaves the specifics of Outland's discovery a mystery, displays her artistic instincts at their best and provides a compelling illustration of the compositional techniques advocated in her essay "The Novel Démeublé."

One intriguing detail, however, remains intact throughout the textual history of *The Professor's House* (or, rather, the limited portion of that history to which we have access), namely, the link between Outland's shadowy discovery and World War I–era aviation. For example, both the Southwick typescript and the first edition indicate that Outland's innovation is "revolutionizing aviation" (42). Though phrased differently in the two versions, Sir Edgar's connection to aeronautical technology is consistent as well. In the typescript, he recognizes Outland's name because "he himself had been in the air branch of the service during the war" (26). In the first edition, Cather makes the same point about the Englishman's wartime affiliation and his prior knowledge of Outland but tightens her military terminology, substituting "Air Service" (meaning, presumably, the Royal Air Force) for "air branch of the service." Moreover, both texts place Sir Edgar in the "construction department" of the RAF, where, it follows, he would have acquired an intimate familiarity with the mechanism bearing Outland's name. Based on this evidence, it appears that Cather's uncertainty regarding the specific nature of Outland's discovery existed side by side with a desire, perhaps sustained from the very beginning of her work on *The Professor's House,* to link Outland's research to early-twentieth-century aviation.

Why aviation? Or, more specifically, why *military* aviation? What might have inspired Cather to select this particular application for Outland's genius? This essay will address these questions by offering a prototype for the Outland engine, a prototype that Cather's readers in 1925 would almost certainly have recognized. Once set alongside this possible source of inspiration, Louie's contribution to the Allied war effort, which he achieves by appropriating Outland's discovery, suddenly emerges as an anything but arbitrary detail in Cather's text. Indeed, Cather's decision to tie Louie's wealth (and Outland's reputation) to a World War I–era aircraft engine stands, when seen in this light, as one of her most inspired artistic touches; arguably no other *kind* of machine would

26

year of the war, when he was barely thirty years of age. ᵃˢ
βefore he dashed off to the front this youngster had discovered
the principle of the Outland vacuum, worked out the construction
of ą bulkʰeaded vacuum, - ~~tehat is, a vacuum protected by a gas~~
~~that does not fill it, the thing~~ that is revolutionizing aviation. He had not only invented it, but, curiously enough for
such a hotₐheaded fellow, ʰe had ₐprotectᵉᵈ it, ~~taken out a pat-~~
~~ent.~~ But he had no time to communicate his discovery or to com-
mercialize it, - simply ~~bɔlxʳᵈ~~ bolted to the front and left the
most important discovery of his time to take care of itself."

Sir ~~Xgʰ~~ Edgar, fork arrested, looked a trifle dazed. "Am I
to understand that it is the ~~âx~~ inventor of the Outland vacuum
you are ~~talking about~~?"

Louie was delighted." Exactly that. Of course you would knᵒʷ
all about it. My wife was young Outland's fiancée,- is virtually
his widow. Before he went to France he made a will in her favor;
he had no living relatives, indeed. Toward the close of the war
we began to sense the importance of what Outland had been doing
in ʰis laboratory, I am an electrical engineer by profession—
we called in the assistance of experts and got the idea over
from the laboratory to the trade. The monetary returns have
been and are, of course, large."

While Louie paused long enough to have some intercourse
with the roast before it was taken away, Sir Edgar remarked
that he himself had been in the air branch of the service during the war, in the construction department, and that it was
most extraordinary to come thus by chance upon the genesis of
the Outland Vacuum.

Fig. 1. Cather's introduction of the Outland engine in the Southwick type-script. Philip L. and Helen Cather Southwick Collection, Archives and Special Collections, University of Nebraska–Lincoln Libraries.

have worked so well in a novel focused on the intersection of technological innovation, war, and commerce.[2]

At first sight, the notion of locating a prototype for the Outland engine, a fictional breakthrough in aviation propulsion, appears dubious. Simply put, no corresponding breakthroughs occurred in actuality, at least not during World War I. As James Woodress and Kari Ronning remark in their explanatory notes for the Willa Cather Scholarly Edition of *The Professor's House,* "There were no radical inventions that revolutionized the aviation industry during the forty years that followed the Wright brothers' first flight in 1902" (344). Although by 1926, one year after the publication of Cather's novel, Pratt and Whitney had devised an engine "fifty times more powerful than the one used by the Wright Brothers," aeronautical engineers still relied upon piston-driven motors to deliver power to propellers (345). In other words, increased horsepower, which boosted airspeed and allowed for the construction of larger aircraft, represented the main achievement of aviation science in the 1910s and 1920s; little else, in terms of the fundamentals of lift and propulsion, separated World War I-era airplanes from the Wright Flyer. Thus, it would seem that the Outland engine, credited in *The Professor's House* with "revolutionizing aviation," is a matter of pure imagination on Cather's part—a rare instance when her creativity operated independently of any prototype.

As it turns out, however, the Outland engine is not entirely divorced from Cather's milieu, for an American aircraft engine *did* receive extensive press coverage during the First World War, as well as numerous (if undeserved) accolades for its purportedly groundbreaking design and topnotch performance. This supposed mechanical marvel was the so-called Liberty engine, one of the United States' most publicized technological contributions to the Allied war effort.

Like the Outland engine, the product of a cowboy turned scientific researcher, the Liberty engine enjoyed a colorful creation story. The circumstances surrounding its development were, in fact, legendary—thanks in part to a government propaganda effort aimed at boosting public confidence in American technological know-how. In May 1917, just one month after the American declaration of war, a new federal task force known as the Aircraft Production Board summoned top engine designers J. G. Vincent (of Packard Motors) and E. J. Hall (of the Hall-Scott Motor Company) to Washington DC. The task set before these engineers was a formidable one: to devise, as quickly as possible, an American aircraft engine that would rival, if not surpass, those designed under wartime pressures by Great Britain, France, and Germany. More specifically, the board required an engine that would "be light in proportion to power" and, perhaps most importantly, "adaptable to quantity production"—adaptable, in other words, to the neo-efficient practices of mass production that were then revolution-izing the American automobile industry (Knappen 77). Anticipat-ing, like most Allied war planners, that the Great War would last into 1919 (if not beyond), the board hoped to build the fledgling American Air Service, which had received almost no funding prior to 1917, into the most advanced organization of its kind, com-plete with American-made aircraft numbering in the thousands. Designed with high-speed production methods in mind, the en-gine created by Vincent and Hall would, the board hoped, literally supply the power for this aerial juggernaut.

On May 29, 1917, board officials brought the two engineers, who had never met before, together in Suite 201 of the Willard Hotel in Washington DC, where the pair were asked to remain until they produced a set of basic blueprints. According to legend, Vincent and Hall worked nonstop from the afternoon of May 29 until 2:00 a.m. the next night and slept only sporadically there-after. Whatever assistance they required, the board provided. Met-allurgists and draftsmen soon filled the suite—along with repre-sentatives of other Allied governments, eager (now that the United States was no longer a neutral power) to share confidential draw-ings of their own aeronautical machinery. After just five days, Vincent and Hall left the Willard Hotel with the design for the new engine in hand.

Subsequent production moved just as swiftly. In July 1917, less than two months after the Liberty engine's birth on paper, an eight-cylinder prototype, assembled by the Packard plant in De-troit, arrived at a test facility in Washington DC. One month later, researchers tested and approved the twelve-cylinder version ulti-mately adopted by the U.S. military. In the fall of 1917, assured of the new engine's sound design, the War Department placed an order for a staggering 22,500 Liberty engines and divided the con-tract among several automobile manufactures, including Packard, Lincoln, Ford, and General Motors. The decision to assign aircraft engine production to American car companies, as opposed to the fledgling American aviation industry, soon met with controversy;

however, the Aircraft Production Board defended this policy based on the enormous scale of the automobile industry's existing facilities and its established methods of high-speed mass production. Detroit proved eager to justify the board's confidence. Asked to supply cylinders for the new engine, items traditionally manufactured through a difficult and time-consuming process, engineers at Ford swiftly devised an improved technique for cutting and pressing steel; as a result, cylinder production rose almost overnight from 151 units per day to more than 2,000 (Knappen 119). Not to be outdone, Lincoln Motor Company completed the construction of a new plant in record time, devoted the entire structure to Liberty engine production, and assembled 2,000 engines in twelve months (104). By the time of the Armistice, the six automobile companies under contract with the War Department had manufactured 13,574 Liberty engines and had reached a combined production rate of 150 engines per day (Hudson 16). Amid the generally disappointing record of American wartime production—by war's end the American army still relied primarily upon with French-made tanks, artillery, and machine-guns—the plentiful Liberty engine stood out as a vindication of American manufacturing methods. But whether the engine actually *worked* remained a matter for debate, as we will see, as the testimony of pilots clashed with that of industrialists.

Not surprisingly, given its propaganda appeal as a supposed triumph of American engineering and modern mass production, the Liberty engine attracted no fewer than sixty-seven articles and editorials in the *New York Times* between July 1917 and December 1918, and thus it is likely that Cather, an avid newspaper reader, knew the engine's history in some detail.[3] Among the *Times* articles that she may have perused are the following eye-catching headlines: "New Motor Developed by Aircraft Production Board," "Perfection of Liberty Motor Announced by Sec. Baker," "Liberty Motor Called Best in World by Experts at Convention of Society of Automotive Engineers," "J. M. Eaton Asserts that German Spies Are Delaying [Liberty Engine] Production," "Battle-planes Equipped with Liberty Motors Are On Way to France Five Months Ahead of Schedule," and "Report of Wholesale Liberty Motor Production Called Bluff by A. H. G. Fokker in Interview

Printed in *Berliner Zeitung*." I cannot say with absolute certainly that Cather read these pieces—or even noticed them. However, the subject of military aviation *did* attract her, as evidenced by her personal copy of *Victor Chapman's Letters from France*, the posthumously published correspondence of a volunteer airman: inside the front cover Cather pasted several news clippings related to famous World War I flyers.[4] In addition, her sensitive and credible portrayal of the pilot Victor Morse in *One of Ours* suggests a deepseated fascination with the world's first air war, a fascination that may have prompted her to scan at least part of the extensive coverage devoted to the Liberty engine in the *New York Times*.[5]

Textual evidence in *The Professor's House* of a link between the Liberty and Outland engines takes two forms: scattered details that appear to have their origin in the real-life story of Vincent and Hall's invention and broad thematic parallels. One especially striking example of the former is Sir Edgar's encounter with the Outland engine while working in the RAF construction department. At first sight, this detail seems rather preposterous (and thus in keeping with the aura of strangeness and the fantastic that surrounds Tom Outland in general). What is an American motor doing in the hands of the RAF? As it turns out, the history of the Liberty engine, which Cather has in this instance explicitly appropriated, provides the answer. In June 1918, the British Air Ministry approved the adoption of the American-made Liberty as an alternative to the high-power aircraft engine manufactured by Rolls Royce, and by September 1918, RAF pilots had field-tested enough of the American imports to conclude (perhaps erroneously) that they functioned at least as well as the Rolls model. As a result, thousands of Liberty engines went into service aboard British aircraft, as well as those of other Allied air services—a fact that Cather's original audience may have considered when evaluating the plausibility of the Outland engine's international success.

Readers of *The Professor's House* in 1925 perhaps also recognized the specter of the Liberty engine, now in a wispier thematic form, amid Cather's oblique account of Louie's war profiteering. Indeed, the controversy that raged throughout 1918 over the quality of the Liberty engine and the motives of its Marsellus-like manufactures is a significant, perhaps even central, "thing not named" in *The Professor's House.* Among war-related machines produced in America during the First World War, the Liberty engine proved one of the most vulnerable to charges of profit-seeking and opportunism on the part of its creators; it was second in this regard only to the American-built aircraft for which it was primarily designed—the De Haviland 4 (or DH-4, also nicknamed the "flaming coffin"), a vehicle whose questionable airworthiness became the subject of congressional inquiry (Fredericks 158). Two years after the war, industrial journalist Theodore Macfarlane Knappen vigorously defended the Liberty engine and its manufactures in his popular book *Wings of War,* a semi-official history of the American contribution to Allied air power. By Knappen's account, the Detroit auto kings were selfless patriots, indifferent to profit, indeed even willing to work at a loss while helping to win the war. The Packard Company, for example, nobly "sacrificed itself for all" by expensively retooling its Liberty engine assembly lines (116). "It is easy," Knappen writes, "to talk of profiteering and to say that all who fought in the war with the forge and the machine fought only for gain . . . but patriotism and the desire to serve at any cost were the dominating motives with thousands of our manufactures. In no effort was this better exemplified than in the conception and production of the Liberty motor" (120). As for the Liberty engine itself, Knappen underscored the reliability of this "great motor" by citing its flawless performance on several celebrated postwar flights, including Capt. E. F. White's nonstop flight from Chicago to New York in April 1919 and the first aerial crossing of the Atlantic, performed by USN Commander Read later that same year. These aeronautical feats were made possible, Knappen insisted, by the same "regular, 'run-of-factory'" engine installed in thousands of Allied aircraft during the war (114).

Later histories offer a different view, both of wartime Detroit and of the Liberty engine. For example, in *The Canvas Falcons* (1970), a general history of World War I aviation, Stephen Longstreet maintains that profit, not patriotism, motivated contract-holding companies, and he cites the Liberty engine, "a shoddy item," as an example of the way that "American war orders made millionaires, but hardly equipment fit to use overseas" (244). Likewise, in his classic history of the AEF, *The Doughboys* (1963), Laurence Stallings paints a largely negative picture of Vincent and Hall's design. According to Stallings, Liberty engine contracts were a financial bonanza for Detroit but only because the engine's operators, who had little confidence in the contraption, were stuck with it. Airmen in France and England, he remarks, claimed the "new engine had a hundred bugs. Less pessimistic pilots said [it] only had seventy-five bugs" (250).

A more balanced, though far from flattering, assessment appears in James J. Hudson's *Hostile Skies* (1968), a history of the American Air Service in World War I. Hudson praises the Liberty engine as an essentially "fine high-horsepower aircraft power plant" but acknowledges the various defects—many of them corrected by the war's end—that resulted from the motor's hasty development and production. Indeed, Hudson recounts that when fitted onto the notorious DH-4, the engine delivered especially questionable performance, as observers learned during stateside test trials (staged while the DH-4 was already entering service overseas) in the spring of 1918. The assortment of mechanical glitches —some attributable to the plane, some to the engine—recorded at these trials by Col. Henry H. Arnold, head of the Division of Military Aeronautics, resemble silent film–era slapstick:

> On April 24th a full throttle test for endurance was made but due to the auxiliary gravity tank failing to function, the plane was forced down after one hour and fifty-two minutes in the air. During this test the radiator shutters broke due to vibration; shock absorber rubbers on the landing gear were stretched too tight, were not large enough, and had to be changed. The radiator shutters would not remain open in the air. The main gasoline tank was leaking badly. On April 25th a half throttle test was made. It was found necessary to descend at the end of two hours due to the fact that five spark plugs had been broken. (qtd. in Hudson 18)

Several days later, the comedy turned deadly as "the test plane went into a spin from 300 feet" and killed the two men aboard (Hudson 18). Although the various mechanical failures associated with Liberty-equipped DH-4s arguably derived more from the airplane than from its power plant (the disastrous placement, for example, of the DH-4's fuel tank in an exposed position between the pilot and observer had nothing to do with the quality of the aircraft's motor), the Liberty engine's association with the "flaming coffin" did little to help its reputation. Ultimately, Vincent and Hall's motor emerged from the Great War under a cloud of ambiguity, a symbol of American engineering and production genius to some, an icon of opportunism to others—a description that also fits the fictional power plant located at the heart of Louie Marsellus's commercial success and Tom Outland's posthumous reputation.

The story of the Liberty engine, then, may have inspired Cather in at least three ways. First, as the only example of American-produced hardware (apart from artillery shells) to see widespread use by other Allied armies, the Liberty engine perhaps provided the basis for creating an American wartime invention that would be well known among multiple nationalities—in sad and ironic contrast, of course, with Outland's largely forgotten (but arguably more admirable) achievements as a self-trained archeologist. Second, the production history of the Liberty would have offered Cather a compelling narrative of wartime big business. In the men who conceived the Liberty engine in just five days, as well as those who oversaw its ultra-accelerated mass production, are displayed all the confidence, energy, and resourcefulness that Cather attributes to Louis Marsellus, an engineer/entrepreneur whose pep and can-do spirit would have been right at home in wartime Detroit. And, third, the controversy surrounding the Liberty engine (and, by extension, the DH-4) may have turned Cather's thoughts to the fuzzy morality of wartime contract procurement. Did the American auto industry "sacrifice itself," as Knappen claims, for the sake of the country? Or was money the real engine at work in Detroit? *The Professor's House* raises similar questions against the same wartime industrial backdrop. Is Louie, who patents a dead man's design, a patriot? Or a profiteer? Did Louie see the value of the Outland engine in terms of its benefit to the Allied war effort? Or its benefit to himself? In these three ways, the story of the Liberty engine apparently offered Cather a rich blend of ideas and issues from which to draw.

The various connections that I have posited do not, however, suggest that Cather built her fictional engine entirely from historical parts. Indeed, she appears to have inverted much of the Liberty engine narrative, in effect, writing *against* or away from her prototype. For example, while the Outland engine employs a new discovery in the field of physics (or is it chemistry?), one so divergent from established understanding that Cather can only call it a "vacuum" and leave it at that, the Liberty engine was anything but experimental. As Knappen explains, the Aircraft Production Board steered Vincent and Hall away from innovations that might slow down the engine's trials and subsequent production. The new engine, the board insisted, "must embody no theory or device that had not already been proved in existing engines. . . . It was not to be an invention, but the simplest and most powerful composite of the best known practice" (77). In other words, Louie Marselluses, not Tom Outlands—practical engineers, not romantic inventors—created the Liberty engine. Vincent and Hall offered nothing visionary in their design; instead, they devised what Knappen praised as the ultimate "producer's engine" (83), subordinating creativity and boldness to the requirements of accelerated mass production. It is also important to note that Outland's invention has none of the "bugs" reported by the Liberty engine's unfortunate operators. Although Mrs. Crane and others question the ethics of Louie's actions in 1917, when he discovers and then takes possession of Outland's scientific "papers," no one in *The Professor's House* contests the quality of the engine that Louie ultimately manufactures—or the genius behind its design. By imagining a truly innovative aircraft engine, one untarnished by accusations of overly expeditious design and production, Cather did more than modify her prototype: she nearly created its antithesis.

More concrete evidence pointing to a link between the Outland and Liberty engines is, I will admit, unavailable—at least for the moment. As far as we know, Cather did not mention the federal Aircraft Production Board, nor its dubious achievements, in her correspondence.[6] Nor do the memoirs of Cather's friends Edith Lewis or Elizabeth Shepley Sergeant indicate whether Cather's fascination with World War I aviation extended into the area of engine development. Nevertheless, the story of the Liberty engine was frequently covered (and to some extent hyped) by a newspaper that we know Cather regularly read. And the thematic connections between Outland's achievement and Vincent and Hall's are hard to ignore: both engines drive a narrative of American ingenuity, modern mass production, profit, and controversy—all set against the background of the War to End All Wars. If I am right, then even the most seemingly fanciful of Cather's fictions—an implausibly revolutionary aircraft engine—has a complex basis in her material culture. Approaching Outland's invention through the prototype that I have offered adds further thematic resonance to *The Professor's House,* especially the novel's otherwise curious references to military aviation, and provides a vivid, albeit speculative, picture of Cather's creative process at work.[7]

NOTES

1. This 204-page typescript was recently acquired by the University of Nebraska–Lincoln as part of the Philip L. and Helen Cather Southwick Collection. I wish to thank the staff of the Archives and Special Collections Department for allowing me to study this extraordinary document. For an excellent discussion of the typescript, see the "Textual Essay" in the Willa Cather Scholarly Edition of *The Professor's House,* 387–430.

2. In their explanatory notes for the Willa Cather Scholarly Edition of *The Professor's House,* James Woodress and Kari Ronning suggest that Cather did not decide upon an aircraft engine until the tenth printing. While it is true that Cather did not use that term in earlier versions of the text, from the beginning she apparently thought of Outland's discovery (whatever it is) as a scientific platform for an advance in aeronautical propulsion. In a paper presented at the most recent International Cather Seminar (June 2005), Nichole Bennett conclusively traced the garbled technical terms that Cather uses, such as "bulkheaded vacuum," to Rudyard Kipling's story "With the Night Mail," which made its American appearance in a 1905 issue of *McClure's.* A work of science fiction, "With the Night Mail" depicts the operation of sophisticated dirigibles in the year 2000 and offers fictional aeronautical innovations, such as "Fleury's Paradox of the Bulkheaded Vacuum," as the basis for the airships' engines.

3. For my tally of news reports, I consulted the *New York Times Index.*

4. This volume is preserved, along with other books from Cather's personal library, in the archives of the Willa Cather Pioneer Memorial in Red Cloud.

5. For a detailed discussion of Morse and his important role in *One of Ours*, see my study *Memorial Fictions* 76–80.

6. No references to the Liberty engine appear in the letters summarized by Janis P. Stout in *A Calendar of the Letters of Willa Cather*.

7. Cather was not the only artist to discover useful material in the story of wartime aircraft engine development. In *Main Street* (1920), Sinclair Lewis inserts references to the federal Aircraft Production Board into his sardonic presentation of Percy Bresnahan, a native son of Gopher Prairie, Minnesota, who has become a millionaire in the Detroit auto industry and is thus Gopher Prairie's only claim to fame. After America enters the Great War, Bresnahan informs his hometown, "I am to go to Washington as a dollar a year man for the government, in the *aviation motor section*, and tell them how much I don't know about carburetors" (296, italics added). Unfortunately, Bresnahan indeed knows little about carburetors — or anything else related to his wartime assignment. He has made millions selling automobiles but has never studied the internal combustion engine. Near the end of the novel, a naval officer in Washington characterizes the Detroit mogul as a "good-hearted idiot" who is "a nuisance in the aeronautic section [because] he doesn't know anything" (453). For readers familiar with the Liberty engine's questionable performance (or with the DH-4 debacle), Lewis's portrait of an Aircraft Production Board member as a well-meaning incompetent was no doubt painfully believable.

WORKS CITED

Cather, Willa. "The Novel Démeublé." 1922. *Willa Cather on Writing: Critical Studies on Writing as an Art*. Lincoln: U of Nebraska P, 1988. 33–44.

———. *One of Ours*. New York: Knopf, 1922.

———. *The Professor's House*. 1925. Willa Cather Scholarly Edition. Ed. James Woodress et al. Lincoln: U of Nebraska P, 2002.

Chapman, John Jay, ed. *Victor Chapman's Letters from France*. New York: Macmillan, 1917.

Fredericks, Pierce G. *The Great Adventure: America in the First World War*. New York: Ace, 1960.

Hudson, James J. *Hostile Skies: A Combat History of the American Air Service in World War I*. Syracuse NY: Syracuse UP, 1968.

Knappen, Theodore Macfarlane. *Wings of War*. New York: Putnam's, 1920.

Lewis, Edith. *Willa Cather Living*. New York: Knopf, 1953.

Lewis, Sinclair. *Main Street*. 1920. New York: Signet, 1998.

Longstreet, Stephen. *The Canvas Falcons: The Men and Planes of World War I.* 1970. New York: Barnes & Noble, 1995.

Sergeant, Elizabeth Shepley. *Willa Cather: A Memoir.* Lincoln: U of Nebraska P, 1967.

Stallings, Laurence. *The Doughboys: The Story of the* AEF, *1917–1918.* New York: Harper & Row, 1963.

Stout, Janis P. *A Calendar of the Letters of Willa Cather.* Lincoln: U of Nebraska P, 2002.

Trout, Steven. *Memorial Fictions: Willa Cather and the First World War.* Lincoln: U of Nebraska P, 2002.

Wartime Fictions
Willa Cather, the Armed Services Editions, and the Unspeakable Second World War

MARY CHINERY

In a 1945 article, *The Saturday Evening Post* reported on wartime efforts to support the troops' morale through reading. In one anecdote, a soldier, lightly wounded in the Philippines and awaiting medical rescue, reached into his knapsack and pulled out a book issued to him by the Armed Services, which he read until help arrived: "Huddled in a muddy foxhole on Leyte with a hole in his ankle, Corp. Erwin Rorick spent the hours before help came reading Willa Cather's *Death Comes for the Archbishop*. He had grabbed it the day before under the delusion that it was a murder mystery, but he discovered, to his amazement, that he liked it anyway" (Wittels 11). Rorick was not alone in being introduced to fiction he would not normally have read. The U.S. government had begun a massive effort to provide reading to the troops in every part of the war theater. As her part of the war effort, Cather agreed to republish some of her works in a highly unusual set of circumstances. One publication was through her old acquaintance Alexander Woollcott, and the other was through the Council on Books in Wartime.

As early as 1939, Cather had understood the gathering gloom in Europe. In *The Writer and Her World*, Janis P. Stout notes, "In March 1939, over a year before she completed *Sapphira*, she told Dorothy Canfield Fisher that having suffered the hardest year of her life, she found consolation in the one activity that could carry her through. She had abandoned the book, she said, but had taken it up again in response to the unspeakableness of another war because the routine of writing provided respite from bad news" (291). In particular, Hitler's march in Europe and France's unsuccessful efforts to resist Nazism contributed to an overwhelming sense of loss. James Woodress explains that "Cather's despair over the fall of France in June [1940] had been followed by the horrendous Battle of Britain, which began in the summer and continued while she was awaiting" the publication of *Sapphira and the Slave Girl* (491). However, Cather's respites were temporary, for in no way did she retreat from the world or the war. Indeed, Cather followed the war closely and in letters specifies battles and key figures. Woodress writes that "Churchill became her hero" and that she felt he was far more prescient about the threat of Hitler than the United States (491). Cather was also worried about her family members who were either fighting in the war or married to someone who was. In one letter, she sent Sigrid Undset an article about a Red Cloud pilot who shot down Japanese planes (Harbison 246).

Cather feared the worst: that civilization as she knew it would be forever changed. Edith Lewis later wrote, "Many people thought she was 'not interested' in the war; but, indeed, she felt it too much to make it the subject of casual conversation." In 1940, "when the French army surrendered, she wrote in her 'Line-a-day,' 'There seems to be no future at all for people of my generation'" (Lewis 184). Cather continued this nearly apocalyptic tone in a 1943 New Year's greeting to her friend Alexander Woollcott,[1] in which she wonders why Earth was not left as empty as the rest of the universe. Woollcott was not a particularly intimate friend, so her confidence to him seems surprising. Yet it was through this New York City acquaintance that Cather made her first contribution to the war effort.

Alexander Woollcott, member of the famed Algonquin Round Table, former drama editor of the *New York Times,* and columnist for the *New Yorker*'s Shouts and Murmurs, was a powerful bon vivant in the New York theater scene. Although it is not certain how Cather and Woollcott met, they certainly attended theater and arts events during the same years. Woollcott was hard to miss in his early career as a theater critic, for he "swept" into front row seats in a black cape and cane (Kaufman and Hennessey xi). In the

1930s, he retired to Vermont, where he held sway over an estate filled with guests. Known for biting reviews, he was loved and loathed by those in the arts scene. His radio show began famously, "This is Woollcott speaking," and his tastes influenced listeners at the most powerful moment of radio, spiking sales of the authors he preferred (Kaufman and Hennessey xv).

Cather, however, was protective of her work and its publication in all forms. More than once she refused to allow him to speak of her books on his radio show, and in a letter to him she made it clear that no radio editions of her work were allowed (February 8, 1935). In 1937 she repeated her refusal to allow anyone to record her fiction to Houghton Mifflin editor Ferris Greenslet, although she later relented for editions of her work for the blind, an "exceptional permission," according to Elizabeth Shepley Sergeant (282).

Indeed, Cather was more scrupulous about her reputation in print. As former managing editor of *McClure's Magazine,* she knew every detail of publishing. She insisted on good typeface and decent paper, indicated by her oversight of all of her editions, from the Benda pen-and-ink drawings for *My Ántonia* to the Autograph series in the 1930s. In general, and perhaps on principle, Cather declined to be published in anthologies. In 1942 she at first refused editor Whit Burnett permission to publish her fiction in the collection *This Is My Best,* explaining that it was impossible for her to anthologize her work, even for a friend, as if it hurt her personally that her works should be in editions in which she did not have total artistic control (April 29, 1942). Burnett countered that perhaps she would allow "Two Friends" to be published, for Cather had already allowed it to be anthologized elsewhere. Eventually, Alfred Knopf himself intervened, suggesting that "Neighbor Rosicky" would be the best choice for the collection (July 18, 1942).

So it is surprising that Cather allowed Woollcott to publish her work in his anthologies, not once but twice. Wollcott's first collection, *Realms of Gold,* did not include any work from Cather, though it is likely that he asked her. Woollcott bravely requested "Old Mrs. Harris" for his *Second Reader,* but Cather flatly refused, though she nonetheless called him a good friend (July 18, 1937). Instead, she allowed "Two Friends," also from *Obscure Destinies,* for the anthology, perhaps because it served her purpose of reintroducing one of her favorite but lesser known stories to a new audience. She was in good company in this volume, with selections from Edith Wharton, Robert Louis Stevenson, Stephen Crane, and even Ernest Hemingway. Woollcott's next project was more complex. *As You Were: A Portable Library of American Prose and Poetry Assembled for Members of the Armed Forces and the Merchant Marine* was developed as a pocket edition to cheer the troops during World War II. Woollcott had been chief war correspondent for the *Stars and Stripes* during World War I, along with other *New Yorker* luminaries such as Harold Ross, founder of the *New Yorker*, and Franklin Pierce Adams, all members of the Algonquin Round Table (Kaufman and Hennessey x).

As part of the war effort, there were a number of attempts to get the troops interesting reading material. One effort, sponsored by the Book of the Month Club, donated subscriptions abroad for the troops, but it was found to be impractical (Miller 2). Another attempt, the Victory Book Campaign, sent books donated by American citizens to soldiers abroad (Miller 1). Cather mentions in a letter to Mary Miner Creighton that she had sent some of her books, though she does not specify if the books were those she owned or had written (Stout, *Letters* 242). The problem with this program was that there were thousands of old, useless books that had to be transported to the soldiers at a time when supplies and space were short (Miller 2).

Woollcott planned a small edition, light to carry, with selections to appeal to young men. To this end, he wrote to hundreds of writers, including his friends Thornton Wilder, Mark Van Doren, and Carl Sandburg, to ask which selections to include in the anthology; "aided by his own prejudices, he would complete the job" (Hoyt 321). Cather, one of his correspondents, suggested that young men would enjoy authors who wrote about things that focused on real life rather than style and form, such as Robert Louis Stevenson, Robert Frost, and Mark Twain. This letter gives us some of Cather's now famous literary insights, including her three favorite novels (a comment she made elsewhere), *The Country of the Pointed Firs*, *The Scarlet Letter*, and *The Adventures of Huckleberry Finn*. But in the same letter she explains her youthful distaste for Sarah Orne Jewett, and she proposed that young men would also not enjoy her work.

Cather seemed completely supportive of Woollcott's project, and though no direct evidence exists, she probably agreed to have her work included not because of her friendship with him but because of her sympathy for the soldiers. The edition resulted in an early collection of America's best-loved literature, a compendium of selections that largely remain famous today: Carl Sandburg's "The Grass," Walt Whitman's "I Hear America Singing," Robert Frost's "Stopping by Woods," and Clement C. Moore's "A Visit from Saint Nicholas." Interestingly, for *As You Were*, Cather chose "Missionary Journeys," the section of *Death Comes for the Archbishop* where Buck Scales nearly kills Father Joseph Valliant and Father Jean Marie Latour, ending with the introduction of Kit Carson. To Cather it may have been the most adventurous part of her novel, suggesting her sensitivity to the needs of the soldiers for interesting material.

Woollcott died in 1943, the same year as the publication of *As You Were*, and thus he did not see the success of the collection, which went though multiple printings, with profits donated to the United Seamen's Fund. But his publisher, Viking, took note of its success, inspiring a new series named after Woollcott's title, *The Portable Library* (Chatterton 40). Trysh Travis explains that "Viking publicity credits Alexander Woollcott with the idea, borrowed from the British *Knapsack Anthology*. But another inspiration [for the Viking portable series] was probably the Council on Books in Wartime's Armed Services Editions (ASES), cheap paperback reprints developed specifically for service personnel. Viking editor Marshall Best served as the secretary of the Council on Books in Wartime and thus was privy to the trade-wide excitement about the ASES" (10). The Viking Portable Library, later headed by Malcolm Cowley, became an American best-selling venture. It published many now-classic American authors, but at the time of their publication in this series, they were often unpopular or out of print (Travis 11).[2]

The other inspiration for the Viking portables, the American Armed Services editions, captured Cather's imagination as well. These paperback books, given to the soldiers fighting abroad, be-

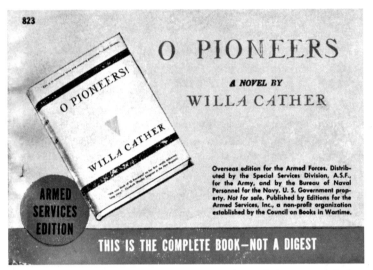

Fig. 1. The front cover of the Armed Services edition of *O Pioneers!* Collection of Steven Trout.

gan after the war and ended in 1947. It was the answer to the previously unsuccessful efforts to transport reading materials cheaply and easily. This project became a massive governmental publication venture, with 123 million copies printed of 1,322 titles (Cole 3).

During the war paper was in short supply and rationed by the publishing houses. On more than one occasion Ferris Greenslet asked Cather if her work could be reprinted on a different imprint, thus saving him paper out of Houghton Mifflin's quota, but Cather nearly always refused. However, in a significant departure from some of her usual publication practices, Cather agreed to publish Armed Services editions of three of her novels: *O Pioneers!*, *My Ántonia*, and *Death Comes for the Archbishop*. Although Elizabeth Shepley Sergeant suggests that Cather needed "a little coaxing from her publishers" for the war editions (271), Cather must not have needed to be convinced for long, for two of her titles appear fairly early in the series, and she had allowed Heinemann, her British publisher, to reproduce a cheaper war edition of *My Ántonia* for the Reader's Union, a British book club (Mignon 500). *Death Comes for the Archbishop* was the first book published in the series. The reason for this selection is uncertain. She had published

"Missionary Journeys" in Woollcott's *As You Were,* and perhaps publishing the rest of the novel made sense to her. But considering her comments to Woollcott about fiction she thought young men would enjoy, she may have viewed the settlement of the Southwest as adventurous.

Sponsored by the Council on Books in Wartime, the Armed Services editions were printed on pulp presses, which were less in use during the war, at a cost of five to ten cents each. The paper was light, so soldiers could easily carry the books. The books were also small, about five inches by three inches, with text in two newspaper style columns per page for easy reading. Longer books used a double imprint of the press, so they were twice the size (Cole 5). Format was set by the war board, and though Cather insisted on which edition was the textual model, she had no editorial control over these books, even though it meant that she could not, for instance, reproduce the Benda drawings for the *My Ántonia* Armed Services edition.

The intention of the Armed Services editions was to make available "good books, both fiction and non-fiction, for the serious reader, as well as books which the serious reader would regard as trash" (Jamieson 19). Daniel J. Miller explains that "maintaining morale among the troops became a primary objective and military officials realized that books could be instrumental in the process" (1). The first selection was a humorous collection of stories, Leo Rosten's *The Education of H*Y*M*E*N* K*A*P*L*A*N,* published in September 1943 (Miller 15). Most genres were represented in the series, including science fiction, westerns, sea stories, popular contemporary fiction, and cartoons for those soldiers for whom reading was difficult (Miller 17). The selection committee "consciously strove to select titles that would appeal to a general audience, [and] the wide breadth of genres encompassed is a remarkable one. Titles range from Faulkner to Margaret Mead to the latest in science fiction and murder mystery" (Miller 12; Wittels 91). Thus, a soldier could both read for entertainment and education. Not surprisingly, racy titles were popular even though they proved not racy at all, such as *Is Sex Necessary?,* by James Thurber and E. B. White, or *Star Spangled Virgin,* by DuBose Heyward (Miller 28–29). More challenging titles included *The Re-*

public of Plato and Virginia Woolf's *The Years*. Very few books were banned, but E. B. White was thrilled when his Armed Services edition of *One Man's Meat* was thought controversial and temporarily halted from distribution (Miller 32). Ironically, *The Letters of Alexander Woollcott* was rejected; the artistic bon vivant who inspired the series was thought "too coy for masculine appeal" (Wittels 92). Cather took no part in the selections, but the series included a number of her favorite authors in the 1,322 titles, such as A. E. Housman, Mark Twain, and Katherine Anne Porter. Cather's dear friend during the war years, Sigrid Undset, agreed to publish *The Bridal Wreath*, the first volume of the *Kristin Lavransdatter* trilogy that brought her the Nobel Prize in literature in 1928. Ninety-nine Armed Services editions were so popular that they were reprinted more than once, such as *A Tree Grows in Brooklyn*, by Betty Smith, *The Robe*, by Lloyd C. Douglas, *White Fang*, by Jack London, *The Yearling*, by Marjorie Kinnan Rawlings, and *Klondike Mike*, by Merrill Dennison. Although these books later became collectors' items, some of them are impossible to find because they were "read to tatters" (Wittel 11). The last edition in the series was Ernie Pyle's *Home Country*, published in 1947.

The popularity of these books has been well documented. David G. Wittels writes that soldiers anxiously awaited their delivery and even split them in half so more than one person could read them, even though it meant that someone began the story in the middle (92). John Cole notes that "One copy of an Armed Services Edition was issued to each soldier as he boarded the invasion barge" before Normandy (9). The C and D series were specifically reserved for the Invasion of Normandy (Hackenberg 18), and Cather's *Death Comes for the Archbishop* was in that series. Letters do not indicate if she knew that fact. Although soldiers were generally instructed to forgo unnecessary items, "the men abandoned souvenirs, spare shoes and blankets, but not a single one of these books was left behind" (Wittels 92). One soldier, Capt. J. H. Magruder, wrote to the *Saturday Evening Post* about the scene of dead men after a battle in the South Pacific. The sad irony of one soldier struck him in particular: "As I looked down at him, I saw something which I don't think I shall ever forget. Sticking from his black trouser pocket

was a yellow pocket edition of a book he had evidently been reading in his spare moments. Only the title was visible—*Our Hearts
were Young and Gay*" (62).

Of the three Cather books published in the series there are sales
records only for *My Ántonia*. In March 1944, "Cather's first royalty check was for 803.38, which meant that 80,338 copies of *Ántonia* had been sold" in a relatively short time (Crane 74). Cather
split the check evenly with Houghton Mifflin (October 13, 1944),
as the governmental contract stipulated. The penny royalty was
from the government; soldiers did not pay for the books, and
they were not available to civilians. Nonetheless, it shows Cather's
popularity among the soldiers and the development of a new fan
base. One of the drawbacks to this popularity was that soldiers
wrote to her. James Woodress explains that "the only contribution
[Cather] could make to the war effort, it seemed, was to respond
to her fan mail from the far-flung battlefields" (500). But she also
"admitted that her awareness of homesick soldiers in foxholes had
become a nervous strain" (Stout 304–05).

Cather does not specify the number of letters she received, but
her correspondence could have been considerable, and she took
it very seriously. Living authors of books published in the Armed
Services editions got anywhere from hundreds to thousands of letters. James Thurber remembers two hundred replies to his six titles
in the series, but H. Allen Smith received five to ten thousand responses from soldiers. Betty Smith, author of the best-selling *A
Tree Grows in Brooklyn*, "received ten times more service mail than
letters from civilians reacting to her novel" (Hackenberg 19).

Cather's preference against being anthologized continued after
this project. Elizabeth Shepley Sergeant bravely volunteered to edit
a Viking Portable edition for Cather, for the new series was renew-
ing the literary reputation of authors who were out of print or out
of fashion. Instead, Cather seemed furious with her old friend for
even considering it. Stout writes that Cather was "amazed that any
self-respecting writer would agree to such a thing" (*Writer* 306).
Sergeant explains that Cather "thundered against the trend to anthologize, to cut books to small pattern for magazines, to reproduce fragments in 'portables.' It's a sorry comment on our times,
she would say, sarcastically—why waste energy wading through

a long novel if you can know the author from a single excerpt?" (282). To Cather, reading itself was a sacred experience. Carefully constructed books and artful fonts preserved the grace and beauty of the relationship between book and reader. Only exceptional circumstances, and the Second World War was one of them, could be worth compromising those values.

In spite of her old-fashioned publishing ideals, Cather nonetheless remained popular after her death in 1947 and long after the war years. The Armed Services editions were arguably a part of that success. By 1948 there were seven million former GIs enrolled in American colleges and universities (Travis 17). These veterans changed the landscape of American education. Miller concludes that the Armed Services editions helped "cement" the post–World War II paperback market (36). Sales of smaller editions skyrocketed and also became part of the textbook industry. The authors who were published in the Viking Portable series and the Armed Services editions were among the better-known authors of the era. Through her heartfelt war effort, Cather became a part of this populist movement.

NOTES

This essay was made possible in part by a Georgian Court University Faculty Summer Research Grant. Special thanks to my research assistant Linda Saraceno.

1. Cather dates this letter December 12, 1943, which Janis P. Stout rightly revises to January 1943. Woollcott died in early 1943, so a December letter to him would have been impossible. See Stout 250.

2. Travis explains that Viking wanted an auspicious beginning to the project, so John Steinbeck inaugurated the series because he was Viking's best-selling author. See Travis.

WORKS CITED

Burnett, Whit. Letter to Willa Cather. June 25, 1942. Archives of Story Magazine and Story Press. CO104 Box 2. Department of Rare Books and Special Collections. Used by Permission of Princeton University.

Cather, Willa. Letter to Alexander Woollcott. February 8, 1935.
Houghton Library. Cambridge MA. b MS Am 1449 (247)
———. Letter to Alexander Woollcott. July 18, 1937. Houghton
Library. Cambridge MA. b MS Am 1449 (246)
———. Letter to Alexander Woollcott. March 17, 1941. Houghton
Library. Cambridge MA. b MS Am 1449 (246)
———. Letter to Alexander Woollcott. December 5, 1942. Houghton
Library. Cambridge MA. b MS Am 1449 (246)
———. Letter to Alexander Woollcott. December 4, 1943. Houghton
Library. Cambridge MA. b MS Am 1449 (246)
———. Letter to Ferris Greenslet. July 18, 1937. Houghton Library.
Houghton Mifflin Papers. Cambridge MA. b MS Am 1925 (341)
———. Letter to Ferris Greenslet. October 22, 1943. Houghton
Library. Houghton Mifflin Papers. Houghton Library, Cambridge
MA. b MS Am 1925. (341)
———. Letter to Ferris Greenslet. October 13, 1944. Houghton Library.
Houghton Mifflin Papers. Houghton Library, Cambridge MA. b MS
Am 1925. (341)
———. Letter to Whit Burnett. April 29, 1942. Department of Rare
Books and Special Collections. Archives of Story Magazine and Story
Press. CO104. Box 2. Used by permission of Princeton University.
Chatterton, Wayne. *Alexander Woollcott.* Boston: Twayne, 1978.
Cole, John Y. "The Armed Services Editions: An Introduction." *Books
in Action: The Armed Services Editions.* Ed. John Y. Cole. Washington
DC. Smithsonian, 1984. 1–12.
Crane, Joan. *Willa Cather: A Bibliography.* Lincoln: U of Nebraska P,
1982.
Hackenberg, Michael. "The Armed Services Editions in Publishing
History." *Books in Action: The Armed Services Edition.* Ed. John Y.
Cole. Washington DC: Smithsonian, 1984. 13–22.
Harbison, Sherrill. "Willa Cather and Sigrid Undset: The
Correspondence in Oslo." *Resources for American Literary Study* 26.2
(2000): 236–59.
Hoyt, Edwin P. *Alexander Woollcott: The Man Who Came to Dinner.*
New York: Abelard-Schuman, 1968.
Jamieson, John. "A History of Armed Services Editions." *Editions for
the Armed Services, A History, Together with the Complete list of 1324
Books Published for the American Armed Forces Overseas.* New York:
Editions for the Armed Services, 1948. 4–31.
Kaufman, Beatrice, and Joseph Hennessey. *Letters of Alexander
Woollcott.* New York: Viking P, 1944.
Knopf, Alfred A. Letter to Whit Burnett. July 8, 1942. Department of

Rare Books and Special Collections. Archives of Story Magazine and Story Press. CO104. Box 2. Used by permission of Princeton University.

Lewis, Edith. *Willa Cather Living.* 1953. Athens: Ohio UP, 1989.

Magruder, Captain J. H. "Epitaph for a Young Marine." *Saturday Evening Post.* July 21, 1945. 62.

Mignon, Charles. Textual Commentary. *My Ántonia.* 1918. Willa Cather Scholarly Edition. Lincoln: U of Nebraska P, 1994. 481–523.

Miller, Daniel J. *Books Go to War. Armed Services Editions in World War Two. An Exhibit at the University of Virginia.* Charlottesville VA. Book Arts P, 1996.

Sergeant, Elizabeth Shepley. *Willa Cather, a Memoir.* 1953. Lincoln: U of Nebraska P, 1963.

Stout, Janis P., ed. *A Calendar of the Letters of Willa Cather.* Lincoln: U of Nebraska P, 2002.

———. *Willa Cather: The Writer and Her World.* Charlottesville: U of Virginia P, 2002.

Travis, Trysh. "The Man of Letters and the Literary Business: Reviewing Malcolm Cowley." *Journal of Modern Literature* 25.2 (2001–02): 1–18.

Wittels, David G. "What the G.I. Reads." *The Saturday Evening Post.* June 23, 1945. 11; 91–93.

Woodress, James. *Willa Cather: A Literary Life.* Lincoln: U of Nebraska P, 1987.

Woollcott, Alexander, ed. *As You Were: A Portable Library of American Prose and Poetry Assembled for the Members of the Armed Forces and the Merchant Marine.* New York: The Viking P, 1943.

Mary Chinery is an associate professor and chair of the Department of English and Communications at Georgian Court University in Lakewood, New Jersey, where she teaches American literature and writing. She received her PhD from Drew University in 2003. She has published articles in *The Willa Cather Newsletter and Review* and *Willa Cather and the American Southwest* (ed. John N. Swift and Joseph R. Urgo, 2002). She is also past president of the New Jersey College English Association.

Debra Rae Cohen is an assistant professor of English at the University of Arkansas and the author of *Remapping the Home Front: Locating Citizenship in British Women's Great War Fiction* (2002). Her two current subjects of research are Rebecca West and the relationship between modernism and radio.

Michael Gorman teaches English and American literature at Hiroshima University in Japan and is completing a PhD dissertation, "Versed in *Country* Things: Pastoral Ideology, Modern American Identity, and Willa Cather," at the University of Tulsa.

Jennifer Haytock is an assistant professor of English at SUNY Brockport. Her book, *At Home, At War: Domesticity and World War I in American Literature* (2003), examines domestic ritual and gender ideology in men's and women's texts about the home-fronts and battle-fronts of World War I. She has also published articles on Ernest Hemingway, Edith Wharton, and Ellen Glasgow.

Pearl James, a visiting assistant professor in English at Davidson College, is currently editing a volume of essays, "Picture This! Reading World War I Posters," for the University of Nebraska Press. She is also writing a book-length study on the representation of World War I in American novels of the 1920s and 1930s.

Celia M. Kingsbury is an assistant professor of English at Central Missouri State University. Her major research interest is World War I literature and culture, especially war propaganda. She is the author of *The Peculiar Sanity of War: Hysteria in the Literature of World War I* (2002), as well as articles and book chapters on the subject of war and propaganda. She is currently working on a project involving World War I propaganda aimed specifically at women and children and popular fiction that mirrors the propaganda.

Susan Meyer is a professor of English at Wellesley College. She is the author of *Imperialism at Home: Race and Victorian Women's Fiction* (1996) and co-editor of *The New Nineteenth Century: Feminist Readings of Underread Victorian Fiction* (1996). Her recent articles include "Craniometry, Race, and the Artist in Willa Cather" (2002), "Imagining the Jews Together: Shared Figures in Edith Wharton and Henry James" (2004), and "Antisemitism and Social Critique in Dickens's *Oliver Twist*" (2005).

Margaret Anne O'Connor is retired from the University of North Carolina at Chapel Hill, where she taught American literature and American studies. Her edited books include *Willa Cather: The Contemporary Reviews* (2001). She now lives in Lake Havasu City, Arizona.

Before returning to academia in 1998, *Wendy K. Perriman* spent fifteen years as an international high school teacher, specializing in English, drama, and dance. She established extracurricular clubs in Germany and England, choreographed many full-scale dance productions, and trained other drama teachers to incorporate movement as part of the National Curriculum. Her dance teams won the YMCA All Germany Command Final in 1993 ("The Dolly Mixtures") and 1984 ("Instep"). Until her recent move to North Carolina she was an assistant professor at Drew University; she is currently working on her second book project, "Willa Cather's Literary Choreography."

Mark A. Robison, an associate professor of English at Union College, is a PhD candidate at the University of Nebraska–Lincoln. His dissertation investigates how the theory and practice of recreation intersect with Cather's life and writing. He has published articles on Cather in *Literature and Belief* and the *Willa Cather Newsletter and Review.*

Ann Romines is the director of Graduate Studies and a professor of English at The George Washington University. She is the author of *The Home Plot: Women, Writing, and Domestic Ritual* (1992), *Constructing the Little House: Gender, Culture, and Laura Ingalls Wilder* (1997), and many essays about American women writers, especially Willa Cather. She edited *Willa Cather's Southern Connections: New Essays on Cather and the South* (2000) and is coeditor of *The Willa Cather Newsletter and Review* and volume editor of the forthcoming Willa Cather Scholarly Edition of *Sapphira and the Slave Girl.*

Mary R. Ryder is a Distinguished Professor of English at South Dakota State University and author of the award-winning book *Willa Cather and Classical Myth: The Search for a New Parnassus* (1991). She has published on Cather in collections of essays and in journals such as *American Literary Realism, Western American Literature,* and the *Willa Cather Newsletter and Review.* Her research has focused on Cather and science; Cather as ecofeminist, poet, and children's author; and Cather's literary connections to Sinclair Lewis, Frank Norris, and Dorothy Canfield Fisher.

Janis P. Stout is professor emerita and dean of faculties/associate provost emerita of Texas A&M University. Her books include *Through the Window, Out the Door: Women's Narratives of Departure, from Austin and Cather to Tyler, Morrison, and Didion* (1998), *Willa Cather: The Writer and Her World* (2000), *A Calendar of the Letters of Willa Cather* (2002), and *Coming Out of War: Poetry, Grieving, and the Culture of the World Wars* (2005).

Steven Trout is a professor of English at Fort Hays State University. He is the author of *Memorial Fictions: Willa Cather and the First World War* (2002) and coeditor of *The Literature of the Great War Reconsidered: Beyond Modern Memory* (2001). His articles on Cather have appeared in *Cather Studies, American Literary Realism,* and *Interdisciplinary Studies in Literature and Environment.* He is currently writing a study of the First World War in American memory, 1919–41.

Page numbers in italics refer to illustrations.